John Hume and the revision of Irish nationalism

Manchester University Press

John Hume and the revision of Irish nationalism

P. J. McLoughlin

Manchester University Press

Manchester and New York

Distributed in the United States exclusively
by Palgrave Macmillan

Published by Manchester University Press
Oxford Road, Manchester M13 9NR, UK
and Room 400, 175 Fifth Avenue, New York, NY 10010, USA
www.manchesteruniversitypress.co.uk

Distributed in the United States exclusively by
Palgrave Macmillan, 175 Fifth Avenue,
New York, NY 10010, USA

Distributed in Canada exclusively by
UBC Press, University of British Columbia, 2029 West Mall,
Vancouver, BC, Canada V6T 1Z2

British Library Cataloguing-in-Publication Data is available

Library of Congress Cataloging-in-Publication Data is available

ISBN 978 0 7190 8689 2 paperback

First published by Manchester University Press in hardback 2010

This paperback edition first published 2012

Printed by Lightning Source

Dedicated with love and respect to my parents,
John and Bridie McLoughlin

Contents

Acknowledgements

This work would not have been possible without financial support from the Arts and Humanities Research Council during my PhD studies, and then the Irish Research Council for the Humanities and Social Sciences and Queen's University Belfast's International Research Initiative, both of which funded post-doctoral positions. Special thanks are due to Richard English and Margaret O'Callaghan, who have been unstinting in their support over many years. I am very grateful to both of them. Similarly, I am indebted to Jennifer Todd and John Coakley, who offered excellent guidance during my time at University College Dublin. Many others provided advice or useful commentary on the work at various stages. In particular, I would like to thank Paula Douglas, Lorenzo Bosi, Christopher Farrington, Mark McNally, Catherine O'Donnell and Tony Wilson. In addition, I am grateful to those who agreed to be interviewed for the book – John Hume himself, but also Gerry Adams, Ben Caraher, Ivan Cooper, Mark Durkan, Seán Farren, Garret FitzGerald, Denis Haughey, Alban Maginness, Eddie McGrady and Mitchel McLaughlin.

Thanks are also due to the staff at Manchester University Press, who have been wonderful in their professionalism and their patience. Similarly, I extend my appreciation to the staff of various libraries and archives: the James Joyce Library at University College Dublin; the Main Library and Séamus Heaney Library at Queen's University Belfast; Belfast's Linen Hall Library, and in particular its Northern Ireland Political Collection; the Belfast Newspaper Library; the Public Records Office of Northern Ireland; and the National Archives of Ireland.

Finally, I am grateful to loved ones who tolerated my preoccupation with this work for extended periods. In particular, I thank Paula, who undoubtedly suffered the most in this regard.

Chapters 1 and 2 of this book draw on an article entitled '"…it's a united Ireland or nothing"? John Hume and the idea of Irish unity, 1964–72', published by Taylor and Francis in *Irish Political Studies*, 21:2 (2006), pp. 157–80. Chapter 3 builds on an article entitled '"Dublin is just a Sunningdale away"? The SDLP and the failure of Northern Ireland's Sunningdale experiment', published by Oxford University Press in *Twentieth Century British History*, 19:4 (2008), pp. 74–96. Elements of

Chapters 5 and 11 draw on an article entitled 'The SDLP and the Europeanization of the Northern Ireland problem', due for publication by Taylor and Francis in *Irish Political Studies*, 24:4 (2009). Part of the Conclusions section borrows from on an article entitled 'Horowitz's theory of ethnic party competition and the case of the SDLP, 1970–79', published by Taylor and Francis in *Nationalism and Ethnic Politics*, 14:4 (2008), pp. 549–78.

P. J. McLoughlin,
Belfast, August 2009

Note on terminology

Although the author does not subscribe to the thesis that the Northern Ireland conflict is religious in motivation, the terms 'Protestant' and 'Catholic', as well the terms 'unionist' and 'nationalist', are used when referring to the two main communities in Northern Ireland. Whilst the latter are, strictly speaking, more accurate in describing an essentially political conflict – a clash of competing national aspirations – the former are also employed to allow for variety of expression in the text. For the same reason, the appellations 'majority' and 'minority' are also used in reference to the unionist and nationalist communities respectively. The terms 'the South', 'the southern state', and 'the southern government' are also used in the interests of variation to refer to the polity more properly known as the Republic of Ireland. However, as far as is possible, only the term 'Northern Ireland' – this being the least politically loaded – is used to refer to the northern polity.

The term 'nationalist' (lower case) is used to refer to any member, members or representatives of the Catholic community in Northern Ireland. It is similarly used to refer to opinion in the Republic of Ireland, or indeed straddling the border in the catch-all term, 'nationalist Ireland'. The term 'Nationalist' (upper case) refers exclusively to the constitutional movement, or its members, which, in various guises and degrees of organisation, represented the majority of Catholics in Northern Ireland from the state's foundation until the outbreak of the Troubles. Although, for the main, it never actually constituted a political party in the full sense of the term – lacking proper co-ordination and a constituency-based organisation – convention is followed in referring to this grouping as 'the Nationalist Party'.

A similar distinction is used with regard to unionist politics. The term 'unionist' (lower case) is used to refer to any member, members or representatives of the Protestant community in Northern Ireland. The term 'Unionist' (upper case) is used only in reference to the Unionist Party, its members or the various governments, formed solely by this party, which administered Northern Ireland until Stormont's collapse in 1972. Hereafter, the term 'Unionist' continues to be used exclusively in reference to the established party which represented the majority of Protestants in

Northern Ireland in the period studied, despite the party's splintering during the breakdown of the Stormont regime. In this, the convention of referring to the main unionist party in the 1970s and 1980s as 'the Official Unionists' is not adhered to.

The only exception to these rules comes when citing an author or political actor who has used the terms differently. For example, when an author or political actor uses the term 'Nationalist' (upper case), but is clearly referring only to a member of the Catholic community rather than a member of the Nationalist Party, any quotation will replicate the original source, this in the interests of scholarly integrity.

Abbreviations

AIA	Anglo-Irish Agreement
ANIA	Americans for a New Irish Agenda
DCAC	Derry Citizens' Action Committee
DFA	Department of Foreign Affairs
DSD	Downing Street Declaration
D/T	Department of the Taoiseach
DUP	Democratic Unionist Party
EC	European Community
EU	European Union
GFA	Good Friday Agreement
HMSO	Her Majesty's Stationery Office
IGC	Inter-Governmental Conference
IIP	Irish Independence Party
IRA	Irish Republican Army
LHL	Linen Hall Library
MEP	Member of the European Parliament
MP	Member of Parliament (Westminster and Stormont)
NAI	National Archives of Ireland
NDP	National Democratic Party
NICRA	Northern Ireland Civil Rights Association
NIF	New Ireland Forum
NIO	Northern Ireland Office
NIPC	Northern Ireland Political Collection
NSMC	North–South Ministerial Council
PD	People's Democracy
PRONI	Public Records Office of Northern Ireland
RTÉ	Radio Telefís Éireann
RUC	Royal Ulster Constabulary
SDLP	Social Democratic and Labour Party
SEUPB	Special EU Programmes Body
TCD	Trinity College Dublin
UUP	Ulster Unionist Party
UUUC	United Ulster Unionist Council
UWC	Ulster Workers' Council

Preface

The traditional nationalist view of Northern Ireland can be summed up in two propositions: (1) the people of Ireland form one nation; and (2) the fault for keeping Ireland divided lies with Britain. (John Whyte)[1]

The principal aim of this study is to assess the degree to which Irish nationalism has departed from these axioms of orthodoxy. It does this by exploring the ideas of arguably the most important Irish nationalist leader of his generation, and certainly one of the most influential politicians of twentieth-century Ireland: John Hume. In doing so, the study considers Hume as an exponent of what is termed 'revisionist nationalism'.

In this, the study looks to reclaim 'revisionism' – a dirty word in the mind of many Irish nationalists. This is a result of the term's intimate association with a particular trend in Irish historiography, a trend which, its proponents claimed, sought to 'professionalise' the study of Ireland's past.[2] The ultimate objective in this endeavour was to create 'value-free' historiography – the implication being that the established narrative of Irish history had been distorted by nationalist ideology. This, it was argued, had produced a politicised version of Ireland's past, which sought to legitimise the nationalist struggle for independence from Britain, and to validate the Irish state that was founded in 1921. As a means to overcome this political distortion, revisionist historians claimed to employ a scientific, systematic and objective approach to the study of Ireland. Through this, they hoped to separate historical fact from nationalist fiction, and so to 'de-mythologise' Irish history.

However, historical revisionism sparked a huge controversy. Critics claimed that behind the assertions of objectivity was a project as ideologically motivated as that which it alleged to expose: if the orthodox narrative of Irish history was tainted by nationalism, then the revisionist interpretation was corrupted by anti-nationalism. As such, the outbreak of the Northern Ireland Troubles in the late 1960s served to pour fuel on a fire of academic disputation. Indeed, the subsequent expansion of the revisionist school was seen by its opponents as further evidence of its reactionary nature and ultimately political bias. Historical revisionists, it seemed, were encouraged in their academic endeavours as a means to extirpate the irredentist logic of the established Irish narrative, believing that this narrative contributed to Catholic rebellion in Northern Ireland, and so threatened political stability across the island of Ireland.

The present study does not deal with this controversial historical debate.[3] However, by insisting on the use of a term so commonly associated with this polemic, there is a need for clarification. This work is not concerned with the contested re-appraisal of Irish history, but rather with the re-articulation of one of the driving forces in the creation of that history: the ideology of Irish nationalism. Of course, the two are not entirely unrelated. Historical revisionism, and the debate which it engendered, has undoubtedly encouraged the reconsideration of certain assumptions in traditional Irish nationalist thinking.[4] But whilst opponents of revisionist historiography have *alleged* its political nature, revisionist nationalism is indubitably political. Where historical revisionism may have been influenced by the ongoing debate over partition and the Northern Ireland problem, nationalist revisionism is unquestionably preoccupied with these issues. Indeed, revisionist nationalism can be defined as the conscious reformulation of Irish nationalist thinking on partition, the Northern Ireland problem, and how the two might be resolved.

As suggested by Whyte, the traditional nationalist perspective holds Britain to be responsible for both the partition of Ireland and the Northern Ireland problem. Though there may always have been Irish nationalists who questioned the reductionism inherent in this interpretation, their voices were largely peripheral in the decades immediately after partition. Indeed, arguably it was only from the 1950s that there occurred significant changes in mainstream nationalist thinking on the subject. Initially, this was most notable within southern Irish nationalism, particularly after Seán Lemass became Taoiseach in 1959. Under Lemass, the Irish government moved away from its established policy – a vociferous anti-partitionism, directed largely at London – and adopted a more pragmatic approach which emphasised the need for co-operation between Dublin and Belfast as a means to the betterment of relations and, through this, the possibility of future Irish reunification.[5] Implicit in Lemass's policy was a recognition that it was unionist attitudes rather than British interests that represented the major obstacle to Irish unity. In this, a tentative shift in southern Irish nationalist thinking was initiated by the Lemass administrations.

At the same time, mindsets within northern nationalism were also in transition. The Irish government's new approach to Northern Ireland may have encouraged this, but opinions amongst the northern minority had already begun to change from the late 1950s.[6] In time, the evolution in northern nationalist attitudes towards partition and the Northern Ireland state would have far greater repercussions than Lemass's revisionism. Indeed, it could be argued that, with the emergence of a reformist northern nationalism in the 1960s, there began a chain of events which ultimately ended in open political conflict in Northern Ireland. This, in turn, caused an immediate retreat to anti-partitionist rhetoric on the part of Lemass's successors in the South.[7] Simultaneously, the onset of the Troubles saw northern nationalism split between those who continued to advocate reform, and those who sought revolution. It is the former trend which this study seeks to explore, examining both the origins and the development of a new form of northern nationalism, which in turn brought lasting changes to the thinking of its southern sister.

To reiterate, the present work concerns itself not with the revision of Irish historiography, but with the revision of Irish nationalist ideology. More specifically, it looks at the leading role which John Hume played in this. However, it does not suggest that he was the sole innovator of revisionist nationalism. Rather, it places Hume in his historical context, appreciating the changes in nationalist thinking – particularly in Northern Ireland – which pre-dated and informed his own political philosophy. Nonetheless, the study does claim that, whilst drawing on a pre-existing or at least incipient revisionism, Hume contributed to, helped to refine, and – most importantly – successfully articulated a new nationalist discourse. In this, it is argued that Hume's most important role was as an exponent of revisionist nationalism.

As well as articulating a new nationalism, Hume sought to persuade others of its merits. Accordingly, the study looks at how Hume engaged with different members of the broad Irish nationalist family – the Irish government, Irish America, and the Irish republican movement. In doing so, it shows how Hume helped to achieve a basic consensus among Irish nationalists – northern and southern, constitutional and physical force, indigenous and diasporic – which was strongly influenced by his own particular brand of revisionist nationalism. Over time, the strength of this consensus also encouraged shifts by the other major parties to the Northern Ireland conflict – the British government and the Ulster unionist community. This helped to create a process which eventually culminated in the signing of the Good Friday Agreement (GFA) in April 1998.

Of course, a host of other factors should be considered in accounting for the changing positions of the British government and the unionist leadership, and thus explaining the emergence of the Northern Ireland peace process.[8] The present work explores only the changes in the ideology of Irish nationalism which underpinned its commitment to this process. But the study is further limited, looking exclusively at the role played by Hume and the party which he helped to found, the Social Democratic and Labour Party (SDLP), in promoting these changes.

Despite this narrow focus, the study does not consider Hume's role in splendid ideological isolation. Rather, it allows for the fact that Hume was a political leader as well as an ideologue, and that his position was, therefore, subject to the political environment in which he was operating. Most obviously, there is need to consider how the events of the Northern Ireland conflict itself affected his thinking. As such, although the work is primarily concerned with Hume's influence on the ideological development of Irish nationalism, by necessity, this is considered in the context of an historical narrative. For the changing position articulated by Hume through the course of the Northern Ireland conflict cannot be understood without reference to the actions of its other participants. For example, it cannot be understood without appreciating the effect on the minority community of British paratroopers' indiscriminate shooting of anti-internment protesters in January 1972; it cannot be understood without considering the implications for reformist nationalism of unionists' overthrow of the Sunningdale Agreement in May 1974; it cannot be understood without recognising the sense of abandonment and growing alienation felt by northern nationalists as the Dublin government largely declined to speak for them in the late 1970s; and it cannot be understood without realising how the self-immolation of ten men in British jails in 1981 transformed the image of the republican movement and its proclaimed cause. The study aims to show how these and other such events seriously impacted on the ideas which Hume was attempting to communicate.

Although adopting a chronological approach to the investigation of Hume's thinking, the study does not claim to provide a comprehensive narrative of the Northern Ireland Troubles. However, it does hope to make an original contribution to the existing literature. For the study explores a very particular perspective on the conflict, and one which has hitherto received insufficient attention. This is the perspective of constitutional, reformist northern nationalism, as embodied in the SDLP, and as led, more than any other individual, by Hume. While this may have been the dominant trend within northern nationalism from the 1960s, the study shows that it could never claim to have held outright hegemony over the minority. Indeed, a small but significant element of the nationalist populace chose violent revolution rather than constitutional reform as the means to political progress, whilst a more considerable number of Catholics remained ambivalent about the former and pessimistic about the prospects of the latter. Accordingly, the study shows how Hume's efforts to revise Irish nationalist thinking were often compromised by the need to maintain political support amongst a community whose allegiance was the subject of an intense, highly emotive, and ongoing battle.

There are already a handful of books on Hume and the SDLP. This study owes a debt to, but also seeks to advance upon, each of them. The two main academic analyses are Ian McAllister's *The Social Democratic and Labour Party* (1977), and Gerard Murray's *John Hume and the SDLP* (1998).[9] Murray's study makes effective use of the SDLP's own papers, lodged with the Public Records Office of Northern Ireland, in order to follow the evolution of the party's political strategy from the 1970s through to 1998. However, in concentrating on this, at times, Murray fails to relate the development of the SDLP to the political events taking place around it. This is most notable in the early part of the book, with the first chapter alone detailing both the origins of the party and its progress as far as the Sunningdale Agreement of 1974. With the approach taken by the present study, this crucial period is given much greater attention. The aim in this is to better understand how the SDLP's formative political philosophy was so adversely affected by events in the early Troubles.

Of course, Murray could rightly point to the fact that the early period of the SDLP is already covered in detail by McAllister's work. However, ironically, McAllister's book lacks exactly that which Murray provides so well, that is focus on the evolution of the SDLP's political programme. Indeed, at times, McAllister can be quite dismissive of the party's strategy, suggesting that the SDLP lacked any coherent policy in its infancy. In this, he fails to give adequate consideration to those party documents that were available even at his time of writing. Similarly, there is little of the voice of the SDLP leadership in McAllister's work. In short, insufficient attention is paid to what the SDLP was actually saying in McAllister's period of study.

This is not to disregard either of these books. Both have great strengths in the areas on which they concentrate. Murray gives an excellent survey of the political debate that took place within the SDLP, particularly in the first two decades of the party's existence. McAllister, meanwhile, provides a detailed organisational analysis of the SDLP, and an insightful account of its socio-political origins and early experience as a party. Indeed, in many respects, the present work seeks to synthesise the different approaches of these two authors: following the evolution of SDLP policy, as does Murray, but closely relating it to the political context in which it took place, as does McAllister.

In its conclusions, too, the present study steers a middle course between Murray and McAllister. Indeed, for whilst the latter can be dismissive of the party's political approach, the former is perhaps overly sympathetic, and at times oversimplifies the course of the SDLP's development. For example, Murray is right to draw attention to a number of internal party papers written in 1971–72, suggesting that these documents informed not only the SDLP's first published proposals, but also much of the party's political approach thereafter. He is also correct in asserting that many of the ideas advanced in these discussion papers were realised in the GFA of 1998.[10] However, in making this argument, Murray is perhaps a little pre-emptive. Although many of the political objectives pursued by the SDLP are indeed present in the 1971–72 documents which Murray cites, some were embryonic at this time, and arguably took further years to mature. The purpose of this work, therefore, is to demonstrate how the SDLP's core political ideas continually evolved and became more defined as the party progressed. However, in doing so, the study rejects the notion implicit in Murray's work, namely that this development was an essentially linear, organic process. By placing the party firmly in its political context – that of the Northern Ireland conflict, and the radicalisation and communal polarisation which it engendered – this work shows how different events impacted on the SDLP's position in such a way that its political approach was not always consistent.

Notwithstanding this qualification of Murray's thesis, the present study ultimately agrees with his rather than McAllister's assessment of the SDLP. For the latter work, produced in the aftermath of the failed Sunningdale Agreement, is markedly critical. Writing during one of the SDLP's most difficult periods, McAllister could not have foreseen the resilience of the party, nor have predicted the arguable vindication of its ideas – much the same as those discredited after Sunningdale – in the later GFA. In contradistinction, Murray was writing close to the completion of the 1998 accord, and this may explain why he is, at times, overly sympathetic to the SDLP. This study looks to strike a balance between these two competing interpretations, recognising the huge imprint of the SDLP's thinking on the GFA as does Murray, but also demonstrating that there were periods of political recidivism as does McAllister.

In contrast to both McAllister and Murray, what is quite different in the methodology adopted by this study is that it seeks to examine the SDLP within the broader context of the Irish nationalist tradition. It does this by taking Hume – as the SDLP's main thinker, strategist and spokesperson – rather than the party itself as the primary subject of analysis. It closely examines Hume's ideas: where they originated, how he articulated them, how he disseminated them, and how he convinced the other foremost members of the Irish nationalist family – the Irish government, the Irish-American political elite, and finally the republican leadership – of their validity. In doing so, it also draws on a number of journalistic biographies of Hume which, although lacking the critical rigour of academic studies, provide a wealth of detail to which this work owes much.[11]

Nonetheless, the study aims to provide fresh insights to Hume's thinking. It does so by closely examining the vast range of writings, speeches, and other forms of commentary which he provided in the course of his long career. In this, too, the study adopts a different methodology to Murray, who has already provided a thorough account of the internal debate within the SDLP by examining the party's own archives. By contrast, this work looks mainly at the public articulation of the SDLP's position, particularly as expressed through Hume. This allows a greater understanding of how the day-to-day events of the Northern Ireland conflict affected the way in which Hume and his colleagues communicated their approach to its resolution. In turn, this approach helps to explain how the founding ideas of the SDLP were often compromised by the extreme political conditions under which the party was operating. However, the study also intends to show that, despite these conditions, ultimately Hume upheld certain key principles proffered from the very outset of his political career – principles which represented significant departures from traditional Irish nationalist thinking, and which fed into and structured the ideological parameters of the Northern Ireland peace process.

Whilst explaining Hume's success in this endeavour, the study will conclude by considering the reasons for his arguable failure in what he intimated was his foremost political objective: the conciliation of the two
communities in Northern Ireland. In essence, it will suggest that Hume's
achievements as a nationalist leader also account for the considerable distrust which he evoked amongst Ulster unionists. However, whilst recognising that Hume was unable to convince unionists of the integrity of his
motives, the study will argue that the political settlement which he helped
to create has provided the most realistic framework for a process of gradual reconciliation between the two main political traditions in Ireland.

Notes

1 J. Whyte, *Interpreting Northern Ireland* (Oxford: Clarendon Press, 1990),
   p. 117.
2 Although the movement came to the fore in the post-war period, its origins
   can be traced back the 1930s and the pioneering work of Theodore William
   Moody and Robert Dudley Edwards. In 1938, Moody and Dudley Edwards
   established the *Irish Historical Studies* journal with the specific intention of
   promoting proper scholarly standards in the writing of Irish history;
   C. Brady, '"Constructive and instrumental": the dilemma of Ireland's first
   "new historians"', in C. Brady (ed.) *Interpreting Irish History: The Debate
   on Historical Revisionism, 1938–1994* (Dublin: Irish Academic Press, 1994),
   pp. 3–4.
3 Texts that do include D. G. Boyce and A. O'Day (eds.), *The Making of Modern Irish History: Revisionism and the Revisionist Controversy* (London:
   Routledge, 1996); and Brady (ed.), *Interpreting Irish History*. Also see the
   recent and interesting arguments on the subject in J. M. Regan, 'Southern Irish
   nationalism as a historical problem', *The History Journal*, 50:1 (2007).
4 Whyte, *Interpreting Northern Ireland*, pp. 122ff.
5 On this see J. Horgan, *Seán Lemass: The Enigmatic Patriot* (Dublin: Gill and
   Macmillan, 1997), ch. 8; and M. Kennedy, *Division and Consensus: The
   Politics of Cross-Border Relations in Ireland, 1925–1969* (Dublin: Institute of
   Public Administration, 2000), chs. 8–11.
6 See below, pp. 2–3, 9–11.
7 R. Fanning, 'Playing it cool: the response of the British and Irish governments
   to the crisis in Northern Ireland, 1968–9', *Irish Studies in International
   Affairs*, 12 (2001), p. 67; Kennedy, *Division and Consensus*, p. 315.
8 On the changes in British policy and unionist politics which prefigured the
   peace process, see F. Cochrane, *Unionist Politics and the Politics of Unionism
   since the Anglo-Irish Agreement* (Cork: Cork University Press, 2nd edn,
   2001); M. Cunningham, *British Government Policy in Northern Ireland,
   1969–2000* (Manchester: Manchester University Press, 2001), chs 3–5; C.
   Farrington, *Ulster Unionism and the Northern Ireland Peace Process*
   (Basingstoke: Palgrave, 2006); and E. O'Kane, *Britain, Ireland and Northern
   Ireland since 1980* (Routledge: Abingdon, 2007).
9 I. McAllister, *The Social Democratic and Labour Party: Political Opposition
   in a Divided Society* (London: Macmillan, 1977); G. Murray, *John Hume and*

the SDLP: Impact and Survival in Northern Ireland (Dublin: Murray Irish Academic Press, 1998).

10   Murray's arguments in this regard are not explicit in his first study of the SDLP, for the simple fact that it was written just before the GFA was concluded. However, he correctly anticipated the SDLP's political vindication, and in a later article, 'The Good Friday Agreement: an SDLP analysis of the Northern Ireland conflict', in J. Neuheiser and S. Wolff (eds), *Peace at Last?: The Impact of the Good Friday Agreement on Northern Ireland* (Oxford: Berghahn Books, 2003), and also in the book which he co-writes with Jonathan Tonge, *Sinn Féin and the SDLP: From Alienation to Participation* (London: O'Brien, 2005), Murray makes clear his belief that the party's earliest policy documents presaged the 1998 settlement in many respects.

11   The first of these studies, Barry White's *John Hume: Statesman of the Troubles* (Belfast: Blackstaff, 1984), remains the most thorough, although Paul Routledge's *John Hume: A Biography* (London: Harper Collins, 1998) is also useful for the later part of Hume's career. George Drower's *John Hume: Peacemaker* (London: Victor Gollancz, 1995) does not provide much that is new on Hume.

Introduction

Northern Irish nationalists were the outright losers in the Anglo-Irish settlement of 1920–21.[1] Southern nationalists attained an independent state, albeit truncated and lacking the full sovereignty of the coveted 'republic' for which many had fought. Ulster unionists also compromised, accepting self-government in a six-county state to avoid coming under a Dublin parliament. But northern nationalists had little say in their fate. Partition left them cut off from the rest of their compatriots in the Irish Free State, and thus overnight they were transformed into a political minority.[2]

Unsurprisingly, northern nationalists' response to the state in which they found themselves was broadly negative. Opposed to partition, but powerless to change it, the minority community largely withdrew into itself. Maintaining their own education system, and their own social and cultural practices, Catholics largely lived apart from the Protestant population of Northern Ireland.[3] At a political level, too, they played little role in the new regime. Initially, the Nationalist Party – the loose grouping of MPs that represented the minority– did not to take its seats in the Belfast parliament, this to demonstrate its refusal to accept the Northern Ireland state. However, even when they did attend Stormont – as a minority group facing an unassailable Unionist majority – the Nationalists found they had little real influence. As a result, they soon retreated back into abstentionism.

Of course, such action was hardly discouraged by the Protestant community, which made little effort to integrate Catholics into state and society in Northern Ireland. Indeed, most Protestants viewed the minority population with suspicion or hostility. Catholics were considered disloyal citizens, a fifth column in Northern Ireland who, in league with Dublin, sought to subvert and ultimately overthrow the Unionist government. Such feeling led to significant discrimination against the Catholic minority, which many Protestants felt could not be trusted to hold positions of influence in Northern Ireland.[4] More generally, discrimination in employment and the allocation of public housing was seen to have a useful side-effect in encouraging Catholic emigration from Northern Ireland. This helped to ease Protestant concerns over the high birth-rate amongst the minority, and so to offset fears of being 'out-bred' by the Catholic population.

The separateness of the two communities was thus maintained by feel-ings on both sides of the religious divide. Most Catholics had no desire to participate in public life in Northern Ireland, a state which they had con-siderable difficulty accepting. Conversely, most Protestants had no desire to encourage Catholics' participation, fearing that this would undermine the state in the long term. As a result, Northern Ireland was a divided but largely stable society in the decades immediately after partition.

This remained the situation until the late 1950s, when there began a gradual shift in nationalist attitudes. Increasingly, Catholic intellectuals began to argue the need to accept the Northern Ireland state, and to work within it to improve their social and economic position.[5] Over time, such arguments gained in legitimacy, and eventually led to the mass mobilisa-tion of the nationalist community behind a civil rights campaign in the late 1960s. With this, the minority appeared to accept partition, but on the condition that it was given equality of opportunity in Northern Ireland.[6]

The orthodox explanation for this transformation in nationalist atti-tudes focuses on the British welfare state, and the related expansion of state education in post-war Northern Ireland.[7] This, it is argued, allowed for the growth of an educated and forward-looking Catholic middle class, which would not allow unionists' opposition – nor indeed the reticence of its own community – to prevent it from playing a fuller role in the state and society of Northern Ireland.[8] This thesis, however, has been shown to be much over-simplified. The British welfare state did help to create a larger, more confident, and more articulate Catholic bourgeoisie, a group less willing to accept discrimination, and eager to secure its share of employment in a greatly expanded public sector. But this alone does not account for the fundamental changes that took place within nationalist politics from the late 1950s.

Firstly, the evolution in nationalist attitudes can be seen as generational, though this can also be related to the British welfare state, under which younger Catholics had been educated, and found an improved standard of living. Indeed, many realised that they were better off than citizens on the other side of the border, with the southern Irish state experiencing severe economic problems in the 1950s. This tended to weaken the northern minority's enthusiasm for joining a united Ireland, and thus helped to rec-oncile them to the Union to some degree. As such, the ameliorative impact of the welfare state made post-war northern Catholics more willing British citizens.[9]

At the same time, this new generation had learnt from, and grown tired of, the sterile politics of traditional nationalism. After forty years spent arguing the illegitimacy of partition, the Nationalist Party had nothing to show for its efforts. Meanwhile, physical-force nationalism had fared no better. Though republican militants mounted a so-called 'border campaign' in 1956–62,[10] this was largely ineffectual, and easily contained by the state security forces. 'The apparent futility of either brand of traditional nationalism', according to John McGarry and Brendan O'Leary, 'and the changed attitudes induced by the welfare state prompted revisionism amongst the Catholic population.'[11] Significant sections of the minority came to accept both the permanence of the Northern Ireland state and the need to work within in to improve their lot.

This shift towards a more reformist outlook was reinforced by changing political priorities in the Irish Republic. Following the economic and emigration crises of the 1950s, when Seán Lemass became Taoiseach at the end of the decade he was focused primarily on the continued survival of the southern state.[12] Accordingly, Dublin was looking to reconcile itself with both London and Belfast in the interests of economic interchange. As such, the Irish government under Lemass began to move away from the anti-partitionism of previous administrations.[13] In turn, the northern minority accepted that any change in its position would have to come within the British political system, and as a result of its own efforts.[14]

But developments in the early 1960s encouraged northern Catholics to feel that a reformist approach might now be a viable option. Most notable was the retirement of the hard-line Unionist leader, Basil Brooke, in 1963. His replacement as Prime Minister, Terence O'Neill, ushered in a new tone at Stormont, one chiming with the times of religious ecumenism in its rhetoric of 'building bridges' between the two communities in Northern Ireland.[15] This led to rising expectations amongst the minority, and a belief that significant change was on its way. Such hopes were further raised the following year, when the Labour Party came to power at Westminster. Labour's victory was aided by strong support from the Irish community in Britain, and amongst the back benches of the new government was a group of MPs who were actively engaging with the reformist elements then emerging among the Northern Ireland minority.[16] This increased pressure on the Stormont government, prompting O'Neill to make further gestures towards Catholic opinion, and thus encouraging the nationalist appetite for reform.[17]

As such, there are a number of factors which have to be considered in accounting for the climate of re-appraisal within the nationalist community in Northern Ireland from the late 1950s. However, it is clear that these factors combined to create a genuine and sustained shift in nationalist attitudes in this period. It is in this context that the politics of John Hume must be examined.

Notes

1 For a background on this, see A. Jackson, *Ireland: 1978–1998* (Oxford: Blackwell, 1999), ch. 5; and J. J. Lee, *Ireland, 1912–1985: Politics and Society* (Cambridge: Cambridge University Press, 1989), ch. 1.

2 Of course, the other principal losers in the partition of Ireland were southern unionists. However, their position differed from that of the northern minority

in two respects. Firstly, they maintained a strong socio-economic standing under the new dispensation, a legacy of the privileged position which Protestants enjoyed in Ireland under the Union. Secondly, being a much smaller minority, southern unionists found it easier to integrate into independent Ireland. This is not to say that they did not experience discrimination or a sense of dislocation in the new and Catholic-dominated state, but ultimately it was easier for them to embrace an Irish identity. For an overview of the Protestant experience in independent Ireland, see J. Coakley, 'Religion, ethnic identity and the Protestant minority in the Republic', in W. Crotty and D. E. Schmitt (eds), *Ireland and the Politics of Change* (London: Longman, 1998).

3   P. Buckland, *A History of Northern Ireland* (Dublin: Gill and Macmillan, 1981), pp. 66–7; J. Tonge, *Northern Irish: Conflict and Change* (Harlow: Pearson Education Limited, 2nd edn, 2002), p. 26.

4   There had been intense debate over the nature and extent of this discrimination. For a flavour of this, see the extended controversy between Christopher Hewitt, Denis O'Hearn and, later, K. A. Kovalcheck that took place in the *British Journal of Sociology* in the 1980s: 32:3 (1981); 34:3 (1983); 36:1 (1985); 38:1 (1987). Also see J. Whyte, 'How much discrimination was there under the unionist regime, 1921–68?', in T. Gallagher and J. O'Connell (eds), *Contemporary Irish Studies* (Manchester: Manchester University Press, 1983). Whyte's conclusion on the discrimination debate, judicious as ever, is that 'the picture is neither black nor white, but a shade of grey' (p. 30).

5   I. McAllister, 'Political parties and social change in Ulster: the case of the SDLP', *Social Studies*, 5:1 (1976); E. Staunton, *The Nationalists of Northern Ireland: 1918–1973* (Dublin: Columba Press, 2001), pp. 220–1; 230ff.

6   This claim is subject to much dispute, and is also related to the controversy on discrimination; see the literature referenced in n. 4. For a more general discussion of the civil rights era and related debates, see T. Hennessy, *Northern Ireland: The Origins of the Troubles* (Dublin, Gill and Macmillan, 2005); and B. Purdie, *Politics in the Streets: The Origins of the Civil Rights Movement in Northern Ireland* (Belfast: Blackstaff, 1990).

7   On this and alternative explanations of the Northern Ireland civil rights movement, see P. Dixon, *Northern Ireland: The Politics of Peace and War* (Basingstoke: Palgrave, 2nd edn, 2008), pp. 84ff.

8   Her Majesty's Stationery Office (HMSO), *Disturbances in Northern Ireland: Report of the Commission Appointed by the Governor of Northern Ireland* [The Cameron Report] (Belfast: HMSO, 1969), Cmnd. 532, paras. 11–12; I. McAllister, *The Social Democratic and Labour Party: Political Opposition in a Divided Society* (London: Macmillan, 1977), pp. 5–7.

9   M. Farrell, *Northern Ireland: The Orange State* (London: Pluto Press, 2nd edn, 1980), p. 189; B. O'Leary and J. McGarry, *The Politics of Antagonism: Understanding Northern Ireland* (London: Athlone Press, 2nd edn, 1996), pp. 157–8.

10   On this, see R. English, *Armed Struggle: A History of the IRA* (London: Macmillan, 2003), pp. 73–6.

11   O'Leary and McGarry, *The Politics of Antagonism*, p. 160.

12   Lee, *Ireland*, pp. 372–3.

13   On this, see H. Patterson, 'Seán Lemass and the Ulster question, 1959–65', *Journal of Contemporary History*, 34:1 (1999).

14 McAllister, *The Social and Democratic Labour Party*, p. 24; O'Leary and McGarry, *The Politics of Antagonism*, p. 156.

15 F. Cochrane, 'The past in the present', in P. Mitchell and R. Wilford (eds), *Politics in Northern Ireland* (Oxford: Oxford University Press, 1999), p. 18.

16 On this, see Purdie, *Politics in the Streets*, ch. 3.

17 P. Bew, P. Gibbon and H. Patterson, *Northern Ireland, 1921–2001: Political Forces and Social Classes* (London: Serif, 2002), pp. 144, 154–6, 167–8; O'Leary and McGarry, *The Politics of Antagonism*, pp. 159, 164, 166.

1

You can't eat a flag

Born into the working-class, Catholic Derry on 18 January 1937, John Hume was by no means predestined to become a politician.[1] Indeed, under the influence of his father, Hume was actively discouraged from any interest in politics.[2] In a story which he often cites, Hume tells of a time when, as a boy of ten, he and his father were observing an election meeting of the Nationalist Party, attended by the customary anti-partitionist rhetoric and flag-waving. As Hume recalled: 'When my father saw that I was affected, he put his hand gently on my shoulder and said, "Son, don't get involved in that stuff," and I said, "Why not, Da?" He answered simply, "Because you can't eat a flag."'[3] Sam Hume was more concerned with bread-and-butter issues than the constitutional question, and this attitude was passed on to his eldest son.[4]

This was evident in Hume's earliest venture into public life. In October 1960, he joined with other local activists to form Derry's first credit union. Seeing the success and rapid growth of this organisation in his home town, Hume became an ambassador for the credit union movement further afield. Throughout the early 1960s, he travelled the length and breadth of Ireland, helping to establish new branches and spreading the creed of the credit union philosophy as a means for communities to help themselves to prosper. Within a few years, Hume had become president of the Irish credit union movement, and vice-president of the world organisation.[5] His work with the movement reflected communitarian and self-help ideas which would remain central to Hume's later political thinking.

For the time being, though, Hume resisted involvement in politics.[6] Nonetheless, he was becoming politicised by various developments in Northern Ireland. Most notable was the controversial Lockwood Report of 1965, which recommended Coleraine as the site for the region's second university. Derry had appeared the more obvious choice, with Magee College already providing a site of third-level education that was open to expansion. As a result, Lockwood met considerable opposition from both religious communities in the city. Encouraged by this, Hume took up the chairmanship of the inter-denominational University for Derry Action Committee, which sought to dissuade the Stormont government from following Lockwood's recommendations.[7]

Hume's belief in the potential of the Action Committee to bring together the two communities in Derry was confirmed by the huge success of a public meeting on the university issue, held at the city's Guildhall. This event saw Nationalist and Unionist politicians sharing the same platform, and speaking to an enthusiastic audience which straddled the religious divide.[8] Hume's first biographer, Barry White, recalls the flavour of the speech which the Action Committee chair made to this audience: 'His theme was the need to unite the two communities, not just for the duration of the university campaign, but for the good of the city in the longer term.'[9] Indeed, Hume hoped that the campaign, created by an issue of common, practical concern, would develop into a more sturdy alliance between the two, arguing that such co-operation could only benefit both sides.[10] This line of reasoning would echo throughout Hume's thinking during the next three decades.

Hume's efforts in the university campaign culminated in his leading a cross-community delegation to Stormont, and his organisation of mass motorcade from Derry to Belfast. This saw an estimated 25,000 people converging on the Stormont estate to demonstrate their support for the campaign.[11] Despite this, the government endorsed the Lockwood Report, and chose Coleraine as the site for the new university. Hume was severely disillusioned. Like many Catholics, he found it difficult not to read Lockwood in a political light. Indeed, for a number of government reports in this period appeared to favour the eastern and predominately Protestant part of Northern Ireland, and to disadvantage the more Catholic western counties. Firstly, the Benson Report of 1963 led to closure of various rail routes in the west, then the Matthew Report selected the Protestant heartlands of North Armagh as the main centre for new urban development, and finally Lockwood chose the unionist town of Coleraine rather than largely nationalist Derry as the site for a new university. Unsurprisingly, Catholics began to see O'Neill's programme of economic 'modernisation' as one designed to consolidate Protestant power and so maintain support for the Ulster Unionist Party (UUP).[12]

This was certainly how Hume presented the case at a public meeting in London which was organised by interested British Labour MPs. This took place only a few months after the university controversy, which Hume claimed had proved the 'last straw' for the people of Derry. 'And so the plan stands clear', he explained:

> The minority in Northern Ireland resides mainly in the western counties of Derry, Tyrone and Fermanagh. To develop those areas is to develop areas opposed to the Government and to lose the few Unionist seats held there. The plan is, therefore, to develop the strongly Unionist Belfast–Coleraine– Portadown triangle and to cause migration from West to East Ulster, redistributing and scattering the minority so that the Unionist Party will not only maintain but strengthen its position.[13]

Hume went on to express his fear that such underhand action by the Stormont government threatened to damage the improved relations that had recently developed between the two communities in Northern Ireland: 'The tragedy is that this plan comes at a time when the ... problem shows more hopeful signs of internal solution than ever before.' Most striking here is Hume's intimation that an 'internal solution' to the Northern Ireland problem was possible, that is a solution which did not affect the border. Indeed, Hume was at pains to stress that it was the communal divide in Northern Ireland – rather than the political divide between the North and South of Ireland – that was his primary concern: 'It is my belief that the problem can only fully be solved by the people there themselves and only then when the mental border that divides the community has been largely eradicated'.[14] Again, Hume expressed sentiments here that would inform his later political thinking.

The challenge to traditionalism

Hume's actions in the University for Derry campaign showed a desire to reach across to the Protestant community, and an eagerness to engage the Stormont government. But neither trait was uncommon to the generation of Northern Ireland Catholics to which he belonged. Indeed, as noted in the Introduction, a number of mutually reinforcing pressures helped forge a more forward-thinking and reformist attitude amongst this generation. This, in turn, led to increasing disenchantment with the established political representatives of the minority, the Nationalist Party.

By the end of the 1950s, the Nationalist Party had become politically moribund. Its singular focus on partition, and its uncooperative attitude towards Stormont, began to be questioned by many in the Catholic community.[15] The first organised expression of this dissatisfaction came with the formation of National Unity in 1959. In essence, National Unity was a pressure group: it did not seek to replace the Nationalist Party, but it did wish to see its reform. In particular, the new group encouraged the Nationalists to create a democratically structured, grass-roots organisation, and to adopt a more constructive approach towards Stormont.[16] However, National Unity did not believe that such a shift should entail the abandonment of the aspiration to a united Ireland. As one of its earliest pamphlets suggested, 'we maintain that while there is room for more co-operation and greater attempts to understand the unionist point of view, it would be fatal to do anything to undermine our ultimate aim and ideal, the unity of Ireland.'[17]

Though firmly committed to this end, National Unity argued that the only way to achieve a united Ireland was to win Ulster Protestants' support. Indeed, one of the group's co-founders, Michael McKeown, felt that this was the chief motivation for National Unity. Recalling the organisation's inaugural meeting, he noted the sense of exasperation with the Nationalist

Party over its failure to adopt any such constructive approach towards Irish
unity: 'There seemed to be no suggestion [amongst the Nationalists] that
they should ever appeal to Unionist voters or make a case on the Protestant
doorstep for a united Ireland. ... [As a result, w]e decided to form an
organisation ... dedicated to the ideal of a united Ireland brought about by
the consent of the majority of the people in Northern Ireland.'[18]

The 'principle of consent' had become a phrase of common political cur-
rency in Northern Ireland by the time McKeown came to write this
account, over a quarter of a century after the formation of National Unity.
But in 1959, the idea that Irish nationalists should – indeed must – gain
the assent of Ulster Protestants for a united Ireland represented a radical
departure. Traditionally, nationalists had denied the unionist community
any right of veto over Irish unity, claiming that the Protestant majority in
Northern Ireland was a position manufactured by partition. But National
Unity suggested that at least a section of this population would have to be
persuaded of the merits of Irish reunification.

From the early to mid-1960s, as debate amongst the Catholic community fermented, National Unity was joined by a number of other groups
encouraging the re-orientation of northern nationalism.[19] Most significant
was the National Democratic Party (NDP), formed in 1965. The NDP was
itself an outgrowth of National Unity, but as an actual political party
rather than a mere ginger group, and by contesting elections and thereby
presenting a potential challenge to the Nationalists, it reflected a growing
impatience with the latter's failure to modernise.[20]

Limited in its organisation, the NDP never represented a serious threat
to the Nationalist Party. However, like National Unity before it, the new
group did have an ideological bearing on the direction of northern nationalist politics in the coming years. Indeed, both the NDP and National
Unity had established a number of core principles which were to inform
progressive nationalism, not just in the 1960s, but also in the decades that
followed. In essence, they advocated constructive political action: participation over abstention. Rather than restating well-worn arguments about
the illegitimacy of partition and the Northern Ireland state, the NDP and
National Unity spoke in favour of working the Stormont system, this to
secure its reform. Towards this end, they sought to create an active, democratic political organisation, and an effective opposition to the Unionist
Party at Stormont. Such an approach contrasted strongly with that of the
Nationalist Party, which had little grassroots organisation, and was largely
abstentionist in its instincts. Also unlike the Nationalists, the NDP
believed that the social and economic conditions of the Catholic community were of greater immediate concern than the constitutional question.
Thus, as with National Unity before it, the NDP maintained the aspiration
to Irish unity, but argued that this could only come about by working
alongside unionists and winning their assent for constitutional change.
Participation, co-operation, and the pursuit of unionist consent for the

creation of a united Ireland were the essential ingredients of a new approach to nationalist politics. Revisionism had taken root.

'The Northern Catholic': a changing disposition?

Such ideas were hugely influential on Hume. Though he was not directly involved in either National Unity or the NDP, he clearly supported their reformist agenda. This was clearly demonstrated by 'The Northern Catholic', a two-part article which Hume wrote for the *Irish Times* in May 1964.[21] In this piece, Hume sought to capture the spirit of change abroad in his community in the early 1960s. This he did, most eloquently, giving an early demonstration of his innate ability to speak for northern nationalists. But in conveying the mood of the minority, Hume also provided the first coherent expression of his own political philosophy, articulating ideas that he would continue to hold to throughout his career. As such, the article deserves detailed consideration.

Hume's immediate objective in this piece was to advertise the change of attitude that was occurring within his community, particularly among those of his own age. 'The crux of the matter for the younger generation', he claimed, 'is the continued existence ... of great social problems of housing, unemployment and emigration. It is the struggle for priority in their minds between such problems and the ideal of a United Ireland with which they have been bred that has produced ... the great political frustration that exists within the Catholic community here.' In Hume's mind, whatever the heresy of this trend, Catholics of his cohort were more concerned for their position *within* Northern Ireland than any prospect of unification with the Irish Republic: 'It may be that the present generation of younger Catholics in the North is more materialistic than their fathers but there is little doubt that their thinking is principally geared towards the solution of social and economic problems. This has led to a deep questioning of traditional Nationalist attitudes.'

Hume was one of those asking questions, particularly of the Nationalist Party, which he felt had failed to challenge the Unionist government in any positive way that might bring practical benefits to the minority: 'Nationalists in opposition have been in no way constructive. ... In forty years of opposition they have not produced one constructive contribution on either the social or economic plane to the development of Northern Ireland ... leadership has been the comfortable leadership of flags and slogans.' However, whilst eager for the Nationalist Party to move beyond its obsession with partition, Hume did not surrender the essential aspiration to a united Ireland. Instead, he questioned the means by which nationalists had traditionally sought to achieve this goal:

> If one wishes to create a United Ireland by constitutional means, then one must accept the constitutional position. ... Such an attitude, too, admits the realistic fact that a United Ireland, if it is to come, and if violence, rightly, is

to be discounted, must come about by evolution, i.e. by the will of the Northern majority. It is clear that this is the only way in which a truly United Ireland (with the Northern Protestant integrated) can be achieved.

In this, following the lead of National Unity, Hume accepted the principle of consent. He recognised that Ulster Protestants' assent was a prerequisite for Irish unity, not just from a moral perspective – believing that it was unjust to coerce unionists into a united Ireland against their will – but also from a practical point of view – acknowledging that without their agreement and thus allegiance such a state could not be 'a truly united Ireland'. In the meantime, Hume had no qualms about accepting the current constitutional position, maintaining that this did not contradict the essential aspiration to Irish unity: 'There is nothing inconsistent with such acceptance and a belief that a thirty-two county republic is best for Ireland'.

Building on the thinking of groups like National Unity, Hume's arguments here represented a clear departure from traditional nationalism, which depicted the British government as the chief impediment to Irish unity, implying that Westminster need only renounce its claim of sovereignty over Northern Ireland in order for that end to be realised. In fact, Hume made no mention whatsoever of Britain in his article. Instead he intimated that it was the Ulster unionist community which represented the primary obstacle to a united Ireland – that it was the attitudes of Protestant Ulster, shaped by its relations with Catholic Ireland, which prevented Irish unity. Implicit in his reasoning was the idea that the ending of partition was not enough to unite Ireland. Division in Ireland constituted more than just a line on a map; the people of the island were divided, and indeed the perpetuation of partition was a reflection more than a cause of this division. The rationale inferred here – which would become more pronounced in and central to Hume's thinking in due course – was that the *people* of Ireland had to be united before territorial unity was worth considering. Towards this end, Hume suggested that, rather than seeking to undo partition, nationalists should afford *de facto* recognition to the Northern Ireland state, and work with it and with unionists for the common good of all. As he saw it, this would serve to break down Protestant prejudices towards the Catholic community, and so make a united Ireland all the more attainable: 'If the whole Northern community gets seriously to work on its problems; the unionist bogeys about Catholics and a Republic will, through better understanding, disappear. It will of course take a long time.'[22]

Hume was not, however, ignorant of the discriminatory practices which prevented his community from playing a more constructive role in public life in Northern Ireland. Thus, he also argued for state authorities to actively encourage Catholics to take up positions in areas where they were underrepresented. But notable in Hume's comments on this matter was his suggestion that, as well as accommodating Catholics *qua* Catholics, unionists had to accommodate them as Irish nationalists: '[T]hey must accept that nationalism in Ireland is an acceptable political belief and that nationally-minded people are entitled to put forward their views constitutionally without prejudice to the right to any position which they might seek.' Again, the similarity with National Unity's arguments is striking: acceptance of and participation in the Northern Ireland state and society should not require the abandonment of Irish nationalism and its ambitions. However, conversely, Hume suggested that nationalists must respect the political rights of the unionist community: 'the Protestant tradition in the North is as strong and as legitimate as our own. Such recognition is the first step to better relations. We must be prepared to accept this and to realise that the fact that a man wishes Northern Ireland to remain part of the United Kingdom does not necessarily make him a bigot or a discriminator.' For Hume, each community had to accept the legitimacy of the other's political aspirations. Such ideas remained central to his later thinking.

The civil rights movement

It was the Unionist government's failure to respond to the reformist tendencies emerging within the minority from the early 1960s that led to the later civil rights movement.[23] Despite various efforts to engage Stormont and to highlight the discrimination which they endured,[24] O'Neill was unwilling or unable to produce the concrete changes which Catholics came to expect from his conciliatory rhetoric. In frustration, the minority now turned to street protest in order to highlight its grievances. In this, the Catholic community was seeking the attention of the British government as much as Stormont, hoping that it would oblige the latter to instigate reform.

Hume's involvement in the civil rights movement may seem a logical progression from his earlier community activism. However, when the Northern Ireland Civil Rights Association (NICRA) was formed in early 1967, he declined an invitation to join, considering the outlook of some of the organisation's founding members to be too radical.[25] Indeed, it was only after witnessing the outcome of the first civil rights march in his home town – the infamous Derry demonstration of 5 October 1968 – that Hume decided to involve himself.

It was the brutal suppression of the Derry protest by the Royal Ulster Constabulary (RUC), and the sudden media interest that followed, which stirred Hume into action. He, like other community activists in the city, sensed that eyes of the world had now turned upon Derry, creating an historic opportunity to press the Stormont government towards reform. Eager to seize this opportunity, Hume immediately contacted former colleagues from the University for Derry Action Committee, and together they sought to wrest control of Derry's burgeoning civil rights campaign from those more radical, confrontational characters who had organised the October march. The outcome of their efforts was the formation of the

Derry Citizens' Action Committee (DCAC), which quickly established itself as the leading organisation in the city's civil rights movement. Seeking to revive the cross-community support enjoyed by the University for Derry campaign, the Protestant activist Ivan Cooper was elected chairman of the DCAC, with Hume acting as his deputy.[26]

Speaking at the first demonstration organised by the DCAC, Hume took the opportunity to refute unionist claims that the civil rights campaign was merely a new approach to the achievement of traditional nationalist ends: 'It has been said against this movement that its purpose is to unite Ireland ... This movement has no political ends. We are not dealing with political issues. Civil rights is not a political but a moral issue. We are seeking fair play for all within the existing state.'[27] Here, Hume addressed the central controversy of the civil rights movement, a controversy which continues to be debated in the literature on Northern Ireland.[28] Hume made clear that the movement was not, in his mind, a means towards Irish reunification. Rather, it represented a demand for reform 'within the existing state'. In this regard, he spoke for many of those involved in the civil rights campaign. Though they may have aspired to Irish unity, activists like Hume were more concerned with the reform of the Northern Ireland state. Indeed, and this was a message which Hume made explicit in his role with the DCAC: 'We are not against Partition, we're for fair play within the existing constitution.'[29]

Following further demonstrations by the DCAC and NICRA, leading in turn to political pressure from Westminster, O'Neill finally announced a reform package on 22 November 1968. However, even moderates within the civil rights movement were disappointed by this package, feeling that it fudged many of their demands. In particular, there was concern that Stormont had failed to produce immediate change in the method of election for local government.[30] This was a crucial issue for the civil rights movement, as the existing system was weighted towards property and business owners, more predominant among the Protestant community. This, and the manipulation of electoral boundaries, had led to serious anomalies in local government, most notably in Derry, where Catholics made up a majority of the population, but the Unionist Party was still able to maintain control of the council. As such, O'Neill's failure to move immediately on the franchise issue, and the questions raised about other aspects of his reform package, meant that his efforts were not met with any great enthusiasm by the Catholic community. Indeed, it was only after the Prime Minister made his famous 'Ulster at the Crossroads' speech on 9 December[31] – an appeal to the civil rights movement, but also to those sections of the Protestant community which were agitating against the prospect of reform – that the DCAC and NICRA reluctantly agreed to a moratorium on all marches for a month. This, it was suggested, would give O'Neill time to prove the sincerity of his efforts, but in the meantime avoid further confrontations between civil rights protesters and loyalist counter-demonstrations.[32]

The tentative truce, however, was broken by the radical student group People's Democracy (PD). PD insisted on the need to maintain pressure on O'Neill, and so organised a four-day march from Belfast to Derry in January 1969. Passing through strongly loyalist areas, the protest provoked considerable opposition, culminating in a particularly vicious assault on the marchers at Burntollet Bridge, just outside of Derry. The attack appeared to be unhindered by the RUC, and was even aided by off-duty members of the reserve police force, the B-Specials. Accordingly, nationalist opinion in Derry was outraged, and when the bloodied marchers finally entered the city on 4 January severe rioting broke out. Shortly afterwards, a group of RUC officers, some inebriated, were involved in what appeared as revenge attacks on houses in the Bogside area. By nightfall on the following day, barricades had gone up around the Bogside, and vigilante groups were patrolling the streets: 'Free Derry' was born.[33]

This proved a crucial turning point in Catholic Derry. Behind the barricades, the moderate DCAC began to lose authority, and more radical, even republican, elements gained sway. The latter fed on the fear and anger that had been generated by the attacks on the Bogside and at Burntollet, incidents which seemed to confirm Catholic perceptions of the RUC and the B-Specials as Protestant and politically partisan outfits. As a result, reform of the Stormont security apparatus now became a key demand of the civil rights movement.[34]

Ulster at the crossroads

It was in this context that the Prime Minister dissolved the Stormont parliament and called an election in February 1969. O'Neill called it the 'crossroads election', as again he appealed for moderation from both communities. In essence, he was seeking a mandate for his policy of piecemeal reform. However, his success in this was questionable, with a number of unionist politicians being elected on an anti-O'Neill ticket. Even within his own party, a significant number of MPs were actively opposed to or refused to support O'Neill's modest reforms. His position continued to deteriorate, and within two months O'Neill was forced to resign as Prime Minister.

The crossroads election also led to change within the Catholic community, with a number of civil rights activists taking seats from the Nationalist Party. Most dramatically, Hume took the Foyle constituency from the Nationalist leader Eddie McAteer. This result in particular suggested a decisive shift amongst the Catholic electorate, effectively decapitating the party which had represented minority since the foundation of Northern Ireland. However, Hume's decision to stand for Stormont, even on a civil rights platform, has to be examined. Indeed, many felt that he was exploiting the reputation he had gained as a civil rights leader, and ultimately betraying the spirit of the movement.[35] Defending his position, Hume suggested that he was in fact advancing the civil rights agenda by bringing it directly into Stormont: 'I had the feeling that the movement on the streets had attained its immediate objectives, and must be consolidated by political advance.'[36] Supporting his claim, it could be argued that by early 1969 the civil rights movement had already run its course as an effective vehicle for change. As street protest continued to degenerate into street violence, it was perhaps natural that Hume and other moderate leaders within the movement would seek to lead the campaign for civil rights into a more peaceable, parliamentary arena.[37]

On the other hand, it was clear from his electoral manifesto that Hume was now moving beyond the civil rights agenda. Indeed, here Hume claimed to seek a mandate from the people to work for the following:

1. The formation of a new political movement based on social democratic principles ...
2. A movement that must provide what had been seriously lacking at Stormont – a strong energetic Opposition to conservatism, proposing radical social and economic policies.
3. A movement that must be completely non-sectarian and committed to rooting out the fundamental evil in our society – sectarian division.
4. A movement that would be committed to the idea that the future of the North should be decided by its people and that there should be no change in its constitutional position without the consent of its people.[38]

Though advancing beyond the aims of the civil rights movement, there were, however, clear limits to Hume's programme. Most notably, he made no mention of Irish unity in his manifesto. Moreover, the very idea of constitutional change was relegated to last place in his list of objectives, and even then the only commitment made was to the principle of consent in determining Northern Ireland's future. In this, again Hume's position can be seen as consistent with that taken by groups such as National Unity since the late 1950s. Following their agenda, he was advocating the creation of a reformist political party that would provide a constructive and energetic opposition at Stormont, pursue a leftist socio-economic agenda, attempt to reach across the sectarian divide, and be committed to the principle that there be no change in the constitutional position of Northern Ireland without the consent of a majority of its people. These standards, as well as providing the essence of Hume's own political philosophy, were to provide the ideological underpinning of the party which he helped to found on the basis of the mandate that he received in the crossroads election.

Notes

1 On Hume's background, see White, *John Hume*, ch. 1.
2 Drower, *John Hume*, p. 36; White, *John Hume*, p. 55.
3 J. Hume, *A New Ireland: Peace, Politics and Reconciliation* (Boulder: Roberts Rhinehart, 1996), pp. 25–6.
4 White, *John Hume*, pp. 7, 55.
5 P. Doherty, *Paddy Bogside* (Cork: Mercier, 2001), pp. 29, 44, 52–3; Hume, *A New Ireland*, pp. 27–8; Routledge, *John Hume*, pp. 38–9; White, *John Hume*, pp. 30–3.
6 White, *John Hume*, pp. 53–5, 56.
7 F. Curran, *Derry: Countdown to Disaster* (Dublin: Gill and Macmillan, 1986), pp. 26, 30–1; Purdie, *Politics in the Streets*, p. 165; White, *John Hume*, p. 38.
8 *Derry Journal*, 9 February 1965; Curran, *Derry*, pp. 31–2.
9 White, *John Hume*, p. 38.
10 *Ibid.*, pp. 38–9.
11 *Derry Journal*, 12 and 19 February 1965; Curran, *Derry*, pp. 32, 33.
12 Curran, *Derry*, p. 33; E. McCann, *War and an Irish Town* (Harmondsworth: Penguin, 1974), pp. 23, 230–1; O'Leary and McGarry, *The Politics of Antagonism*, pp. 164–5.
13 *Derry Journal*, 6 August 1965.
14 *Ibid.*
15 For example, see D. Kennedy, 'Whither northern nationalism?', *Christus Rex*, 8:4 (1959), and G. B. Newe, 'The Catholic in the Northern Ireland community', *Christus Rex*, 18:1 (1964).
16 I. McAllister, 'Political opposition in Northern Ireland: the National Democratic Party, 1965–1970', *The Economic and Social Review*, 6:3 (1975), p. 358; Purdie, *Politics in the Streets*, pp. 54–7.
17 Cited in E. Staunton, *The Nationalists of Northern Ireland: 1918–1973* (Dublin: Columba Press, 2001), p. 231.
18 M. McKeown, *The Greening of a Nationalist* (Dublin: Murlough, 1986), p. 19.
19 B. Lynn, *Holding the Ground: The Nationalist Party in Northern Ireland, 1945–72* (Aldershot: Dartmouth, 1997), p. 232; McKeown, *The Greening of a Nationalist*, pp. 23–5; Purdie, *Politics in the Streets*, pp. 53–4, 200–1.
20 McAllister, 'Political opposition in Northern Ireland', pp. 362–3.
21 The line of argument and all subsequent quotations in this section are taken from the article, appearing in the *Irish Times*, 18 and 19 May 1964. Interestingly, five years earlier, Desmond Fennell, a southern academic and freelance writer, published a series of articles in the *Irish Times* under the same heading as Hume's. In these, Fennell had highlighted some of the early changes in northern nationalist thinking which Hume would explore further in his own article. While Hume's choice of title may have been a coincidence, it is likely that Fennell's writings had some influence on him, if not at this time, then in years to come. Indeed, for both men wrote regularly for Dublin-based papers in the early 1970s, and a perusal of Fennell's columns shows a certain similarity between his and Hume's arguments. This supposition is given credence by the indirect contribution which Fennell made to the SDLP's 1972 proposals, *Towards a New Ireland* (see p. 60, n. 14).

22   As well as following in the footsteps of National Unity, the position advocated
     by Hume in his *Irish Times* article corresponded with the policy then being
     persued by the Irish government under Seán Lemass. As alluded to in the
     Preface, Lemass developed a 'co-operation first' policy, hoping that this would
     lead in time to more friendly relations between Dublin and Belfast, and so
     provide the context of within which reunification might then take place;
     Kennedy, *Division and Consensus*, p. 180; Horgan, *Seán Lemass*, ch. 8.
     Hume's *Irish Times* article must be read in this context. For his arguments in
     favour of nationalists and unionists working together in pursuit of their com-
     mon interests, and his belief that this was the only way in which Irish unity
     might eventually be achieved, clearly coincided with the new thinking on par-
     tition shown by the Lemass government.
23   For a comprehensive account of the civil rights movement, and the various ini-
     tiatives which preceded it, see Purdie, *Politics in the Streets*.
24   See Purdie, *Politics in the Streets*, *passim*.
25   White, *John Hume*, pp. 59, 62.
26   Doherty, *Paddy Bogside*, pp. 60–2; N. Ó Dochartaigh, *From Civil Rights to
     Armalites: Derry and the Birth of the Irish Troubles* (Cork: Cork University
     Press, 1997), pp. 21–2, 23; Purdie, *Politics in the Streets*, pp. 188–90;
     Routledge, *John Hume*, pp. 67–8; White, *John Hume*, p. 64.
27   *Derry Journal*, 22 October 1968.
28   See Hennessy, *Northern Ireland: The Origins of the Troubles*; and Purdie,
     Politics in the Streets. Purdie's study, the most comprehensive on the civil
     rights movement, convincingly refutes the idea that the campaign was a mere
     cloak for traditional anti-partitionist nationalism. Purdie argues that the
     movement was far too disparate, and its development dependent on too many
     other variables, to allow it be considered as a conscious conspiracy to subvert
     the Northern Ireland state (pp. 154, 157–8).
29   *Irish Times*, 22 November 1968.
30   Hennessy, *Northern Ireland: The Origins of the Troubles*, pp. 159–60;
     Ó Dochartaigh, *From Civil Rights to Armalites*, pp. 30–2; Purdie, *Politics in
     the Streets*, pp. 195–6.
31   For a full text of the speech, see T. O'Neill, *The Autobiography of Terence
     O'Neill* (London, Hart-Davis, 1972), pp. 145–9.
32   Ó Dochartaigh, *From Civil Rights to Armalites*, p. 32; Purdie, *Politics in the
     Streets*, p. 195.
33   The Cameron Report, para. 177; Doherty, *Paddy Bogside*, pp. 88–94;
     McCann, *War and an Irish Town*, pp. 51–3; Ó Dochartaigh, *From Civil Rights
     to Armalites*, pp. 33, 39, 40–1; Purdie, *Politics in the Streets*, pp. 213–15.
34   Ó Dochartaigh, *From Civil Rights to Armalites*, pp. 33, 40–7, 52.
35   For example, see the letters to the editor of the *Derry Journal* on 11 and
     14 February 1968.
36   Quoted in Curran, *Derry*, p. 116.
37   McAllister, *The Social and Democratic Labour Party*, p. 24.
38   *Irish News*, 7 February 1969.

2

A united Ireland or nothing

As 1969 unfolded, the situation in Northern Ireland continued to spiral out of control.[1] On the nationalist side, radical leftists and more traditional republican elements both saw the opportunity to encourage disorder and so to further destabilise the state. At the same time, the increasing insurgency of the minority appeared to vindicate loyalist suspicions of the civil rights movement, to feed Protestant fears that the nationalist community was indeed intent on overthrowing the government, and so to strengthen unionist opposition to reform. The growing distrust of 'the other side' allowed extremists in both communities to gain in influence.[2]

This process of polarisation reached a climax in August 1969, when communal mistrust exploded into communal violence. A sustained confrontation between Derry Catholics and the RUC – the infamous 'Battle of the Bogside'[3] – triggered a bout of far more lethal violence in Belfast, where the nationalist community proved particularly vulnerable. Indeed, though homes and lives were lost on both sides of the religious divide, it was Belfast Catholics that suffered much of the worst. The RUC, seemingly unable to stop loyalist attacks on nationalist districts, and in many Catholics' eyes even aiding these assaults, was further discredited.[4] Eventually, the London government was forced to intervene, with the British army arriving on the streets of Northern Ireland in mid-August. Though ostensibly stepping between the two communities, these troops were effectively deployed to protect the minority, significant sections of which now refused to be policed by the RUC. This was an issue which remained central to the Northern Ireland problem over the next three decades.

By the end of the summer of 1969, the situation in Northern Ireland had, therefore, changed dramatically. From a nationalist perspective, mere reform of Stormont was no longer sufficient. Indeed, most Catholics were now looking beyond the Belfast parliament, for their protection as much as for redress of their grievances. August 1969 destroyed any little faith which they previously held in the Unionist government's ability to rule over them in an impartial manner. As Niall Ó Dochartaigh suggests: 'It was no longer a question of adapting Northern Ireland slightly in order to abate Catholic hostility to the state: it had to be changed significantly.'[5]

Clearly, the reformist agenda that had evolved through the 1960s was now being overtaken by the demands of the Catholic masses.

The Social Democratic and Labour Party

The difficulties of reformist nationalism were compounded by its failure to find a common political voice. Fearing the room which this allowed for more radical influences, Hume was striving to remedy the situation. Indeed, immediately after the arrival of British troops in Northern Ireland, he had renewed his appeal – first made during his election to Stormont in February 1969 – for the disparate ranks of the opposition benches to unite under one banner.[6] It was not until the autumn, however, that Hume made any progress towards this end, when he finally persuaded a number of opposition MPs to form a semi-official shadow cabinet, the so-called 'Opposition Alliance'.[7]

It took a further six months of secretive negotiations – again led largely by Hume[8] – before members of this group finally agreed to the establishment of a formal political organisation, the Social Democratic and Labour Party (SDLP). However, even the elongated appellation of the new party told much of the divisions within. Younger figures like Hume and the former Nationalist MP Austin Currie wanted the term 'Social Democratic' in the title, believing this reflected a more moderate, modern, and European agenda. However, the older, more urban members – old-school socialists like Gerry Fitt and Paddy Devlin – were adamant that the word 'Labour' had to be included.[9] Neither side was willing to compromise, and so the new party was bestowed with an arguably tautological title: it was both a 'Social Democratic' and a 'Labour' party.

This dispute reflected wider disagreements, and indeed considerable personal rivalries, amongst the founders of the SDLP. For many months, they had procrastinated over the possibility of coming together, the political priorities of the new party, and – most crucially – who would be leader.[10] Although Hume was clearly the key actor in bringing together the SDLP, the other members were convinced of the need to bring Fitt on board.[11] His position as a Westminster MP, and his contacts amongst the back benches of the British Labour government, were considered crucial for establishing the fledgling party's profile.[12] But Fitt's price for joining was that he would lead the group. In the end, Hume proved willing to defer, but Fitt still took considerable coaxing, and even then seemed uncertain: 'This won't last', he is reputed to have told Devlin, 'but it would be unfair not to try it.'[13]

What united the new alignment, however, was a belief in the principles of the civil rights movement, and in the need to consolidate and secure the reforms which it had achieved. Indeed, the final impetus for the coming together of the SDLP was a fear that loyalist opposition would lead to the toppling of the government and a reversal in the process of change. As Fitt made clear at the party's inaugural press conference: 'We [see] … a very real possibility that there may be a right-wing take-over of the government of Northern Ireland with a consequent interference of the reforms which have recently been placed on the statute book.'[14]

Fitt then went on to read a statement which detailed the aims of the new party. Although drafted by Hume and Currie,[15] this document – which provided the essence of the SDLP's formal constitution – also bore the hallmark of Fitt and Devlin. Indeed, the leftist disposition of the party was given great emphasis as Fitt read out a considerable list of socialistic objectives including the achievement of a fair distribution of wealth, a minimum wage, and the establishment of state industries. Only after detailing these social and economic aims did Fitt finally reveal the SDLP's position on the constitutional question, declaring that the party would seek to 'promote co-operation, friendship and understanding between North and South with the view to the eventual reunification of Ireland'.[16]

In this, the SDLP showed the same order of priorities that Hume had declared in his election to Stormont 18 months earlier: the need for social and economic reform came before any idea of constitutional change. However, unlike Hume's Stormont manifesto, the founding statement of the SDLP did declare the party in favour of Irish reunification. With this commitment, however aspirational, the SDLP could be seen as being a nationalist party from the very outset. But in its approach to Irish unity, the SDLP made a crucial departure from orthodox nationalism. As Fitt went on to explain, the party held that a united Ireland could only be achieved 'through the support of the majority of people in the North and in the South.'[17] Any possible ambiguity in this formulation was eradicated in the choice of words that was used in the SDLP's formal constitution, which declared the party's intention to 'promote the cause of Irish unity based on the consent of the majority of the people in Northern Ireland.'[18] With this, the SDLP followed the path of the NDP and National Unity before it in committing to the principle of consent.

Although building on the ideas of the NDP and National Unity, the SDLP was more explicit in its appeal to the Protestant community. All of the founding members – Hume, Fitt, Devlin, Currie, Paddy O'Hanlon and of course Ivan Cooper, himself a Protestant – had been involved in the civil rights movement, and each had absorbed its idealism. Indeed, the new party hoped to translate the anti-sectarian rhetoric of the civil rights mobilisation into a political movement which spanned the religious divide. 'We are not setting about to set up a Catholic party', declared Fitt: 'We want direct popular support from all sections of the community.'[19] Also, the leftist input of Fitt and Devlin in particular encouraged the new party to believe that this could be achieved by perusing a program of radical social and economic reform.[20] Such an agenda would certainly gain support amongst the disadvantaged Catholic community, but in addition, it was hoped, win votes from Protestant workers alienated by the conservative economic policies of successive Unionist governments.[21] The SDLP's first priority, then, was to continue the process of reform *within* Northern Ireland. The belief was that radical change in the way the two communities lived together there would, in time, lead Ulster Protestants to reconsider their relationship with Catholics across Ireland, and therein open the way towards the reunification of the island.

In the meantime, endorsement of the principle of consent was considered by the SDLP as a guarantee to the Protestant community. Indeed, acceptance of this principle represented *de facto* recognition of the Northern Ireland state. Though it still allowed for the aspiration to Irish unity, such a position implicitly accepted that this was not the wish of a majority in Northern Ireland and that, until it was so, reunification could not be considered. However, following the turmoil of 1968–69, the constitutional question had become all-consuming once again. For this reason, when the SDLP declared its commitment to consent, the unionist community could not see the huge concession which this represented. They could not see past the party's ultimate objective of Irish unity, even if this was conditional upon their agreement. As such, the birth of the SDLP, despite its cross-community aspirations, could only reinforce electoral alignment along confessional lines.

In this respect, the delay in the formation of the SDLP proved particularly costly. Between Hume's call for the creation of a reformist party in February 1969 and the actual establishment of the SDLP in August 1970, much had occurred. Most notably, the violence of August 1969 had led to a revival of traditional Irish republicanism, culminating in the birth of the Provisional Irish Republican Army (IRA) in December 1969.[22] With this, republicans had already established a foothold within the minority community, a position from which they were able to promote their interpretation of the emerging situation, and so attempt to set the agenda for nationalist politics.[23] Thus, from the moment of its inception, the SDLP found a ready-made rival for the leadership of the Catholic community. Moreover, as Eamonn McCann points out, the Provisionals had 'a perfectly coherent and stunningly simple answer to the crisis – smash Stormont and unite Ireland'.[24] This was more immediately intelligible than the incrementalist ideology proffered by the SDLP, especially to nationalists in deprived urban areas, many of whom had seen little gain in the civil rights reforms, and yet had been the main victims of the conflict thus far. Accordingly, as Gerard Murray and Jonathan Tonge suggest: 'Whilst many nationalists endorsed ... the embryonic SDLP, a section of the Catholic working class, disillusioned by political marginalisation, sectarian discrimination and the lack of change, was to prefer armed rebellion.'[25] As a result, the Provisionals were able to condition the words and deeds of the SDLP from the outset.[26]

From reform to repression

By 1970, even moderates within the nationalist community had begun to question the value of the reforms won since 1968. As McGarry and O'Leary explain: 'For Catholics, the institutional nature of the reforms had little immediate effect on their daily experience or life-chances, and consequently did not arouse their enthusiasm.'[27] Structural problems such as unemployment and inadequate housing, the key grievances for the community at large, could not be remedied overnight. But the disproportionate impact which they continued to have on the minority ensured that Catholic resentment did not abate. In other areas, nationalists believed that the Unionist government was reneging on the reforms that had been promised. As a result, nationalists felt that the radical change in the Stormont system which had been envisaged by the civil rights movement was failing to materialise.[28]

Believing that reform had failed, Catholics also sensed the state shifting to a more repressive policy. Both perceptions were related by the minority to the Westminster election of June 1970, won by the Conservatives. Whereas the Labour government had continually pressed the Unionists towards reform, the new British administration felt that to push further might provoke a loyalist backlash, and thus the complete collapse of Stormont. With this, London feared that it would become directly and irrevocably embroiled in the Northern Ireland crisis. As a result, from mid-1970 onwards, Westminster relented in its pressure on the Stormont government and, crucially, allowed it a freer hand in the use of the British army.[29]

By this stage, Stormont faced a growing threat from the Provisional IRA. But allowing the army to take the lead in counter-insurgency operations proved largely counter-productive. The army's heavy-handed and often indiscriminate actions clearly played into the hands of Provisionals. For example, in July 1970, searches for republican arms led to a two-day curfew in the Lower Falls district of Belfast, resulting in the arrest of 300 men, and the death of three civilians. Recalling the impact which this had amongst his constituents, Paddy Devlin wrote that: 'Overnight the population turned from neutral or even sympathetic support for the military to outright hatred of everything related to the security forces. As the self-styled generals and godfathers took over in the face of this regime ... I witnessed voters and workers in the Docks and Falls constituencies turn against us to join the Provisionals.'[30]

The same was occurring in other areas, with the initially warm relations between British troops and the minority rapidly breaking down as the army moved from its initial role – essentially that of peace-keepers and, in reality, protectors of nationalist communities – to one where it increasingly controlled the Catholic populace. Drawing on recent experiences of policing in distant parts of the British Empire, the army acted in an increasingly colonial fashion, and so played into republican hands.

The Provisionals were now able to depict the army – like the RUC before it – as a repressive instrument of the Stormont regime, and a force more intent on preserving the Unionist government than protecting the Catholic community.[31]

All of this naturally impacted upon the infant SDLP. Its position was clearly conditioned by the climate of opinion amongst the minority. However, as it strove to maintain its credibility as a force for political change, the party faced a vicious circle: continuing disorder on the streets undermined the prospects of further reform, the lack of reform increased Catholic disenchantment with the political process, and this disenchantment fed further disorder on the streets.[32] Commenting on the situation in Derry, Eamonn McCann suggested the effect that this was having on Hume's authority amongst his own community, as he struggled to gain recognition of the value of the reforms that had been won:

> 'It should be clear to all people today who say that no change has taken place that this is simply not true' said Hume, with more than a touch of desperation. 'There *have* been changes in this community.' When he walked through the Bogside a few days later John found out what his constituents, who had more than a little experience of reform in the last three years, thought of the 'changes'. 'You'll never get anywhere, Johnnie, by doing the Stormont crawl.'[33]

Pressure on Hume increased dramatically after British troops shot dead two young Catholics in Derry in July 1971. Responding to the resultant upsurge of emotion in the city, Hume and his party colleagues issued an ultimatum to London, demanding a public inquiry into the killings, and threatening to withdraw from Stormont if this was not forthcoming. The British government ignored the demand, and so the SDLP withdrew from the Belfast parliament.[34] Less than a year after its formation – at which time the SDLP had promised to participate in the Stormont system as a means to bring about its reform – the party had been forced to retreat into the traditional nationalist practice of abstentionism.

While Ian McAllister is critical of the SDLP's decision to leave Stormont, he does appreciate the circumstances which led the party leadership to take such action. He is also aware of the role which Hume in particular played in this. Indeed, for it was Hume – in the absence of Fitt and Devlin, both of whom would later question the decision[35] – who was the primary author of the ultimatum sent to London. He decided on this course after making his own inquiries into the shootings, which convinced him that the army was attempting a cover-up.[36] Hume's inquiries would also have made him conscious of the depth of feeling which the killings had produced, and thus the extremely precarious political balance that had emerged in his home town. As McAllister reasons: 'Hume was aware of the danger that constitutional politics could at any time be threatened by the IRA and was equally alive to the tactical fact that the

IRA happened to be not particularly strong in the city just then. The possibility that the future leadership of the Catholic community could be lost by the SDLP was undoubtedly a major factor in the decision.'[37]

This cannot be understated. Indeed, a graphic illustration of the threat to the SDLP's position at this time comes in the fact that, as the party leadership drafted its ultimatum to London in Hume's home in Derry's West End Park, just up the road the Provisional IRA held its first mass rally in the area. This was attended by an estimated 1,500 people,[38] who were openly asked to join the republican movement. The response, wrote Eamonn McCann, was that 'applicants for membership formed a queue.' This helps to explain Hume's desperate decision. For as McCann caustically remarked, the ultimatum was 'a half-despairing attempt to prevent leadership of the Catholic masses passing into the hands of those who advocated taking on the army. All along the SDLP had been fighting to convince their constituents of the efficacy of "parliamentary methods". They realised that if they could not do that they would be swamped by the rising tide of Catholic anger.'[39]

However, this tide became a torrent the following month when, in response to an escalation in the IRA's campaign, the Unionist government introduced a policy of internment. With this, hundreds of Catholics, many innocent of any involvement with the IRA, were incarcerated without trial or due process. Moreover, despite the violence emanating from the Protestant community, no loyalists were interned in the first round of arrests.[40] As such, Catholics saw internment, 'not as a carefully planned and executed military operation against the IRA, but a punitive expedition against their community.'[41] Having already left Stormont, the SDLP was thus forced into an even greater display of disaffection, encouraging its supporters to withdraw from all forms of public office, and joining other opposition groups in calling for a campaign of civil disobedience.[42]

Despite the rapid deterioration of the situation, it was not until the tragedy of 'Bloody Sunday' in January 1972 – when British paratroopers fired on an anti-internment rally in the Bogside area of Derry, resulting in fourteen deaths – that London finally accepted the need to assume direct responsibility for the governance of Northern Ireland. But as well as providing the final nail in the coffin for Stormont, Bloody Sunday also dealt a devastating blow to constitutional nationalism. As with internment, the IRA reaped a bitter harvest from the British army's actions, as scores of young nationalists, convinced of the need to defend their community, swelled the republican ranks.[43] In propaganda terms, too, the Provisional movement gained increasing legitimacy in its claim that, in the face of such state terror, the only option left open to the minority was to rise against it, to overthrow British rule in Ireland, and unite the country by force. This, and the consequent surge in support for revolutionary republicanism, was made clear by Hume in an interview with Radio Telefís Éirann (RTÉ) given on Derry's city walls the day after the tragedy. In this, he famously

declared that: 'Many people down there feel now that it's a united Ireland
or nothing.'[44]

This statement was used against Hume for years afterwards, unionists
claiming that it revealed both his and his party's true colours, namely their
overriding commitment to a united Ireland. In fact, Hume, speaking from
atop of Derry's western wall, was referring to the residents of the Bogside
area below: '*Many people down there* feel now that it's a united Ireland or
nothing'. Hume was talking about the close-knit community which made
up a large part of his constituency, nearly every member of which had just
had a relative, friend or neighbour shot dead by the British army. Thus his
claim that 'it's a united Ireland or nothing' was not a rallying cry, but
simply an interpretation of the existing political situation as he saw it. It
was a comment on the overwhelming disaffection of Catholics from the
Northern Ireland state in the aftermath of Bloody Sunday. Indeed, such was
Catholic hostility to the state at this moment that it threatened to make the
SDLP's reformist project a political irrelevancy. This was the point that
Hume was making. For, although his subsequent words were erased from
unionist memories, he continued his RTÉ interview in saying: 'Alienation is
pretty total and we're all going to have to work very hard to deal with the
situation'.[45] Considering his comments in full and in their proper context, it
is clear that Hume was not, as his detractors have suggested, *calling* for a
united Ireland. Rather, he was making the point that the actions of the security forces had made it near impossible for leaders of the minority to argue
for anything less.

In this respect, Bloody Sunday represented the culmination in a process
of radicalisation of the minority which began with the first attacks on civil
rights marches in 1968. This process, and the gradual recrudescence of traditional republicanism throughout, had a definite impact on Hume's articulation of his position on Irish unity. Indeed, it is worth considering in
some detail the gradual change that occurred during this period in the way
that Hume spoke about Irish unity.

Hume and Irish unity: evolution versus revolution; people versus territory

In a Stormont debate on the Cameron Report[46] in October 1969, Hume
felt the need to respond to Unionist politicians' continued intimation that
the civil rights campaign was a mere cover for the pursuit of the traditional nationalist ends: 'The civil rights movement has stated its aims
clearly again and again. It has been said that it stands for nothing more or
less than full justice and equality for all within Northern Ireland'.[47] For
Hume, unionists' incessant invocation of the constitutional question, their
continued reference to nationalists' failure to accept the border without
qualification, was simply a smokescreen. It was an excuse for the Unionist
government to resist the demand for equal rights in Northern Ireland:

We have often talked about the Constitution of Northern Ireland. Is it not time that someone told us exactly what the Constitution is? How do we recognise a constitution? Do we have to sign something? Most of us have made very clear that we have no wish to change the Constitution of Northern Ireland without the consent of a majority of its people. What exception could anyone take to that position?[48]

In this, Hume defended the right of the nationalists to pursue Irish unity by peaceful means without prejudice to their claim to equality within Northern Ireland:

There are in our community many people who seek to have Ireland reunited. Listening to honourable Members opposite one would think that it was a crime. It is a perfectly acceptable political viewpoint, providing it is put forward in a democratic manner and support for it is sought democratically ...

But some people argue that anyone who does so must be deprived of rights. If someone in Britain campaigned for the establishment of a republic, for a change in the British Constitution, should he be deprived of his rights or freedom of speech?[49]

While reserving the right to seek unification by democratic means, it is clear that at this point in time the goal of Irish unity was very much secondary to Hume's overriding objective, the reform of Northern Ireland. However, seeing that the nationalist aspiration to Irish unity was still being used by unionists as a reason to resist reform, Hume made a quite unprecedented proposal in the aftermath of the Commons debate on Cameron. In a speech in Derry in November 1969 – a speech which has long been overlooked, but which shows his early thinking on Irish unity in an entirely new light – Hume made the case for having a periodic referendum in Northern Ireland on the issue of the border. This was not, however, an attempt to undermine the constitutional *status quo*; in fact it was quite the opposite. Hume was fully aware that such a vote would confirm Northern Ireland's position in the UK. But the idea was that this would then allow elections to be fought on normal political issues. For, as Hume argued, all previous elections in Northern Ireland had, in effect, been made referenda on the constitution, as both Nationalist and Unionist politicians sought to rally support solely on the issue of the border. By having a plebiscite which quite purposely dealt with the constitutional question – and which would clearly show that a majority continued to favour the Union with Britain – Hume hoped to clear the way for political contest on social and economic issues at election time:

It now appears to be agreed on all sides that no change can take place in the existing constitutional position without the consent of a majority of the people in the North, and that any individual or political group has the right to campaign for eventual change of the Constitution ... In the light of this it would seem to follow logically that the constitutional question should be taken out of politics by having a periodic referendum on it, so that elections

could be real elections based on real political issues ... If the achievement
of civil rights and of a just society in Northern Ireland is not followed by
political developments which lead to politics based on normal right or left
political attitudes then the Civil Rights movement will, in the long run, have
been in vain.[50]

The reasoning behind Hume's plebiscite proposal, taken alongside the
arguments which he made in the Commons debate on the Cameron
Report, show that he was still concerned principally with change *within*
Northern Ireland. Though he refused to surrender the ambition towards
Irish unity, he had once again made clear his belief that there should be no
change in the constitution without the assent of a majority in Northern
Ireland. Indeed, he sought to use the principle of consent, operationalised
through periodic referenda on the border, as means to nullify the constitutional question and allow for proper politics, based on bread-and-butter
issues, to develop in Northern Ireland. Whilst he still imagined a day when
the people of Ireland might chose to live under one government, his concern that the partition debate was once again hindering political progress
in Northern Ireland meant that Hume was prepared to kick the constitutional question into the long grass.

The seriousness of Hume's proposal is given evidence by the fact that
he formally submitted his idea to the Crowther Commission on the UK
constitution in February 1970.[51] Despite this, the significance of his suggestion has been largely overlooked. In his proposal, Hume rejected an
essential tenet of traditional Irish nationalism: the idea that the entire
island of Ireland was the only legitimate unit on which to base the exercise of self-determination. In his referendum initiative, Hume was – more
clearly than any nationalist leader before him – accepting the six counties
of Northern Ireland as a valid unit for the exercise of self-determination.
Whilst reserving the right to campaign for change in the *status quo*,
Hume was effectively accepting partition and the Northern Ireland state.

In the months that followed this mould-breaking proposal, Hume's
views changed significantly. The revival of traditional republicanism had a
definite role in this. The rise of the Provisionals undoubtedly impacted on
the political position articulated by Hume. It did not alter the fundamentals of his approach, but it did change his emphasis. For, as the IRA grew
in strength, so Hume's affiliation to the idea of Irish unity became increasingly pronounced. It appears that, as the Provisionals won greater support
in their struggle for a united Ireland achieved by violent revolution, so
Hume felt the need to become more express in his communication of an
alternative approach to reunification won by reform and evolution.

In this, however, Hume's reformism took on a different hue. Previously
he had emphasised reform as an end in itself, with the idea of Irish unity
being secondary to this objective and always articulated in purely aspirational terms. Indeed, as suggested by his proposal for periodic referenda
on the border, Hume hoped to remove the issue of partition from party

politics altogether – this to eliminate unionist objections to, and focus nationalist minds on, the reform of Northern Ireland. But in his pronouncements from early 1970, reform began to be linked to, and indeed presented as a precursor to, reunification.

The first notable example of this tendency came in a lecture which Hume gave at Trinity College Dublin (TCD), in March 1970.[52] Here he declared that: 'The prospect of a Northern Ireland built on equality and justice is one that must affect Ireland as a whole and one which is a necessary prerequisite to the eventual and inevitable marriage of the two parts of Ireland'.[53] But this very predetermined statement was quickly tempered by Hume's subsequent assertion that the achievement of civil rights also obliged the minority to increase its efforts to participate in state and society in Northern Ireland:

> For it goes without saying that those who have fought for civil rights must be prepared to accept civil responsibility. Such acceptance will mean an involvement with the affairs of the North that has not existed before among those opposed to its existence either because they were deliberately prevented or because, and it must be admitted, they did not choose to get involved. We can no longer opt out.[54]

At first, Hume's words appear to be contradictory: on the one hand, he was claiming that reform was a harbinger of Irish unity; on the other, he was continuing to encourage nationalists not only to accept the Northern Ireland state, but to labour for its success: 'In short we must accept the fact whether we like it or not that the Northern State now exists by the will of the majority of its people and that we must involve ourselves at every level of it in order to ensure a better and more prosperous North for all its people'.[55] Hume acknowledged this seeming paradox. But while admitting that acceptance of and involvement in the Northern Ireland state might *appear* to be assenting to partition, in fact, he argued, it was the best way to overcome the division of Ireland. Because for Hume this division was primarily psychological; it was division between the people of Ireland, premised on prejudice and distrust. This, he claimed, could only be overcome by Protestant and Catholic working together to resolve the social and economic problems which both endured and which deepened the enmity between them: 'the Border is not a line on the map. It is mental border built on fear, prejudice and misunderstanding and which can only be eradicated by developing understanding and friendship. This is the real task which faces those who genuinely want to solve the Irish problem. Its weakness is that it is undramatic. Its virtue is that it is the only way.'[56]

When considered more carefully, Hume's argument was not contradictory. He was acceptant of the Northern Ireland state and the constitutional *status quo* precisely because he believed that this was the only way to achieve real unity in Ireland. Nor was Hume's position inconsistent with that which he had previously advanced. Indeed, in his speech to TCD, there were echoes of the article which he wrote for the *Irish Times* six years earlier. But the ideas that were implicit there were made more clear here. In particular, it was evident that Irish unity, in Hume's mind, was more about people than territory: 'For what is Ireland and what is the Border which divides its people ... Ireland is not a piece of earth, Ireland is its people. People of varying traditions and backgrounds who together form the entity know as Ireland, and unity of Ireland really means community of its people.'[57]

If anything had changed in Hume's position it was the enthusiasm with which he was putting forward his case for an Irish unity achieved by reform and evolution. Moreover, it can be argued that this enthusiasm was born out of Hume's concern that the more traditional approach to Irish unification – now being revived by the Provisional IRA – was taking root amongst the northern minority. Such concern was well founded, as over the course of the next twelve months the Provisionals – aided by the British army's indiscriminate and often brutal repression – won increasing support for their cause. As they did so, correspondingly, Hume amplified his argument for a unification achieved by peaceful evolution.

Obviously, the formation of the SDLP in August of 1970 provided a major platform from which to make his case in Northern Ireland, but Hume also saw the need to influence political opinion in the South. Not only was the Irish government essential to any effort to create a united Ireland through a peaceful, gradualist strategy, but the southern polity had also shown that it had yet to divorce itself entirely from the physical force tradition now being reasserted by the Provisional IRA. Indeed, this had been spectacularly demonstrated in May 1970, when Jack Lynch was forced to dismiss two members of his cabinet amidst allegations of a plot to use government funds to import arms for the Provisionals.[58] However, an opportunity to address the more republican-minded sections of southern society – precisely those which might harbour some sympathy for the IRA – was provided in a regular column which Hume wrote the Dublin-based *Sunday Press*[59] from late 1970. From the outset, it is clear that Hume used this column to garner support in the Republic for his reformist strategy. Indeed, his first article for the paper provided his most considered case yet for an evolutionary approach to Irish unity.

That Hume was focused mainly on a southern audience in this article was evident from the opening line: 'Since the North hit the international headlines two years ago, we have had a surfeit of speeches on the border from southern politicians who had been silent on the question for years.' He related this to a well-established tradition of rhetorical anti-partitionism, practised by politicians on both sides of the border: 'Many leaders have come – and gone – protesting their belief in a united country.' But Hume was at pains to point out that 'no party ... in all those years, produced a detailed blueprint for the peaceful reunification of Ireland'.[60] This is precisely what Hume felt was necessary – as a means to persuade unionists that a unitary state was the best option for the people of Ireland, but also to ensure that physical force Irish nationalism did not to gain sway once again.

Hume did not pretend to have already in hand the 'blueprint for the peaceful reunification of Ireland' that he proposed, but he did offer a broad outline of how such a process might unfold. In essence, Hume envisaged Irish unity coming about in three stages. Barry White, Hume's first biographer, referred to this as his 'three Rs' strategy: reform, reconciliation and reunification.[61] Reform, as a means to achieve equal rights in Northern Ireland – a course already begun by the civil rights movement – was the first stage in the process. Indeed, in Hume's mind, parity of treatment was a precondition to the second stage, reconciliation: 'You cannot reconcile with someone who has his boot on your neck'.[62] It was only by facing each other on terms of equality, he argued, that the two communities in Northern Ireland could overcome their differences. But in doing so, Hume imagined that the third stage of the process, reunification, would naturally follow. In this, reform was once again presented as a means to the end of Irish unity, although this was expressed more as a unity of being rather than of territory: 'Full civil rights in the North are an essential prerequisite to the eventual and inevitable coming together of the two parts of Ireland. Reform is therefore the first step in this direction. Reconciliation in the North – the second step – would then be much easier and the third, reunification would be but a matter of time, because the real border, that which divided the people of the North, would be gone.'[63]

However, suggesting that he did not necessarily foresee the dissolution of the Northern Ireland state, Hume claimed that 'the achievement of full justice and equality in the North – and it has still to be achieved – would produce a radical change among those in the North traditionally opposed to the state.' This led him back to the reasoning of his TCD speech of the previous spring, where he argued that the minority should participate in and work for the improvement of the Northern Ireland state: 'People who had fought for civil rights would have to be prepared to accept civil responsibility; to accept that the problems of the North demanded that they get involved at every level in their solution; to eradicate the evils of unemployment and emigration.'[64] Again, this suggests that, whilst Hume may have hoped for some form of political unity in Ireland in the future, his main concern at the present time was to reform and to work the Northern Ireland state for the betterment of all its people.

Despite this, with growing unrest on the streets – increasingly orchestrated by republicans – Hume's strategy of reform and reconciliation as a means to reunification was already being sidelined. In November 1970, again writing in his *Sunday Press* column, Hume referred to both republican violence in Northern Ireland, and to the related 'Arms Trial' in the Republic,[65] when he argued the need for Irish nationalism to finally extricate itself from the physical force tradition: 'To have done so will be to have laid at last the first real foundation of Irish unity since 1921 for such unity can only be achieved by agreement, mutual respect and prosperity in both parts of Ireland.' Hume then continued by arguing the absurdity of any attempt to achieve Irish unity through violence: 'Let us try to understand what the struggle against partition is all about. It is not as the struggle for independence was, a struggle against a foreign and occupying power. It is a struggle to bring together two sections of the Irish people, and how can anyone with the slightest grain of intelligence imagine that violence by one section against another can unite them.' For this reason Hume asserted that: 'The best service indeed that the IRA could give the cause of Irish unity is to disband, for Irish unity will never be achieved by violence'.[66]

It was not until the beginning of 1971, however, that the Provisionals had built up their resources and recruits to the point where they were able to begin in earnest a violent campaign aimed at overthrowing Stormont and forcing an end to partition. But, as they did so, Hume became even more vigorous in articulating his alternative approach, and in February 1971 he produced another considered exposition on the theme of Irish unity. Again this drew on, but also developed, arguments he had previously advanced. But on this occasion he was not writing for a solely nationalist audience. For the magazine in which his article appeared, *Fortnight*, was a publication recently founded by moderates from both sides of the political divide in Northern Ireland.

Not only did this article restate Hume's implacable opposition to a united Ireland achieved by violent means, but it also confirmed, more clearly than ever, that his understanding of Irish unity was quite different from that of traditional nationalist thought. 'Irish Unity', he wrote,

> has come to mean the conquest of one state by the other rather than the partnership of both where both traditions combine in agreement to create a new society in Ireland, a pluralist society where all traditions are cherished and flourish equally ... The border in Ireland is the psychological barrier between two sections of the community in the North built on prejudice, sectarianism and fear. To remove it requires the eradication of sectarianism and prejudice. This can only come through development of understanding and friendship.

Once again, Hume also challenged those who believed that only physical force could achieve a united Ireland, arguing the self-defeating nature of such a strategy: 'It [Irish unity] cannot come about by coercion or violence, because the problem of sectarian division and prejudice is only deepened and strengthened by violence'.[67]

In addition, Hume contradicted those who saw the achievement of a united Ireland as a sectarian reversal for Ulster Protestants, which would see their submergence in a Catholic theocracy: 'It would not resemble in any way the unity that seems to be envisaged by some of those in Dublin who talk of their own people and whose loudly proclaimed republicanism seems to me to be nothing more than the pursuit of Catholic victory'. For Hume, Irish unity would require serious compromise on the part of Catholics, North and South, which would involve a radical reconstitution of the Irish state:

> No-one is entitled to assume that when we talk of unity we are talking of assimilation into the present state south of the border. Such unity as is envisaged would be a unity under an entirely new constitution, one which all sections would have a say in drafting, and one which would provide a framework for a pluralist society in Ireland in which the rights of conscience and religious liberty would be upheld.[68]

By changing the debate in this way, Hume continued to redefine the idea of Irish unity. In his mind, this goal concerned people rather than territory: 'In short to create a truly united country we need a truly united people, not a united piece of earth. In that task we need not to overcome the Northern Protestant but to seek his co-operation, help and assistance.'[69] With this, Hume laid down a challenge which – by citing one of the founding fathers of Irish nationalism, Wolfe Tone – implicitly incited a response from both the republican and the Protestant traditions: 'Is there any other way in which we can create a society in Ireland where Catholic, Protestant and Dissenter can work together as equals for the betterment of us all? Those are the sentiments of a Northern Protestant[70] who founded the republican tradition in Ireland.'[71]

There was, however, a bitter irony to Hume's appeal, for it was only the day after his *Fortnight* article was published that the first British soldier was killed by the IRA. Three weeks later, two RUC officers were shot dead, and therein the Provisionals began a systematic campaign against the security forces in Northern Ireland.[72] Hume's response to these killings was unequivocal: 'If they [republicans] think their methods will unite Ireland under their leadership I want nothing to do with such an Ireland or such a people.'[73]

Hume's next significant discussion of Irish unity came during the opening debate of the new parliamentary session in June. This also happened to be the fiftieth anniversary of the establishment of the Belfast assembly, and Hume used the occasion to question the political progeny of 'a settlement that satisfied no one at the time. Those who fought for the retention of the union with Britain were not satisfied with this settlement because they fought for the union of the whole of Ireland. Neither were those who fought for an independent Irish Republic satisfied because they did not get one, they only got part of it.'[74]

On this basis, Hume again made the case for a reformist nationalism which might refashion the 1920–21 settlement in a way that would satisfy all parties. But more clearly than ever, Hume presented this as an alternative route to Irish unity than that proffered by the Provisionals, whose violent campaign against the Stormont regime was by now in full swing.

Hume sought to stress that an evolutionary approach was not only feasible, but was in fact *the* only feasible way towards Irish reunification. Indeed, Hume clearly felt that it was vital to prove that a vibrant and constructive form of constitutional nationalism could advance this goal. For, in his mind, it was the ineffectiveness of democratic nationalism hitherto which allowed the physical force tradition to prevail:

> those who have put forward this ideal [Irish unity] in the past, and who have said they propose to achieve this ideal by peaceful means, have failed utterly to present any basic strategy, plan or programme before the people who subscribe to this ideal as to how it can be achieved. That failure has made it easier for those who say that violence is the only solution.
>
> We hear often from people who support violent men: 'What were the peaceful men able to do? What were the parliamentarians able to do?' The reason they were able to say that with such conviction is because those who have put forward this ideal in the past, and have advocated peaceful means, have utterly failed to spell out to the people how a peaceful unity can be achieved.[75]

This, clearly, was the role which Hume felt his party should assume. The SDLP had to show how constitutional nationalism, through a coherent, evolutionary strategy, could work towards Irish unity. Only this could deprive physical force nationalism of its rationale and claimed justification. But the logic of Hume's argument also showed how the continued growth of republicanism was forcing him to adopt an ever-more 'unificationist' agenda.

Up until the summer of 1971, Hume continued to advocate his philosophy of reform and reconciliation as a means towards reunification. However, with the upsurge in violence that followed, he quickly retreated from this position. In particular, after the introduction of internment in August, the bitter reaction which this provoked amongst the Catholic community, and the unprecedented expansion of the Provisionals' campaign which this allowed, Hume seemed certain that the reform of Stormont was no longer a viable option. This was clearly evident in two articles he wrote for the *Irish Times* towards the end of 1971. Both pieces showed how far Hume's views of the Northern Ireland state and the possibility of Irish reunification had changed.

In the first article, Hume began by defending the SDLP's resort to abstention from Stormont, arguing the need to demonstrate that the minority had decided on 'a complete withdrawal of consent from the system of government in Northern Ireland'. This system, Hume continued, had proved to be an outright failure. 'On reflection', he considered, 'its failure was inevitable. The very nature of the Northern Ireland State and the manner of its creation made it so.' In this, Hume was beginning to fall back on a more familiar nationalist critique of partition and the Stormont regime, condemning the 'illegal foundations' of a state 'so drawn as to provide a permanent majority for Protestant ascendancy'. Thus, whilst not explicitly calling for an end to partition, Hume's argument was certainly pointing in this direction. Moreover, he believed that thinking within the Protestant community was heading the same way: 'Most Unionists will admit to the inevitability of a united country.' Though he still held that this 'should come by agreement, for the only worthwhile unity is unity by agreement', Hume felt that: 'The search for agreement should begin now. There is little point in evading any further the inevitability on which all are agreed'.[76]

The assumption that a united Ireland was inescapable – and the belief that the Protestant community, deep down, knew this, too – seemed to lead Hume to the erroneous conclusion that unionists would eventually acquiesce. This showed a certain devaluation of Hume's commitment to the principle of consent. For though he continued to emphasise the need for unionists' agreement to Irish reunification, Hume appeared to believe that they could not, ultimately, but agree. Unionists could not withhold their consent forever; they would eventually concede.

As a means to facilitate this end, Hume wanted Westminster to actively promote the goal of Irish unity: 'The British government should declare publicly what is the private conviction of all British parties, that Irish unity is inevitable and that it will take all steps necessary to encourage the agreement that will bring it about.' Although this fell short of the declaration of intent to withdraw from Northern Ireland that the Provisionals were demanding, Hume's request again suggested political regression. For he now putting increasing emphasis on the position of the British government. Where his earlier commentaries had placed the onus on the people of Ireland in overcoming their divisions, here London appeared to be the most important actor in achieving Irish unity: 'The British Government and Parliament should not fear to set in motion the movement towards the inevitable'.[77]

Hereinafter, Hume's focus on Westminster's position on the constitutional future of Northern Ireland, and his emphasis of the need for the British government's support for Irish unity, would be recurring themes in his political discourse. Indeed, he immediately returned to these themes in his second *Irish Times* article, appearing in the paper's final issue of 1971. In this, Hume criticised the Christmas message which Edward Heath had delivered to the people of Northern Ireland the previous week, in which the British Prime Minister reiterated the so-called 'British guarantee' of Northern Ireland's constitutional position within the UK:

> Has it never occurred to him nor to his predecessors that any community of a million people anywhere in the world which receives a permanent guarantee of its supremacy and privileged position from a government like the British Government, backed by the necessary finance, is not going to give any thought whatsoever to any other possible Constitutional position, but that, once the guarantee is withdrawn and it is stated British policy to positively encourage and bring about Irish unity by agreement, many of the million will immediately begin to reconsider their position.[78]

A month later, however, on the walls of Derry, Hume's constitutional musings and his consideration of the role that Britain might play in easing the path towards Irish unity had little place. In the aftermath of the atrocity visited on the Bogside by British paratroopers, few nationalists believed that the Westminster government could play any constructive role in Northern Ireland. Neither was Hume of the mind to reiterate his 'three Rs' strategy: reform and reconciliation as a means to reunification. Instead it was simply 'a united Ireland or nothing'. In this, he was articulating, in the plainest of terms, the base instinct of his own community in the Bogside, but also of nationalists throughout Ireland. He was expressing the belief of many Catholics at this point in time that neither justice nor peace could be obtained whilst Britain remained in Ireland. He was also revealing a fear that a large number of nationalists now felt that the IRA rather than the SDLP offered the only means to remove that impediment.

Notes

1   On this complex process, which can only be briefly detailed here, see Hennessey, *Northern Ireland: The Origins of the Troubles*; and Ó Dochartaigh, *From Civil Rights to Armalites*.
2   S. Wichert, *Northern Ireland since 1945* (London: Longman, 2nd edn, 1999), p. 113.
3   See Ó Dochartaigh, *From Civil Rights to Armalites*, ch. 3.
4   O'Leary and McGarry, *The Politics of Antagonism*, pp. 171, 172.
5   Ó Dochartaigh, *From Civil Rights to Armalites*, p. 140.
6   *Derry Journal*, 19 August 1969.
7   McAllister, *The Social Democratic and Labour Party*, p. 30; White, *John Hume*, p. 96.
8   P. J. McLoughlin, 'John Hume and the revision of Irish nationalism, 1964–79' (unpublished PhD thesis, Queen's University Belfast, 2005), pp. 46ff.; White, *John Hume*, ch. 9; B. White, 'New parties I: SDLP', *Fortnight*, 25 September 1970.
9   A. Currie, *All Hell Will Break Loose* (Dublin: O'Brien, 2004), pp. 156–7; P. Devlin, *Straight Left: An Autobiography* (Belfast: Blackstaff, 1993), p. 142; M. Murphy, *Gerry Fitt: A Political Chameleon* (Cork: Mercier, 2007), p. 156; C. Ryder, *Fighting Fitt: the Gerry Fitt Story* (Belfast: Brehon, 2006), p. 168.
10 Currie, *All Hell Will Break Loose*, pp. 154–8; White, *John Hume*, pp. 97–103.
11 White, *John Hume*, pp. 98, 101.
12 G. Murray, *John Hume and the SDLP: Impact and Survival in Northern Ireland* (Dublin: Murray Irish Academic Press, 1998), p. 87.
13 Quoted in White, *John Hume*, p. 102.
14 *Irish Times*, 22 August 1970.
15 Currie, *All Hell Will Break Loose*, p. 158; White, *John Hume*, pp. 98–9,
16 *Irish Times*, 22 August 1970.
17 *Ibid.*
18 McAllister, *The Social and Democratic Labour Party*, p. 168.

19 *Irish Times*, 22 August 1970; *Belfast News Letter*, 22 August 1970.
20 Devlin, *Straight Left*, pp. 143, 283.
21 McAllister, *The Social Democratic and Labour Party*, p. 60.
22 On this, see English, *Armed Struggle*, ch. 3.
23 P. Bew and G. Gillespie, *Northern Ireland: A Chronology of the Troubles, 1968–1999* (Dublin: Gill and Macmillan, 1999), p. 29; Ó Dochartaigh, *From Civil Rights to Armalites*, p. 256; Murphy, *Gerry Fitt*, pp. 145, 165.
24 McCann, *War and an Irish Town*, p. 86.
25 G. Murray and J. Tonge, *Sinn Féin and the SDLP: From Alienation to Participation* (London: O'Brien, 2005), p. 24.
26 Bew, Gibbon and Patterson, *Northern Ireland, 1921–2001*, pp. 138, 148.
27 O'Leary and McGarry, *The Politics of Antagonism*, p. 175.
28 Ó Dochartaigh, *From Civil Rights to Armalites*, pp. 61, 140–5, 169, 209.
29 C. Kennedy-Pipe, *The Origins of the Present Troubles in Northern Ireland* (London: Longman, 1997), p. 52; Ó Dochartaigh, *From Civil Rights to Armalites*, pp. 228–9.
30 Devlin, *Straight Left*, p. 134.
31 Farrell, *Northern Ireland*, p. 274; Kennedy-Pipe, *The Origins of the Present Troubles*, pp. 54, 176–7; McCann, *War and an Irish Town*, pp. 83, 87, 238; Ó Dochartaigh, *From Civil Rights to Armalites*, ch. 4.
32 Ó Dochartaigh, *From Civil Rights to Armalites*, p. 220.
33 McCann, *War and an Irish Town*, pp. 90–1; emphasis in original.
34 *Derry Journal*, 9 and 23 July 1971; McCann, *War and an Irish Town*, pp. 89–90; Ó Dochartaigh, *From Civil Rights to Armalites*, p. 267.
35 Devlin, *Straight Left*, pp. 155–6; Ryder, *Fighting Fitt*, p. 178.
36 *Derry Journal*, 13 July, 1971.
37 McAllister, *The Social and Democratic Labour Party*, p. 94.
38 Ó Dochartaigh, *From Civil Rights to Armalites*, p. 269.
39 McCann, *War*, p. 90.
40 Kennedy-Pipe, *The Origins of the Present Troubles*, p. 55; H. Patterson, *Ireland Since 1939* (Oxford: Oxford University Press, 2002), p. 222.
41 McAllister, *The Social and Democratic Labour Party*, p. 99.
42 Currie, *All Hell Will Break Loose*, pp. 175, 177; Devlin, *Straight Left*, pp. 161–2; McAllister, *The Social and Democratic Labour Party*, p. 100; Ryder, *Fighting Fitt*, p. 182.
43 English, *Armed Struggle*, p. 151.
44 Quoted in White, *John Hume*, p. 120.
45 White, *John Hume*, p. 120.
46 The Cameron Report was the result of a commission established in March 1969 to investigate the causes of disorder in Northern Ireland up to this point.
47 House of Commons (Northern Ireland) Debates, vol. 74, col. 139; 1 October 1969.
48 *Ibid.*, col. 140; 1 October 1969.
49 *Ibid.*, cols 140–1; 1 October 1969.
50 *Derry Journal*, 11 November 1969.
51 White, *John Hume*, p. 110.
52 The importance which Hume attached to this speech is made clear by the fact that he notified an Irish government official in advance that he was preparing a significant paper for the occasion; National Archives of Ireland (NAI),

Department of the Taoiseach (D/T), 2001/6/513, report by E. Gallagher on Hume's submission to the Crowther Commission; 3 March 1970.

53 *Derry Journal*, 13 March 1970.

54 *Ibid.*

55 *Ibid.*

56 *Ibid.*

57 *Ibid.*

58 See J. O'Brien, *The Arms Trial* (Dublin: Gill and Macmillan, 2000).

59 The *Sunday Press* was aligned to Fianna Fáil, not only the dominant party in the Republic, but also the most vocally anti-partitionist. In writing for this paper, Hume may have felt that he was speaking to a more republican readership, and a more republican political leadership.

60 J. Hume, 'Emotional clap-trap is a waste of time', *Sunday Press*, 4 October 1970.

61 White, *John Hume*, p. 74.

62 Hume, 'Emotional clap-trap'.

63 *Ibid.*

64 *Ibid.*

65 See O'Brien, *The Arms Trial*.

66 J. Hume, 'Violence is not the answer', *Sunday Press*, 22 November 1970.

67 J. Hume, 'John Hume's Ireland', *Fortnight*, 5 February 1971.

68 *Ibid.*

69 *Ibid.*

70 The author assumes that it is Tone whom Hume is citing, for it was Tone who famously spoke of his desire to 'substitute the common name of Irishman in place of the denominations of Protestant, Catholic, and Dissenter'. If so, Hume was wrong in claiming this to be the sentiment of a northern Protestant. Although the majority of his comrades in the leadership of the United Irishmen were from Ulster, Tone was a Dubliner.

71 Hume, 'John Hume's Ireland'.

72 Bew and Gillespie, *Northern Ireland: A Chronology*, pp. 132–3.

73 *Belfast Telegraph*, 3 March 1971.

74 House of Commons (Northern Ireland) Debates, vol. 82, col. 92, 24 June 1971.

75 *Ibid.*, cols. 93–4, 24 June 1971.

76 J. Hume, 'The way forward for Northern Ireland', *Irish Times*, 6 November 1971.

77 *Ibid.*

78 J. Hume, 'United Ireland inevitable: create conditions now', *Irish Times* (Annual Review supplement), 31 December 1971.

3

Dublin is just a Sunningdale away

The collapse of the Unionist government did not halt the SDLP's drift to a more nationalist position. If anything, the political climate in Northern Ireland following Stormont's suspension only led to a further greening of the party. A number of factors contributed to this. Firstly, the prorogation of Stormont had in itself created a sense of euphoria amongst the minority community. Not only did it bring an end to a regime that had come to be despised by even moderate nationalists, but it also appeared to re-open 'the Irish Question' in its entirety. For many nationalists, the fall of Stormont was a mere prelude to the withdrawal of the British state from Northern Ireland and the dissolution of partition. The 'unificationist' feeling amongst the minority, as well as galvanising the republican movement, naturally infected the SDLP as well.

Secondly, the sense of political victory within the Catholic community contrasted strongly with the apparent resignation of unionism. There was some immediate protest against London's imposition of direct rule, but certainly not the widespread Protestant backlash which many had predicted.[1] To some observers, this appeared to suggest that the greater part of the unionist community would now, if not willingly agree to a united Ireland, at least acquiesce in its creation. Indeed, this seemed to be the opinion expressed even by Hume in an interview given to RTÉ shortly after Stormont's suspension. Here, he argued that there were now three possible futures open to Northern Ireland: complete integration with Britain; a restructured Northern Ireland state; or Irish unity. 'The only viable one is the last', Hume claimed, 'and that is what we should be negotiating, as of now.' He also made clear his belief that agreement was possible with 'a significant section of the Northern Protestant community, if there was the right approach now'.[2]

Crucially, elements within the British establishment also appeared to be accepting the inevitability of Irish reunification.[3] This further encouraged the SDLP's shift to a position of effective anti-partitionism. Of particular note was the 'Fifteen Point Plan' which the leader of the opposition, Harold Wilson, presented to Westminster in November 1971. In this, Wilson proposed that the British government initiate a progressive political strategy which would lead ultimately to Irish unity.[4] Whilst the Labour leader claimed to recognise the need for unionist consent for this plan, he failed to explain exactly how this could be achieved.[5] Like Hume, Wilson seemed to assume that Protestants' assent would simply manifest itself somewhere within the process of reunification.

The relative quiescence of the unionist community after Stormont's suspension clearly misled both Irish nationalists and those in Britain who sympathised with the objective of Irish unity. The idea that Ulster Protestants would meekly accept their fate in a united Ireland seriously underestimated their continued hostility towards that end. Bowing to direct rule from London was one thing; submitting to governance from Dublin was an entirely different matter. However, it appeared that events had led even moderate nationalists such as Hume to believe that a sufficient section of the unionist community would now comply with the supposedly ineluctable dialectic of Irish history.[6]

This represented a significant deviation from the revisionist nationalism that had been developed by National Unity and the NDP in the early 1960s. Their vision, seemingly adopted by Hume and the SDLP, had been that the unity of Catholic and Protestant in Northern Ireland was a prerequisite to unity between the North and South of Ireland. However, by 1972, the two communities in Northern Ireland were more divided than ever. At its launch two years earlier, the SDLP had suggested that it would build a bi-confessional support base. At that time, the idea sounded optimistic; now, it appeared unimaginable. Any middle ground which had existed in 1970 had been thoroughly eroded by the violent turn of events, and as it did so the SDLP retreated to more secure, traditional nationalist territory.

Towards a new Ireland or back to the old routine?

Towards a New Ireland, the SDLP's first published policy document, clearly showed how far the party had fallen back on a more conventional nationalism in the aftermath of Stormont's collapse. The document drew on papers written by a number of SDLP members, most notably Ivan Cooper, Ben Caraher and John Duffy.[7] The latter two were former leaders of the NDP, who transmitted much of the thinking of that precursory party to the SDLP.[8] They provided ideas that would shape SDLP policy in its formative years and beyond.[9] In this respect, whilst it was Hume who would become most closely associated with the articulation of the SDLP's political philosophy, it is evident that the party's early programme was influenced by a wider circle of policy-makers.

However, whilst *Towards a New Ireland* incorporated ideas from a number of actors, it was Hume who wrote the final draft,[10] and his particular hand was evident throughout.[11] The paper opened by declaring that not only had the Stormont regime proven itself unworkable, but the 1920 Government of Ireland Act on which it was premised, and in fact the

1920–21 Anglo-Irish settlement in its entirety, had failed. For this reason, it argued: 'Any re-examination [of the 1920–21 settlement] must therefore take place, not in a purely Six County context, but in an Irish context.'[12] In this, the SDLP set its face against any internal solution of the Northern Ireland problem. It implied that the conflict, by its nature and its historical origins, could never be resolved exclusively within existing state boundaries. This notion, like many of the ideas advanced in *Towards a New Ireland*, would remain integral to the SDLP's thinking from hereinafter.

As far back as his seminal 'The Northern Catholic' article, written for the *Irish Times* in May 1964, Hume had argued the need for nationalists to recognise the legitimacy of the unionist tradition and of unionists' desire to maintain the link with Britain. At the same time, he stated that unionists must accept the legitimacy and aspirations of the nationalist tradition.[13] *Towards a New Ireland* offered a way in which such mutual recognition could be achieved, making what was, at the time, still a novel suggestion: joint British-Irish sovereignty over Northern Ireland.[14] Such an arrangement, the paper maintained, 'will take into account the need to give fair expression to the present basic loyalties of both sections of the people of the North [of Ireland]'.[15] However, the integrity of this argument was undermined by the fact that joint sovereignty was proposed only as an interim solution; Irish reunification was the end objective. For, as well as condominium arrangements, *Towards a New Ireland* also proposed the establishment of a 'National Senate of Ireland', whose primary function would be 'to plan the integration of the whole island by preparing the harmonisation of the structures, laws and services of both parts of Ireland'.[16] Notwithstanding this predetermination towards reunification, in further explaining the role of the proposed Senate, *Towards a New Ireland* did at least look to distance the SDLP from a traditionalist conception of Irish unity. Indeed, for here the document was at pains to 'make clear from the outset that the unity that we seek is an entirely new concept and that the New Ireland that should evolve will be one that will still Protestant fears and will have the agreement and consent of all sections of opinion in Ireland'.[17]

In this, the paper echoed arguments which Hume had already advanced in previous discussions of Irish unity, wherein he had proposed a state in which no one culture or ethos was pre-eminent. This pluralist approach suggested a welcome departure from the more narrow conception of nationalism which had come to dominate independent Ireland. However, Hume's line of reasoning, reproduced in *Towards a New Ireland*, also betrayed the limitations of the SDLP's revisionism *vis-à-vis* its understanding of the unionist community. Indeed, for *Towards a New Ireland* suggested that any move towards reunification would have to take account of and address 'Protestant fears' – that is, as distinct from *unionist* fears. Of course, it could be argued that, in the context of Northern Ireland, the terms 'Protestant' and 'unionist', like the terms 'Catholic' and 'nationalist', are synonymous, and as such can be used interchangeably.[18] But in this instance the choice of the term 'Protestant' rather than that of 'unionist' says far more.

Evidently, Hume and his colleagues perceived unionists' opposition to a united Ireland as being primarily religious in its motivation. Following from this was an assumption that an all-Ireland constitution which protected the religious identity and ethos of Ulster Protestants could persuade them to join a unitary state. This suggested that the SDLP doubted the substance of unionists' British identity, believing that they continued to favour the Union with Britain only to avoid submergence in a Catholic-dominated state. This implicit doubt over Ulster Protestants' Britishness allowed the SDLP to imagine a relatively uncomplicated transition to a united Ireland; unity would be achieved if only the Catholic majority on the island could bring themselves to understand and show themselves willing to accommodate Ulster Protestants' religious concerns. This misinterpretation – or at least gross oversimplification – of the essential identity of Ulster unionists[19] in turn served to misguide the SDLP's political strategy.

Towards a New Ireland suggested that, despite their attempts to understand Ulster unionism, Hume and his colleagues still suffered a hangover from the traditional nationalist doctrine fomented by their forebears. The SDLP had failed to overcome the belief that Ulster Protestants were, at the end of the day, fellow Irishmen and women – albeit Irishmen and women of a different religious persuasion. With this came the idea that, while Protestant Ulster had different interests and held different values from those of Catholic Ireland, these were not irreconcilable, and so unionists could be persuaded to join their 'fellow countrymen' in a unified state. This was a notion which, despite the party's rhetoric of recognition and respect for the unionist tradition, continued to inform the SDLP thinking, giving good reason for unionists to doubt that the party truly comprehended their British identity, and thus good reason to distrust its intentions.

Of course, the ideological implications that can be drawn from *Towards a New Ireland* have to be seen in the context in which the document was conceived. For the writing of paper was undoubtedly coloured by the events unfolding around its authors, and particularly the resurgence of republican feeling then apparent amongst the minority community. Indeed, one of the primary progenitors of *Towards a New Ireland*, Ben Caraher, believed that the final draft of the document was conditioned by the strong sense of grievance in the Catholic community at this time, and a resulting concern that radical republicanism would usurp constitutional nationalists' leadership of the minority.[20] When Caraher had initially advanced the idea of a joint sovereignty solution, he did so in the belief that such an arrangement would afford equal recognition to both communities in Northern Ireland. But this notion, he felt, was compromised by the belief that only by providing a means to the ultimate end of Irish unity would *Towards a New Ireland* win full support among nationalists:

[W]hat I was trying to produce was ... a series of political institutions in which ... both national identities were equally represented and equally important. But if this was merely a preparation for a united Ireland, then this made the nationalist identity more legitimate than the unionist identity ... The reason for that was that notion that, in order to have full appeal in the nationalist community, ultimately ... that phrase, 'a united Ireland' ... had to be there.[21]

The inherent 'interimism' of the *Towards a New Ireland* proposals clearly demonstrated the way in which political expediency undermined the more evolutionary aspects of the SDLP's formative philosophy. But it is also clear from the document that the aspiration to Irish unity – and the belief that the people of Ireland, despite their differences, would some day be as one – still held great ideological potency for the SDLP. Evidently, there were psychological limitations to the revision of Irish nationalism in which Hume and his colleagues were engaged. In their minds, a unitary Irish state remained not only a desirable, but also a realisable goal. In this, it can be said that the SDLP had, at this time, failed to come fully to terms with the reality of Ulster unionism.

Towards a New Ireland represented the blueprint for Irish reunification which Hume had first augured in his *Irish Press* column back in October 1970. But it also represented a corruption of his SDLP's founding philosophy. Attempting to sate the appetite for Irish reunification that had grown amidst the Catholic community, and simultaneously trying to stave off the challenge for the leadership of the minority presented by the Provisionals, the document showed a certain disregard for the unionist community. It now appeared that, so focused was the SDLP on proving that it could achieve a united Ireland by peaceful means, the party was overlooking its previous conviction that the best way – indeed the only way – to do this was to win the support of Ulster Protestants. Commenting on *Towards a New Ireland*, an editorial in the *Sunday Independent* articulated this point with great lucidity, suggesting what had become of the SDLP and Hume's 'three Rs' approach as a result of the pressures under which the party laboured:

> the SDLP has become one of the unwilling victims of the violence it has tried to stem. Its original role of a reforming, non-sectarian party, appealing to all sections of the Northern Community, has given way to one which now closely resembles that of the old Nationalist Party, whose politics it formerly condemned. And in the process, its original strategy of reform, followed by community reconciliation, followed eventually by national re-unification, has become blurred.
>
> With the polarisation of the two communities which the IRA has produced (and deliberately produced) it was, perhaps, inevitable that this should happen. ... In essence, the SDLP's proposals ... are a recipe for re-unification, with its former middle strategy of reconciliation abandoned in all but name.[22]

The Irish dimension

Unsurprisingly, the British government rejected the radical ideas of joint sovereignty proposed in *Towards a New Ireland*. Instead, officials in Whitehall and the newly established Northern Ireland Office (NIO) were working towards a seemingly more obtainable objective: a restructured local administration in which representatives from both the Protestant and Catholic communities would share executive power. However, in a government Green Paper outlining this agenda, London did recognise what it termed an 'Irish dimension' to the Northern Ireland problem, suggesting that any new arrangements would have to take account of the region's relationship with the Republic of Ireland.[23] This could be read by the SDLP as a response to the demand in *Towards a New Ireland* that any solution of the Northern Ireland problem should be conceived in an all-Ireland rather than a purely internal context. Accordingly, it led the party to seize upon the notion of an Irish dimension,[24] adopting the phrase as part of its own political nomenclature, and using it henceforth.

Fleshing out the Irish dimension in a subsequent White Paper, the British government offered a 'Council of Ireland' as a forum for North–South co-operation.[25] This, and the promise of a share in executive power by participating in a new Northern Ireland assembly, proved enough to win the SDLP's guarded approval of the White Paper as a basis for formal discussions.[26] But also crucial to the SDLP's re-entry into the political process was the sense that it had the backing of the Irish government. Indeed, Dublin's support was obviously essential if the party was to create the momentum towards Irish reunification that *Towards a New Ireland* had envisaged. However, before further considering developments in the post-Stormont period, it is useful to review the nature of the relationship between the SDLP and the Irish government – or more specifically Hume and the Irish government – up until this point.

Returning to the actual outbreak of the Troubles, it is worth focusing on the numerous reports written by one civil servant working in what was then Dublin's Department of External Affairs – soon to become the Department of Foreign Affairs. From 1969 onwards, Eamonn Gallagher was the most senior Irish official liaising with northern nationalist representatives. His promotion to this position came somewhat by chance. Indeed, he had been working in the trade section of the department until, seemingly of his own initiative, he visited Belfast during the height of the August 1969 violence. After passing on a note of his impressions to his superiors, Gallagher was encouraged to continue making fact-finding missions to Northern Ireland in a more professional capacity. As Ronan Fanning suggests, due to Dublin's sheer ignorance on the emerging situation in Northern Ireland, this quickly led to Gallagher becoming a significant figure in the formulation of the Irish government's policy on 'the Six Counties'. Gallagher's subsequent reports on Northern Ireland were sent on to the Department of the Taoiseach, and 'by October 1969 Jack Lynch was relying on the Department of External Affairs – in effect, on Gallagher – for his speeches on Northern Ireland.'[27] Gallagher's overnight ascension to a position of such importance made his relationship with Hume even more significant.

Gallagher's family was from Donegal, to where he would return most weekends, and it was through his sister, Anna – who lived just across the border from Hume in Letterkenny – that the two men were first introduced.[28] Regular meetings followed, and through this an indirect but important channel between Hume and the Irish government was established. Indeed, Michael Kennedy, as well confirming Gallagher's role in shaping Lynch's response to the growing crisis, asserted that: 'Through Gallagher, he [Hume] became Dublin's number one contact in Derry and his views held an increasing influence over the Dublin government's Northern Ireland policy from this period'.[29]

Even at this early stage of the Troubles, Gallagher showed particular interest in both Hume's approach to Irish unity, and his concern for unionist perceptions of his position on this subject. As Gallagher noted of Hume, 'he follows a deliberate policy of saying nothing about reunification. He even avoids speaking publicly south of the Border so as to preserve himself from any attack on the subject.'[30] When, in November 1969, Hume did make his first controversial statement on the border – with his suggestion for periodic referenda on the issue – Gallagher, noting that the story was not carried in any of the Dublin dailies, eagerly produced for his employers a commentary on Hume's proposal as it had been reported in the *Derry Journal*. Although Gallagher doubted whether Hume's idea would have the effect he intended – that is to take the constitutional question out of everyday politics in Northern Ireland – he felt that the proposal was

> consistent with Mr. Hume's strategy of working towards a decent society within the present system while it reserves the right to change the constitutional basis of the system through normal democratic processes. He does not himself advocate reunification which he believes to be unattainable so long as monolithic policies are followed both by Unionists and Opposition ... By remaining silent on the issue he hopes to attract support from moderate opinion generally in favour of a new deal in the Northern society and thus bring about an easing of community relations; his private opinion is that a normalised society would eventually reconsider the real place of Northern Ireland in an Irish society.[31]

Gallagher's analysis gives credence to the idea that Hume was, at this stage, very much a revisionist in the mould of National Unity – aspiring to and defending the right to advocate Irish reunification, but concerned in the first instance that Northern Ireland should move on from reactionary politics and communal division:

Mr. Hume ... feels ... justified in attempting to shift politics in the direction of positive, social policies in lieu of sterile debate on diametrically opposed principles. In ordinary political circumstances a politician who sought, virtually alone, the middle ground would probably be crushed between the forces on either side of him but ... it is equally possible that Mr. Hume will continue to emerge as a very considerable figure.[32]

Gallagher was quite right to believe that Hume would emerge as 'a very considerable figure'. However, he could not anticipate the severe polarisation of society in Northern Ireland that would follow, forcing Hume to surrender the middle ground for a more orthodox position in order to maintain his ascendancy in his own community.

Having already been provided an *entrée* into government policy-making through Gallagher, Hume's influence in Dublin was further enhanced with the establishment of the SDLP.[33] Indeed, for the party was launched only a few months after the Lynch government had been rocked by the sensational implication of senior ministers in a plot to provide guns to the Provisionals. Justin O'Brien's account of the crisis suggests that, as a result, the embattled Taoiseach saw the emergence of the SDLP as a golden opportunity which he 'grasped as he began to fashion a new response to the Northern question, an approach which led to Hume's eventual domination of Northern nationalist politics.'[34] O'Brien intimates that, as a consequence of the scandal, Lynch felt duty-bound to do all he could to back the SDLP, both as a means to counter the growing threat of the Provisionals, and so as to avoid any further spill-over of the Northern Ireland crisis into the southern state.[35] It was unsurprising, then, that Lynch's government offered unambiguous support for the party's *Towards a New Ireland* paper.[36] By contrast, there were questions raised about the realism of the SDLP document on the Dáil's opposition benches.[37] It is most likely, then, that Hume and his colleagues watched the Irish election of February 1973 with particular interest.

The road to Dublin

The outcome of this election is crucial to understanding the nature of SDLP–Dublin relations in this period. After sixteen years in power, Fianna Fáil was finally removed from office by a coalition of Fine Gael and the Labour Party. However, the new administration, headed by Liam Cosgrave, did not have a commanding majority, holding only a two seat advantage in the Dáil. Nonetheless, the result did open up the possibility of change in the way that Dublin dealt with the SDLP. Indeed, Fine Gael did not have the same historical baggage as Fianna Fáil, whose anti-partitionist reputation, and more nationalist support base, encouraged a robust response to the outbreak of the Troubles. Fine Gael, by contrast, felt much less obligation to take a strong line on Northern Ireland.

Neither could the SDLP take for granted the support of the junior part-ner in the new government. Indeed, despite the organic links between the Labour party and the SDLP's left wing, Labour's spokesperson on Northern Ireland, Dr Conor Cruise O'Brien, had been openly disapproving of the *Towards a New Ireland* proposals.[38] Incensed by this criticism, Paddy Devlin chose to announce publicly that there had been a split with the party which he and his socialist comrade, Gerry Fitt, had previously con-sidered their southern sister.[39] Following on from this, Devlin placed an open letter to Brendan Corish in the *Irish Times*, denouncing the Labour leader for his failure to reprimand O'Brien.[40] However, undeterred, a month later O'Brien clashed with Hume on RTÉ's popular *The Late, Late Show*.[41] Although O'Brien appeared to relish the opprobrium caused by these controversies, some of his party colleagues were less impressed, par-ticularly with a general election on the horizon. They feared that opposi-tion to a northern nationalist party could be portrayed as being pro-partitionist, and thus opposed to the founding ideals of the Irish state. As O'Brien caustically remarked in his recollection of the period: 'In those terms, it has long been mandatory – and remains so – to say "me too" to whatever John Hume says.'[42] After surviving a clumsy attempt by his opponents to expel him from the Labour Party,[43] O'Brien became a minis-ter in the new government, but carried with him a warning of the danger of publicly criticising the SDLP. Nonetheless, it is evident that he and other members of the new cabinet remained more sceptical about the SDLP's approach than the previous administration.

Despite the questions raised over the party's proposals in both London and Dublin, the SDLP went into discussions for a new settlement in Northern Ireland holding to the ideas put forward in *Towards a New Ireland*. In this, the party was arguing for political structures that would be transitional; structures that would expedite the end of Irish reunifica-tion. Indeed, commenting on Whitehall's proposed Council of Ireland, Hume suggested that this body should play essentially the same role as the National Senate augured in *Towards a New Ireland*: examining the laws, structures and services in both parts of Ireland with a view to achieving their harmonisation. 'Once that is done and the problems in the way of unity are removed,' he said, 'that council should have the power to plan a constitution for a new Ireland'.[44]

The SDLP also adhered to the position enunciated in *Towards a New Ireland* on the need for new policing arrangements in Northern Ireland in which the Irish government would have a role.[45] But again it was the party's deputy leader who was most vocal on this matter. Hume's interest in the issue was understandable: large parts of his Derry constituency were still policed by the British army as a result of Catholic residents' enduring hostility towards the RUC.[46] In the various political talks that took place over the following months, it became evident that Hume – more than any of his party colleagues – was convinced of the need to overcome the minority's alienation from the RUC by creating a new force with which Catholics could identify, and which was accountable to both London *and* Dublin.

Even before formal negotiations had begun, however, it was clear that the SDLP was concerned that the new administration in Dublin would undermine its objectives. In a party meeting in early July, concern was expressed about 'the present government's statements on National Unity which indicates [*sic*] a clear drift away from the stance of the last government. ... Equivocation similar to that emanating from the Coalition government could be damaging to us at a time when we appear to be on the verge of a breakthrough.'[47] As a result, the party agreed to send a delegation to Dublin in order seek assurances on the government's position.

Six days later, Hume led an SDLP deputation to a meeting with government ministers at Leinster House. He opened this encounter by expressing the concern which had arisen in his party as a result of the seeming shift in Dublin's Northern Ireland policy towards what was termed 'appeasement' of the unionist community. Hume made it clear that the SDLP expected the government to support its views on the need for a 'real Irish dimension', namely a high-powered Council of Ireland, and radical change to policing in Northern Ireland. In the first instance, it was hoped that Dublin would, alongside London, assume joint responsibility for policing. If this could not be effected, it was expected that the Irish government would have some formal say in the administration of law and order in Northern Ireland through the proposed Council of Ireland.[48]

A few days later, the same message was conveyed to the British government in the SDLP's talks with the Northern Ireland secretary, William Whitelaw.[49] However, in the course of these discussions, the SDLP became further concerned about the intentions of the Irish government. This concern was provoked by Whitelaw's suggestion that Dublin officials had already told London that they did not support the party's position on policing and the need therein for an Irish input.[50]

As a result of Whitelaw's claim, another SDLP delegation was dispatched to Dublin in order to question the coalition government. Here, the Taoiseach assured the party that his administration had not led the British government to believe that it was at odds with the SDLP.[51] Despite this, only a few days later, Cosgrave was dismayed to find reports in the Irish press – based on information leaked by Devlin – which brought public attention to the perceived rift between the SDLP and the government.[52] Interestingly, immediately after these reports, the coalition was seen to swing fully behind the SDLP's line on the Council of Ireland and policing,[53] this after confidential talks took place between the party and the Irish Attorney General, Declan Costello.[54]

It was Hume who instigated this rapid *rapprochement*. He invited Costello to speak to SDLP representatives and members of constituency organisations, and to reassure them of the Irish government's position *vis-à-vis* the political process.[55] Hume may have thought that directly exposing Costello to the feelings of the SDLP rank-and-file would give the government a greater appreciation of the party's position. If this was his intention, it was certainly successful. For, in his report of meetings with various SDLP members, Costello identified considerable hostility towards the government over its failure to back the party in a public manner. He also noted the boldness with which the SDLP was approaching prospective talks with the Unionist Party:

> The view was strongly expressed that it was wrong to approach the negotiations on the basis of ascertaining what would be possible to obtain from the Unionists. The proper approach was to work out what was the way to settle the Northern Ireland problem and demand this solution. The view was expressed that the Unionists had been forced to accept a great deal in the last three years, that it could be said that they had given their retrospective 'consent' to the changes, and that if a strong and firm enough line was taken on the Nationalists' demands that they would be accepted.[56]

These comments demonstrated just how far the principle of consent – the most important departure in the party's founding philosophy – had depreciated within the SDLP's collective mind. It now appeared that 'consent' – and it is perhaps suggestive that Costello also chose to place the word in inverted commas in his report – amounted to unionist acceptance of *faits accomplis*.

Despite the obvious ambitiousness of the party's agenda, Cosgrave acceded to the advice provided by Costello in writing to Gerry Fitt and proposing a more formal liaison between the Irish government and the SDLP. But Cosgrave's letter also recommended that the party should confine its delegation numbers in such talks to a minimum, and expressed the hope the SDLP's relationship with Leinster House could be conducted in a less public manner in the future.[57] Reading between the lines, this suggested the damage done to the government's reputation by Devlin's press leak. As a result, meetings between the SDLP and Dublin became more confidential: the press was no longer informed in advance, and SDLP delegates declined to make comments to the media after they had taken place.[58] However, their silence was a small price to pay for gaining Dublin's undivided attention.

The reason for the Irish government's change in tack can be surmised. Although he did not explicitly say as much in his report, it is likely that Costello found individual SDLP members who, in expressing their dissatisfaction with the coalition government, implied that they might be obliged to turn to Fianna Fáil for support instead. The possibility that the opposition benches could exploit this situation would undoubtedly have weighed heavily on some minds within a coalition whose parties had not experienced office since 1957, and who even now held only a two seat majority. Seemingly confirming this hypothesis, Devlin – who had actually boasted to Costello about his part in the damaging press leak[59] – later admitted that there was 'an element of implicit blackmail' in relations with Dublin at this time.[60] As a result, argues Henry Patterson: 'Fearful of being portrayed as letting the "separated brethren" down, the Irish government's position soon shifted to one of uncritical support for Hume's analysis and prescriptions.'[61] Archival documents detailing the more secretive interactions between the SDLP and the coalition that followed Costello's report seem to support Patterson's opinion. They show Dublin now being far more accommodating of Hume's and his colleagues' demands.

At the end of August, in the first of a series of meetings with the Taoiseach and other government ministers, the SDLP again looked to gain assurances that the coalition wholly supported what the party termed its 'package approach' to negotiations. In this, the SDLP wanted movement on the issues of internment, policing, and the Council of Ireland before it would commit to a power-sharing executive. As Hume emphasised, there was a fear within the party that, if it joined a Northern Ireland government and subsequently found that progress promised on other fronts was not forthcoming, the SDLP would not be able to withdraw without being seen as 'wreckers'. Also expressed was an apprehension that the party leadership might be perceived as being motivated by financial gain if it seemed too eager to form an executive.[62] Clearly, Hume and his colleagues were concerned that the Catholic community might feel they could be 'bought off' by the British government.

Shortly after this meeting, the SDLP forwarded its formal proposals on policing and a Council of Ireland to Dublin. These documents showed the party holding its line in advocating an all-Ireland body with the potential to evolve without hindrance from Westminster, and which would be responsible for policing in both jurisdictions on the island.[63] However, Dublin was still less sanguine than the SDLP, and after a summit meeting between the British and Irish governments in mid-September, Cosgrave sought to inject a sense of realism into the party's thinking. Cautiously, he tried to persuade the SDLP of what had been made clear by Edward Heath in the two premiers' discussions: that Westminster was not prepared to relinquish any power over security in Northern Ireland – an understandable position given the disasters that led to Stormont's abolition – and, as such, could not countenance any role for the Council of Ireland in policing the region.[64]

In spite of Cosgrave's counsel, the SDLP persevered. After further discussions with Whitelaw, Hume felt that the British government was coming round to his arguments. In particular, he believed that the NIO was becoming more receptive to the idea of a Council of Ireland with responsibility for law and order in Northern Ireland, but only if this meant that the southern Irish police force, the Garda Síochána, would also come under the new body's control.[65] Hume's interpretation suggests that the British government was perhaps interested in an arrangement that would tie its Irish counterpart into more effective policing of the border, as IRA activists continued to escape to the Republic after launching attacks in

Northern Ireland. However, in relaying this information to Dublin ministers in a meeting in October, Hume immediately sensed their apprehension to any deal which would allow for a British influence in affairs south of the border as a *quid pro quo* for an Irish say in Northern Ireland. Nonetheless, he continued to make his case for an all-Ireland approach to law and order. Hume felt that this would help to overcome nationalists' hostility to the security apparatus in Northern Ireland, and could also be sold to unionists on the grounds that it would facilitate the pursuit of IRA suspects who sought refuge in the South. Again, he claimed that British officials had shown interest in this idea as a way to win unionist approval for new policing arrangements, but Hume was clearly concerned that Dublin would not seize the opportunity which he perceived.[66]

His concern was well founded, and Hume and his colleagues were sorely disappointed with the proposals which the Irish government put before its British counterpart shortly afterwards. These suggested that the police in both Northern Ireland and the Republic should regularly account to the proposed Council of Ireland, but that the North–South body would exercise no real authority over either force.[67] The SDLP's response once again showed that it was prepared to bring into question the coalition's nationalist credentials, claiming that British officials had been correct to suggest that the Irish government was not fully behind the party. The SDLP described the coalition's proposals as 'generally partitionist and [indicative] that Dublin may not be sincere in its approach to Irish unity.' Once more, a veiled threat was made to imply that the SDLP might have to turn to Fianna Fáil for support instead.[68]

Again the SDLP's concern was for how the northern minority would perceive the structures being proposed. The party was adamant that the Council of Ireland should have real responsibility for policing, claiming that '"accounting" is meaningless', and that unless it had genuine authority, the new institution 'would be regarded as "collaboration" in the Provo. sense of the word'. Meanwhile, responding to the coalition's suggestion of special courts for the trial of political offenders in both jurisdictions, the SDLP argued that these would 'hardly be identifiable to the man in the street as all-Ireland courts'.[69] This provided further evidence of the electoral importance which the party now attached to the 'Irish dimension'. There appeared to be a genuine fear within the SDLP that, unless it won significant political gains for the minority, the party would lose support to the IRA. This type of anxiety was undoubtedly encouraging the SDLP to peruse an increasingly nationalist agenda.

The SDLP's outburst provoked another *volte-face* by the coalition, which now promised to create a new policing authority in the Republic, a means to circumvent the constitutional problems involved in allowing the Garda Síochána to be directed by any body other than the government.[70] With a similar institution already in existence in Northern Ireland since reforms in 1969, it was felt that this would provide for symmetrical arrangements which would both come under the Council of Ireland. As a result, Irish officials were able to report back to the cabinet of the SDLP's seeming satisfaction with the government's new proposals.[71]

Having secured the coalition's compliance, the SDLP could now concentrate on its talks with the British government and the Unionists. Already the SDLP had given some ground here, having at least begun discussions on the formation of the executive prior to agreement on a Council of Ireland. Now, with the Irish government seemingly locked into their strategy, Hume and his colleagues appeared more confident of their position, and in late November of 1973 the SDLP finally agreed to join a power-sharing administration in Northern Ireland. The party only did so, however, on the understanding that the Council of Ireland and all other outstanding issues would be addressed at a tripartite conference – between the executive elect and the two governments – to be convened the following month. Only then would the executive actually take office.

The Sunningdale experiment

This conference, held at Sunningdale Civil Service College, Berkshire, was designed to put into place the final pieces of the political settlement outlined by the British government White Paper which had been published in the spring. In short, this meant finding agreement on the exact nature and powers of the proposed Council of Ireland; deciding Dublin's relationship to Northern Ireland in the context of the new political arrangements; and resolving law and order arrangements, both within Northern Ireland and in a cross-border context. Following four arduous days of talks, a joint communiqué announced that agreement had been reached.

The actual negotiation of the Sunningdale Agreement[72] has been well documented in a number of first-hand accounts.[73] There is, therefore, little need to recount the talks in detail, suffice to say that most of these memoirs, and indeed many academic commentaries, concur in depicting the SDLP – and Hume particularly – as the driving force at the Sunningdale conference. Accordingly, they tend towards the conclusion that the Unionists were outnegotiated, implying that the agreement made was significantly more favourable for the SDLP.[74]

Given the ever-increasing momentum of the party in the run-up to the conference – and particularly its success in securing a united front for Irish nationalism by co-opting the Dublin government into its strategy – it is easy to accept the idea that the SDLP forced an unfair settlement onto the UUP at Sunningdale. However, the memoirs of the Unionist leader, Brian Faulkner, flatly contradict this interpretation: 'all of us in the Unionist deputation were convinced that we had come off the best at Sunningdale ... We felt elated and expected our success to be recognized. One member of our delegation remarked that Sunningdale would go down in history as a Unionist victory.'[75]

It is fair to say that the Unionists conceded much ground at Sunningdale. But this judgement is made with consideration of what the Unionist Party had until the suspension of Stormont in 1972, namely a state system over which it had complete hegemony.[76] In this, it could be said that the Unionists had a lot more *to concede* than the nationalist participants at Sunningdale. However, on the core constitutional issues, they surrendered very little, and so Faulkner had good reason to feel victorious. The 1973 Agreement in no way changed the existing relationship between Belfast and London: Northern Ireland was to remain part of the UK so long as a majority in the region so desired. Moreover, to all intents and purposes, this was accepted by the Irish government. Although the Irish constitution did not allow Dublin to give formal, *de jure* recognition of Northern Ireland's position within the UK,[77] in a solemn declaration included in the Sunningdale communiqué, the Cosgrave government accepted the *status quo*, and the fact that it could not change without the consent of a majority in Northern Ireland.[78]

Of course, the obvious question over the constitutional integrity of Northern Ireland was that posed by the Council of Ireland – particularly since Hume and his party had, from the time that the institution was first proffered, championed the body as an engine of Irish reunification. However, despite the strongly 'unificationist' intentions of the SDLP as it went into the conference, the all-Ireland structure actually agreed at Sunningdale could *not* be a mere harbinger of Irish unity. Firstly, although the Council of Ireland had administrative functions in a number of areas, the principle of consent was built into its workings in that the executive arm, the Council of Ministers, had to operate on the basis of unanimity.[79] As a result, no decision with regard to North–South relations could be taken without Unionist agreement. Though they would be outnumbered on the Council of Ministers by nationalist representatives – that is SDLP and Dublin ministers combined – the Unionists could not be overrun. They could resist any act of 'harmonisation' which they felt compromised the constitution of Northern Ireland. Secondly, those fields in which the Council of Ireland did have competence were limited to anodyne areas of common interest between North and South such as trade and tourism.[80] Furthermore, this range of fields could not be extended without the assent of the Northern Ireland Assembly, where unionists had a clear majority. This gave Ulster unionism a double veto over the power of the proposed Council.[81]

This explains why Faulkner had such confidence in the deal he made. Moreover, whilst he accepted that his community came to quite a different verdict on Sunningdale, Faulkner remained unrepentant of his part in the Agreement: 'All this may seem in retrospect ironic and unreal. But I do not think if one examines the balance-sheet our conclusions can be shown to have been poorly judged.' Indeed, and it is very difficult to contradict his final appraisal of the Agreement:

nothing agreed on at Sunningdale infringed on the powers of the Northern Ireland Assembly by which everything would have to be approved and delegated. Given the overwhelming Unionist composition of that body and the unanimity rule in the Council of Ministers we were satisfied that the constitutional integrity of Northern Ireland was secure. ... [T]he Council of Ireland was not the massive Trojan Horse people were led ... to believe. ... We had ... control over the direction and pace of its developments and ... its establishment would in no way compromise ... [our] position as citizens of the United Kingdom.[82]

However, it was not this interpretation of Sunningdale that won out amongst the unionist community. Rather it was 'Trojan Horse' argument which Faulkner alluded to, epitomised by the loyalist declaration that 'Dublin is just a Sunningdale away'. With this rallying slogan, opponents of the Agreement turned the untimely Westminster election of February 1974 into an effective referendum on Sunningdale. Coming together as the United Ulster Unionist Council (UUUC), anti-Agreement unionists won eleven of the twelve Westminster seats in Northern Ireland, and showed a clear majority of the Protestant community in opposition to Sunningdale.[83] Using this as a mandate for further action, loyalist activists and paramilitaries coalescing under the banner of the Ulster Workers' Council (UWC) organised a general strike. Crucial to its success were loyalist workers' positions in key utilities, which allowed them to disrupt power supplies and bring Northern Ireland to a standstill. In London, meanwhile, the February election had led to the formation of a minority Labour government. Its insecurity undoubtedly added to its unwillingness to intervene and to save Sunningdale. In the end, the UWC strike forced Faulkner and his ministers to resign, and the Sunningdale experiment collapsed.

The SDLP and Sunningdale

In the period that followed Sunningdale's demise, the SDLP showed tremendous resentment towards the British government for its failure to stand against the UWC strike.[84] Hume especially was unflinching in his criticism: 'The greatest factor of all [in the fall of Sunningdale] ... was the lack of will on the part of the British Government ... to face up to the Loyalists and instead to adopt a policy of inaction and delay which could only lead to the collapse of the Executive'.[85] Hume believed that a decisive move by the British army against loyalist road blocks set up during the early days of the strike would have saved Sunningdale.[86]

However, whilst the UWC strike was, in its initial stages, undoubtedly enforced by loyalist intimidation, it went on to win the support of a wider range of unionist opinion.[87] This confirmed the result of the Westminster election three months earlier, which suggested that it was not just loyalists who had turned against Faulkner, and that more moderate sections of the Protestant population were also concerned about Sunningdale.[88] It was probably this realisation that the Agreement had already lost legitimacy amongst the greater part of the unionist community which led the new Labour government to conclude that the executive was doomed, thus explaining the absence of any genuine effort to avert its fall.[89]

But the collapse in unionist support for Sunningdale was, essentially, caused by a misinterpretation of the Agreement. As reasoned above, the threat which Sunningdale posed to the Union was more imaginary than real. The Agreement did not alter in any way the existing constitutional relationship between Belfast and London, and the Council of Ireland could not have brought about the dissolution of partition without the consent of unionist representatives. However, any sensible reading of Sunningdale was overshadowed by the apocalyptic rhetoric of the UUUC.

At the same time, Protestant anxieties were heightened by nationalists' interpretation of the Agreement, which seemed to vindicate the loyalist view. In this regard, the SDLP must share the blame for the failure of Sunningdale. Rather than a framework within which nationalists, North and South, might co-operate with unionists and gradually persuade them of the value of Irish unity, the Sunningdale Agreement was extolled as a mere precursor to that seemingly inescapable end. It was this – the party's presentation of Sunningdale, rather than the actual content of the Agreement – which brought its ruin by providing a ready-made propaganda package with which loyalists were able to raise the spectre of Hibernia irredenta and the idea of the impending destruction of Ulster unionism.

The most memorable and oft-cited example of this faux pas was provided by the SDLP's Hugh Logue, when only a month after the Sunningdale conference he told a Dublin audience that the Council of Ireland was 'the vehicle that would trundle Unionists into a united Ireland'.[90] As argued above, the Council of Ireland, functioning on a basis of unanimity, and incapable of expansion without assent from the Northern Ireland Assembly, could not 'trundle Unionists into a united Ireland' – at least not without their agreement. However, the conclusion that was drawn from Logue's comment was that unionists could not but agree to join a united Ireland; soon enough they would submit to the supposedly irresistible logic of Irish unity. In this, despite recognising the need for unionist consent for the creation of a united Ireland, Ulster Protestants' right to actually withhold that consent did not – judging by the party's rhetoric – seem to be within the SDLP's comprehension at this time. Thus the party's most important principle was compromised by the SDLP's presentation of Sunningdale.

But why was the party so willing to play the role required by loyalists? Why did the SDLP feel the need to portray the Sunningdale settlement, erroneously, as simply a stepping-stone towards a united Ireland? In answering these questions, the political climate within which the party was operating needs to be considered. For this helps to explain the SDLP's continued deviation from its formative philosophy.

First and foremost, there was the issue of the SDLP's participation in a Stormont administration. For many Catholics, the very name, 'Stormont', had become a byword for discrimination and repression. Although the new dispensation could be seen as much reformed in nature – not least in guaranteeing seats for nationalists in its executive office – there remained problems related to the *ancien régime*, most notably the continuation of internment without trial. This emotive issue had dogged the SDLP since the very first arrests in August 1971, after which the party had sworn not to enter into any political dialogue until all internees were released. After the suspension of Stormont, the SDLP changed tack, arguing that it would negotiate an end to internment as part of overall settlement. However, the party left Sunningdale with only a promise from the British government that it would phase out the policy as the security situation allowed.[91] By joining an administration that continued to practise detention without trial, Hume and his colleagues appeared to be turning their backs on the principles which they had loudly proclaimed during the civil rights period.

Related to internment was the issue of policing, and it was this – rather than the Council of Ireland or Dublin's recognition of Northern Ireland – that had been the main debating point at Sunningdale, delaying the conclusion of the conference by some thirty hours.[92] As noted, Hume had been the main advocate of policing reform in negotiations prior to Sunningdale, even demanding that the Council of Ireland be given responsibility for law and order on both sides of the border as a means to overcome the northern minority's alienation from the security forces. By all accounts, he pushed the Sunningdale conference to breaking point on this issue. Indeed, in an effort to secure the changes which he deemed necessary, Hume stayed up all night, and was still negotiating with Heath at seven in the morning on the final day of the conference. Ultimately, Hume's intransigence exasperated even own party colleagues,[93] but his position on policing was undoubtedly informed by the experience of his own community in Derry. Since the early days of the Troubles – from the suppression of the first civil rights march in the city in October 1968, to the infamous 'Battle of the Bogside' in August 1969 – Derry nationalists had come to reject the Stormont security forces outright. The failure to produce radical reform in this area[94] ensured that they, and Catholic communities across Northern Ireland, continued to withhold their consent to be policed by the RUC. This created the state of disaffection and, in parts – particularly areas of Hume's constituency – outright lawlessness in which the IRA was able to sustain itself. Accordingly, Hume was convinced that the reconstitution of the RUC and the agencies of its control was vital to any solution that would deliver lasting peace.

But despite this conviction, and his arduous efforts, Hume failed to achieve any real change to policing in Northern Ireland at Sunningdale. The simple reason was that, just as Hume saw the need for a complete restructuring of policing in Northern Ireland in order to undermine the IRA, so British officials believed in the need to maintain current security arrangements as the only way to contain republican violence. The British government could not countenance any security reform which would unsettle unionists and thus diminish the efficacy of the overwhelmingly Protestant RUC, a force on which Westminster still heavily relied in order to police Northern Ireland. William Whitelaw had made this clear in a discussion with the Irish Foreign Minister, Garret FitzGerald, a month before the Sunningdale conference, when he explained his opposition to the SDLP's demands for a change in the name of the RUC. The force's name, the Northern Ireland Secretary declared, was 'like the "Ark of the Covenant" for many', and to change it, he claimed, would precipitate the resignation of 300 of his best officers.[95] Despite Whitelaw's departure from the NIO prior to Sunningdale, at the December talks Heath steadfastly maintained the line that there could be no concession on policing. Unsurprisingly, Faulkner was also vehemently opposed to further changes to the RUC, or to any role for the Irish government in the force's control. But it was the obduracy of the British government over policing that ultimately defeated the SDLP's ambitions. In this, contrary to accounts that depict the Sunningdale negotiations as a broad success for the party, on what proved to be the decisive issue at the conference, it was the SDLP that was forced to back down.[96]

The vigorous struggle which the SDLP had fought in the run-up to Sunningdale – persuading the Irish government to link the Garda Síochána to the Council of Ireland, and believing that the British government would then do likewise with the RUC – had all been in vain. Whether or not the NIO genuinely considered the possibility of such a *quid pro quo* in order to obtain better policing of the southern side of the Irish border is a moot point; when all the cards were on the table at Sunningdale, it was clear that Heath – still mindful of such disasters as the introduction of interment and Bloody Sunday – was not prepared to relinquish any control over security in Northern Ireland, nor even to give Dublin the kind of consultative role that Margaret Thatcher would concede in the Anglo-Irish Agreement a decade later. As such, the best the SDLP could obtain in the Sunningdale Agreement was a vague commitment that 'the governments concerned will cooperate under the auspices of the Council of Ireland through their respective police authorities'. Following from this, an extremely tenuous association between state security in Northern Ireland and the Irish government was achieved through the provision that appointments to the Northern Ireland police authority would 'be made after consultation with the Northern Ireland Executive which would consult with the Council of Ministers of the Council of Ireland'.[97] These arrangements fell short of even the Irish government's pre-Sunningdale proposal that the police forces in both jurisdictions should regularly account to the Council of Ireland – memorably dismissed by the SDLP as '"collaboration" in the Provo. sense of the word' – never mind the party's original hope of gaining an actual role for Dublin in the control of the security apparatus in Northern Ireland.

The SDLP's failure at Sunningdale to secure any real change to the administration of law and order in Northern Ireland was critical. In particular, the party's inability to resolve the highly emotive issue of internment meant that, on taking office, Hume and his colleagues found themselves part of what was, for many nationalists, a punitive Stormont regime – precisely that which they had repudiated in their withdrawal from the Belfast parliament only three years earlier. As a result, the SDLP was left open to criticism from republicans and other radicals in the nationalist community, who had long predicted that the party would fall into line as an instrument of British state strategy and a proponent of the political status quo.[98] This, in turn, helps to explain the particularly defensive behaviour of the SDLP at this time. For the party's response to the criticism it received over Sunningdale was to hold all the more tenaciously to its increasingly nationalist credentials, and especially to the idea that the Council of Ireland would deliver Irish unity. Indeed, in this regard, it should be remembered that Hugh Logue's famous comment that the Council was 'the vehicle that would trundle Unionists into a united Ireland' was made in direct response to a republican heckler amongst his audience, who accused the party of 'selling out' on the national issue.[99]

In summary, the Sunningdale Agreement was not quite the success for the SDLP that has sometimes been suggested. Rather, it was the way that the party presented the settlement that so prejudiced unionist opinions. For even before the Agreement was announced, Sunningdale was effectively 'pre-sold' to nationalists on the premise that it would prepare the way for Irish reunification. Indeed, since the collapse of Stormont, the SDLP's entire political strategy appeared predetermined towards the creation of a united Ireland. This was a consequence of attitudes in both communities in Northern Ireland during this period. On the nationalist side, the radicalisation of the minority produced by events like internment and Bloody Sunday, followed by the rising levels of expectation engendered by Stormont's collapse, was found difficult to sate with the reformist, gradualist doctrine originally proffered by SDLP. At the same time, support had grown for the republican movement in its promise to overthrow the British state, end partition, and lead nationalists directly into a united Ireland. Fearing that it would lose authority amongst the minority, this caused the SDLP to adopt a more dynamic language, which portrayed the negotiation of a new political settlement as an incontrovertible process towards Irish reunification. Meanwhile, within the unionist community, the division and demoralisation that followed Stormont's demise had led Hume and his colleagues to the erroneous conclusion that a significant section of the Protestant population would now acquiesce in the reunification of Ireland if nationalists, North and South, seized the initiative and set in motion such a process.[100] In both respects, the evolutionary and consensual approach to Irish unity within the SDLP's original thinking was effectively eclipsed.

The irony in this is that Sunningdale was, arguably, very much in keeping with the revisionist ideas that had initially influenced Hume his party: on the one hand, the Agreement gave *de facto* nationalist recognition of partition and the Northern Ireland state, seeking its reformation rather than is abolition; on the other, by bringing the two communities in Northern Ireland together in a new government, and by facilitating North–South co-operation through the Council of Ireland, the Agreement provided a constitutional framework within which nationalists might overcome unionists' distrust and, in time, demonstrate the value of an increasingly integrated island. But it could not bring unionists into a united Ireland without their assent. Sunningdale was premised on the fundamental axiom of revisionist nationalism: the principle of consent.

However, whilst consonant with the party's formative philosophy, the Sunningdale Agreement was, to a significant degree, misrepresented by the SDLP. Both the opportunities afforded and the pressures endured by the party in the period following Stormont's collapse had led the SDLP to stray from its founding principles, to overstate the dynamic and the nationalist potential of the Sunningdale experiment, and so to debase the project in unionist eyes. For though the Agreement proposed that that their consent was necessary for the creation of a united Ireland, the SDLP's rhetoric in reference to Sunningdale implied that it did not believe unionists had any right to withhold this assent. Thus, from a unionist perspective, the party's strategy appeared as one of coercion rather then persuasion, and compulsion rather then consent. Divided and disorientated by the end of Stormont, the Protestant community was reunited and refocused by Sunningdale, and this led to a triumphant intransigence that would govern unionist politics for the remainder of the decade.

Notes

1 Bew and Gillespie, *Northern Ireland: A Chronology*, p. 48; Hennessey, *Northern Ireland: The Origins of the Troubles*, pp. 228ff., 309ff.
2 Quoted in White, *Hume*, p. 127.
3 P. Bew and H. Patterson, *The British State and the Ulster Crisis: From Wilson to Thatcher* (London: Verso, 1985), pp. 39–40; Bew, Gibbon and Patterson, *Northern Ireland, 1921–2001*, pp. 156, 160–1; Dixon, *Northern Ireland*, p. 114.
4 Bew and Patterson, *The British State*, p. 40.
5 Bew and Gillespie, *Northern Ireland: A Chronology*, p. 42.
6 For similar thinking on the part of a senior southern Irish politician, see Garret FitzGerald's *Towards a New Ireland* (Dublin: Gill and Macmillan, 1972), which was written at the time of Stormont's collapse.
7 Murray, *John Hume and the SDLP*, pp. 13–18.
8 Ben Caraher; interview with author, Belfast, 25 June 2004.
9 As suggested in the Preface, whilst Murray is right to emphasise that much of the SDLP's political thinking can be traced to unpublished party papers, written by figures like Caraher and Duffy in 1971–72, he perhaps overestimates

the degree to which these ideas had matured, and thus overstates the case that the documents can be related to the Good Friday Agreement of 1998; Murray, 'The Good Friday Agreement', p. 51; Murray and Tonge, *Sinn Féin and the SDLP*, pp. xiv, xvi, 27–9, 200–2. Although many of the SDLP's ideas find their genesis in these discussion papers, the party's outlook would continue to evolve and to be shaped, not always in a wholly progressive manner, by the political developments that unfolded around it.

10 Devlin, *Straight Left*, p. 185; Murray, *John Hume and the SDLP*, p. 17.
11 This is most obvious when the document is compared to the aforementioned articles which Hume wrote for the *Irish Times* in the latter part of 1971; see the *Irish Times*, 6 November 1971, and 31 December 1971.
12 SDLP, *Towards a New Ireland* (Belfast: SDLP, 1972), p. 1.
13 See above, pp. 12–13.
14 Paddy Devlin claims that the idea of joint sovereignty first came from a Belfast doctor, Paddy Lane, who passed on to the SDLP a paper which argued the merits of such an arrangement. But it seems that it was the academic and free-lance writer, Desmond Fennell, who, through Ivan Cooper, converted the party to the idea of condominium; Ivan Cooper; interview with author, Derry, 30 June 2004; Devlin, *Straight Left*, p. 185; D. Fennell, *The Revision of Irish Nationalism* (Dublin: Open Air, 1989), p. 39.
15 SDLP, *Towards a New Ireland*, p. 4.
16 *Ibid.*, p. 6.
17 *Ibid.*
18 Indeed, the present author does exactly that.
19 For discussions of Ulster unionist identity, and complex interaction of politics and religion therein, see C. Coulter, 'The character of unionism', *Irish Political Studies*, 9 (1994); and J. Todd, 'Two traditions in unionist political culture', *Irish Political Studies*, 2 (1987).
20 Murray, *John Hume and the SDLP*, p. 18.
21 Ben Caraher; interview with author, Belfast, 25 June 2004.
22 *Sunday Independent*, 24 September 1972.
23 HMSO, *The Future of Northern Ireland: A Paper for Discussion* (Belfast: HMSO, 1972), paras. 76–8.
24 *Irish News*, 8 November 1972.
25 HMSO, *Northern Ireland: Constitutional Proposals* (London: HMSO, 1973), Cmnd 5259, para. 109.
26 *Irish Times*, 23 March 1973.
27 R. Fanning, 'Playing it cool: the response of the British and Irish governments to the crisis in Northern Ireland, 1968–9', in *Irish Studies in International Affairs*, 12 (2001), p. 80.
28 P. Arthur, *Special Relationships: Britain, Ireland and the Northern Ireland Problem* (Belfast: Blackstaff, 2000), p. 105; Fanning, 'Playing it cool', p. 80.
29 Kennedy, *Division and Consensus*, p. 323.
30 NAI, Department of Foreign Affairs (DFA), 2000/5/48, report by E. Gallagher on Hume's review of Terence O'Neill's *Ulster at the Crossroads* for the *Irish Times*, 28 October 1969.
31 NAI, DFA, 2000/5/48, report by E. Gallagher on Hume's proposal for a border poll, 13 November 1969.
32 *Ibid.*

33 By this point, Gallagher had introduced Hume to the rest of the staff at Iveagh House, and it is notable that, hereinafter, almost every major statement which he made was meticulously recorded by officials there. See NAI, DFA, 2001/43/1396.
34 O'Brien, *The Arms Trial*, p. 163.
35 *Ibid.*, pp. 153, 185–6.
36 NAI, DFA, 2003/17/319, government press release, 28 September 1972.
37 *Irish Press*, 25 and 27 September 1972; *Irish Times*, 25 and 26 September 1972.
38 *Irish Press*, 25 September 1972.
39 *Irish Times*, 3 October 1972.
40 *Ibid.*, 13 October 1972.
41 *This Week*, 16 November 1972.
42 Conor Cruise O'Brien, *Memoir: My Life and Themes* (London: Profile, 1999), p. 338.
43 *Ibid.*, pp. 339–40.
44 *Belfast Telegraph*, 29 May 1973.
45 SDLP, *Towards a New Ireland*, pp. 5, 11–12.
46 Hume continually had to speak out against the activities of the British army in areas such as the Creggan, which the state continued to control only by such an extensive military presence that everyday life was constantly disrupted for the residents there; for example, see the *Irish Independent*, 5 October 1973.
47 Minutes of meeting of the SDLP assembly party, 6 July 1973; cited in Bew and Patterson, *The British State*, p. 72, n. 81.
48 NAI, D/T, 2004/21/670, minutes of meeting between government ministers and SDLP delegation, 12 July 1973. It is not clear from this source whether the word 'appeasement' was used by Hume, or was a term chosen by the minute-taker at the meeting to capture the essence of what the SDLP deputy leader was saying at this point. Either way, it is suggestive of the party's considerable concern.
49 *Irish News*, 17 July 1973.
50 NAI, D/T 2004/21/670, minutes of meeting between government ministers and SDLP delegation, 26 July 1973.
51 *Ibid.*
52 *Sunday Press*, 29 July 1973; *Sunday World*, 29 July 1973.
53 *Financial Times*, 30 July 1973.
54 *Irish Independent*, 30 July 1973.
55 NAI, D/T, 2004/21/624, report by D. Costello on meetings with SDLP, 30 July 1973.
56 *Ibid.*
57 NAI, D/T, 2004/21/670, letter from Cosgrave to Fitt, 2 August 1973.
58 *Irish Press*, 30 August 1973; *Irish News*, 7 September 1973.
59 NAI, D/T, 2004/21/624, report by D. Costello on meetings with SDLP, 30 July 1973.
60 Quoted in Bew and Patterson, *The British State*, p. 72, n. 84.
61 Patterson, *Ireland Since 1939*, p. 238.
62 NAI, D/T, 2004/21/670, minutes of meeting between government ministers and SDLP, 29 August 1973.

63 NAI, D/T, 2004/21/670, SDLP, 'Proposals for A Council of Ireland by the Social Democratic and Labour Party', 15 September, 1973; SDLP, 'The Police Service of Northern Ireland', 16 September 1973.

64 NAI, D/T, 2004/21/670, minutes of meeting between government ministers and SDLP, 20 September 1973.

65 NAI, D/T, 2004/21/670, minutes of meeting between government ministers and SDLP, 12 October 1973.

66 *Ibid.*

67 NAI, D/T, 2004/21/670, letter including proposals document from C. V. Whelan to Dr D. O'Sullivan, 26 October 1973.

68 NAI, D/T, 2004/21/625, report by S. Donlon on meeting with Hume, Paddy Devlin, Gerry Fitt, Austin Currie and Ivan Cooper, 30 October 1973.

69 *Ibid.*

70 NAI, D/T, 2004/21/624, report of the legal committee on the implications of reform of the security forces in Northern Ireland.

71 NAI, D/T 2004/21/625, letter from S. Donlon to Dermot Nally, 6 November 1973.

72 In truth, Sunningdale was only, in the words of one senior official, 'an agreement to reach an agreement'; K. Bloomfield, *Stormont in Crisis: A Memoir* (Belfast: Blackstaff, 1994), p. 203. There was understanding that a second conference would be held in early 1974, at which a formal accord based on the December communiqué would be signed by the two governments and the participating parties. However, the second conference never took place. Despite this, convention is followed in referring to the December communiqué as 'the Sunningdale Agreement' in the main text here.

73 See Bloomfield, *Stormont*, pp. 185ff; Currie, *All Hell Will Break Loose*, ch. 19; Devlin, *Straight Left*, pp. 203ff.; B. Faulkner, *Memoirs of a Statesman* (London: Weidenfeld and Nicolson, 1978), ch. 17; G. FitzGerald, *All in a Life: An Autobiography* (London: Gill and Macmillan, 1991), pp. 210ff.; E. Heath, *The Course of My Life: My Autobiography* (London: Coronet, 1998), pp. 243–4; B. McIvor, *Hope Deferred: Experiences of an Irish Unionist* (Belfast: Blackstaff, 1998), pp. 100–5; and O'Brien, *Memoir*, pp. 350–3.

74 Bew and Gillespie, *Northern Ireland: A Chronology*, pp. 74–5; Bew and Patterson, *The British State*, p. 64; Dixon, *Northern Ireland*, pp. 144–5, 156–7; R. F. Foster, *Luck and the Irish: A Brief History of Change, 1970–2000* (London: Allen Lane, 2007), p. 118; A. Jackson, *Home Rule: An Irish History, 1800–2000* (London: Weidenfeld and Nicolson, 2004), p. 315; Murphy, *Gerry Fitt*, p. 198; Patterson, *Ireland Since 1939*, p. 239.

75 Faulkner, *Memoirs*, pp. 236–7.

76 See O'Leary and McGarry, *The Politics of Antagonism*, ch. 3.

77 The only way that the coalition could have given unambiguous recognition of Northern Ireland's status would have been to hold a referendum to allow the deletion of the Republic's constitutional claim to sovereignty over the whole of Ireland. However, it is likely that the government would have lost such a referendum, with the political opposition, Fianna Fáil, mobilising the country in defence of the claim which its founding father, Éamon de Valera, had written into the constitution. As such, Cosgrave decided against such a move; Faulkner, *Memoirs*, pp. 231, 247; FitzGerald, *All in a Life*, pp. 223–4.

78 Dublin Stationery Office, *Agreed Communiqué issued following the Conference between the Irish and British Governments and the parties involved in the Northern Ireland Executive (designate) on 6th, 7th, 8th, and 9th, December, 1973* [the Sunningdale Agreement] (Dublin: Dublin Stationery Office, 1973), article 5.
79 *Ibid.*, article 7.
80 *Ibid.*, article 8.
81 FitzGerald, *All in a Life*, p. 209. One senior NIO official went so far as to describe the Council of Ireland as 'a sham', arguing that the need for unanimity meant that there was no threat to the unionist position; cited in Bew and Patterson, *The British State*, p. 73 (n. 107).
82 Faulkner, *Memoirs*, pp. 237, 253.
83 S. Elliott and W. D. Flackes, *Northern Ireland: A Political Directory, 1968–1999* (Belfast: Blackstaff, 1999), p. 537.
84 Bew, Gibbon and Patterson, *Northern Ireland, 1921–2001*, p. 190.
85 *Irish Times*, 15 November 1975.
86 Routledge, *John Hume*, p. 137.
87 J. Ruane and J. Todd, *The Dynamics of Conflict in Northern Ireland: Power Conflict and Emancipation* (Cambridge: Cambridge University Press, 1996), p. 133.
88 McAllister, *The Social Democratic and Labour Party*, p. 143.
89 M. Cunningham, *British Government Policy in Northern Ireland, 1969–2000* (Manchester: Manchester University Press, 2001), p. 17; Patterson, *Ireland Since 1939*, p. 240.
90 Quoted in Bew and Gillespie, *Northern Ireland: A Chronology*, p. 77. There is some controversy over exactly what Logue said, and he has sought to clarify his comment on numerous occasions since (for example, see Murphy, *Gerry Fitt*, p. 218). However, this is how Logue's words were reported, and certainly how they were remembered by unionists.
91 Devlin, *Straight Left*, p. 210.
92 Currie, *All Hell Will Break Loose*, p. 235; FitzGerald, *All in a Life*, p. 217.
93 Currie, *All Hell Will Break Loose*, p. 239; Devlin, *Straight Left*, p. 209; FitzGerald, *All in a Life*, pp. 216–21.
94 On the Hunt reforms of October 1969, and the reasons why they failed to gain Derry Catholics' assent for new policing arrangements, see Ó Dochartaigh, *From Civil Rights to Armalites*, pp. 140–4.
95 NAI, DFA, 2004/15/23, minutes of a meeting between FitzGerald and Whitelaw, 8 November 1973.
96 Faulkner, *Memoirs*, p. 236; FitzGerald, *All in a Life*, p. 221.
97 *Agreed Communiqué*, article 15.
98 Bew and Patterson, *The British State*, pp. 65–6; Murphy, *Gerry Fitt*, pp. 191, 192, 221.
99 T. P. Coogan, *The Troubles: Ireland's Ordeal 1966–1996 and the Search for Peace* (London: Hutchinson, 1996), p. 209; Dixon, *Northern Ireland*, p. 147.
100 Jackson, *Home Rule*, p. 318; White, *Hume*, p. 127.

4

The two traditions

The collapse of the Sunningdale Agreement dealt a massive blow to the SDLP. All that the party had worked for in the two years since Stormont's collapse was, within just two weeks, swept away by the UWC strike. Nonetheless, after holding a series of internal party talks to decide the best way forward, Hume and his colleagues emerged from the ruins of Sunningdale with a renewed commitment to the basic formula behind the 1973 Agreement: executive-level power-sharing and an institutionalised Irish dimension.[1] Indeed, within a month of the Sunningdale's demise, the SDLP released a policy statement which made clear that there would be no departure from the party's essential political programme:

> The SDLP stands firmly by the policies ... for which we have received a clear mandate. We regret the suggestions that because of the fall of the Northern Ireland Executive's [sic] new policies must be found. ... We shall not be deterred ... from our conviction that the only basis for a solution to the problems of this community must be partnerships between both sections of the Northern community and between both parts of this island based on agreement.[2]

Notwithstanding the claim that there would be no change in the party's core policies, this statement paid less attention to the Irish dimension, and the press was quick to note the omission of any specific reference to the abortive Council of Ireland. However, the SDLP soon dismissed any suggestion that this should be read as a weakening of the party's commitment to North–South institutions. 'The Irish dimension is fundamental to SDLP policy', Austin Currie declared: 'Whether or not it is realised in a Council of Ireland or any other structure is a matter for discussion.'[3] Currie's statement was considered particularly important in the light of the controversial comments made by Liam Cosgrave a few days earlier. In these, the Taoiseach had suggested that the citizens in the Republic of Ireland did not desire 'unity or close association with a people so deeply imbued with violence and its effects', and that the ongoing conflict in Northern Ireland was 'killing here the desire for unity which has been part of our heritage'.[4] This was widely read as a signal that Dublin was looking to distance itself from Northern Ireland in the aftermath of the failed Sunningdale initiative, and so to effectively foreclose the Irish dimension. Unsurprisingly, therefore, Cosgrave's words caused considerable disquiet within the SDLP.[5]

Asked about the implications of the Taoiseach's remarks during an interview on RTÉ radio, Hume rejected the idea that the nationalist aspiration towards a united Ireland might be weakening. Instead, he claimed that there was still a desire, perhaps not for immediate unity, but for an eventual 'coming together' of the two parts of the island. However, further explaining this opinion, Hume made clear that his idea of a united Ireland was quite different from the traditional ideal. 'A coming together', he said, 'must mean an agreed Ireland. If we get an agreed Ireland that is unity. What constitutional or institutional forms such an agreed Ireland takes is irrelevant because it would represent agreement by the people of this country as to how they should be governed.'[6]

The implication in this – that Irish unity as understood by Hume and his colleagues might not entail the creation of an actual unitary state – was given further substance in the SDLP policy statement that followed. In this, the party argued that Irish reunification should not mean annexation of Northern Ireland by the Republic: 'The term "United Ireland" can mean many things to many people and is capable of many interpretations. The SDLP has always made it clear that it does NOT desire a take-over of the North by the South and that any coming together must be on the basis of agreement.' Echoing Hume's words from the previous day, the statement continued to say that: 'The institutional or constitutional form is not the most important issue. What is important is that such institutions should have the agreement of the people of the North and of the South. Agreement is the essence of any real unity and we cannot see how anyone in the North can object to working for an agreed Ireland with institutions acceptable to both parts of the country.'[7]

In this, there was a conscious reinterpretation of the meaning of Irish unity. This was clearly expressed with a mind to address the fears which Sunningdale had raised amongst the unionist population – particularly the idea that they were being corralled into an all-Ireland state against their will. Instead of this, the SDLP's statement made plain that the party's key objectives were power-sharing and an Irish dimension. Indeed, again endorsing Hume's earlier comments, the party suggested that agreement around these terms would *in itself* constitute Irish unity. This contrasted strongly with the discourse that the SDLP had employed in its approach to Sunningdale, wherein power-sharing and all-Ireland institutions were presented as essentially transitionary structures which would prepare the way for the formal reunification of the island.

In summary, the post-Sunningdale period saw SDLP hold to its immediate political aims; the party was still convinced of the essential rectitude of its programme. However, the SDLP did begin to think more seriously about its strategy – about its implications and its presentation – than had previously been the case. In this, there appeared a deliberate effort by the party to both assure unionists of its intentions, and persuade them of its proposals. Much of the ideas which emerged from this rethink would continue to evolve and to shape SDLP policy in the coming years. As they did, Hume's intellectual dominance within the party would become increasingly apparent.

The Constitutional Convention

Surprisingly soon after the collapse of Sunningdale, the new Northern Ireland Secretary, Merlyn Rees, launched a fresh political initiative. The Constitutional Convention was a forum to which the local parties would be elected with the aim of devising a system of devolved government for themselves. However, the background to the British government's second attempt to produce a settlement of the Northern Ireland conflict was, at least from the SDLP's perspective, not entirely encouraging. To begin with, the Protestant community was hardly in the mood for political compromise. Indeed, buoyed by their defeat of Sunningdale, unionists of all shades became increasingly intransigent from the mid-1970s, convinced that if they held out long enough, the British government would either restore an essentially majoritarian Stormont system, or fully integrate Northern Ireland into the UK.

In addition, there was a question mark over London's sincerity in the new initiative. The White Paper outlining the terms of the proposed Convention did recommend power-sharing and an Irish dimension,[8] but the Wilson government's failure to uphold these elements as they appeared in the Sunningdale Agreement left the SDLP doubting that the same administration would support them now. Moreover, the fact that the new initiative placed the onus on the local parties to find an agreement on these terms – with the British government effectively rescinding its role as chair of the settlement process – gave further cause for concern.[9]

Hume was particularly unimpressed. His prediction of the likely outcome of the Constitutional Convention was bleak and, as it transpired, remarkably prescient:

> If anything can be foreseen clearly … it is the scenario which will follow the proposed convention election. The strategy of the UUUC could not be clearer. They will talk to no one before the elections for the simple reason that such talks would clarify their real objectives. After the elections, with the hope for a comfortable majority … [the UUUC] will simply announce that they are the majority and that majority rule will be restored.

However, Hume was also worried about London's likely response to such an outcome: 'What will the British Government do then? Will they confront and defeat this further challenge to their authority? Or will they instead announce their withdrawal, pointing out that they have done all in their power including giving the people of Northern Ireland the opportunity to sort matters out for themselves?'[10]

The concern which Hume expressed here was far from rhetorical. Indeed, following the collapse of the Sunningdale Agreement, many commentators believed that the Northern Ireland problem had exhausted the patience of both the London government and the British public. As a result, some saw the Constitutional Convention as merely a political device, a means to buy time for Whitehall as it prepared the ground for a withdrawal.[11]

As his comments suggested, Hume was particularly anxious of this prospect. Whatever his previous ideas for a planned and piecemeal reunification of Ireland, he feared the consequences of an immediate evacuation of British troops from Northern Ireland. However, others in his party were less concerned, even asking Dublin to prepare contingency plans for such a scenario, and to discuss these with London. The Irish government swiftly rejected this suggestion, precisely because it feared to encourage thoughts of a withdrawal within Whitehall.[12]

In retrospect, the prospect of a British withdrawal from Northern Ireland seems hard to believe. However, at the time, there was evidence to support the idea that this was London's intention. Most notable was the unusual armistice that emerged between republicans and British security forces in the run-up to the Constitutional Convention. This resulted from the unexpected announcement of an IRA ceasefire in December 1974, leading in turn to clandestine contacts between republicans and officials from the NIO.[13] Even more surprising was the fact that these contacts, and a general cessation of hostilities between the IRA and British army, continued through to early 1976.[14] This raised considerable concern, particularly in Dublin, that the NIO was actually negotiating the terms of a withdrawal with the republican movement.[15] Such fears were further stoked when Rev William Arklow – a Protestant clergyman involved in the negotiation of the initial IRA ceasefire – publicly endorsed the idea that the Provisionals had received a commitment on British withdrawal in the event of the failure of the Constitutional Convention.[16] Whatever the truth of this assertion, it gave further reason to believe that the Wilson government was considering the possibility of pulling out of Northern Ireland. This, undoubtedly, impacted on the thinking of Hume and his colleagues.[17]

Abstention once again?

Given the ominous backdrop to the initiative, there were thoughts within the SDLP of boycotting the Convention elections.[18] In public, Hume remained non-committal, simply emphasising the need for London to clarify its commitment to the principles of power-sharing and an Irish dimension as outlined in the Convention White Paper. '[B]efore the elections take place', he suggested, 'Britain must say what it will do in the event of the loyalists at the Convention rejecting these terms.'[19] However, without such clarification, Hume was one of the voices within the SDLP who was arguing that the party should abstain from the Convention. On this occasion, he was in a minority, with most senior members of the opinion that this would portray the SDLP as the intransigent party. There was also a fear that a boycott of the Convention would play into republican hands, and a concern that the Provisionals might actually seize the opportunity to put forward their own political representatives for election.[20]

Eventually, Hume was persuaded that it was best for the SDLP to contest the Convention elections, and his change of heart was clearly demonstrated by an article he wrote for the *Sunday Press* in the spring of 1975. This piece suggested that, whatever his doubts about the new initiative, Hume was determined to make it work: 'Most people in the North, in spite of the pessimism that surrounds the Convention and in spite of well-founded reservations that most people have about it, hope that it is an opportunity that will be taken to give the North a new beginning.' However, in order to avail of this opportunity, Hume argued that each party at the Convention would have to seriously question its existing political outlook: 'If we are to succeed, then no shibboleth, no conditional attitude, or no handed-down political dogma must be left unexamined or unchallenged, for we know that they have failed us in the past, and they will fail us again.'[21]

From this, Hume moved to a theme that would become increasingly prevalent to his public discourse hereinafter. This was the theme of 'the two traditions' in Ireland:[22] 'If one word can sum up our problem it is division. Division not by a line in the map, but by two powerful traditions that inhabit this island. ... The only possible approach to a solution is to reject conflict and pursue the path of partnership between our two traditions.'[23] Such partnership, Hume felt, would best be achieved by essentially the same formula that had produced Sunningdale: 'Partnership between our two traditions – both within the North through power-sharing, and between North and South through the Irish dimension – accepting and respecting our differences will in time build trust and confidence to replace distrust and prejudice.' However, whilst continuing to advocate power-sharing and an Irish dimension, Hume was at pains to stress that an agreement based on these terms should not be seen as a means towards traditional nationalist ends: 'Out of it will emerge a new society both in the North and in Ireland which may well bear little relationship to the dreams that have always been wrapped up in our respective flags. The constitutional form that it takes will be irrelevant for it will have been built and freely agreed between both our traditions.'[24]

The SDLP's manifesto for the Convention election, *Speak with Strength*, took a similar line, again proposing power-sharing and an Irish dimension as the cornerstones of any new settlement, but without prescribing the particular structures that would give them political expression. This, McAllister feels, was as an indication of the SDLP's flexibility and willingness to negotiate around these terms.[25] Also, echoing Hume's arguments in his *Sunday*

Press article, there was a studied emphasis on the duality of the Northern Ireland situation: 'There is an Irish Dimension to the problem. There is a British Dimension to the problem. Any solution must take account of both.'[26] In this, the SDLP returned to the logic of its first political proposals, the *Towards a New Ireland* paper of 1972, suggesting the need for structures which would accommodate the identities of both communities in Northern Ireland. However, unlike its predecessor, *Speak with Strength* did not advocate such structures as part of an interim arrangement that would eventually give way to a unified Ireland. In this, it seemed the SDLP had learned from Sunningdale. The Protestant mobilisation against the Agreement – if seen as a reaction to the perceived threat of Irish reunification – may have led Hume and his colleagues to the realisation that unionists' British identity was not something that they were about to abandon any time soon. Accordingly, in *Speak with Strength*, the 'British dimension' was given equal billing alongside the Irish.[27]

The conciliatory overtures of *Speak with Strength*, and the generally more considered discourse of the SDLP in the run-up to the Convention election, seemed to have little impact on unionist opinion. The UUUC, standing on a platform of outright opposition to both power-sharing and any form of Irish dimension, won an overall majority of votes cast, and 47 of the 78 seats available in the new forum.[28] The UUUC took this as a mandate to obstruct any constitutional change, and instead to push for a return to a majoritarian Stormont – much as Hume had predicted at the outset of the initiative.

Despite this, Hume looked to reassure SDLP supporters that there would be no compromising of the party's own electoral mandate: 'We ... are going to the Convention with the clear understanding that any solution must take account of two basic principles – power-sharing and an Irish dimension.'[29] Any suggestion that the latter would be abandoned in order to facilitate the former was also dismissed. Hume argued that the political identities of both communities would have to be given equal recognition if there was to be a durable settlement: 'Any solution which does not take account of the Irish dimension is doomed to failure. SDLP policies clearly commit the Party to a solution that takes account of both basic loyalties in the community and both must be taken into account if any solution is to be found.'[30] But still, neither he nor his colleagues gave any indication of the particular structures that might give institutional expression to these principles. The SDLP remained studiously vague, seeming to confirm McAllister's opinion that party was trying to demonstrate an open-mindedness – a willingness to consider any agreement that allowed some form of power-sharing and an Irish dimension. This suggested a conscious departure from the dogmatic approach which preceded Sunningdale, where the SDLP had vigorously pursued the exact political institutions that it thought most appropriate.

Unity in diversity

This should not be taken to suggest that the SDLP were unengaged from the Constitutional Convention. But Hume's mind in particular was working on a different level in this period. This was most apparent in a speech which he gave to the Convention in its early stages. Drawing on the article he wrote for the *Sunday Press* three months earlier, it appeared that this address had been some time in gestation, and followed much deep thought on Hume's part. Clearly, its primary objective was to rouse the various parties to the Convention, encouraging them to seize the opportunity presented to establish a genuine and just peace in Northern Ireland.

Hume began his speech with a theme which held great resonance, particularly given the manner in which Sunningdale was undermined by its portrayal as simply a staging post on the road to a united Ireland. This was the theme of misrepresentation:

> One of the great weaknesses and causes of failure in this community has been that the ideals which different sections of it have held have been misrepresented by other sections. I am prepared to accept that my colleagues and I may and do misrepresent the ideals and attitudes of those who sit opposite. I am certain that they misrepresent ours, not perhaps through any malice but through sheer misunderstanding.[31]

Evidently, Hume wanted to bring an end to this misrepresentation and misunderstanding by making it clear what the intentions of his party were, hoping that unionists would respond in kind, and that through this exchange a climate of trust might develop in which a new political settlement would be easier to construct and maintain.

Revisiting his 'two traditions' discourse, Hume argued that it was not difference *per se* which created conflict in Northern Ireland, but rather the way that difference was dealt with:

> It often seems ... that the division which exists here is at the root of our problem. Perhaps it is not so much in the division as in our approach to its solution that we make mistakes. ... The question we must ask ourselves is, 'Should we seek to end that diversity or end the division by conquest or by domination?' In effect, that is what both traditions in Ireland have tried to do for centuries. ... The questions we should be asking ourselves are, 'Are we right to think that our tradition, whatever it is, is the only one? Are we right in thinking that a solution can only be based on the recognition of one tradition?'

For Hume, it was this cultural supremacism that led to conflict: 'I believe that both traditions are guilty of this basic exclusivist approach which feels that one tradition can exist only by getting rid of the other or by dominating the other.'

Drawing examples from other countries throughout the world, Hume maintained that the diversity of a society need not be a debilitating factor:

If countries like India with its teeming millions and diverse traditions, or Canada with its differing national traditions, or the United States with so many races, were to adopt the attitude of mind which both sections in this island, in their traditional approach, have adopted, where would they be? Instead they sought to find a Constitution to which all gave their loyalty and in which all traditions were respected and allowed to flourish – not one mould but a diversity; unity in diversity. We have to try to do the same but … in order to do so we need to rethink our position.

In this, Hume was calling, quite explicitly, for political re-appraisal by unionist and nationalist alike: 'not only have both traditions on this island got to rethink their position but we have got to re-examine the fundamentals of our traditions, including the basic political commandments that have been handed down to us.'

Hume also drew on history to point out the problems with the way both traditions had sought to maintain themselves in the past:

The Loyalist tradition in Ireland … has always rightly sought – I emphasise rightly – to protect its basic traditions and rights … Sadly, we believe that in protecting them they have taken a course which has been wrong. … Your tradition has lived under many different constitutions on this island but it has always had one thing in common, that you sought to protect yourselves by retaining power and protecting ascendancy. Today you can do likewise. You can retain control. You can retain power. … But … you will fail. It has failed before and it will fail again because it is an approach which seeks to exclude other traditions and in the end will lead only to the grave, to death, destruction and conflict.

For Hume, the best way for the loyalist tradition to maintain itself was simply to have confidence in itself and in the demographic realities of unionism. This, he argued, provided a better guarantee than any British government ever had: 'The real security your tradition has rests in your own strength and numbers and in nothing else.' To Hume, then, the best way forward for the unionist community was to find agreement with those with which it shared the island of Ireland, and to work with them to overcome their mutual distrust and prejudice: 'In the end the real protection the majority tradition in this part of the island has rests in its own numbers, not in defensiveness or siege mentality but in positively coming out, working in co-operation and partnership with the other tradition and building an entirely new society.'

At the same time, Hume argued the need for his own tradition to change. Irish nationalists also had to consider the same destructive tendency and the same exclusivism which history had witnessed in their approach:

We have been handed down a set of political dogma that has served us badly. … We have been given an exclusivist notion of Ireland which excludes and wants to exclude the million people in the northern part of Ireland who have every right to be there. The exclusivism, that undefined Irishness to which if you do not ascribe you do not belong, is the same thing again – ascendancy of one tradition over another. ... [B]ut we know for certain that if we do we shall fail because it, too, leads only to conflict and to the grave.

It was on the basis of these arguments that Hume again asserted that the Sunningdale formula provided the best way to progress. Through power-sharing and an Irish dimension – and therein a partnership of equality between the two traditions in Ireland – Hume felt the past approach of domination and conflict, fuelled by ignorance and mistrust of the other, could be overcome: 'We must form a partnership between both sections if we are to go anywhere, if we are to develop trust and confidence to replace the distrust, the fear and the prejudice that have poisoned our past.' However, once more, Hume was keen to stress that co-operation between the North and South of Ireland was not simply the means towards traditional nationalist ends: 'We do not see the process of partnership leading to some ulterior ultimate objective.'

This particular comment led to a predictable call from the unionist benches of the Convention: 'Have you given up that objective?' However, Hume was unwilling – and, if he hoped to maintain political support, unable – to explicitly renounce the aspiration to a united Ireland. Nonetheless, he responded with the conciliatory tone common to all of his and his party's statements since the collapse of Sunningdale, suggesting that Irish unity was, for the SDLP, essentially about agreement and recon-ciliation between the different peoples of Ireland:

> What we see is a partnership between both of the traditions here and between both parts of this island leading to a new situation. It is not a form of territorial unity because territorial unity is meaningless. ... [T]he ultimate objective as we see it – we are talking about a completely new definition of unity in this island – is unity in diversity, in the acceptance and the marrying of differences for our common good so that at the end of the day we have an agreed society, North and South, and agreed institutions in the North supported not only by the entire population of the North but by the entire population of the South.

In Hume's mind, this – the southern state's acceptance of new structures of governance – was also necessary if there was to be a stable and lasting settlement: 'For the first time in our history we would have the entire pop-ulation of this island respecting the institutions that exist, North and South.' But for this to happen, Hume felt, the rethink which he was pro-posing would have to extend to the Republic of Ireland: 'The Government, the political parties and the people there have to ask themselves where their political dogma and political commandments have led them or led us in the North.'

However, despite his emphasis on the Irish dimension, Hume did not ignore the unionist perspective: 'There is [also] a British dimension ...

because the majority has said it wishes to retain such a dimension.' With this, Hume initiated an idea which he would continue to develop in the coming years, that of a comprehensive Anglo-Irish approach to the Northern Ireland problem, which would maximise political consensus for a new settlement:

> we cannot ignore the fact that this problem not only affects us [in Northern Ireland] ... but that there is a British Dimension and an Irish Dimension. It affects both these islands ... Therefore, we must also look at what our relationships are going to be with the rest of these islands. ... We should try to get a situation in which our institutions are supported not only by ourselves but by the people of Britain and the people of Ireland as a whole. The only thing then missing would be the full loyalty of the people of the North.

This last element, Hume felt, would eventually be achieved through a process of practical co-operation between the two communities in Northern Ireland, leading in time to their reconciliation: 'That can only be found by working together in partnership in the administration of our affairs. ... Constitutions, systems of government, do not give us the security we need. ... These are only opportunities, frameworks. The real thing to give us security is the people here having faith in one another, living on the same piece of earth and having the trust to work together.'

Some unionist politicians welcomed Hume's speech,[32] perhaps seeing in it a genuine attempt to move beyond the well-worn debate over partition, and even a reluctance by Hume to discuss Irish unity in any sense that would imply actual political union between the two parts of Ireland. Others, however, seized on this suggestion, even interrupting Hume's address to suggest that he explicitly forsake the idea of a united Ireland.[33] Indeed, even when he had finished his speech, Hume was immediately faced with a question from the unionist benches: 'Does what he has just said mean that he repudiates his words of three years ago? He said then, "A united Ireland or nothing."'[34] Hume showed great patience as, not for the first time, he tried to put this infamous comment back into its proper context. However, in doing so, he refused to meet unionist demands by renouncing the aspiration to Irish unity: 'My remark was not as the Member has quoted it, but I make no apology. ... I simply remind the Member of the circumstances in which my statement was made. Thirteen people had been killed in my constituency ... In answer to questions I said that the feeling of the people in the area was such that they would accept nothing but a particular solution.' But also notable was the way that Hume chose to end the exchange. For here he emphasised that, whatever his comments in the past, he was currently concerned more with the problem in *Northern* Ireland: 'Today we are discussing the future of *this part of Ireland*.'[35] Hoping that unionists would also focus on this discussion – instead of persistently returning to the issue of partition – Hume finished by saying: 'It is an important debate. We could all rake over the ashes of the past.'

It may be misleading to read too much into these closing comments. But considering Hume's speech in its entirety, it is fair to suggest that he was trying to draw a line under the approach adopted by his party since the fall of Stormont, when the creation of new structures of governance for Northern Ireland was inextricably and explicitly linked to a process of Irish reunification. Of course, Hume would not – and, as suggested, if he wished to retain support in his community, could not – renounce the aspiration to Irish unity. However, it did appear that he was attempting to move beyond the strategy pursued up until Sunningdale, where he had demanded that the end-goal of any new settlement must be a united Ireland. Indeed, it seemed that Hume was trying to exorcise the 'interimism' of his approach to Sunningdale, hoping that this would encourage unionists to enter into arrangements which, though not predetermined towards reunification, would facilitate the rebuilding of relations between what he termed the two traditions in Ireland. In this, it appeared that Hume had reverted to the revisionist nationalism of his early political career, where the aspiration to Irish unity was never abandoned, but the more immediate goal was reform and reconciliation in Northern Ireland.

The unionist veto

If Hume was trying to scale back the significance of the Irish dimension, and if he was seeking to blunt the unificationist intent of his previous approach, hoping that this would encourage a more compromising attitude among unionists, he was to be sorely disappointed. The Constitutional Convention clearly showed that the UUUC was unwilling to countenance power-sharing with nationalists even within a purely internal political arrangement. This became plainly obvious when one of the UUUC leaders, William Craig, precipitated his own political demise after proposing such an accommodation.

Craig appeared to accept as genuine the more conciliatory approach which the SDLP had adopted since Sunningdale, declaring that the party 'has satisfied me at least and, I think, the great majority of the people that it is prepared to accept the decision that Ulster remains inside the United Kingdom for as long as the majority of our people want that.'[36] On this understanding, Craig had suggested that an 'emergency coalition' be formed with the SDLP until the security situation in Northern Ireland had been brought under some measure of control. Of course, this proposal would have been extremely difficult for the SDLP to accept, as it did not offer even rhetorical recognition of the Irish dimension, nor an institutionalised form of power-sharing, with no guarantee of nationalist participation in government after the 'emergency' had ended.[37] However, before any serious discussion of the idea could take place, Ian Paisley came out against it. This, in turn, led the rest of the UUUC's Convention representatives to abandon Craig. In the end, he was the only UUUC member to vote in favour of the coalition proposal, and in doing so this former doyen of the unionist right effectively ended his political career.[38]

By November, the UUUC had used its majority within the Convention to pass its own report containing proposals for a settlement of the Northern Ireland problem, presenting this document as if it were an agreed submission from the forum as a whole.[39] The report rejected power-sharing and any Irish dimension, advocating the restoration of Stormont with an essentially majoritarian model of government. The document also explicitly refuted the two traditions thesis advanced by Hume and his party. Indeed, it appeared to deny even the idea that Northern Ireland was a divided society.[40]

However, despite the now obvious futility of his initiative, Rees recalled the Convention for a second sitting, hoping that the parties could find some form of agreement which would allow the SDLP to participate in government.[41] But the second phase of the Convention, beginning in February 1976, and ending the following month, proved equally fruitless. As had been the case during its first sitting, the violence and disorder taking place outside the Convention continued to cast a shadow over proceedings. Indeed, on the day that the first direct talks between the SDLP and the UUUC were due to take place, news broke of the death of Frank Stagg, an IRA prisoner who had been on hunger strike in an English jail. Catholic districts across Northern Ireland erupted, and rumours circulated suggesting that SDLP members living in affected areas would be physically prevented from leaving their homes:

> The SDLP once again saw Catholic support slipping away from them towards the republican movement. Not only was the atmosphere therefore unconducive to compromise, but there must have been at least a shadow of doubt in the minds of the SDLP leaders as to whether a calmly worked out political solution with the loyalists, even if it were feasible, would not put them farther out of touch with grass-roots Catholic opinion.[42]

But the SDLP had little need to worry in this respect: a calmly worked out political solution with the UUUC was not feasible. Indeed, it was impossible, and after a frank exchange between Hume and Harry West, where the UUUC leader admitted that there were no circumstances in which he and his colleagues would serve in a cabinet alongside the SDLP, the party walked out of the talks.[43] Finally, Rees was forced to dissolve the Constitutional Convention.

During the closing stages of the initiative, Hume had made clear his frustration and disillusionment. His comments at this time provided a stark contrast to those made near the start of the Convention, when he had spoke in encouraging terms of the opportunity to move on from past approaches and establish a new partnership between the two traditions in Ireland. All such optimism had now evaporated, and Hume had little that was positive to say about his political counterparts:

the UUUC after the election last year ought simply to have posted their manifesto to the British Government ... and saved us the expensive charade which this Convention has been. They ought to have done that because ... [t]hey have worked from the beginning purely and simply for the implementation of their electoral manifesto and have ignored everyone else.

Hume also lamented the fact that, despite his earlier plea for open-mindedness from all parties to the Convention, the UUUC continued – willfully it seemed – to misinterpret the SDLP's position: 'We are not asking Members opposite to join us in a united Ireland. We are asking them to form the sort of partnership which any country or community, faced with the problems which we face, would form.'[44] Again this strongly implied that, in contrast to his SDLP's approach up until Sunningdale, power-sharing in Northern Ireland rather than unification with the South was now the party's chief priority.

Despite the collapse of the Convention, Hume's closing comments appeared to impact on some unionist representatives. Indeed, for during the forum's final days, senior figures in the UUUC made unofficial contacts with the SDLP.[45] This, in turn, led to private talks between Hume and Devlin for the SDLP, and the Rev Martin Smyth and Capt Austin Ardill of the UUUC. As outlined in a statement released at the end these discussions, Hume and Devlin used the dialogue to assess unionist objections to the Sunningdale formula 'and to make constructive proposals designed to answer those objections and to give necessary assurances.' This resulted in considerable concessions from the SDLP. Indeed, though still formally committed to the principles of power-sharing and an Irish dimension, Hume and Devlin gave far less emphasis to the latter. In addition, and perhaps more importantly, they proposed that a democratic check be built in to any new settlement: 'These arrangements should be subject to a Constitutional review at the end of the life of the second parliament. This would enable a thorough review to take place with the working of a new system and meet the objection that power-sharing is unworkable or that some ulterior motive lies behind it.'[46] Clearly, the aim of the proposal was to deflect unionist arguments that the SDLP's strategy was still predetermined towards a united Ireland. But Murray argues that the downgrading of the Irish dimension in these talks was also significant: 'There was some recognition by the SDLP that power-sharing had to work over a period of time before an Irish dimension could evolve.'[47]

Optimistic about the progress made in the discussions, Smyth and Ardill had returned to the UUUC seeking approval for their continuation. However, as Devlin recalled: 'Yet again Paisley delivered the knock-out upper-cut, leaking the details of the talks and pile-driving the rest of the [UUUC] coalition into bringing them to an inconclusive end. That proved to be the last formal political initiative I was involved in.'[48] It also proved to be the last serious engagement between the SDLP and Ulster unionism of any shade for the remainder of the decade.

Murray suggests that the breakdown of the talks with Smyth and Ardill convinced the SDLP that unionists were simply not prepared to compromise in the current political climate. As a result, the dispirited party decided that what it saw as a 'unionist veto', exercised continuously since May 1974, had to be broken if progress was to be made. This, the SDLP believed, could only be achieved if the British government was prepared to alter its policy in a way that would oblige unionists to enter into serious negotiations. Until this change was effected, Hume and his colleagues felt there was no point in further talks with unionist representatives. Accordingly, the SDLP now called upon the British government to assume proper responsibility for Northern Ireland, to take decisive political action to bring about a just settlement, and to show that it was prepared to face down the unionist veto over the implementation of such a settlement.[49]

In this, Hume and his party were returning to a more patently nationalist position. Having previously suggested a willingness to compromise on the Irish dimension – with all discussions since Sunningdale focusing mainly on the prospect of power-sharing – elements within the SDLP would soon begin to push for Dublin's reintroduction to the political process. In line with this, Hume also began to revert to the position first articulated in *Towards a New Ireland*, and particularly to the claim in this document that the Northern Ireland problem could not be resolved exclusively within existing state boundaries. At the same time, Hume would return to another of his earlier themes: Britain's constitutional guarantee to the majority in Northern Ireland. For it was this, he felt, that was the real source of unionist obstinacy. Indeed, in Hume's mind, the British guarantee and the unionist veto had become inextricably linked. Whilst Westminster continued to offer an unqualified commitment to uphold unionists' essential political preference – that is the Union with Britain – he believed that they would never feel any need to compromise with the minority community. Once again, Hume's thinking was moving towards a more familiarly nationalist mode, as his focus turned away from the unionist community, and began to fix instead on the role of Britain.

Notes

1 Devlin, *Straight Left*, p. 252.
2 PRONI D/3072/4/1/1, SDLP press release, 'SDLP offers agreed Ireland', 18 June 1974.
3 *Irish Times*, 19 June 1974.
4 *Ibid.*, 14 June 1974.
5 *Ibid.*; McAllister, *The Social Democratic and Labour Party*, p. 150. See also Arthur, *Special Relationships*, pp. 181–2, on Dublin's apparent abandonment of the SDLP in the aftermath of Sunningdale.
6 *Irish Times*, 17 June 1974.
7 PRONI D/3072/4/1/1, SDLP press release, 'SDLP offers agreed Ireland' (emphasis in original).

8   HMSO, *The Northern Ireland Constitution* (London: HMSO, 1974), Cmnd 5675, para. 45, clauses (a) and (c).
9   Devlin, *Straight Left*, p. 253; S. Farren and R. F. Mulvihill, *Paths to a Settlement in Northern Ireland* (Gerrards Cross: Colin Smyth, 2000), p. 80; McAllister, *The Social Democratic and Labour Party*, p. 147.
10 *Irish Independent*, 9 July 1974.
11 Bew and Gillespie, *Northern Ireland: A Chronology*, pp. 95, 97, 104; Bew and Patterson, *The British State*, p. 78.
12 FitzGerald, *All in a Life*, pp. 252, 255.
13 It seems that republicans were amongst those who believed that the failure of Sunningdale had exhausted London's patience with Northern Ireland. Accordingly, they were prepared to suspend their military campaign and enter into talks with the NIO, believing that they were negotiating a process of British withdrawal. Although the British side later claimed that the purpose of the talks was simply to divide the republican leadership, there is some evidence to suggest that the Wilson government did, at this time, give genuine thought to the idea of disengaging from Northern Ireland. If so, it seems that London soon realised that such a move would unleash a far worse conflict which would destabilise the whole of Ireland. Accordingly, it was decided that staying in Northern Ireland, if only to contain the problem, was the least dangerous option available; P. Bew, *Ireland: The Politics of Enmity, 1789–2006* (Oxford: Oxford University Press, 2007), pp. 516–23; Bew and Gillespie, *Northern Ireland: A Chronology*, pp. 97, 99–101.
14 However, there were continued infringements and breakages of the ceasefire; see Bew and Gillespie, *Northern Ireland: A Chronology*, pp. 98–111.
15 FitzGerald, *All in a Life*, pp. 258–61.
16 Bew and Patterson, *The British State*, p. 82; FitzGerald, *All in a Life*, pp. 259, 261; McAllister, *The Social Democratic and Labour Party*, p. 149.
17 FitzGerald, *All in a Life*, p. 255.
18 Bew and Patterson, *The British State*, p. 82.
19 *Belfast Telegraph*, 9 December 1974.
20 Murray, *John Hume and the SDLP*, p. 33.
21 *Sunday Press*, 16 March 1975.
22 This concept – or the same idea expressed in different terms – began to appear in Irish nationalist commentaries some time before the outbreak of the Northern Ireland conflict. Indeed, John Whyte highlights the 1950s in particular as a period in which mainly southern writers such as Michael Sheehy and Donal Barrington began to consider the problem of partition in terms of 'two distinct peoples in Ireland'. In this interpretation, partition was not imposed upon Ireland by the British government, but rather an inevitable response by London to the seemingly irreconcilable differences of these two 'peoples': Irish nationalists and Ulster unionists. As can be seen below, Hume built upon these arguments in developing his own particular 'two traditions' discourse; Whyte, *Interpreting Northern Ireland*, pp. 119–20; see also, P. J. McLoughlin, '"Humespeak": the SDLP, political discourse, and the Northern Ireland peace process', *Peace and Conflict Studies*, 15:1 (2008), pp. 101–6.
23 *Sunday Press*, 16 March 1975.
24 *Ibid.*
25 McAllister, *The Social Democratic and Labour Party*, pp. 58, 152.

26 SDLP, *Speak with Strength* (Belfast: SDLP, 1975), p. 3.
27 *Ibid.*, p. 6.
28 Bew and Gillespie, *Northern Ireland: A Chronology*, pp. 102–3.
29 *Belfast Telegraph*, 7 May 1975.
30 *Irish News*, 22 May 1975.
31 This and all subsequent quotations from Hume in this section are taken from the same speech. This can be found in the Northern Ireland Constitutional Convention Debates, pp. 283–7, 19 June 1975.
32 *Irish Independent*, 20 June 1975; Merlyn Rees, *Northern Ireland: A Personal Perspective* (London: Methuen, 1985), p. 200.
33 Northern Ireland Constitutional Convention Debates, pp. 285, 286, 19 June 1975.
34 *Ibid.*, p. 287, 19 June 1975.
35 Author's emphasis. The use of this phrase did seem deliberate, for Hume had used it previously in his speech; Northern Ireland Constitutional Convention Debates, p. 286, 19 June 1975.
36 Northern Ireland Constitutional Convention Debates, pp. 337–8, 1 October 1975.
37 Currie, *All Hell Will Break Loose*, pp. 295–6, 299; McAllister, *The Social Democratic and Labour Party*, p. 155.
38 Dixon, *Northern Ireland*, pp. 163–4; McAllister, *The Social Democratic and Labour Party*, pp. 154–5; O'Leary and McGarry, *The Politics of Antagonism*, pp. 201–2.
39 McAllister, *The Social Democratic and Labour Party*, p. 156.
40 HMSO, *Northern Ireland Constitutional Convention Report: Together with the Proceedings of the Convention and other Appendices* (London: HMSO, 1975), paras 4, 8.
41 Bew and Gillespie, *Northern Ireland: A Chronology*, pp. 107–8, 110.
42 McAllister, *The Social Democratic and Labour Party*, p. 158.
43 *Ibid.*, pp. 158, 189 (n. 38).
44 Northern Ireland Constitutional Convention Debates, pp. 970–1, 977, 2 March 1976.
45 *Irish Times*, 10 June 1976.
46 PRONI, D/3072/4/3/1, SDLP press release, 'Joint Statement by Mr. John Hume and Mr. Paddy Devlin', 8 September 1976.
47 Murray, *John Hume and the SDLP*, p. 38.
48 Devlin, *Straight Left*, p. 264.
49 Murray, *John Hume and the SDLP*, pp. 38–40, 41–2.

5

An agreed Ireland

Between the collapse of the Constitutional Convention in March 1976 and the election of Margaret Thatcher in May 1979, the British government failed to produce any serious political initiative on Northern Ireland. Lacking in ideas, the serving Labour administration appeared happy to simply contain the ongoing conflict. However, it was not British troops that led this more military approach to the problem. Through a policy of 'Ulsterisation', British soldiers began to be replaced by indigenous forces, namely the RUC and Ulster Defence Regiment, in the front line of the battle against the IRA. As Paul Arthur explains, this policy offered London considerable advantages in its propaganda war with republicans: 'the use of locally recruited security forces allowed the problem to be presented to international observers as an internal one between conflicting Irish groups, and hence downplayed the role of Britain and the army as part of the equation. ... But it was a policy that entailed high risks because, essentially, it was concerned with managing, rather than resolving, the conflict.'[1]

London's shift from a strategy of conflict resolution to one of conflict management was to have serious repercussions for the SDLP. Indeed, the political inertia of the late 1970s saw the party become increasingly impotent in the eyes of the Catholic community. In this context, there was a growing concern that support for the SDLP might begin to be transferred to the Provisional movement.[2] As Hume commented in early 1977: 'The terrible danger is that if constitutional political parties such as the SDLP are seen to be having no success people will turn away in another direction, and the only direction being offered is the gun.'[3]

Hume and his colleagues also had reason to doubt Dublin's commitment to Northern Ireland in this period. Like its British counterpart, the Irish government appeared to have little idea as to the way forward after unionists' vehement rejection of the Sunningdale Agreement. Indeed, Dublin's approach from the mid-1970s seemed to confirm the thinking of an Irish policy document that was leaked to the press shortly after Sunningdale's demise. This paper had proposed that the government take a 'low profile', and avoid any reference to the Irish dimension that might 'reduce the chances of power-sharing, and increase Loyalist strength'.[4] Accordingly, the leak suggested that Dublin was now purposely distancing itself from

Northern Ireland, this to assuage the fears that Sunningdale had stoked in unionist hearts, and so create a more compromising attitude amongst the majority community. However, Irish government policy did little to encourage unionist conciliation, and only fed nationalist alienation.

This, in turn, affected the SDLP. Indeed, the political disengagement of the two governments, and the growing disaffection amongst the minority, seemed to fuel dissension within the party's rank and file. In particular, the SDLP's green wing – led by the increasingly influential figure of Séamus Mallon – was in a state of considerable agitation in the late 1970s.[5] This was most evident in the growing call from party members for a British declaration of intent to withdraw from Northern Ireland. Whilst many advocating this line did so from a traditionalist standpoint, other less nationalist elements in the party, for example Paddy Devlin, also considered the idea in terms of the negotiated independence of Northern Ireland.[6] Indeed, the red and green wings of the SDLP now appeared united in their frustration with the British government and its apparent failure to create the conditions for a just settlement in Northern Ireland. It was this which led figures like Devlin to consider such drastic vistas as independence.[7]

As a result, at the SDLP's sixth annual conference in December 1976, over 100 delegates, and ten of the seventeen former Convention representatives, backed a motion calling for a British declaration of intent to withdraw from Northern Ireland.[8] Arguing against the motion, Hume continued to hold a revisionist line, suggesting that it was not the British presence that was the main problem, but rather the division that existed between the two communities: 'Whether the British are in or out, the problem is how we solve that ... If we can provide a general agreement between our own people, the British presence will be irrelevant.'[9] To this end, Hume asserted that power-sharing and an Irish dimension – the 'partnership strategy' as it had become known in SDLP parlance – was still the way to proceed: 'Let not frustration be the basis of Party policy ... The present policy is best, and people are turning away from it because they are disheartened at its lack of success to date. ... [I]t's not that partnership has been tried and failed. It has never been tried.'[10]

However, other party members who addressed the conference were vehemently critical of Hume's position. Paddy Duffy was one such person: 'I used to accept John Hume and the dogma that fell from his lips. In later days I have come to realise that John Hume can be wrong. There are other thinkers who are capable of appreciating when Hume ... and others are wrong.'[11] Such open criticism of Hume's standing in the SDLP was unprecedented, and was interpreted by the press as a genuine challenge to his hitherto dominant position in terms of the formulation of party policy.[12]

Facing reality?

The disaffection within the party rank and file had a definite impact on the SDLP's political direction in this period. This was clearly evident in *Facing Reality*, a policy document which originated from a paper prepared by Hume for a meeting of the SDLP executive in August 1977.[13] *Facing Reality* represented a culmination of the frustration that had been building in the SDLP over the previous three years. Indeed, the paper began by stating that the time which had elapsed since the fall of Sunningdale had been one of outright political stalemate. This it attributed to the intransigence of unionism, and the inaction of the British government. The latter party, the document suggested, was either unwilling or unable to produce a settlement in the region. 'In the light of these developments,' the paper claimed, 'the SDLP have carried out a major review of the situation'.[14]

This review amounted to an upgrading of the Irish dimension, and a reassertion of the party's opposition to any internal settlement of the Northern Ireland problem. 'Attempts to solve the problem in a purely British context', it asserted, 'have failed and will continue to fail.'[15] Although this had clear echoes of the party's first published policy document, *Towards a New Ireland*, *Facing Reality* suggested more than a simple retreat to the SDLP's unificationist approach of the early 1970s. Indeed, the paper represented a strategic re-appraisal of party policy, inspired by the continued obduracy of unionist politicians, and their refusal to countenance even an internal power-sharing arrangement with nationalists. This led the SDLP to argue for the re-introduction of the Irish government into the political process, suggesting that London and Dublin should work together to advance a political settlement in Northern Ireland even in the absence of unionist support. To this end, although *Facing Reality* called for quadripartite talks, it also stressed that, irrespective of their outcome, the two governments should press on with the process.[16] By intimating that the two governments should act over the heads of intransigent unionists, *Facing Reality* thus set the SDLP on the path towards a major re-thinking of its political programme. In the coming months, the party would increasingly withdraw its interest, or rather its belief, in the feasibility of negotiating a local settlement for Northern Ireland. Instead, the SDLP began to promote an inter-governmental, Anglo-Irish approach to the problem, seeing this as the only way towards political progress in the existing climate.

A third way?

In an interview with the *Irish Times* in early 1978, Hume sought to justify the policy shift signalled by the *Facing Reality* document. As had been suggested in the paper itself, Hume stressed that it was unionist intransigence, encouraged by the unimaginative stance of the British government, which had forced the change on the SDLP: 'Unionist politicians have completely refused to budge and we believe the major reason for this is that Britain has refused to state its long-term intentions.' Following from this, Hume argued that the British government now had three options open to it. The first was to maintain its present position, providing what the SDLP saw as an unconditional commitment to the unionist community, the guarantee of Northern Ireland's position within the Union: 'The first thing that can be said about that is that, as a basis of policy, it had produced neither peace nor stability nor justice in Northern Ireland. So it's not unreasonable for us to ask that it be re-examined. While that commitment remains, unionists have no reason to look at any other alternative, so a re-examination of that is the first thing we suggest.'[17]

Hume proposed that the second option available to the British government was that traditionally advanced by nationalists: withdrawal from Northern Ireland. But in discussing this option, Hume appeared to confirm the idea that *Facing Reality* had been adopted specifically to head off the support for such a drastic prescription as had grown amidst the frustrated ranks of the SDLP.[18] For here it is clear that, rather than speaking to the London government, Hume was appealing to the disaffected members of his own party, and to the nationalist community at large:

> Does everybody think [that in the event of a British withdrawal] the unionist population will be prepared, like lambs, to sit around the table? ... [T]here is a serious risk that a significant number of them would not do so but would react violently. That being the case, the action and reaction that we all know about would take place and we would be left, at best, with a re-partitioned Ireland ... With such a serious risk of violence, no serious political party could take that approach.[19]

Now clearly addressing those more radical elements of his own party, Hume continued in his rejection of any policy dedicated solely towards the withdrawal of the British state from Northern Ireland: 'The second weakness in that approach, for a political party, is that a party which commits itself to a declaration of intent by the British as a first step to progress completely handcuffs itself if that declaration is not made. If it's not made then ... you're saying no progress can be made.'

At this point, Hume came to the third course of action which he saw as being open to the British government. This, for Hume, represented a third way between the first and second options – those preferred by uncompromising unionists and traditional nationalists respectively: 'The third option open to the British government is to declare that its objective in Ireland is the bringing together of both Irish traditions in reconciliation and agreement.' In this, Hume was reviving an idea which was first articulated in the aftermath of Sunningdale's collapse,[20] and subsequently developed in *Facing Reality*. This was the notion of an 'agreed Ireland'.

In *Facing Reality*, it had been argued that:

While remaining in Northern Ireland ... [the British government] should promote reconciliation and an end to divisions among all Irish people, leading to
the establishment of structures of government which allow both traditions in
Ireland to flourish freely and to live together in unity and agreement. ... The
end result of such a policy, pursued rigorously and positively over a number
of years would undoubtedly be an agreed Ireland; the essential unity of whose
people would have evolved over the years.[21]

In his interview with the *Irish Times*, Hume was also looking to convince
Westminster that this pursuit of an agreed Ireland was the best way forward: 'We believe that this should be the basis of British policy now,
instead of the maintenance of the Union. They should commit all their
resources, all their powers of persuasion towards that end in the same way
as they have committed all their resources in the past to maintaining the
Union.'[22]

Paul Bew and Henry Patterson, whilst recognising that Hume's enunciation of an agreed Ireland was a way to mitigate the pull from the SDLP's
green wing, are scathing of the whole notion. To them, Hume's agreed
Ireland was simply a united Ireland dressed up in a more liberal discourse:

Hume ... was one of those [in the SDLP] acutely aware the dangers of being
manoeuvred into a position from which all one could do was to demand
withdrawal. He was completely incapable however of doing more than produce superficially new and attractive versions of what were in fact traditional
nationalist notions. This is the significance of his ponderous adumbration of
a 'third way' between the status quo and a demand for a declaration of intent
– the notion of an 'Agreed Ireland'.[23]

It is fair to say that, in the late 1970s, as in the early part of the decade,
Hume's and his party's ambition towards Irish unity was articulated, less as
an aspirational, and more as immediate political objective. But this ambition was encouraged by the sense that, since the collapse of Sunningdale,
the British government had decided to extricate itself from or at the very
least quarantine the Northern Ireland problem. The minimisation of its military commitment achieved through Ulsterisation, and the abandonment of
any serious political strategy in the region, had led significant elements
within the SDLP to push for a formal declaration that disengagement was
in fact the real purpose of British policy.[24] In addition, the growth in support for this option reflected disaffection among the party's political constituency. Increasingly policed by the Protestant community as a result of
Ulsterisation, and still lacking any say in the governance of Northern
Ireland, by the late 1970s the minority had found that its position under
the direct rule of Westminster was little different from that endured under
the old Stormont regime. Indeed, in many respects, it was worse, as significant sections of the Catholic population lived with the constant surveil-
lance, day-to-day inconvenience, and at times brutality of the state security
apparatus.[25] The cumulative effects of this were reflected in survey data

from the period, which suggested that as many as two out of every three
nationalists now supported the view that the British government should set
a specific date by it which it would withdraw from Northern Ireland.[26]
Considering such feeling amongst the Catholic community, it becomes
easier to understand how even moderates in the SDLP such as Eddie
McGrady began to consider that the departure of the British state might be
the only way to improve the situation. As McGrady later explained: 'There
was total frustration in our community, and it was quite obvious that the
British were not going to ... or were not capable of, helping us; so therefore
they became a hindrance.'[27]

It was this sense of desperation amongst the minority which had given
rise to the independence lobby within the SDLP. But it was against this
lobby that more far-sighted members of the party, figures like Hume,
struggled to communicate a less drastic political strategy. Rather than
pushing for a British withdrawal – an option which Hume always
regarded as likely to result in an escalation of the conflict – he and other
SDLP leaders sought to articulate an approach which would allow for the
ultimate disengagement of the British state, but ensure that stable and
accepted political structures were put into place first. It is in this context
that Hume's enunciation of an agreed Ireland, achieved by a concerted
strategy of inter-governmental co-operation, should be considered. For the
agreed Ireland policy was a means to stave off the challenge from the more
hard-line nationalism then asserting itself within the SDLP and the broader
Catholic community. It was also a means to re-engage the two governments with the Northern Ireland problem, and so end the minority's isolation. With the benefit of hindsight, it can be argued that Hume's strategy
was successful in both respects.

Bew and Patterson claim evidence of the continued greening of the SDLP
in its 1978 conference, where a motion endorsing British disengagement
was passed with only two dissenters.[28] However, this should not be seen a
triumph for the independence lobby, but rather a subtle victory for the
more moderate line being advanced by Hume and aided, most notably, by
Austin Currie. Indeed, it was Currie's Coalisland branch of the SDLP that
proposed this motion, which was clearly contrived to endorse British withdrawal only 'as part of an overall political solution which would provide
guarantees for both traditions in the North'. The motion also called for 'a
quadripartite conference of the two sovereign Governments in London and
Dublin and representatives of the two traditions in the North with a view
to finding a permanent solution to the Irish problem.'[29] In this, rather than
advocating an unconditional British withdrawal from Northern Ireland,
Currie's motion rallied the party conference behind Hume's idea of an
agreed Ireland achieved through the engagement and sponsorship of the
two governments. Currie was keen to stress this, arguing that what he proposed was not a 'mere "Brits out" motion' such as that advanced by more
hard-line elements of the SDLP: 'Committed as we are to an agreed Ireland

based on partnership between its different traditions we have a positive view of British disengagement. We oppose and abhor simplistic "Brits out" type slogans which masquerade as a policy.' Currie also made clear that it was the British government's indifference to the Northern Ireland problem which had forced the SDLP's change in approach. With Westminster's failure to produce any constructive policy of its own, he claimed, the party believed that the best the British government could do now was to help establish the conditions for an agreed Ireland in which it would act as guarantor for the unionist community.[30]

Given the growth in support for the SDLP's independence lobby from the mid-1970s,[31] the overwhelming support for the 1978 motion on disengagement should actually be seen as a remarkable success for party moderates. Indeed, this motion served to steer the disaffected ranks of the SDLP behind a more constructive Anglo-Irish approach to the problem, and to restore party unity after a period of serious division. Nonetheless, this did involve a compromise between the competing wings of the SDLP. The greens had gained some ground, forcing the party leadership to move away from the policy pursued since the fall of Sunningdale, which had focused essentially on the prospect of power-sharing in Northern Ireland, with the Irish dimension receiving only rhetorical recognition. Now, the SDLP was returning to a stronger line on the Irish dimension, and indeed was reverting to its pre-Sunningdale position in emphasising the eventual departure of the British state from Ireland.

In this respect, the Bew and Patterson critique of Hume's agreed Ireland has some credibility. Indeed, from a unionist perspective, there appeared to be little difference between an agreed and a united Ireland – both, it seemed, involved the eventual dissolution of the Union with Britain.[32] Moreover, the way in which Hume spoke of an agreed Ireland in the late 1970s – with the onus he placed on the British government in facilitating this end – did seem at odds with his original thinking. Indeed, in his earliest commentaries on the problem, Hume had sought to remove Britain from the equation, and focus on relations between the two communities in Northern Ireland.[33] But now he and his party were moving away from the idea of dialogue with unionists, and instead looking to London – in conjunction with Dublin – to provide at least the initial impetus towards a solution.

In the SDLP's defence, it could be reasoned that such a change had been forced upon the party. For it is fair to say that, since Sunningdale, the unionist leadership had blocked all political movement in Northern Ireland. From the SDLP's perspective, this intransigence was bolstered by the British government's unconditional commitment to the maintenance of the Union.[34] With such a guarantee, the SDLP argued, unionists would never feel any obligation to enter into meaningful negotiations with the nationalist community. It was this which led Hume and his colleagues to effectively abandon efforts to reach a compromise with unionism, and instead concentrate on changing the position of the British government. Similarly, it was clear that unionists' opposition to even internal power-sharing with the minority – an opposition made evident time and again since 1974 – had caused the SDLP to revert to its previous conviction that the Northern Ireland problem could not be resolved within the confines of existing state boundaries. For a brief period after Sunningdale, the party had suggested a willingness to scale back the significance of the Irish dimension of any settlement. However, such an approach – compounded by Dublin's effective abandonment of the SDLP at this time – had clearly demonstrated the political impotence of the party.

This was something which Hume and his colleagues could not ignore, particularly as electoral polls began to show a decline in support for the SDLP,[35] and after a rival political group, the Irish Independence Party (IIP), was launched in October 1977. Although the new party was short-lived, it did secure votes among more nationalist sections of the Catholic elec-torate, and even led to defections from the SDLP's North Antrim branch.[36] For the first time since its formation, the SDLP realised that it could face an electoral challenge for the leadership of the minority, and thus could not take its support base for granted. All things considered, therefore, the political situation in the late 1970s – as the situation in the early part of the decade – made some hardening of the SDLP's position inevitable.

The evolution of the Anglo-Irish strategy: a new approach towards a new Ireland

Going into 1979, the SDLP continued to develop an Anglo-Irish strategy which would, if necessary, see the British and Irish governments imposing new political structures over the heads of the Northern Ireland parties. Indeed, as suggested by Murray's extensive analysis of internal party dis-cussion papers, the SDLP had – for the time being at least – abandoned altogether the idea of creating new local institutions. The party believed that the polarisation of society in this period, and the influence of extremists on both sides of the political divide, made agreement within Northern Ireland impossible. As such, the SDLP saw a 'top-down' inter-governmental approach as the only way forward at this time.[37]

The integrality of this strategy to the SDLP's thinking was made evident in an important speech which Hume gave in Waterville, Co. Kerry, in September 1979. Here, Hume used the stage – a conference on American–European relations – to challenge both the British and Irish governments, demanding that they accept their responsibilities in Northern Ireland, and launch a joint initiative to break the political deadlock. 'London', he asserted,

> exercises a frayed and somewhat reluctant sovereignty in Northern Ireland
> while Dublin maintains a frayed and somewhat reluctant claimed sovereignty.

Events ... cry out for joint decisive action and underline the Republic's essential role in helping to solve the Northern Ireland problem. There will be no progress until that need is publicly acknowledged in both capitals.[38]

Once again, Hume emphasised that both governments had their own specific roles to play:

The British government should acknowledge that the basis of their policy is unworkable ... The basis of that policy is, in fact, an unconditional guarantee of support to one section of the community, the unionists, at the expense of the other. This has ensured both the alienation of the minority and the unwillingness, indeed inability, of unionist political leaders to have any meaningful dialogue with anyone about the problem.[39]

Meanwhile, with the Dublin government, Hume stressed the need to reappraise and clearly articulate its understanding of Irish unity: 'Are the government parties and people of the Republic prepared to accept the sacrifices involved in real unity? Do they accept that the goal is a pluralist Ireland, one that is dominated by no section or tradition? ... [I]t is long past the time when the meaning of unity should be spelt out. Agreement yes, coercion no.'[40]

But as well as their individual obligations, Hume emphasised the overriding need for the two governments to act in concert:

The time has come for a positive and decisive initiative. It must be taken by both governments acting together. They should firstly make it clear that there are no longer any unconditional guarantees for any section of the Northern community. There is only a commitment to achieve a situation in which there are guarantees for all. Secondly they should make it clear that there is in fact no solution but only a process that leads to a solution. They should declare themselves committed to such a process, a process of integration of the differing traditions on the island, a process designed to lead to an agreed Ireland with positive roles for all.[41]

Hume's Waterville speech was, in fact, a showcase for the document that enshrined the SDLP's Anglo-Irish strategy as official party policy. Indeed, Hume's address employed much of the arguments and even the phraseology that was found in this paper. After extensive drafting, this seminal document was eventually presented to, and overwhelmingly endorsed by, the SDLP's annual conference in November 1979.[42]

Towards a New Ireland, re-employing the title of the party's first published position paper, was arguably as important as the 1972 document in the evolution of the SDLP's political programme. It began by making clear the SDLP's continued commitment to its partnership strategy: 'This approach necessarily means partnership between the differing traditions in the North and partnership between both parts of Ireland.' In this, it reaffirmed that power-sharing and an Irish dimension remained the SDLP's ultimate objectives. However, the party argued that, despite its persistent efforts to negotiate a settlement around these terms – and notwithstanding its flexibility as to how they might find institutional expression – unionist intransigence and British indifference had made the realisation of the partnership strategy impossible.[43]

For this reason, the SDLP believed that it had been forced to reconsider its position. It now felt that the search for agreement between the local parties had become pointless, and so had turned to an inter-governmental approach to the problem, the validity of which it was keen to emphasise:

> [T]he problems of Northern Ireland can only be solved by joint Anglo-Irish action ... between both governments. ... Indeed what we ask them to recognise is that the Northern Ireland problem is their common problem ... which can not be tackled successfully except through a joint, agreed approach. But if the Irish government has – as has been recognised even by the unionist parties – a central role to play in creating peace in the North, they must surely have a joint political role to play with the British government in creating the institutions of lasting peace.[44]

With this, the party came back to the issue of the British guarantee, which it now saw as the primary impediment to political progress in Northern Ireland. The SDLP wanted this guarantee to be revised in some way which would, without threatening the essential interests of unionists, oblige them to compromise with Irish nationalism. In short, the SDLP wanted an assurance from the two governments that the interests of both communities in Northern Ireland would be safeguarded in any proposed settlement:

> As a first step they should make it clear that there are no longer any unconditional guarantees for any section of the Northern community, but rather a commitment to achieve a situation in which there are guarantees for all. The British government must acknowledge that the basis of its policy is ... an unconditional guarantee to support one section of the community – the unionists – at the expense of the other. This has ensured both the alienation of the minority and the unwillingness – indeed inability – of the unionist parties to enter into any meaningful dialogue about the problem. Such a guarantee is an open invitation to intransigence ... It must be re-examined.[45]

At the same time – and again clearly echoing Hume's Waterville speech – *Towards a New Ireland* underlined the need for the Dublin government to revise its understanding of Irish unity, to re-articulate it in a way that was not threatening to unionists' interests, and to stress that it could only come about with their assent. This, like the re-formulation of the British guarantee, was also held to be of utmost importance in the effort to overcome unionist obstinacy:

> The Irish government ... must acknowledge that its claim to unity, while it remains undefined ... is interpreted by many unionists as a real threat. They

must clearly demonstrate that they are prepared to accept the sacrifices involved in real unity, including the social changes which will demonstrate that Irish life is not dominated by any one section or tradition. Unity must come, and be seen to come, by agreement.[46]

In summary, *Towards a New Ireland* argued that the two governments should work together to re-structure the Northern Ireland problem in such a way that would, in turn, encourage compromise at a local level. By going over unionists' heads, the SDLP recognised that such an approach might evoke greater resistance in the short term. However, the party hoped that, if those interested in political progress in Northern Ireland pressed on with their efforts, this would eventually persuade refractory unionists to join them in shaping future constitutional arrangements.

> short-sighted intransigence must not be allowed to postpone the political, eco-nomic and social stability which the people of Ireland, North and South, so desperately want and deserve. No longer can the veto of one small section of the Irish people be allowed to condemn the vast majority on the island, who wish to live in peace and agreement, to further decades of suffering and strife. The process must start and the dialogue continue without them while leaving the door open for their eventual participation.[47]

While *Towards a New Ireland* made clear the SDLP's belief in an Anglo-Irish approach to political progress, it was less prescriptive than its 1972 namesake in deciding what should be the final outcome. Rather than endorsing any one solution, the paper suggested that whatever new struc-tures emerged from a comprehensive political process – open to all parties, but led by the two governments – would prove acceptable to the SDLP. Evidently, more important than the particular solution arrived at was the framework in which it was conceived. For Hume and his colleagues, that had to be an Anglo-Irish framework.

Reviewing the SDLP's political evolution in the late 1970s, it can be said that, although it was a severely testing time for the party, it was also a pro-ductive period in terms of policy formulation. Indeed, the immense pressures on the party at this time forced the SDLP to seriously reconsider its approach. However, the change that took place did not represent a policy overhaul. The Irish dimension had long been integral the party's philosophy, but from the late 1970s – in the face of unionist obduracy and British indif-ference – this aspect of the SDLP's thinking was given greater emphasis. In this, it can be argued that the change in policy in this period represented a shift in the SDLP's strategy rather than its end-goal. The party had not aban-doned its belief in the need for co-operation between the two communities in Northern Ireland, and between the North and South of Ireland. Rather, it had re-evaluated the means by which this end might be attained. As Murray suggests: 'The SDLP were not negating the principle of partnership govern-ment, but rather reappraising its method of achieving this policy.'[48]

Hume was central to this shift. Though he was not the main author of *Towards a New Ireland*, Hume had contributed to the paper.[49] Moreover, it was he who had set the party on the road towards its Anglo-Irish strategy with the document he presented to the SDLP executive two years previously – the paper which formed the basis of *Facing Reality*. This renewed the party's commitment to the Irish dimension, and was the first SDLP document to intimate the need to work on an inter-governmental level – even if this meant advancing without unionist support in the short term. In addition, Hume's importance in the redirection of the SDLP was evident in the leading role he played in promoting the party's Anglo-Irish strategy among a wider audience.[50] But as well as his role in the conception and propagation of the Anglo-Irish strategy, Hume would also guide the SDLP towards its realisation.

Hume takes the helm

As suggested, the SDLP's movement towards an Anglo-Irish approach, though essentially the product of a strategic re-appraisal, was also meant to mollify the party's rebellious green wing. However, whilst this may have maintained the essential unity of the SDLP, it also led to the defection of two of its most senior founding members, Paddy Devlin and Gerry Fitt. Devlin left in 1977, after launching a public tirade against the policy document that prefigured *Facing Reality*. In a lengthy statement released to the press, Devlin had detailed his objections to the shift in party policy which this paper signalled. Primarily, he rejected the demand for Dublin's re-introduction to the political process, and the related implication that new structures of governance for Northern Ireland should be imposed even in the absence of unionist support. Devlin believed that this negated the SDLP's commitment to the principle of consent: 'The present policies [adopted] do not suggest a better way of securing the consent of the majority for political change, or a better method to work for the best interests of the people in the present situation.'[51]

Devlin's statement also noted the drift away from the socialist ideals which he especially had infused in the SDLP at its inception, and the party's failure to reach across the sectarian divide – another founding and yet unfulfilled ideal. However, in addition, Devlin's critique made veiled references to Hume's increasing influence over the SDLP.[52] In later years, Devlin would emphasise that it was the party's shift to the right – in terms of both its socio-economic outlook and its constitutional proposals – that precipitated his departure.[53] But his comments at the time made clear that Hume's growing dominance within the SDLP was also a crucial factor.

Fitt resigned from the SDLP two years later. The trigger for his departure was the reaction of his colleagues to the fresh political initiative launched by Humphrey Atkins, the new Conservative government's Northern Ireland Secretary, in November 1979. Aitkins proposed a conference of interested parties to discuss the possibility of achieving devolution, but the exact terms of the forum were left suitably vague in the White Paper outlining the initiative: 'Its task will be to establish the highest level of agreement ... which will best meet the immediate needs of Northern Ireland.'[54] Though it paid lip-service to the aim of creating institutions that would 'safeguard the interests of the minority',[55] the paper made no specific commitment to executive-level power-sharing. This, of itself, was enough to cause anxiety amongst the SDLP. But even if power-sharing had been guaranteed, the party would still have been wary to commit to the Aitkins initiative. For the shift in SDLP policy that had taken place over the previous two years had led to the shelving of its plans for power-sharing, with priority now being given to the establishment of the Irish dimension. Indeed, many in the SDLP, including Hume, felt that this might be the only way to compel unionists to accept a genuine role for nationalists in the governance of Northern Ireland. As such, the complete neglect of the Irish dimension in Aitkins's proposals ensured that they would be immediately rejected by the SDLP. The only surprise was that this response also precipitated the departure of the party leader.

Fitt had been willing to talk with unionists, even without reference to the Irish dimension, in the hope that some form of power-sharing might be agreed. The majority of his colleagues, however, were not as pliant, nor as optimistic that unionists were ready to compromise. Moreover, the Atkins initiative was formally launched only a fortnight after the SDLP's annual conference had overwhelmingly endorsed the Anglo-Irish strategy recommended in *Towards a New Ireland*. Accordingly, it would be most difficult for the party leadership to now accept a wholly internal approach towards a solution, especially when the reasoning behind the policy change – and indeed the protracted internal debate which preceded it – had concluded that such a course was ultimately unviable.

In response to his colleagues' negative reaction to the Atkins initiative, Fitt announced his resignation from the SDLP, leaving the way open for Hume's election as party leader. His first job in the post was to defend the SDLP's decision to reject the Atkins talks. Hume blamed the extreme limitations of the initiative for the party's reaction, stating that what was on offer was 'a pale reform of the old Stormont system'. The complete exclusion of the Irish dimension in the terms of reference for Aitkins's conference had made his party's participation impossible, Hume argued.[56]

Like Devlin before him, Fitt declared the continued greening of the SDLP, and the consequent dilution of its socialism, as the reason for his leaving the party: 'I have never been a Nationalist to the total exclusion of my Socialist beliefs. The SDLP is nationalist.'[57] Again, though, Hume's intellectual influence over the party appeared to contribute to Fitt's decision. Indeed, in truth, Hume had always been the motivating force behind the SDLP, and the party's chief policy-maker. As Austin Currie recalled: 'For quite a while that Hume was deputy leader, he was effectively leader of the party in thinking and strategic terms, because that wasn't Gerry's forte.'[58] Fitt was more of a figurehead, with his prominence at Westminster being a crucial factor in winning him the leadership at the time of the SDLP's formation.[59] However, it was a role he never embraced,[60] leaving Hume to act as *de facto* leader long before he took formal charge of the party.

Hume and the leadership of the SDLP: retreat from revisionism?

At the time of his departure, Devlin had criticised the SDLP's neglect of its leftist ideals, but also Hume's direction of the party towards an inter-governmental, Anglo-Irish approach to the Northern Ireland problem. In Devlin's view, this – and the related assumption that new modes of gover-nance might have to be introduced even in the absence of unionist support – undermined the principle of consent. This charge deserves consideration, for the change in SDLP policy did involve a re-appraisal of the party's most fundamental axiom. However, given the political situation which the SDLP faced in the late 1970s, many in the party felt that such a shift was unavoidable.

Since the collapse of the Sunningdale Agreement, the leadership of the unionist community had shown itself incapable of offering any form of compromise to the SDLP. Indeed, at the Constitutional Convention of 1975–76, unionist politicians had made it clear that they would not share power with nationalists even in a purely internal settlement. Unionists were unwilling to move, and the British government, it seemed, had no intention of moving them. Indeed, from the SDLP's perspective, the British position at this time served to buttress the wall of unionist obstinacy. Westminster still promised that there would be no change in the constitu-tional status of Northern Ireland without the agreement of a majority of its citizens. However, unionists had taken this to mean that there should be no change at all in Northern Ireland without their assent. To Hume and his colleagues, the British guarantee provided the majority with the sense that it could oppose any alteration in the governance of the region. Corre-spondingly, the principle of consent – the acceptance that Irish unification could not take place without unionists' agreement – had become a veto on *all* political progress.

The persistent exercise of this veto had seriously affected the SDLP. Unable to secure any political change in the late 1970s, the party had become largely impotent in nationalist eyes. It was this, more than any other factor, which led to the greening of the SDLP, and caused the party to move away from an absolutist interpretation of the principle of consent. Thus, while Hume and his colleagues still accepted that there could be no change to Northern Ireland's place in the Union without the consent of a majority, they were no longer prepared to allow this interdict to be an obstacle to any change at all in the region. Unionists' assent was essential for the creation of a united Ireland, but it was not seen as a precondition to the reframing of the Northern Ireland problem.

Nonetheless, it was clear that any new structures created by the British and Irish governments would, ultimately, need to win unionists' endorsement. However, the SDLP hoped that, by beginning a process towards this end, those more pragmatic elements within unionism would eventually see the sense in playing their part in the shaping of such developments. In the meantime, unionists would have to be shaken from their steadfastness by decisive action from the two governments. It had to be made clear that the current *status quo*, or indeed the *status quo ante* 1972, was inadmissible. Denis Haughey, SDLP chairman for much of the 1970s – and one of Hume's confidants – thus explained that the party had not abandoned its overall objectives:

> in the late '70s the SDLP took the view that: 'We haven't given up on power-sharing but for the moment it doesn't look as if there's anybody prepared to share power with us, and therefore what we have to do is create a new overall structure ... ' [We were] trying to change the external circumstances that bore down on Northern Ireland so as to effect the pressure for change in thinking within Northern Ireland. We had the feeling ... that if a firm partnership was established between the two governments, based on certain principles, that unionists would become convinced there is no route-map which would lead us back to the past, we have got to accept that circumstances have changed, and that that would lead to a change in thinking within the unionist community, and lead to the emergence of a sufficient element to make power-sharing possible.[61]

However, the SDLP also believed that a new Anglo-Irish framework to the problem would better accommodate the interests and identities of both communities in Northern Ireland. This approach fitted with the 'two traditions' model which Hume had been developing since the fall on Sunningdale, and which would become increasingly common to the thinking of the SDLP under his leadership. With this model, the conflict in Northern Ireland was seen to result from a clash between two religio-national identities, both equally legitimate, and both in need of equal recognition and accommodation if the problem was to be resolved. At present, the identity of Ulster unionists was fully recognised and accommodated through the Union with Britain. However, the same could not be said for the minority's Irish nationalist identity. But by bringing the Dublin government into the process – by giving realisation to the Irish dimension – Hume believed that the identity of the nationalist community in Northern Ireland would be successfully accommodated. It was on these grounds that he appealed to the British government to work with its Irish counterpart, and in this to affirm the Irish dimension and the validity of the minority community's sense of itself. In Hume's mind, it was the failure to do so which led to nationalist disaffection from the Northern Ireland state: 'The problem here cannot be solved on the basis of one identity alone and either wittingly or unwittingly, British politicians run the risk of promoting violence in the North by not accommodating the two different identities in it.'[62] For Hume, any new structures of governance for Northern Ireland had to give equal recognition to the identities of both communities, and this made the logic of an Anglo-Irish, intergovernmental approach self-evident.

Hume's two-traditions discourse also augmented his early depiction of the problem as one of a divided people rather than a divided territory. This thesis, prefigured by intellectuals and activists in the 1950s,[63] had moved nationalist thinking away from its traditional fixation on partition and the role of Britain. Instead, the problem was seen as being essentially indigenous to Ireland: it was a consequence of the fundamental divisions that existed between the people of Ireland. In this interpretation, partition was a symptom rather than a cause of the conflict.

Hume's earliest writings on Northern Ireland appeared to endorse this thesis. However, with London re-engagement with the region from 1969, and particularly after the Conservatives came to power the following year, Hume began to reconsider Britain's role in the problem. As the Heath administration moved away from a strategy of reforming to one of simply maintaining the Stormont system, Hume started to question the origins of this system in the 1920–21 settlement. In doing so, he did not conclude that the British government was the primary cause of the contemporary conflict. However, Hume did evoke a more familiarly nationalist narrative in citing Westminster's part in creating and maintaining the Northern Ireland state, and thus manufacturing and sustaining a unionist majority which used its dominant position to subordinate the minority and resist political change.[64] In order to overcome this imbalance, Hume decided that only a fundamental reworking of the 1920–21 settlement – one which would bring Dublin into the political equation, and allow the minority to pursue its national ambitions – would create the basis for equality in Northern Ireland, and therein a context in which reconciliation between the two communities could take place.

Hume believed that such a situation had been achieved in Sunningdale. However, the Wilson government's failure to uphold this settlement – in Hume's eyes, Westminster's capitulation to the unionist veto over political change[65] – made Britain part of the problem once again. This perception was reinforced by the British approach after Sunningdale, which seemed to accept unionists' unwillingness to compromise, concede that no new settlement could be created, and simply adopt an strategy of conflict containment. With this, though Hume still believed that division in Ireland was essentially aboriginal, he decided that British policy was now an obstacle to its resolution. Thus, he did not, like those more traditional elements of his own party, see the British presence as *the* cause of conflict in Northern Ireland, but did conclude that the Westminster government was still central to the problem. Accordingly, in Hume's mind, it had to be central to its solution, too.[66] In this, Hume became convinced that the British government still had a primary role to play in facilitating the process of accommodation between the two communities in Northern Ireland. But it could not do this, he felt, while it upheld the will of one at the expense of the other.

This brought Hume back to *the* central theme in the SDLP's discourse at the close of the 1970s: the British guarantee. Whilst London continued to provide an unconditional guarantee of Northern Ireland's place in the UK, he believed that unionists would never have feel obliged to offer any compromise to the minority. Under Hume, therefore, the SDLP's primary objective was to change the nature of the British guarantee in a way that would encourage unionists to rethink their position. As Hume explained shortly after becoming party leader:

> As long as unionists have that guarantee, genuine dialogue will not take place because unionists are going into the unknown. Genuine dialogue has never taken place between the two sections of the community here. It will only take place when that guarantee has gone. The goodwill which would generate from such dialogue would produce the type of Ireland we would all want to see – an Ireland with no one dominating.[67]

The Irish Question: a British problem?

Even before taking charge of the SDLP, Hume had produced a considered case against the British guarantee and what was, in his mind, a direct product of that guarantee: the unionist veto. In 'The Irish Question: a British problem', an article which was published in the highly prestigious *Foreign Affairs* journal in late 1979, Hume bluntly argued that 'the two greatest problems in Northern Ireland are the British guarantee ... and the unionist dependence on it'.[68] This essay set the co-ordinates of the SDLP's course under Hume, articulating a political approach which the party would pursue doggedly through the early 1980s.

Hume's article represented an appeal to various parties. First and foremost, it was an appeal to the British government. Hume was calling on London to recognise Northern Ireland as 'a British problem'. As argued above, this did not represent a retreat to orthodox nationalism, which saw the British presence alone as the cause of conflict in Northern Ireland. Indeed, Hume continued to reject such a view: 'This analysis of things ... affords a simple view of a highly complex situation'. Nonetheless, Hume's position in this article did mark the outer limits of his revisionism: Britain was not the sole cause of the problem in Northern Ireland, but it was still 'a central protagonist, and must therefore be centrally involved in the solution'.[69] In essence, Hume was looking to re-engage the British government with the Northern Ireland problem after a lengthy period of effective political indifference.

As a prerequisite to political progress, Hume again emphasised the need for Westminster to revise its constitutional guarantee to Northern Ireland:

> the reiterated guarantee [maintains] that Northern Ireland shall remain part of the United Kingdom so long as a majority of the electorate of Northern Ireland so desire. ... [This] has provided the basis for a half a century of injustice, discrimination and repressive law, a situation in which the minority community ... have been persistent losers and victims. ... 'The British guarantee', as it is called, proved to be a guarantee of permanent exclusive power to one side, the Unionists, and a guarantee of permanent exclusion from power to the other, the Catholic minority.[70]

In this, Hume implied that the British guarantee was a source of sectarianism in Northern Ireland, encouraging unionists to maintain their numbers and their solidarity – and thereby maintain the Union – through exclusivist, hegemonic and discriminatory practices.[71] Moreover, whilst London continued to uphold the guarantee, Hume argued that there was 'no incentive for unionists to enter into genuine dialogue with those with whom they share the island of Ireland.'[72] Rather, their stance would remain wholly defensive, resistant of any negotiation with nationalists on the subject of how they might live together: 'the politics of the besieged'.[73]

Following from this, Hume addressed unionists themselves. In doing so, he argued the unreliability of the British guarantee, suggesting that Ulster Protestants' best assurance lay in their own strength as a community. Continuing this line of argument, Hume called upon unionists to shake free of their dependence on the British government, and instead 'to believe in themselves as their own best guarantors in a future shared with the other people of the island of Ireland'. However, Hume was also conscious of the part which nationalists had to play in helping unionists to do this. Thus, he appealed to his own tradition, too: 'Unionists fear that they would be culturally and racially overwhelmed by the Catholic nationalist majority if they were to join the rest of the island. Would they? This is the challenge laid down to Irish nationalism, to Dublin, [and] to the nationalist community in Northern Ireland.'[74]

In this regard, Hume was adamant that nationalists must recognise and seek to address the genuine fears of the unionist community. Most obviously, there was the need to end the IRA's campaign of violence. For this, Hume argued, 'more than any recent development, set back and distorted the cause of Irish nationalism in the eyes of Unionists'. Also, in considering republicans' rationale for violence, Hume again made clear that, whatever the changes in his own thinking regards to the role of Britain, he was still fundamentally at odds with their traditional nationalist conception of the conflict: 'For the Provisionals, the Irish problem is the British presence in Ireland – nothing more; remove that presence, they claim, and the problem will quickly be solved by the establishment of a united, independent Irish state.' Hume continued to contest this interpretation, suggesting that a British withdrawal would not lead to Irish reunification, but rather a civil war which would engulf the whole island.[75] In arguing thus, he reaffirmed his belief that division in Ireland went beyond partition; it had far deeper roots in the feelings of the people of the island.

At the same time, Hume highlighted the fundamental contradiction in the republican movement's armed campaign: 'The Provisional wing of the Irish Republican Army believes Irish unity will be secured by waging war against a British establishment which clearly had no fundamental opposition to Irish unity, while they ignore (and, in their campaign against Britain, further incite) those who most adamantly resist the imposition of unity, the one million Protestant majority.'[76] Pre-empting a line of argument he would take directly to the Provisional movement in the late 1980s, Hume was suggesting that London had no interest in the continued partition of Ireland, and that the primary obstacle to Irish unity was not, therefore, the British state, but rather the Protestant community, who still desired its presence in Northern Ireland. This showed that Hume's thinking remained revisionist in its core assumptions.

As well condemning the republican movement, Hume also considered the failings of constitutional nationalists. In particular, Hume returned to his argument that, if Dublin was serious about Irish unity, it would have to demonstrate to Ulster Protestants that the state which it envisaged could accommodate their tradition, too: 'Unionists have a right to be convinced that the South is serious when it declares its intention to embody pluralist values in the law of the United Ireland to which it aspires. So far, the evidence for these intentions is inadequate.' Also, Hume felt it was necessary to convince unionists that the nationalist aspiration to unity was not simply a territorial ambition, and that their assent was, therefore, essential: 'Statements which contain hints of irredentism, of conquest, of compulsion, do not promote a policy of unity; moreover, they give comfort to the men of violence. The Irish government ... [should] clarify, if necessary *ad nauseam*, its commitment to unity by agreement, only by agreement, and through reconciliation.'[77]

In summary, Hume's article made clear his belief that all parties to the Northern Ireland conflict had much to do to bring about its resolution. Agreement between the two communities was obviously essential, but he also argued the importance of the British and Irish governments in facilitating this end. However, as the title of the piece suggested, it was Britain – as the sovereign power, and indeed the most powerful actor in the conflict – that Hume felt held the main responsibility in terms of advancing agreement. Nonetheless, continuing to emphasise his Anglo-Irish approach, Hume also argued the need for recognition of the Northern Ireland problem as one shared by Britain and Ireland – a problem which could, therefore, only be solved in a wider British–Irish space, and with the commitment of both governments: 'It is time the British and the Irish took each other – and our common crisis – seriously. ... The time has come for a positive and decisive initiative. It must be taken by both Dublin and London acting together.'[78]

In this, Hume believed that the primary aim of the two governments should be to remove what he and his party saw as the main obstacle to agreement: the British guarantee and the resultant unionist veto: 'They should first make it clear that there are no longer any unconditional guarantees for any section of the northern community. There is only a commitment to achieving a situation where there are guarantees for all.' But even then, Hume believed that agreement would not be immediate. Indeed, a settlement would only arise from a process of political negotiation: 'they [London and Dublin] should make it clear that there is in fact no pat solution. They should declare themselves committed to such a process, a process designed to lead to an agreed Ireland with positive roles for all. They should invite all parties to participate in this process, the process of building a new Ireland.'[79]

There is good reason for paying such attention to this article. Indeed, it represented an effective manifesto for the SDLP under Hume. Much that was discussed in the paper – the need to engage London; the need to change the British guarantee and, *ipso facto*, remove the unionist veto; the need to engage Dublin; the need for Irish nationalists to rethink their aims and methods and to clearly outline their intentions to the unionist community; and finally the need for a process of reconciliation rather than a given settlement – all of this informed the SDLP's political approach in the 1980s. Moreover, many of the ideas outlined in the article were actually realised in this decade, through the Anglo-Irish process initiated by the two governments in 1980, the New Ireland Forum convened by the Dublin government in 1983, and, most crucially, the Anglo-Irish Agreement that was brokered in 1985.

Notes

1   Arthur, *Special Relationships*, pp. 164–5.
2   Murray, *John Hume and the SDLP*, pp. 223–4, 230.
3   *Irish News*, 1 February 1977.
4   *Irish Times*, 25 September 1974.
5   On Mallon's rise to prominence in the SDLP, and the greening of the party commonly associated with this, see Currie, *All Hell Will Break Loose*, pp. 303ff.; Murray, *John Hume and the SDLP*, pp. 46, 53–5; and White, *John Hume*, pp. 197ff.
6   Murray, *John Hume and the SDLP*, pp. 46–52.
7   For Devlin's position on an independent Northern Ireland, see his article in the *Irish Times*, 3 December 1976.
8   *Irish Times*, 6 December 1976.
9   *Sunday Press*, 5 December 1976.
10 Quoted in Murray, *John Hume and the SDLP*, pp. 48–9.
11 *Irish Times*, 6 December 1976.

12 *Ibid.*, 11 December 1976.
13 Currie, *All Hell Will Break Loose*, p. 303; Murray, *John Hume and the SDLP*, p. 60.
14 SDLP, *Facing Reality* (Lurgan: Ronan Press, 1978).
15 *Ibid.*
16 *Ibid.*
17 *Irish Times*, 16 February 1978.
18 Austin Currie's memoirs make clear that this was Hume's intention in drafting *Facing Reality*, and the party's intention in endorsing the document; *All Hell Will Break Loose*, pp. 304, 306.
19 *Irish Times*, 16 February 1978.
20 See above, p. 66.
21 SDLP, *Facing Reality*.
22 *Irish Times*, 16 February 1978.
23 Bew and Patterson, *The British State*, p. 99.
24 At the time when the idea of an independent Northern Ireland was being seriously discussed within the SDLP, comments made by Séamus Mallon and Paddy Devlin suggested that, while each supported this option for different reasons, both were influenced by the belief that the British state was, in effect, already withdrawing from the region. In this, it seemed that leading figures of the independence lobby were looking for honesty from the British government as much as anything else. See the *Irish Times*, 6 and 11 December 1976.
25 On the methods of state security in Northern Ireland in 1970s, and the excessive use of special measures against the Catholic community, see K. Boyle, T. Hadden and P. Hillyard, *Ten Years on in Northern Ireland: The Legal Control of Political Violence* (London: Cobden Trust, 1980).
26 E. Moxon-Browne, *Nation, Class and Creed in Northern Ireland* (Bodmin: Robert Hartnoll, 1983), p. 118.
27 Eddie McGrady; interview with author, Downpatrick, 25 August 2004.
28 Bew, Gibbon and Patterson, *Northern Ireland, 1921–2001*, p. 194.
29 SDLP, *SDLP Eighth Annual Conference Agenda and Other Reports* (Lurgan: SDLP, 1978), p. 14. For Currie's own account of the background to this crucial motion, see *All Hell Will Break Loose*, pp. 307–8.
30 *Irish Times*, 6 November 1978. This account of the conference shows that the success of Currie's motion was not easily achieved. Indeed, both moderates and more hard-line party members had been involved in the manipulation of the conference schedule as they sought to ensure that their respective proposals gained adequate attention. As it transpired, the battle of wills was won by the former.
31 After the narrow defeat of the lobby at the 1976 conference, further motions for British withdrawal had been put forward at the 1977 meeting. However, these were withdrawn amidst allegations of arm-twisting from the party leadership; *Irish Press*, 7 November 1977; *Irish Times*, 7 November 1978.
32 Garret FitzGerald, who was very close to Hume in this period, suggests that his development of the agreed Ireland schema was strongly influenced by the belief that the British government was intent on withdrawing from Northern Ireland in the late 1970s; FitzGerald, *All in a Life*, pp. 252, 255. This would help to explain the way that, at this time, Hume articulated the concept of an agreed Ireland in a way which suggested a settlement that would, ultimately,

allow for British disengagement from the island – albeit with London retaining a role as political guarantor of the unionist community. Specifically, Hume seemed to be thinking in terms of a federal Ireland in this period (see his comments in the *Irish Times*, 16 February 1978, and 9 May 1978).

33 *Irish Times*, 18 and 19 May 1964.
34 Murray, *John Hume and the SDLP*, pp. 39–40, 41–2.
35 P. Mitchell, 'The party system and party competition', in P. Mitchell and R. Wilford (eds), *Politics in Northern Ireland* (Oxford: Westview Press, 1999), p. 98.
36 Murray, *John Hume and the SDLP*, pp. 68–70.
37 *Ibid.*, pp. 77–80.
38 *Irish Times*, 24 September 1979.
39 *Ibid.*
40 *Ibid.*
41 *Ibid.*
42 *Ibid.*, 5 November 1979; Murray, *John Hume and the SDLP*, pp. 78–81.
43 SDLP, *Towards a New Ireland: A Policy Review* (Belfast: SDLP, 1979).
44 *Ibid.*
45 *Ibid.*
46 *Ibid.*
47 *Ibid.*
48 Murray, *John Hume and the SDLP*, p. 61.
49 *Ibid.*, p. 81.
50 His interview with the *Irish Times*, in which he sought to defend and to clarify the proposals in *Facing Reality*, came after a party meeting which decided 'to lobby at home and abroad' to win support for the paper; *Irish Times*, 16 February 1978. Hume's Waterville speech, delivered to a conference on American–European relations, was obviously part of this effort.
51 *Irish Times*, 26 August 1977.
52 *Ibid.*
53 Devlin, *Straight Left*, pp. 277–8; Murray, *John Hume and the SDLP*, p. 66.
54 HMSO, *The Government of Northern Ireland: A Working Paper for a Conference* (London: HMSO, 1979), Cmnd 7763, para. 3.
55 *Ibid.*, para. 9.
56 *Irish Times*, 23 November 1979.
57 *Ibid.*
58 Quoted in Murray, *John Hume and the SDLP*, p. 87.
59 Murray, *John Hume and the SDLP*, p. 87.
60 Murphy, *Gerry Fitt*, pp. 79, 158; Ryder, *Fighting Fitt*, pp. 167, 168.
61 Denis Haughey; interview with author, Cookstown, 30 July 2004.
62 *Irish News*, 9 May 1978.
63 See above, p. 79, n. 22.
64 See in particular his comments in the *Irish Times*, 1 June 1971; and J. Hume, 'The way forward for Northern Ireland', *Irish Times*, 6 November 1971.
65 See the *Irish Times*, 15 November 1975.
66 J. Hume, 'The Irish question: a British problem', *Foreign Affairs: An American Quarterly Review*, 58:2 (1979), p. 307.
67 Quoted in Murray, *John Hume and the SDLP*, p. 94.
68 Hume, 'The Irish question: a British problem', p. 306.

69   *Ibid.*, p. 307.
70   *Ibid.*, pp. 302–3.
71   On this, also see Hume's comments in the *Irish Times*, 31 December 1980.
72   Hume, 'The Irish question', p. 303.
73   *Ibid.*, p. 305.
74   *Ibid.*, p. 306.
75   *Ibid.*, pp. 306–7.
76   *Ibid.*, p. 302.
77   *Ibid.*, p. 309.
78   *Ibid.*, pp. 301, 309.
79   *Ibid.*, pp. 309–10.

6

Internationalising the conflict

As well as addressing those directly involved in the Northern Ireland conflict, Hume's 1979 *Foreign Affairs* article was written in order to appeal to
the world beyond Britain and Ireland. This was evident merely in the fact
that the paper appeared in a prestigious international journal, but also,
more explicitly, in the piece's frequent references to the 'friends of Britain
and Ireland'. In case these friends should miss their cue, copies of Hume's
paper were also posted out to a number of senior politicians and opinion-
formers in Europe and the US.[1]

This was just one example of the efforts which Hume was making to
'internationalise' the Northern Ireland conflict in the late 1970s. Joseph
Ruane and Jennifer Todd suggest that this was a conscious strategy on
Hume's part, and a response to the political stalemate which emerged after
the collapse of Sunningdale. It was, they argue, an attempt by Hume to
change the balance of power in the region. He was seeking to build an
international coalition which would support the constitutional nationalist
case, thus counterbalancing the strength of the British–unionist axis, and
so helping to break the latter's veto over political change in Northern
Ireland.[2]

As was made evident in Hume's *Foreign Affairs* article, it was the
European Community (EC) and the US who were the most important
actors in this game plan. Indeed, Hume's paper made numerous references to the practical help and support which each could provide in the
search for peace in Northern Ireland. But he also suggested that the EC
and the US government had already begun to play some positive role in
the region.[3] However, here Hume was being diplomatic. He had already
done much groundwork in terms of bringing both a European and an
American influence to bear on Northern Ireland.

The European dimension

After the collapse of Constitutional Convention in 1976, Hume had found
himself unemployed for the first time in his career. It was with some grat-
itude, therefore, that the following year he took up a position working
as a political advisor to Dick Burke, Ireland's EC Commissioner for

Transport, Trade and Administration.[4] 'That ... was very valuable to me', Hume later recalled: 'I built a lot of major contacts in Europe and I got to know the European scene inside out.'[5] The experience of the Brussels bureaucracy which he gained whilst working for Burke, added to Hume's fluency in French, meant that he was well positioned to begin working the EC machinery towards his own ends after he was elected to the Strasbourg parliament in June 1979.

With the SDLP already a member of the European Confederation of Socialist Parties,[6] Hume was able to sit with the largest, and therefore most powerful, political bloc in the EC parliament. This in itself gave the SDLP considerable influence at Strasbourg, as it could now expect socialist parties from every other member state to support its line on the Northern Ireland problem. However, during his time working as an advisor in Brussels, Hume had also established close personal relations with senior figures from the Confederation. As such, on election to Strasbourg, he was immediately offered a place on the Socialists' front bench, acting as the group's treasurer.[7] Given that the SDLP provided only one parliamentary seat to the Socialists, this suggested the favour which Hume had already won amongst leaders of the European left, favour which he was keen to exploit in his efforts to internationalise the Northern Ireland problem. Thus, within six months of his election to Strasbourg, Hume, with the full backing of the Socialist bloc, was able to put forward a resolution calling for an investigation into the ways that the EC could help the Northern Ireland economy. The subsequent Martin Report (1981) met with some opposition from the German and Danish governments, who were concerned about existing strains on the EC budget. However, further lobbying by Hume – aided partly by the former German Chancellor, Willy Brandt – helped to win officials from both countries over. As a result, Northern Ireland first began to receive special economic assistance from the EC.[8]

This breakthrough was also notable in that Hume was able to secure support for the Martin Report from the two Ulster unionist members of the European parliament, Ian Paisley and John Taylor.[9] This marked out an approach which Hume would continue to pursue throughout his long career as a member of the European Parliament (MEP). He was always eager to work alongside his unionist co-representatives, their united front helping to maximise the funding which Brussels gave to Northern Ireland. This approach, in conjunction with Hume's lobbying skills, and his particular influence amongst Strasbourg's Socialist group, would help to provide many millions more in special aid to assist the Northern Ireland economy. In this, Hume's motive was ultimately political, albeit non-partisan in this instance. He recognised the part which social deprivation played in feeding violence and extremism on both sides of the divide in Northern Ireland, and so sought European aid to help counter this. However, in articulating his case for extra funding, Hume showed that his essential attitude towards Europe was fundamentally different from that of his unionist colleagues. Indeed, unlike Paisley and Taylor, Hume was a passionate supporter of European integration.[10] Thus, in seeking aid from Brussels, he would cite the founding ideals of the EC project, and articulate the aim of increased economic equality between the various regions of Europe as a basis for greater political integration.[11] Hume clearly wanted financial assistance to help Northern Ireland's immediate economic problems, but also to help fulfil the integrationist ideal of political harmony in Europe.

In addition, Hume sought to make Brussels a source of diplomatic pressure on London, and a means to steer the British government towards a more progressive policy on Northern Ireland. Most significant in this respect were the efforts he made to bring the problem to the attention of the EC's Political Affairs Committee. This ended with the Committee commissioning an inquiry into the economic but also the *political* aspects of the Northern Ireland conflict. Paisley and Taylor were outraged, as was the Thatcher government, all arguing that an investigation dealing with the internal political affairs of a member state was beyond the competence of the EC. However, despite efforts by London and the unionist MEPs to stifle the initiative, Brussels pushed ahead with the inquiry. The ensuing Haagerup Report (1984), though cautious in its analysis, notably reflected the SDLP's position by endorsing an Anglo-Irish approach to the resolution of the problem. This, and other aspects of Hume's European lobbying, clearly played a part in nudging the British government towards the Anglo-Irish Agreement which was signed a year later.[12]

The American dimension

Hume viewed the US in similar terms to the EC, as a source of both economic and political support in his efforts to resolve the Northern Ireland problem. Through numerous trips to America in the early 1970s, he had managed to build up a myriad of business contacts. He exploited these to the full during his time as Minister for Commerce in the Sunningdale administration, securing thousands of new jobs for Northern Ireland during the executive's short life.[13] However, equally notable were Hume's efforts among the US business community in the 1980s, when he campaigned *against* the so-called 'MacBride Principles'. These provided a code of conduct for American firms operating in Northern Ireland, apparently designed to increase Catholic representation in the workforce. However, rather than preventing discrimination, Hume felt that the MacBride Principles served to discourage new investment because of the added obligations they placed on potential employers. In this regard, he argued that depriving Protestants of jobs would not alleviate the lot of unemployed Catholics.[14] Clearly, Hume's first and foremost commitment was to the politics of economic well-being for both communities in Northern Ireland.

Hume also demonstrated this commitment in September 1983, when he travelled alongside Paisley during an American investment tour. This decision helped to restore Paisley's US visitor's visa, which had been revoked because of the Democratic Unionist Party (DUP) leader's extreme speeches. Although SDLP colleagues and some of his American supporters were annoyed at the move, Hume was unrepentant.[15] For him, it was more important to show that representatives of the two communities were agreed on the urgent need for economic assistance in Northern Ireland: 'What we set out to do was to demonstrate that in spite of our political differences there would be a welcome from both sections in Northern Ireland to any inward investment.'[16]

Hume also recognised the huge political power that might be exercised through the US. Accordingly, he consciously sought to cultivate Irish-America during the 1970s. He began at the very top, with the most senior surviving member of the Kennedy dynasty. Edward Kennedy had shown an interest in Northern Ireland from the time of the civil rights movement, but, with the onset of the Troubles, he betrayed a largely traditionalist interpretation of the problem, calling for the withdrawal of British troops and the reunification of Ireland. Particularly in the aftermath of Bloody Sunday, Kennedy became openly critical of the London's role in Northern Ireland, depicting the situation as 'Britain's Vietnam' and, unsurprisingly, attracting much media attention in the process.[17]

Hume felt that Kennedy's concern was genuine, but could be re-directed towards more constructive ends.[18] As a result, shortly after the Bloody Sunday killings, Hume travelled to the US to meet the Democratic figure-head and other American leaders.[19] An in-depth briefing on the situation in Northern Ireland ended with an agreement that Hume would keep Kennedy informed of further developments.[20] Following on from this, on a trip to Europe in late 1972, Kennedy invited Hume to meet him in Bonn in order to discuss the British government's forthcoming proposals for a new settlement in Northern Ireland.[21] Over dinner, Hume was able to persuade Kennedy of how he might better use his influence to bring about a just solution in Northern Ireland. Kennedy remembers this meeting as a crucial turning point, which in time gained Hume access to the corridors of power in Washington: 'Ever since that evening I have had enormous respect for John, his courage and his leadership. He has had a profound influence on my thinking and on the attitudes of the Congress and the American Government towards the conflict; he has often been called the 101st Senator from Northern Ireland.'[22]

In 1976, Kennedy helped to gain Hume a temporary fellowship at Harvard University. This position gave Hume access to a whole network of influential Americans, just as his work under Dick Burke helped him to establish connections among the Brussels elite. Most notably, through Kennedy, Hume was able to extend his contacts to other senior Irish-American Democrats, including the Speaker of the House, Thomas P. 'Tip' O'Neill; the Governor of New York, Hugh Carey; and Senator Daniel Moynihan.[23] Along with Kennedy, this coterie became known as 'the Four

Horsemen' – after the University of Notre Dame's famous quarterback line[24] – and the influential tetrad were to prove central to Hume's American strategy.[25]

Hume's objective in the US was two-fold. Firstly, he hoped to combat the base, republican instincts of the Irish diaspora in America. 'They always had a romantic notion of Ireland', Hume suggested, 'and a very simplistic one: "Get the British out and the problem will be solved."'[26] Having converted the Horsemen from such views, Hume sought to use them as his mouthpiece in the US, through which he tried to turn other Irish-Americans away from supporting republicans. In particular, he wanted to stop the crucial flow of US dollars to the IRA. Secondly, Hume sought political backing from the Irish-American elite, conscious of the huge power they might wield in supporting the SDLP and pressing the constitutional nationalist case on the British government.

Hume's impact in America was enormous. As Arthur observes: 'His message was carried by the Horsemen all the way to the White House and his imprint can be seen in every major statement of American foreign policy on Ireland from the late 1970s onwards.' However, Arthur also notes the crucial support provided by the Dublin government and its Washington Embassy.[27] The Irish Department of Foreign Affairs, then working under Garret FitzGerald, was similarly committed to shutting down the Provisionals' financial life-line and engaging Kennedy and his cohorts in efforts to pressurise London.[28] Nonetheless, FitzGerald was generous enough to recognise that it was Hume, first and foremost, who steered Irish-America away from its instinctive empathy with the republican position: 'The turning round of American opinion was a John Hume achievement ... We continued that, but I think that in fairness John Hume really deserves credit for the first turning round of the Americans which is then reinforced; '74 onwards we were playing our part.'[29]

Michael Lillis and Seán Donlon, two senior diplomats dispatched to the US by FitzGerald, were the most notable actors playing the part for the Irish government.[30] They established a close working relationship with Hume,[31] and together this triad proved highly adept in directing the efforts of interested Irish-American politicians such as the Horsemen,[32] and in countering Britain's Washington Embassy in its attempts to keep the Northern Ireland problem from the attention of the White House. Their efforts also helped to stymie support for militant republicanism, with Hume particularly eager to encourage sympathetic Irish-Americans to invest in the Northern Ireland economy rather than to donate to US affiliates of the Provisional movement.[33]

Hume saw the potential of the Four Horsemen speaking to Irish-America with one voice. Accordingly, it was he, with the help of Lillis, who was the organising force behind a joint statement from the Horsemen made on St Patrick's Day 1977.[34] This denounced all organisations who were engaged in violence in Northern Ireland, but also those in America who helped to fund their activities.[35] Following on from this, Kennedy and O'Neill in particular were eager to do more. Thus, at the suggestion of Hume, and again with the help of Lillis, they began working on a much more ambitious project to bring the American Presidency in on the act.[36] Despite London's attempts to frustrate the initiative, on 30 August 1977 Jimmy Carter made a highly significant speech on the Northern Ireland problem. Though concerned British officials had managed to tone down the language of the statement, the work of Hume and Lillis was still evident. As well as condemning the violence, Carter recognised the need for Dublin's involvement in any viable solution, and emphasised the need for 'a form of government in Northern Ireland which will command widespread acceptance throughout both parts of the community' – a diplomatically-phrased endorsement of power-sharing. Carter also made an offer of economic assistance from the US in the event of a political agreement, a suggestion which came directly from Hume.[37] Moreover, the American government remained true to this commitment, with a most generous aid package demonstrating its approval of the 1985 Anglo-Irish Agreement.[38]

It was, however, the political significance of Carter's speech that represented the greatest victory for Hume. As Adrian Guelke has noted, 'the novelty of the declaration was that it treated the situation in Northern Ireland as a legitimate concern of American foreign policy.'[39] In this, the initiative represented a genuine watershed. It overturned British assertions that Northern Ireland was a wholly internal matter, and broke the non-interventionist mould set by the Anglophile American State Department in deference to its main Cold War ally. Carter's speech was, therefore, a crucial development for the SDLP at a time when it found itself to be virtually impotent on the domestic front. The President's words gave the demoralised party a much-needed boost following years of political inertia in Northern Ireland.

But the Carter initiative did not provoke London into the pro-activism which Hume and his American allies had imagined. This led the Four Horsemen to repeat their St Patrick's Day statement the following spring. Again they condemned the IRA, but this time added criticism of unionist and British intransigence. In 1979, their St Patrick's Day declaration having now become an annual tradition, the Horsemen went further in their opprobrium of British obstinacy. Allusions were made to recent revelations of police brutality in Northern Ireland, and to 'a policy of conspicuous tilt in favour of the majority and to the detriment of the minority'.[40] Following on from this, Hume suggested to O'Neill the idea of leading an American delegation to Northern Ireland to coincide with the upcoming Westminster election. O'Neill went one better, visiting Northern Ireland, but also travelling to London to discuss the conflict with the leaders of the main British parties.[41]

Exasperated by the lack of response, in June 1979, O'Neill announced his support for a Congressional movement to ban the sale of arms to the

RUC. The proposal had been instigated by the more republican-minded Irish-American lobby, but O'Neill's backing proved crucial to it success.[42] In effect, the ban represented an indictment of the RUC's human rights record, and a huge embarrassment to the British government, which was also fearful that a contest for the Democratic presidential nomination might bring the Carter administration further into the thrall of Irish-America. It was no surprise, then, when a new initiative was finally announced by the British government in October 1979, the significance of which it was notably eager to impress upon American opinion, with Mrs Thatcher even telling the *New York Times* that she would impose a settlement on local parties if necessary.[43]

As it transpired, the proposals that arose from this initiative proved unsatisfactory from the SDLP's perspective.[44] Nonetheless, it was London's first serious engagement with Northern Ireland in over three and half years. In this respect, by the end of the 1970s, it seemed that Hume's internationalisation strategy had begun to pay dividends – a fact which he tentatively recognised in his *Foreign Affairs* article.[45] This was particularly important to the SDLP at a time when, following the failure of Sunningdale and the collapse of the Constitutional Convention, the party found itself in a political wilderness. Though the SDLP remained convinced of the essential rectitude of its political programme, it found itself incapable of achieving its implementation. It was this which had led Hume to look further afield for help. His success in building support networks in both the EC and the US meant that, on becoming SDLP leader, Hume was in a position to begin mobilising an international coalition behind the party. This was to prove crucial to the realisation of the SDLP's strategy in the 1980s and beyond.

Notes

1   *Irish Times*, 9 November 1985.
2   Ruane and Todd, *The Dynamics of Conflict*, pp. 133–4; J. Ruane and J. Todd, 'The Northern Ireland conflict and the impact of globalisation', in W. Crotty and D. E. Schmitt (eds), *Ireland on the World Stage* (London: Longman, 2002), p. 119.
3   Hume, 'The Irish question', pp. 312–13.
4   Routledge, *John Hume*, p. 154; White, *John Hume*, p. 202.
5   Quoted in Drower, *John Hume*, p. 84.
6   SDLP, *A New Horizon* (n. p.: 1979), p. 2.
7   White, *John Hume*, pp. 205, 229.
8   J. Mitchell and M. Cavanagh, 'Context and contingency: constitutional nationalists in Europe', in M. Keating and J. McGarry (eds), *Minority Nationalism and the Changing International Order* (Oxford: Oxford University Press, 2001), p. 258; White, *John Hume*, pp. 229–30.
9   P. Hainsworth, 'Northern Ireland in the European Community', in M. Keating and B. Jones (eds) *Regions in the European Community* (Oxford: Clarendon, 1985), pp. 110–11.

10   See Chapter 11 on this and how European integrationist ideology also greatly
     influenced Hume's political philosophy.
11   Murray, *John Hume and the SDLP*, pp. 211–12; SDLP, *A New Horizon*,
     pp. 3–4.
12   A. Guelke, *Northern Ireland: The International Perspective* (Dublin: Gill and
     Macmillan, 1988), pp. 159–60; D. Kennedy, 'The European Union and the
     Northern Ireland question', in B. Barton and P. J. Roche (eds), *The Northern
     Ireland Question: Perspectives and Policies* (Aldershot: Avebury, 1994),
     p. 179.
13   Devlin, *Straight Left*, p. 223; Drower, *John Hume*, p. 79; White, *John Hume*,
     pp. 158, 160, 187–9.
14   *Irish Times*, 24 September 1987; Murray, *John Hume and the SDLP*, p. 237;
     A. J. Wilson, *Irish-America and the Ulster Conflict, 1968–1995* (Belfast:
     Blackstaff Press, 1995), p. 270; Routledge, *John Hume*, pp. 14, 195. As
     Arthur notes, Hume's reward for his opposition to the MacBride Principles
     was to be called 'England's main propaganda expert in the United States of
     America' in a letter to the *Derry Journal* written by Fr Seán McManus, a
     leader of the republican lobby in the US; Arthur, *Special Relationships*,
     p. 276, n. 78.
15   Routledge, *John Hume*, p. 195; White, *John Hume*, p. 251.
16   *Irish Press*, 29 September 1983.
17   Coogan, *The Troubles*, p. 408; R. B. Finnegan, 'Irish-American relations', in
     Crotty and Schmitt (eds), *Ireland on the World Stage*, p. 99; White, *John
     Hume*, pp. 184–5.
18   Murray, *John Hume and the SDLP*, pp. 222–3; White, *John Hume*, p. 186;
     Wilson, *Irish-America*, p. 115.
19   *Irish Independent*, 22 March 1972; *Irish Times*, 22 March 1972.
20   *Derry Journal*, 24 March 1972.
21   *Irish Independent*, 22 November 1972.
22   E. Kennedy, 'Foreword' to Hume, *A New Ireland*, p. 7.
23   Drower, *John Hume*, p. 80; Murray and Tonge, *Sinn Féin and the SDLP*,
     p. 86; Wilson, *Irish-America*, p. 130.
24   A. Guelke, 'The United States, Irish Americans and the peace process',
     International Affairs, 72:3 (1996), p. 529.
25   For an insight into the role played by the Four Horsemen in the late 1970s,
     and the influence of Hume over Kennedy in particular, see D. McKittrick,
     'Horsemen of the Irish Apocalypse', *Irish Times*, 6 September 1979.
26   Quoted in Drower, *John Hume*, p. 79.
27   Arthur, *Special Relationships*, p. 139.
28   Murray, *John Hume and the SDLP*, p. 227; Patterson, *Ireland*, pp. 255–6.
29   Garret FitzGerald; interview with author, Dublin, 22 March 2004. See also
     FitzGerald's memoirs, *All in a Life*, pp. 347–8, on this.
30   R. Fanning 'The Anglo-American alliance and the Irish question', in J. Devlin
     and H. B. Clarke (eds), *European Encounters: Essays in Memory of Albert
     Lovett* (Dublin: UCD Press, 2003), p. 207.
31   Donlon actually knew Hume from their time together at Maynooth College,
     and had become close to the SDLP during the run-up to the Sunningdale
     Agreement, when he was the most senior Irish official liaising with the party.
     He subsequently became a crucial figure in Hume's quest to re-orientate

Irish-American opinion on Northern Ireland. However, it has been suggested that the relationship was two-way, and that the pair's common educational background allowed Donlon to exercise a considerable intellectual influence over Hume; Ben Caraher; interview with author, Belfast, 25 June 2004.

32 On the co-operative 'triangle' between the SDLP, Dublin officials, and Irish-American politicians, see R. J. Briand, 'Bush, Clinton, Irish America and the Irish peace process', *The Political Quarterly*, 73:2 (2002), pp. 173 ff.

33 FitzGerald, *All in a Life*, p. 349; Murray, *John Hume and the SDLP*, pp. 227–8; White, *John Hume*, p. 191; Wilson, *Irish-America*, pp. 129–30.

34 FitzGerald, *All in a Life*, p. 348; White, *John Hume*, p. 191; Wilson, *Irish-America*, p. 132.

35 Arthur, *Special Relationships*, p. 139.

36 Wilson, *Irish-America*, pp. 134–5.

37 *Irish Times*, 31 August 1977; Fanning 'The Anglo-American Alliance', pp. 208–9; White, *John Hume*, pp. 192, 193; Wilson, *Irish-America*, pp. 134–6. For a first-hand account, see Donlan's own recollection of the initiative, 'Bringing Irish diplomatic and political influence to bear on Washington', *Irish Times*, 25 January 1993.

38 Finnegan, 'Irish-American Relations', p. 104.

39 Guelke, 'The United States, Irish Americans and the peace process', p. 529.

40 *Irish Times*, 17 March 1979.

41 Wilson, *Irish-America*, pp. 155–6.

42 Briand, 'Bush, Clinton, Irish America and the Irish peace process', p. 175; Wilson, *Irish-America*, pp. 159–61, 163.

43 Briand, 'Bush, Clinton, Irish America and the Irish peace process', p. 176; Guelke, 'The United States, Irish Americans and the Peace Process', pp. 530–1.

44 See above, p. 93.

45 Hume, 'The Irish Question', pp. 301, 310–11, 312, 313.

7

The totality of relationships

As seen in Chapter 5, during the late 1970s, Hume and the SDLP had increasingly argued the case for Northern Ireland to be considered as a problem shared by Britain and Ireland – a problem which could, therefore, only be solved through joint action by the British and Irish governments. As a result, Hume and his colleagues were greatly encouraged by the significant developments in Anglo-Irish relations that took place in the early 1980s. Firstly, in May 1980, talks were held in London between the two heads of government, Charles Haughey and Margaret Thatcher. This was followed by a further summit meeting in Dublin in December, at which Thatcher recognised the 'unique relationship' between Britain and Ireland, and the two leaders agreed on the need to consider 'the totality of relationships within these islands'.[1] Hume was clearly delighted, describing the Dublin meeting as a 'significant and important milestone' on the road to a solution in Northern Ireland.[2] However, this joy was short-lived, with tensions between the two governments quickly returning with the onset of the republican hunger strikes.

Between May and August of 1981, ten republican prisoners fasted to death in an effort to regain the 'special category status' which the British government had previously afforded them, but which had been removed five years earlier as part of a 'criminalisation' strategy.[3] In this, republicans were looking to recover a position wherein the state had, in effect, recognised them as being politically motivated. Though the hunger strikers failed in this objective, they transformed the image of the Provisional movement. By evoking a powerful tradition of Irish nationalist martyrdom, they gained sympathy and support far beyond the republican heartlands, amongst more moderate sections of the minority community, and voters in southern Ireland. This was spectacularly demonstrated when the leader of the hunger strikers, Bobby Sands, was elected to the Westminster parliament, and two other protesters won seats in Dáil Éireann.

The inflexibility of the British government clearly contributed to this crisis. Related to the subject of the prisoners' status were a number of individual demands concerning the conditions of their captivity. These concerned issues such as the prisoners' right to wear their own clothing and freedom of association. The Irish government viewed these lesser

demands in humanitarian terms, and felt that they offered room for compromise. But true to her reputation, Thatcher refused to grant any concessions made under duress.[4] As the death toll increased, this approach
caused disbelief amongst nationalists, with even the head of the Irish
Catholic Church, Cardinal Tomás Ó Fiaich, openly criticising the Prime
Minister's 'rigid stance'.[5] However, this rigidity posed a particular dilemma
for the SDLP. By opposing the republican candidates who stood for election in this period, the party feared that it would be seen as supporting
Thatcher's uncompromising attitude towards the hunger strikers.[6] In the
highly emotional atmosphere that went with the crisis, Hume worried that
this would lead sections of the Catholic community to disown the party.[7]
'The SDLP would have been accused of lifting the siege of pressure on the
British', he later explained: 'That would have reverberated through other
elections. It was a no-win situation. We would have drowned in the deluge
... [and] become one more victim of British policy.'[8] But by abstaining
from these critical contests, the SDLP allowed the emergence of a serious
political challenge. The Provisionals, surprising themselves as much as the
British government, discovered that they had significant electoral support
amongst the Catholic community. Seeking to build on this, the movement's
political wing, Sinn Féin, subsequently announced that it was willing to
contest elections in Northern Ireland. Suddenly, the SDLP faced a con-
tender for the leadership of the minority.

In the short term, the hunger strikes appeared to destroy any hope of
political progress in Northern Ireland, as the period saw a further polarisation of the two communities. However, with the benefit of hindsight, it
can be argued that the crisis actually served to break the political stalemate
which had held since the mid-1970s. For though the episode put immediate strain on Anglo-Irish relations, London and Dublin were soon forced
to overcome their differences.[9] Indeed, the astonishing rise of Sinn Féin in
the aftermath of the hunger strikes caused considerable panic in both capitals. There was now a genuine fear that the moderate nationalism of the
SDLP would be eclipsed by the radical republicanism of Sinn Féin.[10] Thus,
it was the growth of Sinn Féin which provided the initial rationale for the
Anglo-Irish Agreement (AIA) of 1985, and the precursory New Ireland
Forum (NIF) of 1983–84.

The New Ireland Forum

Cynical commentators saw the NIF merely as an attempt by the Irish
establishment to 'save' the SDLP. By bringing the northern party into conference with its southern sisters – Fianna Fáil, Fine Gael, and the Labour
Party – it was thought that the initiative would boost the SDLP's political
credibility, and so aid in its electoral struggle with Sinn Féin. However, the
origins of the NIF predate the rise of political republicanism. Indeed, since
the late 1970s, the SDLP had been arguing the case for a formal alliance

between constitutional nationalists in both parts of Ireland, with the idea that this would help press the British government into adopting a more progressive policy on Northern Ireland.[11] Such ideas met with words of approval in Dublin, but no concrete action. However, after the emergence of Sinn Féin as a political force, the need for the latter became obvious.

By this stage, the SDLP was in serious difficulties. In April 1982, the new Northern Ireland Secretary, James Prior, had announced a plan for 'rolling devolution'. This involved the election of a new Belfast assembly, which would work gradually towards agreement on how devolved powers should be exercised. The SDLP had immediate concerns: the new initiative offered little recognition of any Irish dimension to the problem, and did not guarantee executive-level power-sharing.[12] As a result, senior members of the SDLP, including the deputy leader, Séamus Mallon, advocated a complete boycott of the proposed assembly. However, with Sinn Féin now openly challenging the party for the leadership of the Catholic community, Hume worried that the SDLP would be seen as ceding ground to the republican position.[13]

In the end, Hume proposed a compromise to his divided party: the SDLP would contest the election for Prior's assembly, but not to take its seats. Instead, the party would use the election to secure a mandate for what it called the 'Council for a New Ireland'.[14] The SDLP's manifesto outlined the purpose of this:

> It is ... time for those who believe in a New Ireland to spell out their propos-
> als in some detail. Towards that end it is the intention of the SDLP following
> the election to propose to the Irish government the setting up of a Council for
> a New Ireland made up of members of the Dáil and those mandated in this
> election. The Council should have ... the specific task of examining the obsta-
> cles to the creation of a New Ireland and producing ... an agreed blueprint so
> that a debate on real alternatives can begin within the Anglo/Irish framework.[15]

Hume's idea addressed the SDLP's immediate concerns, but also more long-standing strategic and ideological objectives. Whilst abstaining from Prior's assembly, participation in an all-Ireland convention would allow the party to remain engaged in a political process. This would help the SDLP to maintain its profile at a time when Sinn Féin was dominating the headlines. However, Hume also hoped that the proposed Council of Ireland would create the nationalist alliance which the SDLP had long spoken of as a means to pressurise London and change British policy on Northern Ireland. In addition, and as suggested in the party's manifesto, the SDLP intended that the scheme would produce a serious debate on the 'obstacles to the creation of a New Ireland' – namely the institutions and practices of the Irish state, and the ideas of Irish nationalism more gener-ally, which had contributed to the conflict and political stalemate in Northern Ireland. In this, the rationale behind the initiative echoed ideas which Hume and the SDLP had been articulating throughout the 1970s.

It is also fair to say that the SDLP's proposal matched the thinking of the Fine Gael leader, Garret FitzGerald, who returned to power in Dublin in November 1982. The previous month, in the assembly election in Northern Ireland, further fears had been raised for the SDLP, which won only 18.8% of the poll, whilst Sinn Féin shocked many commentators by achieving 10.1%.[16] This suggested that republicans now had the support of approximately a third of all Catholics casting their vote. As a result, the new Taoiseach was eager to aid the SDLP. However, even before his return to office, FitzGerald had been considering a scheme similar to the SDLP's proposed Council for a New Ireland. The principal difference in FitzGerald's thinking is that he was opposed to the idea of a solely nationalist convention. He knew that unionist participation was unlikely, but felt it important that proceedings should – at least in principle – remain open to their contributions. For this reason, FitzGerald also opposed the use of the word 'council' in the title of any such initiative, fearing that this would stir Protestant memories of Sunningdale's Council of Ireland.[17] Accordingly, the 'New Ireland Forum', as it became, finds its parentage in the thinking of both Hume and FitzGerald.[18]

However, despite FitzGerald's intentions, the NIF was an essentially nationalist exercise. Unsurprisingly, the UUP and DUP both opposed the initiative, but to FitzGerald's disappointment, the Alliance Party also declined to play any role in its proceedings.[19] As a result, the NIF was comprised of the four main constitutional nationalist parities in Ireland, with Sinn Féin purposely excluded because of its support of the IRA. For the southern parties, the Forum was an additional burden to their existing duties in the Dáil and, in the case of Fine Gael and Labour, to their responsibilities in government. For this reason, all deserve credit for the time and effort that they devoted to the initiative, especially as it ran on some months longer than was originally anticipated. However, the SDLP's situation was very different. Having abandoned Prior's Belfast assembly, Hume and his colleagues were able to devote all of their energies to the NIF. They also had the incentive to do so, seeing it as a unique and unprecedented opportunity to influence southern opinion on the Northern Ireland problem.[20] At the same time, the Forum offered the chance to engage the Irish political establishment after a period in which, beyond expressions of sympathy for northern nationalists, it had effectively withdrawn its interest in the conflict. The hunger strikes, the rise of Sinn Féin, and the destabilising impact which all of this had in the Republic,[21] was forcing the Dublin elite to listen. In turn, the SDLP intended to be heard.

The NIF convened in May 1983, and in his opening speech Hume outlined his own understanding of its aims: 'The world is looking at this Forum today, but there are two particular audiences to whom we must address ourselves, the unionists of the North and the British people and Government.'[22] Hume saw the NIF as a way to prompt a change in British policy on Northern Ireland, and in turn to affect attitudes in the unionist community. However, if it was to achieve this end, he believed that the Forum would also have to win the support of the international community: 'We must mean business and the world must see that we desperately mean business.'[23] To show that the NIF meant business, Hume stressed one thing above all else: unity of purpose: 'Let no one underestimate the power and strength of democratic consensus in this Forum. Let no one doubt its impact on British and international opinion.'[24] The need for an agreed nationalist approach to the Northern Ireland problem was something which Hume emphasised time and again through the duration of the NIF.[25]

As well as demonstrating unanimity, Hume felt that the Forum should show that Irish nationalists were serious about compromise. This, he believed, was also crucial if the initiative was to elicit a response from the British government, and encourage a dialogue with Ulster unionism. However, in discussing the latter, Hume showed that his own thinking had perhaps progressed since the 1970s. At that time, when considering the unionist character, he and his colleagues had tended to focus on religion.[26] But here, Hume recognised a greater depth to unionist identity:

> The Protestant ethos I am talking about is not merely theological ... It contains also and perhaps more importantly a strong expression of political allegiance to Britain which we cannot ignore and which we cannot wish away any more than unionists can wish away our deep commitment to Irish unity. This intractable difficulty we must face squarely in this Forum ... How would we propose to give to unionists an adequate sense of security – physical, religious, political, economic and cultural – in a new Ireland? Are we, the nationalists of Ireland, prepared to pay the painful political and economic price this will involve?[27]

This was a crucial statement. In a way more explicit than at any previous point in his career, Hume was recognising that unionists had an attachment to Britain which was as authentic as the nationalist attachment to the ideal of Irish unity. He was asking his fellow nationalists to accept this reality and so, through the Forum, to show that they were interested in an agreement which would not only safeguard unionists' religious interests, but also protect their political identity.

This set the tone for the NIF, which spent the next twelve months discussing the ways in which Irish nationalists could accommodate the unionist tradition.[28] In doing so, the Forum received over 300 submissions from outside actors, and conducted hearings with a range of these. Most notably, there were extended consultations with the Catholic hierarchy and representatives of the main Protestant churches. This led to considerable debate on the thorny issue of church–state relations in Ireland. In addition, economic experts were commissioned to measure the cost of the Northern Ireland conflict and assess the financial implications of a range of alternatives to the constitutional *status quo*.[29] However, an early leak to the *Irish Press* revealed that the NIF was structuring its discussions around three specific constitutional proposals: the traditional nationalist preference of a unitary Irish state, a federal or confederal arrangement between the two parts of Ireland, and a system joint British–Irish authority over Northern Ireland.[30]

In order to prevent further leaks – but also to speed the proceedings of what was becoming a far more arduous task than had originally been anticipated – the NIF became increasingly controlled by a steering committee comprised of the four party leaders.[31] Through this, the preferences of each became more apparent. Hume believed that the final report from the Forum should be analytical rather than prescriptive, establishing a framework for negotiations with the British government and unionists that would, in time, lead to a comprehensive settlement. If the report recommended any given 'solution', it would, he felt, only invite instant rejection. Accordingly, he wanted the report left open to discussion rather than specifically endorsing any of the three constitutional options being considered by the Forum.[32]

FitzGerald and the Labour leader, Dick Spring, also favoured an open-ended report. However, Haughey seemed intent on using the NIF for party political ends, namely to assert Fianna Fáil's traditional position as keeper of the nationalist faith.[33] As a result, he was adamant that the report should endorse the unitary state model.[34] But it is also clear that Haughey had some support from members of the SDLP, including Séamus Mallon, with whom he had a close relationship.[35] These divisions within NIF – but also within the SDLP – caused considerable delays in the effort to produce an agreed final report.[36]

Finally, in May 1984, the Forum reached its conclusion and presented its report. Here, it seems, Haughey had allowed a more aspirational commitment to a united Ireland.[37] However, in return, he gained a more ambiguous formulation on the principle of consent: 'The particular structure of political unity which the Forum would wish to see established is a unitary state, achieved by consent and agreement, embracing the whole island of Ireland'.[38] Moreover, in the post-Forum press conference, Haughey undermined the entire rationale of the initiative by presenting the unitary state model as if it was the only serious proposal being offered by nationalists: 'It is not an option – it is the wish of the parties to the Forum …Neither of these other two arrangements, federation or joint sovereignty, would bring peace or stability to the North.'[39] Furthermore, he openly rejected the idea that the unitary model would require the consent of a majority in Northern Ireland: 'nobody is entitled to deny the natural unity is unification of Ireland. … The Forum wish to see established a unitary state; I don't believe that the consent or agreement of anyone is required for that.'[40] Unsurprisingly, the media focused on these comments rather than the more nuanced statements of Hume, FitzGerald and Spring.

Evaluating the New Ireland Forum report: revisionist or traditionalist?

For Hume and the SDLP, the principle aim of the NIF was to create agreement among constitutional nationalists as to how they should best approach the Northern Ireland problem. Such a consensus, Hume felt, would help to mobilise international opinion, and thus force the British government to respond in a positive manner. Similarly, FitzGerald was determined that the Forum would produce an agreed report, believing that this would provide him with both a negotiating mandate and a set of principles on which he could base talks with the British government.[41] However, it is clear that this overriding urge towards consensus served to compromise the revisionist potential of the NIF.

In order to achieve an agreed report which all parties to the Forum could sign up to – and in particular to ensure that Haughey and Fianna Fáil would accept the document – numerous concessions were made to traditional nationalist thinking.[42] This was most evident in the third chapter of the report, which described the origins of the Northern Ireland conflict. In doing so, it employed a broadly orthodox nationalist narrative, with 1920 taken as the point of departure, and partition presented largely as a British imposition. This act, it argued, had created a sectarian, one-party state in Northern Ireland, and a minority population whose mistreatment was largely ignored by Westminster. Accordingly, the British government received much of the blame for the outbreak of violence in 1969.[43]

FitzGerald in particular was worried about this section of the report, feeling that it would antagonise British readers. However, he allowed it to pass in the hope that the latter sections of the report would be shaped by the more progressive elements in the NIF. Above all, FitzGerald, along with Hume, was focused on fifth chapter of the report, which both identified as being the most crucial.[44] This chapter described the 'Present Realities and Future Requirements' of the problem, realities and requirements which it argued would have to be addressed in order to resolve the conflict.[45] In contrast to the historical section of the report, the fifth chapter offered a more revisionist interpretation, suggesting that the contemporary conflict was, in essence, motivated by a clash of identities and aspirations that were indigenous to Ireland. In doing so, it echoed the two traditions thesis articulated by Hume, and a similar 'two identities' interpretation offered by FitzGerald,[46] arguing that Ulster unionism and Irish nationalism were both equally legitimate political outlooks, and that each would have to be equally accommodated in any workable settlement: 'The validity of both the nationalist and unionist identities in Ireland and the democratic rights of every citizen in this island must be accepted; both of these identities must have equally satisfactory, secure and durable, political, administrative and symbolic expression and protection.'[47]

The bi-national logic of this assertion would inform various political developments in the coming years. However, in the meantime, despite the call for the equal accommodation of both identities in Ireland – and indeed despite Hume's own appeal at the outset of the Forum for nationalists to recognise the reality and depth of unionists' Britishness – it was only in the joint authority proposal that the report really met this ambition. This model was the one most favoured by Hume and FitzGerald,[48] and the essential rationale of Forum report – overshadowed by Haughey's emphasis on the unitary state option – certainly points in the direction of an intergovernmental arrangement. Of course, even joint British–Irish authority over Northern Ireland was a highly ambitious objective, but the arguments supporting this proposal offered a radical departure from traditional nationalism. For implicit in this option was an acceptance that a British withdrawal from Northern Ireland was not necessary for a solution to the conflict. In this regard, what is also notable about this model is that, although it drew on ideas first articulated by the SDLP in 1972, the Forum version omitted a key feature of the scheme outlined in the party's *Towards a New Ireland* document. Indeed, for that had suggested condominium only as interim arrangement, advocating a 'National Senate of Ireland' which would oversee the harmonisation of structures in the two parts of the island with a view to their eventual unification. However, in a review of the *Towards a New Ireland* document which the SDLP submitted to the NIF, the party had admitted that interim structures were 'inherently unstable', and thus advocated a joint-governmental system as a permanent solution.[49] The Forum report also presented joint authority as a lasting arrangement, providing no mechanism to integrate the two parts of Ireland. In this, it appeared to accept the reality, but also the durability, of unionists' British identity. Unlike the SDLP's position in 1972, there was no assumption that this identity would somehow diminish through a process of Irish reunification. Instead, the Forum's model of joint authority offered institutions that would give equal recognition to the political identities of both communities in Northern Ireland on a permanent basis.[50]

FitzGerald and Hume felt that the joint authority proposal was the only specific option offered by the NIF that the British government might respond to.[51] Even in this, they were optimistic, but hoped that London would engage in discussions that would lead to a system of government approximating joint British–Irish administration over Northern Ireland. However, Thatcher subsequently rejected all three constitutional options of the Forum report in her infamous 'out, out, out' press conference of November 1984. This dealt a terrible blow to the efforts of those involved in the initiative. In a single statement, Thatcher seemed to dismiss twelve months of labour on the part of Irish nationalists.[52] Given that the Forum was, very consciously, designed to show the value of constitutional nationalism, this represented a particular setback for the SDLP in terms of its struggle with Sinn Féin. Indeed, republicans gleefully seized on Thatcher's comments, citing them as evidence that purely peaceful methods could not move the British government, and that the SDLP was, therefore, politically redundant.

However, in spite of appearances, the Forum had not been a futile exercise. Though Thatcher had rejected the three specific models proposed by its report, there remained a fourth suggestion which had not been ruled out. For, as well as positing three particular constitutional options, the report had stated that the participants to the NIF 'also remain open to discuss other views which may contribute to political development'.[53] Though this was only one line in the report, it was far from insignificant, or unintentional. Indeed, Hume had actually refused to commit to the report unless Haughey agreed to its inclusion.[54] As Hume later explained, there was a particular reason for this obduracy: 'There were four proposals in the Forum report, not three. The fourth one was there because some of us foresaw that she [Thatcher] might say "out, out, out". The fourth one was if people refused our proposals, we would like to know what theirs were ... We would listen to any proposals that would lead to political development and progress.'[55]

The 'open' option of the NIF report was clearly a far-sighted stratagem on the part of the more progressive authors of the document. For it was difficult for the British government to reject an openness to discussion without appearing completely intransigent. Moreover, this option allowed the other party leaders to mitigate Haughey's traditionalist representation of the Forum report. Indeed, Hume, FitzGerald and Spring all emphasised the open-ended nature of the document, and continually referred to the 'realities' and 'requirements' identified by chapter 5 as providing an appropriate basis for discussion.[56] Most notably, speaking at a Westminster debate on the report shortly after its publication – and notably before Thatcher's rejection of its three specific models for a solution – Hume suggested that:

> The most important aspect of the report is not the three options, but the views of Irish nationalists about the ways in which realities must be faced if there is to be a solution. We also say that we are willing to examine other ways of accommodating those realities and requirements. ... I invite the House to read chapter 5 of the report carefully. It contains a list of realities which must be faced if we are to solve the problem. ... [T]he only major proposal in the Forum report is to get the governments together to create the framework and atmosphere in which the realities can be discussed to bring an end to Irish problem.[57]

By stressing this open-ended interpretation of the report, the more revisionist participants in the NIF were able to retain the moral high-ground. As a consequence, international opinion fell behind the initiative, reacting strongly against Thatcher's rejection of the report, and sympathising with what was seen as a genuinely conciliatory effort on the part of Irish nationalists.[58] Most notable was opinion in the US, where Hume's Democratic allies had now joined with representatives of the Republican Party to establish a bi-partisan lobby group, the Friends of Ireland.[59]

Hume had gained their approval for the Forum even before it was convened, and subsequently the group made sure to keep informed of the initiative's progress.[60] As a result, when Thatcher carelessly rebuffed the
Forum report, she immediately invited on herself the wrath of Irish-
America. Thus, it came as no surprise when, in the aftermath of Thatcher's
comments, Ronald Reagan – prompted largely by the irate Friends of
Ireland – personally praised 'the Irish statesmen for their courageous and
forthright efforts recently embodied in the report of the New Ireland
Forum'.[61] It is unlikely that such a statement by the American President
went unnoticed in London.

In this, although the initiative seemed to run aground with Thatcher's
rejection of the three Forum proposals, the Prime Minister's remarks actually proved to be a turning point. The negative impact of her comments
gave FitzGerald diplomatic leverage which he used to push for negotiations with the British government. At the same time, he found the Iron
Lady to be much more conciliatory after her 'out, out, out'-burst.[62] Thus,
albeit in a manner less direct than the SDLP had imagined, the Forum was
successful in forcing London to begin reconsidering its position on the
Northern Ireland problem.

In summary, the NIF brought together a number of strategic and ideological threads which Hume and the SDLP had been working on for some
years. Firstly, it involved Dublin in the party's efforts to press the British
government to change its policy on Northern Ireland. Moreover, despite
her seeming rejection of the Forum report, Thatcher was eventually
obliged to respond in a way that opened the path to formal intergovernmental negotiations, thereby reviving and even galvanising the Anglo-Irish
process favoured by the SDLP. In addition, the Forum allowed the party to
influence the Dublin elite in its thinking on Northern Ireland. As result,
hereinafter, successive Irish governments saw the conflict in terms which
were, to a large degree, shaped by Hume and his colleagues.[63] Relating to
this, the NIF also initiated a process of re-appraisal among Irish nationalists. Despite the limitations of this effort which were suggested by the
actual Forum report, Irish nationalism had finally began to think seriously
about how it could be more accommodating of Ulster unionists. Clearly,
this was a process which would continue in the coming years.[64] But even
judging the Forum in it own terms, the initiative did represent a sincere
attempt to refashion Irish nationalism and its relations with the unionist
tradition in such a way that might allow for political progress in Northern
Ireland.

In the final analysis, the need for agreement between the various parties
in the NIF served to compromise its output, with large parts of its report
giving ground to the traditional nationalist perspective. However, the essential impulse for the initiative, and key arguments in its report, were revisionist. As John Whyte suggests, the Forum moved towards a recognition of
the rights and identity of the unionist tradition. This also represented a shift

away from orthodox nationalism in its focus on Britain as the primary cause of the conflict, and an acceptance that political divisions in Ireland were, in essence, endogenous: 'the report does not see the British presence as being at the heart of the Northern Ireland problem. The core is seen as lying in the clash of two identities.'[65] This allowed Whyte to dismiss interpretations of the NIF which focused solely on the traditional elements in its report,[66] or which accepted Haughey's presentation of the document as a simple statement in support of Irish reunification. Instead, Whyte's judicious conclusion on the NIF report was that 'the innovations in its approach decisively outweigh the continuities with old-style nationalist views.'[67]

The Anglo-Irish Agreement

As noted above, though Thatcher had rejected the three specific models proposed by the Forum report, its authors had also declared their openness to discussion of other options addressing the 'realities' and 'requirements' of the Northern Ireland problem which they had identified. On this basis, FitzGerald felt that he could engage with the British government whilst retaining the report as a guide to negotiations.[68] In doing so, he was particularly keen to emphasise what the NIF had termed the 'alienation' of the minority from state institutions in Northern Ireland.[69] Following this 'alienation thesis', FitzGerald and his officials had argued the need for Dublin to play some formal role in the governance of the region. This, it was claimed, would provide political recognition of the minority's Irish identity. However, it would also help to reform the Northern Ireland state, particularly in areas which had an impact on the daily lives of those in the Catholic community, like policing and the administration of justice. Changes in these areas, it was suggested, would help to reduce nationalist disaffection, and so stymie support for radical republicanism.[70]

Although Thatcher had explicitly rejected the idea of joint British–Irish authority over Northern Ireland, it is clear from these arguments that FitzGerald was still perusing an agreement along these lines. Moreover, in making his case to British officials, FitzGerald had been led to believe that some such arrangement – perhaps not termed joint authority, but producing much the same effect – was possible.[71] However, through the course of the negotiations, and as Thatcher was more directly involved, it became obvious that she was extremely reluctant to allow Dublin to play any formal political role in Northern Ireland. Her approach was more minimalist, as she sought only an agreement which would provide greater security co-operation from the Irish government.[72]

The AIA, signed by the two governments at Hillsborough Castle on 15 November 1985, represented a compromise between the respective positions of FitzGerald and Thatcher.[73] FitzGerald did not get the joint authority arrangement which he had hoped for, but neither did Thatcher win Dublin's agreement to closer security co-operation without a political *quid pro quo.* This came in the form of an Inter-Governmental Conference (IGC), the most important institution to be established by the AIA, which gave Dublin a formal right to consultation on British policy in Northern Ireland.[74] Through this, although London would retain ultimate power in the region, the Irish government was given a voice in the affairs of Northern Ireland. In effect, the IGC made Dublin the mouthpiece of the minority's grievances, and the guardian of its essential interests.

How is it, though, that Thatcher, an ardently pro-Union Prime Minister, came to sign what amounted to the most significant compromise with Irish nationalism since the Anglo-Irish Treaty of 1921? Her security concerns account for much of her motivation, but they do not tell the whole story.

As suggested, it was the growth of Sinn Féin which provided the primary rationale for FitzGerald in both convening the NIF and then seeking an agreement with the British government that would aid the SDLP.[75] However, the threat from Sinn Féin also helped FitzGerald to persuade Thatcher of the need for radical reform in Northern Ireland.[76] But the Prime Minister herself saw the need for change in aftermath of the hunger strikes. Indeed, though she may have won the battle in her refusal to submit to the hunger strikers' demands, arguably Thatcher lost the war. For the popular mobilisation of republicanism, made manifest in the rise of Sinn Féin, served to undermine her claim that the Provisionals were merely a criminal gang with no political support. As such, despite her opinion of Northern Ireland as essentially a security problem – and indeed despite her deep aversion to the idea of Catholic 'alienation'[77] from the state – Thatcher could not afford to ignore the radicalisation of the minority community in the early 1980s. She had to find some way to address this, even if it meant involving the Irish government.

There was, however, another, more crucial motivation for Thatcher's consenting to the AIA: international opinion. Of course, British policy in Northern Ireland had met with criticism from the international community since the outbreak of the Troubles. However, the demand to adopt a more conciliatory approach, and one which had the agreement of the Irish government, had grown stronger from the early 1980s, particularly as emotive images of the republican hunger strikers were broadcast around the world. Over time, this obviously impacted on Thatcher's thinking.

As demonstrated in the previous chapter, Hume had played a major part in directing international interest in Northern Ireland into constructive channels. For example, as already noted,[78] he had promoted the EC to commission the Haagerup Report of 1984, which clearly reflected the SDLP's thinking in endorsing an Anglo-Irish approach towards the resolution of the conflict. This, undoubtedly, encouraged London to adopt a more bilateral strategy, if only to insulate itself from further criticism from the international community.[79] However, even more important in achieving the AIA, but again related to Hume's internationalism, was American pressure to this end.

After Ronald Reagan was elected to the White House in 1981, Washington had withdrawn from the tentative involvement in Northern Ireland that had been initiated by the Carter administration. Indeed, even during the critical period of the hunger strikes, Reagan refused to make any comment on Thatcher's stance.[80] However, as noted above, by now Hume's allies, the Four Horsemen, had been joined by other interested Irish-American politicians – Republicans as well as Democrats – in the Friends of Ireland group. Through the Friends of Ireland, Hume and the Irish government still enjoyed some influence over the White House. Indeed, as already recorded, it was only after pressure from the Friends that Reagan responded to Thatcher's dismissal of the NIF options, and personally endorsed the work of those involved in the initiative.

However, Reagan's public comments on the NIF belied the private efforts which Irish-America made to turn Thatcher around. For, after her rejection of the NIF proposals, both Hume and FitzGerald had contacted the Friends of Ireland, hoping that they could the help move the situation forward. The Friends' intervention – aided by some crucial string-pulling on the part of Dublin's former Ambassador to America, Seán Donlan – led Reagan to voice his concern over the Anglo-Irish process during a meeting with Thatcher in December 1984. It was most notable, then, that a month later the British government tabled new proposals for an Anglo-Irish accord, proposals which accepted the need for Dublin's involvement in Northern Ireland, and which formed the essence of the agreement signed the following November.[81]

Clearly, the US played a significant role in nudging the British government towards the AIA. The 'special relationship' with the US – and Thatcher's own close relationship with Reagan – was being disturbed by an increasingly irksome Irish-American elite, acting largely at the behest of Hume and the Irish government. This appears to have been a crucial factor in persuading the Prime Minister to allow Dublin a foot in the door to Northern Ireland. Indeed, shortly after her resignation in 1990, when a close colleague asked Thatcher why she had ultimately committed to the AIA, her succinct reply told all: 'It was the pressure from the Americans that made me sign that Agreement.'[82]

The SDLP and the Anglo-Irish Agreement

Overall, the SDLP also played an important part in bringing about the AIA. Hume and his colleagues provided the initial impetus for the accord in their promotion of an Anglo-Irish approach to the Northern Ireland problem from the late 1970s; a political blueprint in their contribution to the NIF report; and perhaps the final, vital pressure on the British government via their American allies. However, it also appears that, through Dublin, the SDLP leadership had a more direct role in the shaping of the AIA. Indeed, from the outset of negotiations between the two governments, FitzGerald had consulted extensively with Hume and other senior members of the SDLP.[83] It is this which leads McGarry and O'Leary to their conclusion that

> the decisive actor in the making of the Agreement was the SDLP and its leader John Hume. ... [A]s instigator of the Anglo-Irish discussions and the New Ireland Forum ... and as an actively consulted adviser to the Irish government throughout the negotiations, Hume contributed more than any other political leader on the road to Hillsborough. ... To Ulster unionists Hume was the evil genius behind the Agreement.[84]

McGarry and O'Leary are not alone in this interpretation. Indeed, even academics dismissive of his thinking admit that 'Hume was very successful in ensuring his own definition of the problem was to a large degree influential in the framing of the Agreement.'[85] This definition of the problem had been distilled in the NIF report. In essence, it suggested that any solution had to recognise and to accommodate the identity and aspirations of both communities in Northern Ireland, and the logic of this argument clearly informed the AIA. Indeed, the preamble to the accord – apparently drafted with particular reference to the NIF report[86] – saw the two governments

> [r]ecognising the need for continuing efforts to reconcile and to acknowledge the rights of the two major traditions that exist in Ireland ... Recognising that a condition of genuine reconciliation and dialogue between unionists and nationalists is mutual recognition between and acceptance of each other's rights ... [and r]ecognising and respecting the identities of both communities in Northern Ireland, and the right of each to pursue its aspirations by peaceful and constitutional means.[87]

Comparing this declaration with the 'Northern Catholic' article which Hume wrote for the *Irish Times* over two decades earlier – a piece in which he had argued the need to accept the legitimacy of both the nationalist and unionist tradition, and the right of each to follow its political ambitions by constitutional means[88] – shows how his most formative thinking had fed into the highest level of political exchange between London and Dublin.

But Hume's influence went beyond the rhetorical commitments of the AIA. It was what the Agreement symbolised, and also what it promised in practical terms, that won his party's support for the accord. Most importantly, more than a decade after the demise of Sunningdale, it re-established the Irish dimension, something which the SDLP had long argued was a *sine qua non* for any solution to the Northern Ireland problem. Dublin's involvement in the governance of the region, in however limited a way, was interpreted by the SDLP as a recognition of northern nationalists' Irish identity. As Hume would later argue: 'Nationalists could now finally raise their heads knowing their position was, and was seen to be, on an equal footing with that of unionists.'[89] However, Hume and his colleagues also looked forward to the reforms which they hoped the Irish government would bring though its role in the IGC. Indeed, for under terms of the Agreement, the IGC was to concern itself with a range of issues that had a direct impact on the daily lives of those in the minority community, from policing and security arrangements, to matters of fair employment and cultural expression.[90] The SDLP believed that changes in each of these areas would make the symbolic equality of the AIA a more real experience for Catholics in Northern Ireland.

However, despite the potential of the AIA, it should be remembered that the SDLP had anticipated a more significant role for Dublin in the administration of Northern Ireland. Like the Irish government itself, Hume and his party had hoped that Dublin would, in effect, act as joint authority in the region, particularly in matters of policing and justice. But the Irish government gained no executive power in Northern Ireland, and the AIA promised only that the IGC would consider reform of policing and judicial arrangements.[91] As such, Dublin and the SDLP were still anxious to see what changes would actually be achieved in these areas.

In spite of this, both the Irish government and the SDLP were willing to accept the AIA as a step forward. Thus, Hume tended to describe the accord as 'the framework for a solution, not the solution'.[92] However, this was very much the type of framework that he and his party had been arguing for since the late 1970s, namely an intergovernmental framework, wherein Dublin had a recognised role in the process towards a solution. The IGC, limited as it was, provided such a role. In the famous phrase of Bew, Gibbon and Patterson, the governance of Northern Ireland became 'Direct rule with a green tinge'.[93]

As such, despite its limitations, Hume embraced the accord, arguing that it served to recast the Northern Ireland problem in a new Anglo-Irish paradigm. As he explained to the British parliament: 'This is the first time that we have had a real framework within which to address the problem. The problem is not just about relationships within Northern Ireland ... it is about relationships in Ireland and between Britain and Ireland. Those interlocking relationships should be addressed within the framework of the problem ... and that is the British-Irish framework.' At the same time, Hume welcomed the Agreement's acceptance of the legitimacy of the aspirations and identities of both communities in Northern Ireland, arguing that this provided the only basis for a peaceful settlement: 'The recognition of the equal validity of both traditions removes for the first time every excuse for the use of violence by anybody in Ireland to achieve his objective. A framework for genuine reconciliation is provided. Both sections of our community can take part in it.'[94]

However, Hume's comments here also suggested that he saw the intergovernmental framework of AIA as providing a means towards an eventual deal between the two communities in Northern Ireland. In this, Hume's thinking appears to have been in tune with some of the chief

architects of the Agreement.[95] Indeed, after conducting extensive research
into the making of the accord, McGarry and O'Leary concluded that it
was specifically designed in such a way as to 'coerce the unionists into
accepting a new version of the Sunningdale agreement of 1973–4.'[96] In
support of their case, McGarry and O'Leary can point to the clause in the
AIA which committed both governments to a form of devolution which
involved 'co-operation of constitutional representatives within Northern
Ireland of both traditions there'[97] – in other words, communal power-
sharing. In addition, the AIA promised that, in those areas where the two
communities could agree to share power, Dublin's influence would lapse.[98]
McGarry and O'Leary suggest that this provision was intended to compel
unionists to work with the minority as a means to limit the role of the
Irish government in Northern Ireland. Accordingly, they characterise the
AIA as an attempt at 'coercive consociationalism'.[99]

If this was the aim of the Agreement, it did not work quite as planned.
Indeed, the Protestant community was implacably opposed to any involvement of the Irish government in the administration of Northern Ireland.
Accordingly, unionist leaders organised a mass campaign of protest against
the London–Dublin 'Diktat',[100] refusing to enter into any negotiations –
with either nationalists or the British government – until it was revoked.
As such, any idea that the AIA would produce a power-sharing settlement
between unionists and the SDLP appeared highly optimistic in the period
immediately after the accord was signed.

Despite this, Hume felt that the unionist community would eventually
negotiate with the SDLP. His confidence stemmed from the belief that the
Agreement had achieved another of his party's long-standing objectives. This
concerned Britain's constitutional guarantee to the majority in Northern
Ireland, which Hume felt had become an obstacle to political progress in the
region. Indeed, from the late 1970s, he had continually argued the need for
London to revise this commitment.[101] In Hume's mind, with unqualified support for their basic position – namely the desire to remain part of the United
Kingdom – unionists had no incentive to negotiate with the nationalist community. The British guarantee thus underpinned a unionist veto. However, in
the AIA, by involving Dublin in the governance of Northern Ireland, Hume
believed that London had changed the nature of its guarantee to the majority, and that this would end the unionist veto over political progress in the
region. Thus, shortly after the Agreement was signed, he suggested that
'there aren't any unconditional guarantees anymore. I think it has been
made clear to the unionists that they don't have a veto over British policy in
Northern Ireland. … I think that is what is very significant. In many ways it
may turn out to be more significant than the Agreement itself. The guarantee is no longer an unconditional guarantee.'[102]

Again, McGarry and O'Leary are supportive of Hume's interpretation
here. By bringing Dublin into the structures of governance in Northern
Ireland, they argue that London had signalled its commitment to radical

reform, even in the face of unionist resistance. Thus, 'whilst the unionist guarantee remained ... unionists would have no veto, tacit or explicit, on policy formulation within Northern Ireland. ... The Union was preserved, but without an Ulster unionist veto on its structure.'[103]

In spite of this, Hume maintained that the AIA did not impinge on the essential rights or identity of the unionist community. Rather, by removing their veto over political progress, it had merely established a level of equality between unionists and nationalists, the only basis on which Hume felt that they might enter into meaningful dialogue:

> This Agreement has taken nothing away from the Unionists. It has simply created a framework for equality for the first time ... By standing behind it and implementing it and eliminating the Unionist veto on change, the British government will take a major step towards peace and stability in Ireland.
>
> ... [T]he Unionist people ... will finally embrace real politics, real dialogue and sit down with the rest of us to begin the long process of breaking down the barriers of prejudice and mistrust which for so long have disfigured this country.[104]

Indeed, so optimistic was Hume of this prospect that, when he saw tentative movements within unionist politics in spring of 1986, he suggested that there would be inter-party talks by end of summer.[105] However, such predictions proved highly premature, and as it transpired, the AIA led to something quite different from talks between the SDLP and unionists.

Notes

1 *Irish Times*, 9 December 1980.
2 *Irish News*, 23 January 1981.
3 Cunningham, *British Government Policy in Northern Ireland*, pp. 24–5.
4 Arthur, *Special Relationships*, pp. 177–8; O'Kane, *Britain, Ireland and Northern Ireland Ireland since 1980* (Abingdon: Routledge, 2007), pp. 21, 22; M. Thatcher, *The Downing Street Years* (New York, HarperCollins, 1993), p. 390.
5 Cited in Bew and Gillespie, *Northern Ireland: A Chronology*, p. 151. However, it has also been suggested that Ó Fiaich, strongly nationalist in his political outlook, may have given encouragement to the republican protesters in the comments which he made. This claim is perhaps more valid in relation to the earlier 'dirty protest' of 1978; Bew and Gillespie, *Northern Ireland: A Chronology*, pp. 129–30; Patterson, *Ireland Since 1939*, pp. 252–3.
6 Murray, *John Hume and the SDLP*, p. 107.
7 Routledge, *John Hume*, pp. 174, 177.
8 Quoted in P. O'Malley, *The Uncivil Wars: Ireland Today* (Belfast: Blackstaff, 1983), p. 124.
9 O'Kane, *Britain, Ireland and Northern Ireland*, pp. 20–1.
10 Bew and Gillespie, *Northern Ireland: A Chronology*, p. 167; Bew, Gibbon and Patterson, *Northern Ireland, 1921–2001*, p. 202; FitzGerald, *All in a Life*, pp. 462, 496–7; Thatcher, *The Downing Street Years*, p. 395.
11 Murray, *John Hume and the SDLP*, pp. 72–3, 135.

12 O'Kane, *Britain, Ireland and Northern Ireland*, pp. 31, 34.
13 Murray, *John Hume and the SDLP*, pp. 116–17; White, *John Hume*, p. 240.
14 Routledge, *John Hume*, p. 183; White, *John Hume*, p. 241.
15 SDLP, *Stand Firm – Vote SDLP* (Belfast: SDLP, 1982).
16 Bew and Gillespie, *Northern Ireland: A Chronology*, p. 166.
17 FitzGerald, *All in a Life*, pp. 462ff.
18 This was not the only way in which the two leaders shared a similar mindset. Indeed, FitzGerald can also be seen as a revisionist nationalist in his thinking. Moreover, through their first contacts during the outbreak of the Troubles, and then in their co-operation in the negotiation of the Sunningdale Agreement, Hume and FitzGerald had fostered a close working and even personal relationship. This, and their very similar thinking on Northern Ireland, helped in the advancement of many of the SDLP's goals in the 1980s; see Routledge, *John Hume*, pp. 123ff., and FitzGerald, *All in a Life*, *passim*.
19 Two members of the UUP made submissions in an individual capacity, but otherwise the NIF's deliberations 'lacked a significant unionist input and its report suffered accordingly'; Arthur, *Special Relationships*, pp. 187, 199.
20 Murray, *John Hume and the SDLP*, p. 123.
21 The most striking example of this tendency was the election of two of the hunger strikers to Dáil Éireann in June 1981, which helped to dislodge the incumbent Fianna Fáil government. However, FitzGerald also notes the problems which the Irish authorities had in dealing with protests relating to the hunger strikes; FitzGerald, *All in a Life*, p. 374.
22 J. Hume, opening speech to the New Ireland Forum, 30 May, 1983, in Dublin Stationery Office, *New Ireland Forum Public Sessions*, *1–13* (Dublin: Dublin Stationery Office, 1984), p. 22.
23 *Ibid.*, p. 21.
24 *Ibid.*, p. 24.
25 See, for example, his comments in the *Irish Times*, 30 January 1984.
26 See above, pp. 41–2.
27 Hume, opening speech to the New Ireland Forum, p. 23.
28 For a detailed account of the proceedings of the NIF, see Arthur, *Special Relationships*, pp. 190ff. For an official record, see Dublin Stationery Office, *New Ireland Forum Public Sessions*, *1–13*.
29 Arthur, *Special Relationships*, pp. 194, 199–201. The economic studies also demonstrated that the NIF was trying to engage with unionists' considerable material reasons for opposing any move towards a settlement with Irish nationalism.
30 *Irish Press*, 18 August 1984; White, *John Hume*, pp. 255–6.
31 Arthur, *Special Relationships*, pp. 193–4; White, *John Hume*, pp. 256–7.
32 *Irish Press*, 20 February 1984; White, *John Hume*, pp. 256, 261.
33 Arthur, *Special Relationships*, p. 193.
34 *Irish Times*, 3 May 1984.
35 *Irish Press*, 20 February 1984; Arthur, *Special Relationships*, pp. 197, 286 (n. 73); Murray, *John Hume and the SDLP*, p. 142; White, *John Hume*, pp. 261ff. However, Murray and White also highlight the crucial role which Mallon played in negotiating an eventual compromise between Haughey and the other party leaders, thus avoiding a breakdown in the initiative, and helping to produce an agreed report.

36 *Belfast Telegraph*, 7 April 1984; *News Letter*, 17 April 1984; Arthur, *Special Relationships*, pp. 198, 201–2.
37 See Arthur, *Special Relationships*, pp. 203–4, on the on final wrangles between the participating parties and the interesting last-minute changes that were made to the wording of the report.
38 Dublin Stationery Office, *New Ireland Forum Report* (Dublin: Dublin Stationery Office, 1984), article 5.7.
39 *Irish Times*, 3 May 1984.
40 Quoted in FitzGerald, *All in a Life*, p. 492.
41 FitzGerald, *All in a Life*, pp. 460ff.
42 Patterson, *Ireland Since 1939*, p. 295.
43 Dublin Stationery Office, *New Ireland Forum Report*, articles 3.1–3.12.
44 FitzGerald, *All in a Life*, pp. 486, 490, 491; White, *John Hume*, pp. 261, 266.
45 Dublin Stationery Office, *New Ireland Forum Report*, article 5.3.
46 See FitzGerald, *All in a Life*, p. 411. The interpretation which FitzGerald presented here shows the commonality between his and Hume's understanding of the Northern Ireland conflict. Their closeness of thinking clearly helped to determine the content of the crucial fifth chapter of the Forum report.
47 Dublin Stationery Office, *New Ireland Forum Report*, article 5.2 (4).
48 *Irish Press*, 20 February, 1984; FitzGerald, *All in a Life*, pp. 464, 469–70.
49 Murray, *John Hume and the SDLP*, p. 128; Murray and Tonge, *Sinn Féin and the SDLP*, p. 126.
50 The wording of the report also appeared to recognise this as an advantage which the other two constitutional arrangements proposed by the Forum could not offer: 'There would be no diminution of the Britishness of the unionist population [under joint authority]. Their identity, ethos, and link with Britain would be assured by the authority and presence of the British government in the joint authority arrangements'; Dublin Stationery Office, *New Ireland Forum Report*, article 8.7.
51 *Irish Press*, 20 February 1984; FitzGerald, *All in a Life*, p. 464.
52 For Hume's initial and largely outraged reaction to Thatcher's comments, see the *Sunday Press*, 25 November 1984.
53 Dublin Stationery Office, *New Ireland Forum Report*, article 5.10.
54 White, *John Hume*, pp. 264, 265–6. On this subject, also see Arthur, *Special Relationships*, p. 204; and FitzGerald, *All in a Life*, p. 489.
55 Quoted in Murray, *John Hume and the SDLP*, p. 145.
56 FitzGerald, *All in a Life*, pp. 486, 491–2; K. Boyle and T. Hadden, *Ireland: a Positive Proposal* (Harmondsworth: Penguin, 1985), pp. 21–2.
57 *Hansard*, sixth series, vol. 63, col. 57, 2 July 1984.
58 Guelke, *Northern Ireland*, p. 97.
59 Arthur, *Special Relationships*, pp. 148, 217; O'Cleary, *The Greening of the White House: The Inside Story of How America Tried to Bring Peace to Ireland* (Dublin: Gill and Macmillan, 1996), p. 30.
60 *Irish Press*, 30 December, 1983; Wilson, *Irish-America*, pp. 240–1.
61 *Irish Times*, 3 December 1984.
62 FitzGerald, *All in a Life*, pp. 461, 524, 527; G. FitzGerald, 'The origins and rationale of the Anglo-Irish Agreement of 1985', in D. Keogh and M. H. Haltzel (eds), *Northern Ireland and the Politics of Reconciliation* (Cambridge:

Cambridge University Press, 1993), p. 197; O'Leary and McGarry, *The Politics of Antagonism*, pp. 218–19 (n. 30).

63 Murray, *John Hume and the SDLP*, pp. 123, 141.

64 For examinations of the continued change in southern Irish nationalist ideology in the years after the NIF, see K. Hayward, 'The politics of nuance: Irish official discourse on Northern Ireland', *Irish Political Studies*, 19:1 (2004); and G. Ivory, 'Revisions in nationalist discourse among Irish political parties', *Irish Political Studies*, 14 (1999).

65 Whyte, *Interpreting Northern Ireland*, p. 140.

66 See, for example, C. O'Halloran, *Partition and the Limits of Irish Nationalism* (Dublin: Gill and Macmillan, 1987), pp. 194–210.

67 Whyte, *Interpreting Northern Ireland*, p. 140. See also O. MacDonagh, 'What was new in the New Ireland Forum?', *The Crane Bag*, 9:2 (1985), for a considered appraisal of the of the NIF. MacDonagh similarly reads between the lines of the NIF report to see the beginnings of decisive shift in Irish nationalist thinking.

68 FitzGerald, *All in a Life*, pp. 497ff.

69 Dublin Stationery Office, *New Ireland Forum Report*, article 5.1 (1).

70 FitzGerald, *All in a Life*, pp. 473ff.; FitzGerald, 'The origins and rationale of the Anglo-Irish Agreement', pp. 198, 201; O'Kane, *Britain, Ireland and Northern Ireland*, pp. 57–9.

71 FitzGerald, *All in a Life*, pp. 463–4, 477–8, 494–6. FitzGerald also tried to persuade Thatcher that a joint authority arrangement need not entail a dilution of British sovereignty in Northern Ireland: 'I saw it simply as a method that the British government might chose to adopt in the exercise of its sovereignty in order to regulate the affairs of one part of the kingdom'; FitzGerald, *All in a Life*, p. 501. However, both governments knew that any formal role for Dublin in the administration of Northern Ireland – and indeed even the very limited voice which it did acquire in the AIA – would represent a conditioning if not a dilution of British sovereignty in the region.

72 Thatcher, *The Downing Street Years*, p. 385.

73 For greater detail on the negotiations that led to the AIA, and the vital role which government officials as well as the two premiers played in these, see O'Kane, *Britain, Ireland and Northern Ireland*, pp. 43ff. FitzGerald, *All in a Life*, ch. 16, also provides a richly detailed account, whereas Thatcher's *The Downing Street Years*, pp. 396–402, is much briefer.

74 The IGC actually built on an informal arrangement set up after a summit meeting between Thatcher and FitzGerald in November 1981, the Anglo-Irish Inter-Governmental Council. This forum brought senior officials from the two governments into frequent contact, and thus aided the process which subsequently produced the AIA. Indeed, in some respects, the AIA can be seen to have simply institutionalised that process by establishing a standing secretariat to service the IGC. The secretariat was located at Maryfield, just outside Belfast, and thus saw Irish government officials permanently based in Northern Ireland for the very first time. Dublin had argued for such a physical presence to act as a visible sign of the representation of the nationalist minority, hoping that this would reduce their alienation from state structures in Northern Ireland. However, it was this same presence that so outraged unionist opinion.

75 FitzGerald, *All in a Life*, pp. 462ff.
76 Thatcher, *The Downing Street Years*, p. 395. This also explains why FitzGerald advised Hume not to inform Thatcher when they saw that Sinn Féin's challenge to the SDLP was receding in the approach to the local elections of May 1985; FitzGerald, *All in a Life*, 529.
77 Apparently Thatcher rejected this term also because of its 'Marxist' connotations; O'Leary and McGarry, *The Politics of Antagonism*, p. 241 (n. 16).
78 See above, p. 107.
79 Guelke, *Northern Ireland*, p. 160; Kennedy, 'The European Union and the Northern Ireland question', p. 179.
80 Murray, *John Hume and the SDLP*, p. 234.
81 P. Bew, H. Patterson, and P. Teague (eds), *Northern Ireland: Between War and Peace: The Political Future of Northern Ireland* (London: Lawrence and Wishart, 1997), p. 59; Briand, 'Bush, Clinton, Irish America and the Irish Peace Process', p. 177; S. Donlon, 'Bringing Irish diplomatic and political influence to bear on Washington', *Irish Times*, 25 January 1993; J. Dumbrell, 'The United States and the Northern Ireland conflict, 1969–94: from indifference to intervention', *Irish Studies in International Affairs*, 6 (1995), p. 119; Finnegan, 'Irish-American Relations', p. 103; FitzGerald, *All in a Life*, pp. 461, 527; Wilson, *Irish-America*, pp. 243–5.
82 Quoted in A. McAlpine, *Once a Jolly Bagman: Memoirs* (London: Weidenfeld and Nicolson: 1997), p. 272.
83 *Irish Times*, 17 August 1985; *Irish Press*, 12 November 1985; Currie, *All Hell Will Break Loose*, pp. 346–7, 353; FitzGerald, *All in a Life*, pp. 499ff., 511, 536ff., 565–6.
84 O'Leary and McGarry, *The Politics of Antagonism*, p. 238.
85 P. Bew and H. Patterson, 'The new stalemate: unionism and the Anglo-Irish Agreement', in P. Teague (ed.), *Beyond the Rhetoric: Politics, the Economy and Social Policy in Northern Ireland* (London: Lawrence and Wishart, 1987), p. 43.
86 FitzGerald, *All in a Life*, p. 543.
87 HMSO, *Agreement between the Government of the United Kingdom of Great Britain and Northern Ireland and the Government of the Republic of Ireland* [The Anglo-Irish Agreement] (London: HMSO, 1985), Cmnd. 9657.
88 See above, pp. 12–13.
89 Hume, *A New Ireland*, p. 64.
90 The Anglo-Irish Agreement, articles 5(a) and 6–8.
91 *Ibid.*, articles 7–8. During the negotiation of AIA, FitzGerald had continually pushed for reform in the methods of state security and the administration of justice in Northern Ireland. However, London refused to make any concrete commitment to change in these crucial areas. As a result, sections of the SDLP, including the deputy leader, Séamus Mallon, had to be persuaded by Hume and the Irish government before they would accept the proposed agreement; O'Leary and McGarry, *The Politics of Antagonism*, p. 241 (n. 21).
92 Quoted in O'Leary and McGarry, *The Politics of Antagonism*, p. 220.
93 Bew, Gibbon and Patterson, *Northern Ireland, 1921–2001*, p. 209.
94 *Hansard*, sixth series, vol. 87, cols. 780, 783, 26 November 1985.
95 FitzGerald, *All in a Life*, p. 531; D. Goodhall, *The Anglo-Irish Agreement of 1985 and its Consequences* (Liverpool: Liverpool University Press, 1995), pp. 4–5, 9, 11; O'Kane, *Britain, Ireland and Northern Ireland*, pp. 60–2.

96 O'Leary and McGarry, *The Politics of Antagonism*, p. 234.
97 The Anglo-Irish Agreement, article 4(c).
98 *Ibid.*, articles 2(b), 5(c), 10(b).
99 O'Leary and McGarry, *The Politics of Antagonism*, p. 220.
100 On this, see F. Cochrane, *Unionist Politics and the Politics of Unionism since the Anglo-Irish Agreement* (Cork: Cork University Press, 2nd edn, 2001), ch. 4.
101 See above, pp. 89ff.
102 Quoted in Murray, *John Hume and the SDLP*, p. 152.
103 O'Leary and McGarry, *The Politics of Antagonism*, pp. 226, 227.
104 *Guardian*, 21 January 1986.
105 *Observer*, 27 April 1986.

8

No selfish strategic or economic interest

Republicans understood the Northern Ireland conflict in imperial terms. Historically, Britain had always held economic interests in Ireland, and partition, republicans believed, served to secure those interests. Indeed, partition allowed the British government to maintain a foothold in Ireland – notably in the region with the most advanced industrial base – and a position from which it could continue to influence economic activity across the island. Similarly, republicans felt that London had strategic interests in Ireland. In the context of the Cold War, and whilst the Irish government refused to join the NATO alliance, Britain needed to maintain a military presence on the island.[1] It was this, republicans argued, which legitimised their campaign of violence against the British state. History, both in Ireland and the rest of the colonial world, showed that the British would not be moved by anything less. A united Ireland could only be achieved by physical force.

The SDLP had always opposed this interpretation. However, in the aftermath of the AIA, Hume began a concerted effort to overturn the republican reading of the Northern Ireland problem, and violent strategy which flowed from this. In doing so, Hume went as far as to suggest that the AIA was, in effect, a statement of British neutrality *vis-à-vis* the possibility of Irish reunification:

> the British government have declared themselves neutral in the basic quarrel between us [the two communities in Northern Ireland] ... The British government has declared that Irish unity is a matter for those Irish people who want it persuading those who don't. ... Is Provisional Sinn Féin prepared to join us in taking up the peaceful challenge implicit in the British declaration on Irish unity? Do they not agree that declaration removes all justification for the use of violence?[2]

What is most significant here is that Hume was openly addressing the republican movement, asking it to consider the political implications of the AIA. In doing so, he drew particular attention to the first article of the Agreement. Clause (a) of this article had confirmed the position of Ulster unionists, with both the British and Irish governments recognising that there would be no change in the status of Northern Ireland without the consent of a majority among its population. But clause (c) appeared to endorse the nationalist position, accepting the right to establish a united Ireland if majority consent was secured. Of course, previous agreements and declarations by the British government had made similar statements, but what was new here is that London also explicitly committed itself to support and to legislate for a united Ireland should the consent of a majority be forthcoming.[3] 'This', Hume argued, 'is a clear statement by the British government that it has no interest of its own, either strategic or otherwise, in remaining in Ireland. It is a declaration that Irish unity is a matter for Irish people, for those who want it to persuade those who don't.'[4]

In this, Hume engaged with and explicitly contradicted the republican, imperialist interpretation of the Northern Ireland problem. In his mind, London held no self-interest in Northern Ireland. Rather, it was the wishes of the majority in Northern Ireland which maintained the British presence there. Accordingly, Hume suggested that the British government would accept a united Ireland if only nationalists could persuade unionists to consent to that end. As such, he argued that 'the agreement [the AIA] ... removes completely the slightest justification for the use of violence in Ireland to achieve political objectives.'[5]

In public, republicans rejected Hume's reading of the AIA. However, behind closed doors, it seems that his arguments had some impact. As Hume recalls: 'I got a message from a priest who told me that what I was saying [about the AIA] was very interesting to Sinn Féin and that they would like to talk to me about it'.[6] The priest in question was Fr Alec Reid,[7] from the Clonard Monastery in West Belfast. During his time at Clonard, Reid had earned himself a reputation as a mediator, particularly in his efforts to resolve feuds between rival republican factions.[8] In the process, he established relations with leading members of Sinn Féin, most notably Gerry Adams, and subsequently used these contacts in an attempt to steer republicans towards a more political strategy. With this in mind, Reid had been much encouraged by the NIF of 1983–84. He saw in this an example of how Irish nationalists of various shades could combine and, potentially, offer an alternative to the armed strategy currently being pursued by republicans. As a result, in the years after the Forum, Reid began to put out feelers towards the SDLP, culminating in his letter to Hume.[9]

Hume had rejected previous overtures from Sinn Féin,[10] but was currently receiving information from different sources to suggest that changes were taking place within the political wing of republicanism. Accordingly, he felt that some form of dialogue might now prove useful. Thus, after consulting with Reid and other members of the Clonard Monastery, Hume eventually agreed to private discussions with Adams, their first meeting taking place in September 1986.[11] Hume's objective in these talks was to bring an end to republican violence. However, he knew that this could not be achieved overnight, and indeed did not even broach the subject of an IRA ceasefire at this early stage. Instead, discussions focused on the AIA, with Hume seeking to persuade Adams that the accord was, effectively, a statement of British neutrality *vis-à-vis* Irish unity. Despite Adams's problems with this analysis, the two leaders found their talks productive, and after a time they agreed to more formal discussions which would include delegations from their respective parties.[12]

The SDLP–Sinn Féin talks

The SDLP–Sinn Féin talks of 1988 wholly contradicted the intended outcome of the AIA. The British and Irish governments had hoped that the Agreement would marginalise republicanism, strengthen the SDLP, and thus help ease the path towards negotiations between moderate elements from the two communities in Northern Ireland. Similarly, Hume had believed that, by standing firmly behind AIA, the British government would force a more pragmatic unionism to emerge, one which was prepared to enter into serious negotiations with the SDLP.[13] However, three years on from the AIA, unionists were still refusing to participate in any talks whilst the institutions of accord remained intact. Meanwhile, on the other side of the equation, the AIA failed to reduce support for political republicanism. Though it may have helped to halt the advance of Sinn Féin, the Agreement did not roll back the republican vote.[14] Indeed, Sinn Féin continued to win approximately a third of the nationalist ballot, and in the general election of 1987 Adams held the Westminster seat for West Belfast with an increased majority. With this, it became clear the Sinn Féin had established itself as a significant political player. Though not strong enough to displace the SDLP, it had the potential to destabilise any agreement which the more moderate party might seek to negotiate. This, undoubtedly, impacted on Hume's thinking, causing him to reconsider his previous strategy, which was geared solely towards an accommodation with moderate unionism.[15] He now accepted that Sinn Féin would also have to be brought in to any political settlement that was to prove successful in the long run. Arguably, Hume was the first senior actor involved in the Northern Ireland problem to recognise this reality.[16]

The talks between the SDLP and Sinn Féin were prefaced by an exchange of letters by Hume and Adams on 17 March. These letters were intended to summarise what had already been discussed by the two leaders in their private meetings, and so prepare the ground for the larger delegation talks. Hume's letter, though only a few pages long, deserves close examination.[17] Indeed, it captures the essence of the revisionist nationalist outlook, in both its explanation of the causes of the Northern Ireland conflict, and its assertion that the problem could only be resolved by a peaceful, reconciliatory strategy.

In the first part of his letter, Hume focused upon the means and the motives of the republican movement. He began by questioning the claim that the IRA's campaign of violence was merely a reaction to the British military presence in Northern Ireland. As Hume pointed out, the British government could easily argue the reverse, that the ongoing presence of its army was required to combat republican violence. For Hume, therefore, it was too simple to say that the situation of conflict in Northern Ireland was the responsibility of one side alone. With this argument, he challenged a core republican conviction, and simultaneously advanced a central claim of revisionist nationalism: 'It is not an answer to suggest that the British presence is the primary source of our problems, and therefore the cause of all the violence.'[18]

In addition, Hume questioned the efficacy of the IRA campaign in relation to its proclaimed objective. Firstly, he asked whether republicans truly believed that the British government would ever concede a military defeat in Northern Ireland. Even if it did, Hume argued that a British withdrawal would not presage Irish reunification. Instead, it would create a power struggle, and an even bloodier conflict between the two communities in the region.[19] In this, Hume suggested that the republican campaign actually subverted the aim of Irish unity.

The second part of Hume's letter offered an alternative explanation of the Northern Ireland problem, and an alternative, political approach towards its resolution. This explanation was based on the revisionist idea that the conflict was a product of internal, communal divisions rather than external, political interference. Outlining this thesis, Hume echoed arguments which he had been making since the early 1970s: 'Ireland is first and foremost its people, the territory is secondary since without its people the territory isn't much different from any other piece of earth. The tragedy is that the <u>people</u> of Ireland are deeply divided and have been deeply divided for centuries on some very fundamental matters.'[20]

On this basis, Hume was able to engage with what was, for republicans, a central political principle: national self-determination. As recently as 1987, in a paper entitled *A Scenario for Peace*, Sinn Féin had reiterated the traditional nationalist position on self-determination. In this, it cited the Westminster election of 1918, where the original Sinn Féin party, standing on a platform for independence from Britain, had won a clear majority of the vote in Ireland. From a republican perspective, the British government's refusal to accept this poll, and the subsequent partitioning of the island, represented a denial of Irish democracy and self-determination.[21]

In his letter to Adams, Hume responded to this case by accepting the idea of Irish self-determination, but suggesting that its source of legitimacy lay in the *people* of Ireland rather than any territorial unit: 'it is the <u>Irish people</u> who have the right to self-determination.' Unfortunately, he continued, 'the Irish <u>people</u> are divided on how to exercise the right to self-determination ... [and] the right to sovereignty. It is the search for agreement among the Irish people on how to exercise these rights that is the real search for peace and stability in Ireland.'[22]

Republicans, of course, were looking for more than peace and stability in Ireland. They wanted the political reunification of the island, seeing this as the only means to fulfil the act of self-determination expressed in 1918. Hume accepted this ambition, but argued that it could only be achieved by first winning the agreement of Ulster Protestants. However, if such agreement was secured, then he felt that the British government would be legally bound to accept it. In this, Hume came back to the AIA, again highlighting the British commitment in the accord to facilitate Irish reunification in the event of majority support in Northern Ireland: 'the present British government has made clear in an internationally-binding agreement that if such agreement on the exercise of self-determination took the form of Irish unity that they would in fact endorse it.'[23]

With these arguments, Hume sought to reinforce the revisionist idea that it was not Britain, but rather divisions within Ireland, which maintained the partition of the island. The means towards Irish reunification, therefore, was to address these divisions, and specifically to address Ulster Protestants' fears of such a prospect. But if this was done by peaceful means, Hume argued, then the British government would willingly withdraw from Northern Ireland. Indeed, this was the key argument which Hume was making to Sinn Féin: 'Britain is now saying that she has no interest of her own in being here and that her only interest is to see agreement among the people who share the island of Ireland.'[24]

Adams's letter to Hume was much shorter, but included a position paper outlining his party's understanding of the conflict and the means to its resolution. Unsurprisingly, this document contradicted much of what Hume had said in his letter. In essence, it restated a colonial interpretation of the Northern Ireland problem, arguing that the British government did have self-interests in the region, and that its pursuit of those interests was the primary cause of the conflict: 'given the lengths to which Britain goes to remain here ... one can only conclude that it believes it is in its interests to maintain the Union, to finance the Union, to let its soldiers die for the Union'.[25] For this reason, Sinn Féin continued to defend the armed struggle, arguing that this was the only means to loosen London's grip on Northern Ireland.[26] Thus, Sinn Féin explicitly rejected Hume's neutrality thesis: 'Britain's continuing involvement in Ireland is based on strategic, economic and political interests.'[27]

The dialogue between the SDLP and Sinn Féin continued until mid-August, and involved the exchange of a series of discussion papers. Despite this, the two parties failed to move beyond their basic disagreement over the role of Britain in Northern Ireland. In the SDLP's final contribution to the talks, the party recognised this, and the fact that it had failed to persuade the republican delegation of its arguments: 'Our most significant difference [with Sinn Féin] ... is the degree to which we believe that British policy towards Ireland is *now* neutral and agnostic ... We accept that to date Sinn Féin remain unconvinced of our belief.'[28] However, even in this there was a note of optimism – a sense that, 'to date', republicans were unconvinced, but might yet be won over. Indeed, for through the course of the talks, Sinn Féin had shown signs of increasing interest in the SDLP's arguments.[29]

In essence, Hume and his colleagues felt that republicans were asking them to provide greater proof of their claim of British neutrality. The SDLP accepted this challenge, but suggested that, if its thesis was proven, this in turn would require Sinn Féin to support efforts towards an IRA ceasefire: 'if our belief [in British neutrality] is correct, then the IRA's stated justification for their campaign is removed ... The question is, if our belief is correct, do Sinn Féin accept that the consequences for the IRA campaign are as we state and would they ask the IRA to cease its campaign. If so, then it would be our responsibility in the SDLP to demonstrate to Sinn Féin that our belief was correct.'[30]

From these comments, it is clear that the SDLP did not believe its dialogue with Sinn Féin had been wholly unproductive. Though the talks had not achieved an end to republican violence, Hume and his colleagues appeared unwilling to abandon all hope of such an outcome. However, it is also clear that they saw the need to provide further evidence for Hume's neutrality thesis, and in this to convince republicans of the viability of a peaceful approach towards Irish unity.

The birth of 'pan-nationalism'?

Hume and the SDLP faced enormous criticism for talking to Sinn Féin, particularly from the unionist community.[31] At this time, with the IRA still committed to its campaign of violence, any form of contact with republicans was deemed unacceptable. However, unknown to the public, during its talks with the SDLP, Sinn Féin had also held meetings with representatives of the Irish government. Again, Alec Reid was central to this initiative. Shortly after his first meeting Hume, Reid had approached the Fianna Fáil leader, Charles Haughey, also asking him to open up a dialogue with republicans.[32] Given his own history,[33] Haughey was extremely cautious, but whilst the media was focused on the public talks with the SDLP, he did allow intermediaries to hold secret discussions with Sinn Féin.[34] These talks also ended with little progress, as the Dublin representatives seemed doubtful that Adams and his colleagues had the ability to move the IRA towards a ceasefire. Under these circumstances, the government could not continue the dialogue. However, again the discussions were not completely fruitless, establishing lines of communication that would later prove useful. Most notably, Reid remained an informal conduit between Sinn Féin and Fianna Fáil.[35]

By approaching both Hume and Haughey, it is clear that Reid was trying to create the basis of an alternative strategy for republicans.[36] He was hoping to show how the various strands of Irish nationalism might come together to devise a peaceful means of political progress. In his first letter to Hume, Reid outlined his thinking in this regard: 'the nationalist parities,

North and South, would agree, through dialogue between themselves, to ... a common nationalist policy of aims and methods for resolving the conflict and establishing a just and lasting peace. This would mean that ... the nationalist parties would make an ad hoc agreement to combine their political forces and to act in unison in a common campaign for reconciliation and peace.'[37]

Reid's proposal obviously interested Hume. Indeed, it matched his own thinking in the NIF of 1983–84, where Hume had already helped to establish a common approach to the Northern Ireland problem amongst constitutional nationalists. Reid had been impressed by this achievement, and it clearly informed his own discussions with the republican leadership.[38] As a result, the example of the NIF was also evident in Reid's proposal to Hume. From this, Hume could see that Sinn Féin was becoming interested in the idea of a combined nationalist approach. Like Reid, he believed that this might demonstrate to republicans that there was a viable alternative to armed struggle.

Accordingly, in his discussions with Sinn Féin, Hume continually referred republicans to the possibility of working with other nationalists to find an equitable solution to the Northern Ireland problem. Indeed, in the letter which prefaced these talks, Hume ended by proposing 'a conference table, convened by an Irish Government, at which all parties in the North with an electoral mandate could attend'. In effect, Hume was suggesting a reconvention of the NIF, but this time open to Sinn Féin's participation. Like the original Forum, unionists would also be invited, but, anticipating their refusal, Hume argued that Sinn Féin should nonetheless 'join with the Irish Government and other nationalist participants in preparing a peaceful and comprehensive approach to achieving agreement'. However, the price of entry to this convention was also made clear: 'It would be understood that if this conference were to happen that the IRA would have ceased its campaign.'[39] Clearly, Hume was endorsing Reid's thinking, suggesting that republicans could exchange the armed struggle for a place in a broader nationalist coalition, which would then push for a just settlement of the Northern Ireland problem.

Of course, Hume could not speak for the Irish government in making this proposal. Moreover, it is clear that Dublin, at this stage, had serious doubts about republicans' ability to move towards a peaceful political approach. However, this is the thinking which informed Hume's efforts in the following years, in both his continued dialogue with Adams, and his attempts to re-engage the Irish government in a way that would show it to be supportive of such a strategy. It is also the thinking that underpinned the IRA ceasefire of August 1994, and within two months of this Sinn Féin was given a place at a conference convened by the Irish government, the Forum for Peace and Reconciliation.[40] Arguably, this did not have quite the political impact as the NIF. However, symbolically, it served the same purpose as the convention proposed by Hume in 1988. Effectively, republicans were invited into the nationalist family, with Dublin accepting its role as the head of clan, and its duty to show that constitutionalism could produce real political progress. However, for the meantime, the Irish government remained wary. As yet, it was not convinced that the republican movement was ready to make the transition to peaceful politics.[41] At this stage, only Hume was prepared to believe that this was possible.

Hume's role in this period – firstly his discussions with Sinn Féin, and subsequently his overtures to the Irish government – saw his stock fall further amongst the unionist community. From a Protestant perspective, Hume came to be seen as the central figure in construction of a 'pan-nationalist front'. Even this term – used more by unionist commentators – suggested a profound distrust of Hume's intentions. 'Pan-nationalism' was perceived as the uniting of nationalist forces, North and South, as a means to undermine the Northern Ireland state, both from within and without. It was, in short, an irredentist alliance.[42] In addition, Hume's initiative had an historical resonance, evoking comparison with the 'New Departure' of 1879, when Charles Stewart Parnell had won the support of the Fenians for his Home Rule movement. Of course, judicious historians have noted that this combining of militant and constitutional factions is a phenomenon that is not limited to the nationalist tradition in Ireland. Nonetheless, they have tended to judge Hume's efforts in the same light: 'successive generations of constitutional politicians have been augmented by their association with the hard men'.[43] The implication is clear: by drawing republicans into a political strategy, Hume was seeking to sharpen the edge of Irish nationalism.

However, a very different interpretation of Hume's thinking from 1988 can be offered. This requires consideration of what Hume had achieved hitherto. For, as noted, even before his engagement with republicans, Hume had already created an informal alliance between the various factions of Irish nationalism, culminating in the NIF. At the same time, Hume had cultivated American support for this alliance. And it was this – the NIF, with vocal encouragement from Irish-America – which had helped to achieve the most significant advance for Irish nationalism since partition, the 1985 AIA. If the British government had been moved by Irish nationalism, it was not by 'the hard men', but by the combined efforts of its constitutional representatives.

In his talks with Sinn Féin, Hume suggested that republicans could join in this alliance. However, he also made clear that that they would have to accept its commitment to purely peaceful methods. As such, republicans would be adding to the numbers in this coalition, but they would not be bringing any cutting edge. Rather, they would be removing what Hume had long argued was the greatest weakness of Irish nationalism, its resort to political violence.[44] As such, the only way that republicans would strengthen this alliance would be in moral terms, by showing that Irish nationalists of all shades were united behind a peaceful strategy.

This interpretation contradicts the view that Hume's engagement with Sinn Féin represented a strategic shift – the first stage in the creation of a 'pan-nationalist front', the combined force of which would dismantle partition. Rather, it could be said that Hume was applying principles to which he had always adhered. Moreover, it can be argued that, in the course of his career, these were principles which had helped deliver the only moments of significant progress in Northern Ireland, from the reforms of the early civil rights movement, through to the AIA of 1985. For these advances were achieved through the combination of nationalist energies in a peaceful political strategy, and the mobilisation of international support on this basis. What was different in the aftermath of the AIA is that republicans were now giving signals to suggest that they could be willing to work with such an approach. Of course, they might present this as a way towards the ending of partition, but it was surely evident to the republican leadership that aligning with constitutional nationalists would require a dilution of its ambitions. Indeed, for though co-operation between different nationalist groupings had produced change, it was in a reformist rather than a revolutionary direction. As such, the idea of 'pan-nationalism' – though understandably unnerving unionists – was actually the means by which republicans could be coaxed into participation with a peaceful and more moderate political programme.

Hume's thinking from 1988 did not, therefore, represent a fundamental departure. Rather, it signalled a change in approach towards the same end. Hume had not abandoned the hope of reaching an accommodation with the Protestant community. However, as they continued to rail against the AIA, he saw little evidence that unionist politicians were ready to talk with the SDLP. Even if they did, and a political settlement was achieved, Hume felt that it would not bring stability, and certainly not reconciliation. Indeed, while there were those on both sides in Northern Ireland who were prepared to engage in political violence, the two communities would remain polarised. Denis Haughey, one of Hume's closest aides at this time, thus explains that his motives in talking to Sinn Féin were twofold. First and foremost, Hume's aim was to bring an end to violence. However, this objective was also considered with a view as to how it might facilitate agreement between the two communities, including their political extremes:

> Hume was electrified by the thought of turning off the violence and saving human life ... [But, h]e was fitting that into a framework of thinking which I think could be summarised roughly like this: the middle ground is not taking shape in the way that we [in the SDLP] hoped it would as a consequence of the Anglo-Irish Agreement, and it isn't going to take shape, because of the divisive effect upon opinion being generated by the violence ... and for as long as that violence goes on we are not going to get a sufficiently strong middle ground to mount any kind of structure of power ... [However,] if we are going to switch off the violence, we have got to offer these guys [republicans] something; we have got to offer them a place in the scheme of things ... it has got to be inclusive.[45]

Hume was not, therefore, seeking to strengthen the nationalist position in 1988. Indeed, arguably the power of a united Irish nationalism had already been demonstrated in the achievement of the AIA. However, since then, the limitations of a strategy involving only constitutional nationalists had also been exposed. Dublin's involvement in the governance of Northern Ireland was leading to the better management of the problem, but this of itself could not deliver a solution – that is an agreement between the two communities. Moreover, whilst republicans remained outside the political process, they could continue to frustrate any movement towards this end. However, by bringing them into the nationalist mainstream, Hume felt that he could end republican violence, and so create the conditions for a settlement with unionists. Pan-nationalism – or whatever term might be applied to Hume's strategy – was not about overpowering Ulster unionism. Rather, it was about providing republicans with a credible alternative to the armed struggle, one which could achieve real progress in Northern Ireland, and so prove the efficacy of peaceful political action. For Hume believed that it was only after the violence had ended that it would it be possible to conduct genuine negotiations and create a durable political agreement between the two communities. However, despite his intentions, Hume's dialogue with republicans was bound to raise unionist fears. For this reason, subsequent contacts with Adams were conducted in private.

Looking to London

As a result of the SDLP–Sinn Féin talks, Hume came to believe that the republican movement was in a state of political transition. Though they had formally rejected his interpretation of the AIA, Hume felt that Adams and his colleagues were at least interested in the idea that the British government was essentially neutral on the future of Northern Ireland. 'In failing to persuade Sinn Féin of this analysis', he recalled, 'it was my understanding that its members deemed the evidence to support the SDLP contentions insufficient'.[46] In effect, Hume felt that republicans were 'demanding that I prove British neutrality'.[47] Accordingly, he now turned to London, hoping that the British government would offer validation of the arguments which he had presented to Sinn Féin.

Hume was greatly aided in this objective by the appointment of Peter Brooke as Northern Ireland Secretary in July 1989. Where his predecessor, Tom King, had criticised the SDLP–Sinn Féin dialogue, Brooke was more positive. As a result, Hume kept him informed of the secret discussions which he continued to hold with Adams in the aftermath of the 1988 talks. By this means, Hume encouraged the new Northern Ireland Secretary to believe that change was taking place within the republican leadership.[48] Of course, British intelligence may have been telling Brooke a similar story, and it was around this time that he sanctioned the opening of a line of communication between MI5 and the republican movement.

Unknown to the public, this secret channel had been used before by the British government – most recently during the hunger strikes in the early 1980s – but had lain dormant since. For this reason, it has been suggested that Brooke authorised its reactivation as a means to investigate the claims which Hume was now making.[49]

All of this provides the background to the highly significant speech which Brooke made on 9 November 1990. Although delivered to his own electoral constituency in London, the contents of this speech were clearly intended for republican consumption. Indeed, it later transpired that a copy of the speech was forwarded in advance to Sinn Féin by means of the intelligence channel which Brooke had recently re-opened.[50]

Brooke began his speech by accepting the legitimacy of the aspiration towards a united Ireland, but arguing that violence could only thwart this ambition: 'a 32 County State could never be created by force or advanced by putting a union of territories before a union of hearts and minds ... a desire for unity to be pursued in this way can only deepen division.'[51] In this, there was already a certain similarity to the kind of language used by Hume in his discussion of Irish unity. However, even more striking were Brooke's comments on the AIA, where specific terms from Hume's 1988 letter to Adams were clearly evident:[52] 'Article 1 of the Agreement – registered at the United Nations as a binding international treaty – acknowledges that the status of Northern Ireland can only be determined by the people of Northern Ireland themselves.' With this, Brooke was insisting that the British government presented no barrier to a peaceful evolution of relations in Ireland that would lead to the eventual reunification of the island:

> the obstacle to the development of a new and more inclusive Irish identity if people want this for themselves is not to be sought in Great Britain. ... [I]ndeed the government has made clear on several occasions, notably in the signing of the Anglo-Irish Agreement, that if, in the future, a majority of the people of Northern Ireland clearly wish for and formally consent to the establishment of a united Ireland, it would introduce and support in parliament legislation to give effect to that wish.

Clearly – and quite explicitly – Brooke was affirming Hume's interpretation of the AIA, and his understanding of the British government's position on Northern Ireland as a consequence of the accord. Thus, Brooke summarised, 'it is not the aspiration of a sovereign, united Ireland against which we set our faces, but its violent expression.'

However, the single most important part of Brooke's speech came in the finale: 'The British government has no selfish strategic or economic interest in Northern Ireland'. Comparing this formula to the terms in which Sinn Féin had previously rejected Hume's neutrality thesis,[53] there is an unmistakable similarity. Clearly, Hume was telling Brooke what republicans needed to hear a British minister say.[54]

Notes

1   A more detailed exposition of such arguments can be found in G. Adams, *The Politics of Irish Freedom* (Dingle: Brandon, 1986), pp. 90–9.

2   Linen Hall Library (LHL), Northern Ireland Political Collection (NIPC), P4496, address by Hume to the 16th annual conference of the SDLP, 21–23 November 1986.

3   In the Sunningdale Agreement, the British government promised to support a united Ireland if a majority in Northern Ireland so consented, but did not make the express commitment to *legislate* for such change that was included in the AIA. More importantly, the premature demise of Sunningdale meant that, unlike the AIA, the 1973 accord was never lodged with the United Nations. As such, Sunningdale never attained the same standing in international law that was afforded to the AIA. This – the internationally binding nature of the AIA – was a point that Hume was keen to emphasise in subsequent talks with Sinn Féin; see below, p. 141.

4   *Irish Times*, 13 September 1986. Hume made similar arguments in the early 1980s (see his interview with Séamus Deane and Barre Fitzpatrick in *The Crane Bag*, 4:2 (1980), p. 39). However, following the AIA, it was clear that he intended to use the specific commitment that was made by the British government in this accord in order to support his position.

5   *Irish Times*, 13 September 1986.

6   Quoted in E. Mallie and D. McKittrick, *Endgame in Ireland* (London: Hodder and Stoughton, 2001), pp. 80–1.

7   On Reid's crucial role in the gestation of the Northern Ireland peace process, see G. Adams, *Hope and History: Making Peace in Ireland* (Dingle: Brandon, 2003), *passim*; E. Mallie and D. McKittrick, *The Fight for Peace: The Secret Story Behind the Irish Peace Process* (London: Heinemann, 1996), *passim*; and E. Moloney, *A Secret History of the IRA* (London: Allen Lane, 2002), *passim*. The latter work all but ignores Hume's role in the development of the peace process, suggesting that Reid, Adams and, interestingly, Charles Haughey were the key figures in this. Whilst Reid and Adams were undoubtedly crucial to the politicisation of the Provisional movement, the present study aims to show that it was Hume, far more than Haughey, who helped to facilitate republicans' entry into the democratic mainstream. This interpretation is confirmed by Adams's account, which notes that he and Reid were engaging with Hume some time before Reid held talks with Haughey, and suggests that the latter discussions were of far less significance (Adams, *Hope and History*, pp. 40–8). However, apart from this, it is difficult to challenge Moloney's extraordinary account, as it draws on a number of undisclosed and therefore unfalsifiable sources.

8   Mallie and McKittrick, *The Fight for Peace*, pp. 67–8.

9   Adams, *Hope and History*, pp. 34, 36–42.

10 On an abortive effort to speak directly with the IRA leadership in 1985, see Routledge, *John Hume*, pp. 207–9.

11 Drower, *John Hume*, p. 133; Adams, *Hope and History*, pp. 42–3; T. Hennessy, *The Northern Ireland Peace Process: Ending the Troubles?* (Dublin: Gill and Macmillan), pp. 39–40.

12 Adams, *Hope and History* pp. 43, 57; Routledge, *John Hume*, p. 218.

13 *Guardian*, 21 January 1986.

14 Dublin had hoped that the outworking of the AIA would produce radical reform in Northern Ireland – particularly in the crucial areas of security policy,

policing, and the administration of justice – and that this would help erode support for Sinn Féin. However, given the strength of the unionist reaction to the accord, it seemed that London wanted to limit or at least to play down the reforms which flowed from the AIA, this so as not to further antagonise the Protestant community. As a result, FitzGerald suggests that even those changes that were achieved through the AIA were not fully appreciated by the minority, and thus did not radically change voting patterns within the community; FitzGerald, *All in a Life*, pp. 572–5. Also see O'Kane, *Britain, Ireland and Northern Ireland*, pp. 78–9, 90–1, on this.

15 Bew, Patterson and Teague, *Between War and Peace*, p. 73.
16 Mallie and McKittrick, *The Fight for Peace*, p. 180.
17 Hume also stressed the importance of this document in later years: 'The basic principles of that first letter remain central to … the peace process to date'; Hume, *A New Ireland*, p. 115.
18 LHL, NIPC, P3395, letter from Hume to Gerry Adams, 17 March 1988, pp. 1–2.
19 *Ibid.*, pp. 2–3.
20 *Ibid.*, p. 3; emphasis in original.
21 Sinn Féin, *A Scenario for Peace* (Belfast: Sinn Féin, 1987), pp. 2–3.
22 LHL, NIPC, P3395, letter from Hume to Adams, 17 March 1988, p. 3; emphasis in original.
23 *Ibid.*, p. 4.
24 *Ibid.*
25 LHL, NIPC, P3394, Sinn Féin, 'Towards a strategy for peace', 14 March 1988, p. 3.
26 *Ibid.*, pp. 7–10.
27 *Ibid.*, p. 12.
28 LHL, NIPC, P3395, SDLP, 'Response to questions raised in discussion and previous Sinn Féin papers', 11 July 1988, p. 7; emphasis in original.
29 See LHL, NIPC, P3394, and in particular the opening to Sinn Féin's third written contribution to the talks, 'Persuading the British – a joint call', June 1988.
30 LHL, NIPC, P3395, SDLP, 'Response to questions raised in discussion and previous Sinn Féin papers', 11 July 1988, p. 5.
31 Coogan, *The Troubles*, p. 395; Murray, *John Hume and the SDLP*, p. 197; Routledge, *John Hume*, pp. 216–17.
32 Adams, *Hope and History*, pp. 47–8.
33 See O'Brien, *The Arms Trial*.
34 Adams, *Hope and History*, p. 80.
35 Mallie and McKittrick, *The Fight for Peace*, pp. 85–90; M. Mansergh, 'Mountain climbing Irish-style: the hidden challenges of the peace process', in M. Elliott (ed.), *The Long Road to Peace in Northern Ireland* (Liverpool: Liverpool University Press, 2002), p. 110. For a more considered reading of these early contacts between Sinn Féin and Fianna Fáil, see C. O'Donnell, 'Fianna Fáil and Sinn Féin: the 1988 talks reappraised', *Irish Political Studies*, 18:2 (2003).
36 Mallie and McKittrick, *Endgame*, p. 80. However, it should be said that Reid acted only after sounding out Adams and other senior republicans, a number of whom were already talking of such an 'alternative method'. Reid clearly encouraged such thoughts; Adams, *Hope and History*, pp. 29, 36; Coogan, *The Troubles*, pp. 389–90.
37 Cited in Adams, *Hope and History*, p. 42.

38 Adams, *Hope and History*, pp. 34, 36.

39 LHL, NIPC, P3395, letter from Hume to Gerry Adams, 17 March 1988, p. 5.

40 Clearly, this was part of a deal which Dublin offered to republicans in an effort to secure a ceasefire, for the commitment to hold such conference was evident in the precursory Downing Street Declaration of December 1993. John Major suggests that Albert Reynolds was adamant about including this commitment in the Declaration, this despite unionists' particular opposition to the idea (J. Major, *The Autobiography* (London: HarperCollins, 1999), pp. 452, 453). This suggests the importance which republicans came to attach to such an initiative, and it seems that its origins can be traced back to the proposal made by Hume in 1988.

41 Mallie and McKittrick, *The Fight for Peace*, p. 90; M. Mansergh 'The background to the Irish peace process', in M. Cox, A. Guelke and F. Stephen (eds), *A Farewell to Arms?: From 'Long War' to Long Peace in Northern Ireland* (Manchester: Manchester University Press, 2000), p. 17.

42 Cochrane, *Unionist Politics*, pp. 305, 306, 321.

43 Jackson, *Home Rule*, pp. 381–2.

44 Hume, 'The Irish question', p. 306.

45 Denis Haughey; interview with author, Cookstown, 30 July 2004.

46 J. Hume, 'A New Ireland in a new Europe', in Keogh and Haltzel (eds) *Northern Ireland*, p. 228.

47 Hume, *A New Ireland*, p. 115.

48 Mallie and McKittrick, *The Fight for Peace*, pp. 96, 104; Routledge, *John Hume*, pp. 218, 233.

49 Mallie and McKittrick, *Endgame*, p. 153. Moloney maintains that, working through Reid, Adams was in contact with the British government from as early as 1986. However, even in his own account of this dialogue, Maloney appears to accept that it was agents from British intelligence, rather than governmental ministers, that responded to any correspondence from Adams (Moloney, *A Secret History of the IRA*, pp. 246–59). The channel sanctioned by Brooke was clearly of a different order, as it showed that the British government rather then just its intelligence agencies was now interested in what was happening within republicanism.

50 Adams, *Hope and History*, p. 97.

51 *Irish Times*, 10 November 1990. The subsequent quotations from Brooke's speech are all drawn from the same source.

52 See above, p. 141. In particular, note Hume's description of the AIA as 'an internationally-binding agreement', something which Brooke was also remarkably keen to emphasise.

53 See above, p. 141.

54 Mallie and McKittrick, *Endgame*, p. 83; Mallie and McKittrick, *The Fight for Peace*, p. 108; Routledge, *John Hume*, p. 234. Moloney suggests that Hume persuaded Tom King to make a similar statement regarding British interests in Northern Ireland, but that this was sent as a private message to Adams (Moloney, *A Secret History of the IRA*, pp. 254–5). Brooke's very public declaration obviously had far greater significance than King's clandestine communication.

9

Two balls of roasted snow

As well as the disavowal of any selfish British interest in Northern Ireland, the other major development during Peter Brooke's time as Secretary of State was his success in bringing together the local parties for their first formal talks in a over a decade. This only became possible after unionists accepted that their campaign of opposition against the AIA had come to naught. Despite vehement protests from the Protestant community – and indeed, despite her own misgivings over the results of the accord[1] – Thatcher would not renege on the Agreement which she signed.[2] Meanwhile, in the working of its institutions, Anglo-Irish co-operation over Northern Ireland – though not without its difficulties – steadily improved.[3] By the late 1980s, unionist politicians had accepted that the only way to check the Dublin government's increasing influence in Northern Ireland was to negotiate with the SDLP, and to find new political structures through which the two communities could share power in the region.[4] In this, it can be argued that McGarry's and O'Leary's thesis of 'coercive consociationalism' was borne out, albeit not in the time-frame, nor in quite the manner, that the architects of the AIA might have imagined.

When the Northern Ireland parties did finally sit down together in June 1991, their discussions were organised on the basis of what was known as 'the three strands'. The use of the three strands schema suggested the influence of the SDLP, which still refused to take part in negotiations geared towards an internal settlement of the Northern Ireland problem. Instead, the party had argued that talks should address political relations at three levels: between the two communities in Northern Ireland; between the North and South of Ireland; and between Britain and Ireland. This evoked an approach which was first suggested in SDLP discussion papers in the early 1970s,[5] but which had become a more prominent part of the party's public discourse in the aftermath of the AIA.[6] At the SDLP's insistence, Brooke accepted that talks should proceed on this basis,[7] telling the House of Commons that 'discussions must focus on the three main relationships: those in Northern Ireland ... among the people of the island of Ireland; and between the governments'.[8] The influence of the SDLP – even in the terms which Brooke chose to use here – suggested the party's strengthened position in the aftermath of the AIA. Having established a significant Irish dimension in the 1985 accord, Hume and his colleagues did not feel obliged to surrender this in return for power-sharing in a purely internal constitutional arrangement. Instead, they saw the AIA as a base-line from which to negotiate a more comprehensive settlement of the Northern Ireland problem.[9] Accordingly, Hume would talk of 'transcending' rather than replacing the AIA.[10] Evidently, he had in mind some form of agreement that would give nationalists a role in the administration of Northern Ireland, but still involve the Irish government.

Unionists, on the other hand, were only beginning to accept the inevitability of sharing power with the SDLP; they had yet to face the reality that Dublin would retain a role in Northern Ireland. This partly explains the limited progress of the Brooke talks: unionists were still finding difficulties in engaging with the Irish dimension. Nonetheless, Brooke's successor as Northern Ireland Secretary, Patrick Mayhew, began a fresh round of discussions in April 1992, these organised on the same three-strand basis as the previous talks. This time round, some progress was achieved. Indeed, unionists participated in Strand Two of the talks – those concerning relationships between the North and South of Ireland – and, for the first time since Sunningdale, even entered into discussions with Dublin ministers. However, now the SDLP began to prove difficult, submitting proposals to the talks which outlined a most elaborate scheme of government for Northern Ireland. This involved a six-person executive comprised of three locally elected members, one representative each from the British and Irish governments, and also one from the European Commission.[11] Unionists naturally rejected such ideas, but London also appeared unimpressed at what were seen as overly ambitious, and indeed highly impractical, proposals. Hume, however, stood firmly behind the SDLP's submission, and it is for this reason that he took much of the blame, particularly from unionist commentators, for the breakdown of negotiations.[12]

So ambitious were the SDLP's proposals at the Mayhew talks that there is some question about how realistic the party was being in tabling them. At the time, there was even a suggestion that the SDLP, and in particular Hume, was not as interested in these talks as might previously have been the case.[13] Such indifference was considered all the more surprising because it came at time when unionist politicians, after years of obstruction, were starting to show signs of genuine flexibility. Much to the annoyance of the British government, it seemed that the roles of the SDLP and the unionist parties had suddenly reversed. But if Hume was less than focused on these discussions, the possible reason – more obvious with the benefit of hindsight – is that he had his eye on a bigger prize. For at the same time as the Mayhew talks, Hume was still involved in secret discussions with Gerry Adams, these aimed at bringing an end to the IRA's campaign of violence, and drawing republicans into the political process.

'Hume–Adams'

As early as the Brooke talks of 1991, Hume had begun to question the idea that a workable political agreement could be achieved under the conditions then prevailing. Whilst unionists were still debating the modalities of the talks, outside of the process, the IRA showed an undiminished capacity for violence, and its political counterpart continued to speak for a significant section of Catholic opinion. As a result, Hume concluded that a new settlement could not be created or sustained without republican involvement. However, more positively, Hume believed that such a prospect was becoming less fanciful. Indeed, his ongoing talks with Adams convinced Hume that thinking within republicanism was continuing to shift.[14] In particular, he was encouraged by the impact which the Brooke statement of November 1990 had made within republican circles.[15] For Brooke's declaration appeared to vindicate many of the arguments which Hume had put to Sinn Féin two years earlier. Most notably, Brooke's assertion that the British government had 'no selfish strategic or economic interest in Northern Ireland' seemed to confirm Hume's interpretation of London's position and the possibility of a united Ireland achieved by peaceful means. British intentions, he could argue, should now be tested by an IRA ceasefire.

Of course, to achieve this end, Hume knew that he needed more than the words of one British minister. For though the republican leadership was certainly interested in what Brooke had said, the movement's rank and file would need something more substantial if it was to be convinced that there was a genuine alternative to the armed struggle.[16] Accordingly, following the collapse of the Brooke talks in the autumn of 1991, Hume began to focus again on efforts to persuade republicans that such an alternative did exist. In doing so, he returned to the papers which his party had received from Sinn Féin during the 1988 talks. Drawing on these, Hume drafted a new document, 'A Strategy for Peace and Justice in Ireland'.[17] His thinking was that this paper would provide the basis for a joint British–Irish declaration, outlining each government's position on Northern Ireland, and the means by which the conflict might be resolved.[18]

Two aspects of Hume's document were of particular importance. Firstly, he wanted the British government to restate that 'they no longer have any selfish political or strategic interest in remaining in Ireland'.[19] Hume hoped that a formal declaration of this position – made at the highest level of the British government – would finally convince republicans that London was essentially neutral on the future of Northern Ireland, and thus remove their rationale for armed struggle. The second point of note in Hume's paper was the way he dealt with the issue of Irish self-determination. For this, too, was a subject of great import for republicans. Indeed, alongside the debate over British interests in Northern Ireland, it had been the main point of discussion during the SDLP–Sinn Féin talks of 1988.[20]

In the 1988 talks, Hume had accepted the principle of Irish self-determination, but suggested that the people of Ireland were divided over the means to its expression. Resolving the problem, he had argued, would involve a search for agreement between the people of Ireland on this crucial issue.[21] Sinn Féin, however, had problems with this approach. For Adams and his colleagues, accepting the need for unionist agreement, without conditions, meant accepting the 'loyalist veto'.[22] Unless the British government recognised the whole of Ireland as the legitimate unit for the exercise of Irish self-determination, then unionists – with their 'artificial' majority in Northern Ireland – could still deny northern nationalists their rights in this regard.

In the draft document, which he produced in autumn 1991, Hume returned to this debate. In doing so, he took the first tentative steps in an effort to bridge the gap between republicans' belief in the whole of Ireland as the appropriate unit for the exercise of self-determination, and his own emphasis on the need for unionist consent for any such act. Hume did this by making a case for what he termed 'agreed self-determination'.[23] Like his concept of an 'agreed Ireland',[24] this would involve a settlement which encompassed the whole of the island, but create institutions which had the assent of both political traditions.[25] Through a process of negotiation, Irish nationalists and Ulster unionists would jointly determine the political structures under which they would live. This, therefore, was the ultimate purpose of Hume's declaration initiative: to make the British and Irish governments co-sponsors of a process that would lead to 'agreed self-determination' in Ireland.

Of course, the ideas that Hume was considering here were still in gestation. However, over the course of the next two years, they inspired a series of intense and intricate negotiations, firstly between himself, republicans and the Irish government, and subsequently between Dublin and London, with some input from unionist and loyalist representatives. The final outcome of this was the Joint Declaration for Peace – or the Downing Street Declaration (DSD) as it is more commonly known – made by the British and Irish governments in December 1993. This included key elements of the draft document which Hume had produced in autumn 1991, albeit developed and modified by various actors, most notably officials from the two governments. There is not room here to detail the clandestine and convoluted process by which this occurred, and any account is bound to prove unsatisfactory: so many different actors contributed to this process – and so many different drafts and redrafts were exchanged between these actors – that it is impossible to say with any certainty who is responsible for what in the final product.[26] Despite this, it is worth considering the part which Hume and Adams played in creating the essential dynamic towards the DSD.

The first the public knew that the two were still in dialogue was in April 1993, when Adams was spotted going into Hume's house in Derry. From here on, media interest played a huge part in propelling what was hitherto a highly secretive enterprise involving Hume, republicans and the Irish government. At present, the public knew nothing of the latter's role, but even the idea that Hume and Adams were in discussion caused a media frenzy. In response, the two leaders decided to issue a joint statement, attempting to explain the purpose of their talks, and trying to quell the speculation surrounding them.

This statement, and the talks from which it emanated, were dubbed by the media as the 'Hume–Adams initiative', or more simply, 'Hume–Adams'. However, a number of commentators were critical of the initiative, suggesting that the discussions saw Hume surrendering ground to Adams.[27] In particular, there was concern over Hume's engagement during these talks with the subject of self-determination. For many, this was, by definition, a republican concept and, by considering it in an all-Ireland context, it was felt that Hume was moving towards a republican interpretation of the problem.[28] For this reason, Conor Cruise O'Brien – a long-standing critic of Hume, and a leading commentator in the Irish media in early 1990s – insisted on calling the initiative 'Adams–Hume' rather than 'Hume–Adams'. His appellation, O'Brien suggested, better described who was the 'predominant partner' in the talks.[29]

O'Brien's chief concern was with a line in the first Hume–Adams statement of April 1993: 'We accept that the Irish people as a whole have a right to national self-determination.'[30] To O'Brien, this single sentence amounted to 'a declaration of war against unionists, and against the existence of Northern Ireland. ... This formula represents what has *always been the policy of Sinn Féin-IRA*. It is the classic republican formula ... Hume simply signed the dotted line.'[31] However, this reading of the statement overlooks the movement which Adams, in turn, was making towards Hume's perspective, which emphasised the need to find agreement on the means by which Irish self-determination could be exercised. For the statement continued: 'The exercise of self-determination is a matter for agreement between the people of Ireland. It is the search for that agreement and the means of achieving it on which we will be concentrating ... We both recognise that such a new agreement is only achievable and viable if it can earn and enjoy the allegiance of the different traditions on this island.'[32] Of course, there is no explicit recognition here of the need for the consent of a majority in Northern Ireland in order to bring about constitutional change. Indeed, as O'Brien himself noted,[33] any such move by Adams at this early stage of the peace process would have brought an immediate end to his leadership of the republican movement. But it is clear that Hume was gently nudging Adams in this direction. He was steering Adams towards his idea of 'agreed self-determination', an exercise which required the assent of Ulster unionists.

'Hume–Adams', however, was only the public face of a complex political process that involved a variety of actors. Most notably – but unknown

to most contemporary commentators – this process already involved the
Irish and even the British government. Indeed, directly after Hume produced his first draft of a possible joint declaration in autumn 1991, he had
brought it to Dublin. Henceforth, he worked in collaboration with Irish
officials to amend and redraft various versions of a potential statement to
be made by the two governments.[34] Via Hume, these documents were
being passed on to Adams, but by this stage the Irish government had itself
began to re-engage with the republican movement through Fr Alec Reid.
In addition, from early 1992, versions of these texts were being sent to
London,[35] which was also communicating with republicans through the
intelligence channel opened by Brooke in 1990. However, despite this
complex network of clandestine activity, there was no visible movement
towards a joint declaration by the two governments.

The main reason for the delay was British reluctance to endorse the initiative. Firstly, John Major's government found it hard to believe that the
republican movement was interested in peace. This was understandable,
especially as the IRA was, at precisely this time, increasing the scale of its
attacks on British towns and cities.[36] In addition, Major had serious misgivings about the documents which he was receiving from Dublin and,
through the NIO, from Hume: 'They were utterly one-sided, so heavily
skewed towards the presumption of a united Ireland that they had no
merit as a basis for negotiation.'[37] Cleary, on the Irish side of the initiative,
the possibility of an IRA ceasefire was obscuring all other considerations,
and particularly the lengths to which London could go in any declaration.
However, it is also possible that developments at Westminster were limit-
ing Major's room for manoeuvre. With a diminishing parliamentary
majority, Tory rebels were causing considerable difficulties over the government's European policy, and in July 1993, Major was forced to rely on
the support of Ulster Unionist MPs in a vote of confidence relating to the
Maastricht Treaty.[38]

Observing such developments, Hume became increasingly frustrated. He
felt that the situation at Westminster was preventing Major from acting on
the declaration initiative, and that this would undo the patient work which
he and the Dublin government had made towards achieving an IRA ceasefire. Accordingly, in mid-September, Hume travelled to London in order to
speak to Major directly, and to impress upon him the opportunity for
peace which he perceived to be within reach. However, Hume emerged
from 10 Downing Street seemingly in a state of even greater frustration.
Thus, when waiting reporters mentioned the growing criticism of his talks
with Adams, Hume brusquely responded by saying that he did not give
'two balls of roasted snow' for those questioning his judgement.[39]

Despite his effort to move the process forward, the British government
still seemed unwilling to act. As a result, by the end of September, Hume
was persuaded by Adams to issue another joint statement.[40] In this, the
two leaders suggested that they had made considerable progress in their

discussions, and intended to forward a report of their position to the Irish government for its consideration.[41] This was disingenuous: Dublin was already well aware of the state of play between Hume and Adams.[42] What the two were doing here was making the public aware that a serious initiative was in hand. The idea in this was to mobilise popular opinion,[43] thus pressing the Irish and in turn the British government to deliver a joint statement. However, whilst this may have worked in nationalist Ireland, the reaction was not the same in Britain, or amongst the unionist community. Indeed, Adams's public association with the process made it far more difficult for Major to endorse[44] – especially at a time when he was experiencing problems with the Tory right and, as a consequence, relying on Unionist support at Westminster. Accordingly, as Eamonn O'Kane has suggested, although the Hume–Adams dialogue provided the essential motivation for the initiative, ironically, it now became an obstacle to efforts to produce a joint declaration by the two governments.[45]

To make matters worse, an extremely vicious cycle of violence now broke out in Northern Ireland, making October 1993 one of the bloodiest months in the whole of the Troubles. In one attack on the Shankill Road, the IRA claimed to have missed its intended target – a meeting of loyalist paramilitary leaders – when a bomb killed nine Protestant civilians. One of the IRA men involved, Thomas Begley, also died in the explosion, and at his funeral Adams took his turn in carrying the coffin. Although it was standard practice for the Sinn Féin leader to play such a part at republican funerals, this was seen in the unionist community and in the British media as a cruel endorsement of an overtly sectarian act of violence. Now it seemed impossible that Major could make a declaration that was seen as being any way related to Adams. As if to reinforce this point, a few days later, when opposition MPs at Westminster suggested that the government should engage with republicans, Major's response was unequivocal: 'If the implication ... is that we should sit down and talk with Mr Adams and the Provisional IRA, I can only say that that would turn my stomach ... we will not do it'.[46]

Increasingly desperate, Hume again travelled to Downing Street, pleading with Major to take up the joint declaration initiative, and telling the assembled media that there would be 'peace within the next week' if he did so.[47] However, by this stage, the British government appeared to have abandoned the idea that the republican movement could be enticed into a democratic process, and Major now sent an entirely new proposal to Dublin. Although this was also premised on the idea of a joint declaration, Irish officials were dismayed to find that it offered nothing of substance to republicans. Instead, the new British document was aimed at re-launching the talks process between Northern Ireland's constitutional parities.[48]

Hume was shattered. His long and arduous efforts to achieve an IRA ceasefire seemed to have come to naught. In the course of these efforts, he had faced fierce criticism.[49] Particularly in recent months, as the death toll multiplied, Hume had come under increasing pressure over his ongoing talks with Adams. With the Shankill bombing, and Adams's carrying of Begley's coffin, the Sinn Féin leader was vilified, but Hume, by association, was also condemned. Moreover, it was not just unionists and British commentators who castigated the SDLP leader. By this stage, the Dublin government also began to distance itself from Hume, and sections of the Irish media seized the opportunity to attack a politician who commanded enormous respect among people in the Republic.[50] The abuse took its toll: in early November, Hume collapsed and was hospitalised.[51] Both he and his initiative with Adams appeared to be finished,[52] but there was to be one more twist in the tale.

Hume's decision to release another statement with Adams in September 1993 has been rightly questioned. If the British government had subsequently moved on the joint declaration initiative, it would have been seen as working to a nationalist or even republican agenda. Major would have had serious difficulties selling this to his own party, but certainly could not bring Ulster unionists along with such a move. Hume was surely aware of this. However, his decision on the September statement was made after he was informed of the secret intelligence channel through which the British government had been communicating with republicans. One of the individuals involved in this channel – a former priest based in Derry – told Hume of its existence because he felt that the British government was ignoring an offer of a temporary ceasefire which the IRA, through the channel, had already made to London. Hume chose not to publicise this information, but knowing that the British government was talking to republicans – and now aware that Major also knew an IRA ceasefire was possible – he felt obliged to put some pressure on London.[53]

However, it was not the September statement, but rather the public disclosure of the back channel two months later, that finally forced the British government to act. Rumours that London had been talking to republicans began to build in early November, but the government flatly denied these suggestions. On one such occasion, a DUP delegation had met Major at Downing Street, and was specifically assured that the government was not talking to the IRA.[54] As such, when the *Observer* ran a full story on the back channel a few days later,[55] Major found himself in an extremely difficult situation. In particular, there was concern over the suggestion that a meeting between republicans and a government agent had taken place only days after the Warrington bombing of March 1993[56] – an attack which killed two children, and caused public outrage in Britain and Ireland. Such revelations were made worse by the fact that, only weeks before the publication of the *Observer exposé*, Major had told the Commons that it would turn his stomach to talk to republicans. The validity of this statement was now called into question: representatives of his government had been communicating with the republican movement, and over a sustained and particularly violent period.[57]

Arguably, the only way to justify these contacts was to show that London's sole intention had been to secure an IRA ceasefire. The best way to prove this, of course, was to make a public declaration of the government's position, and one which openly appealed to republicans to pursue a peaceful path. Previously, Major had feared the effect that such a declaration would have on Protestant opinion, particularly whilst he was relying on votes from the UUP in the Commons. But now it was likely that unionists were more concerned for what the government had been saying to republicans behind closed doors. It suddenly seemed wiser for London to speak to Sinn Féin in an open manner, and to hope that this would reassure unionists that the government had no other motive than to end IRA violence.

Also crucial was the way that the *Observer* report was received in Dublin. Here, the Taoiseach, Albert Reynolds, had come under enormous pressure – from the general public, and from his own party – over his handling of the joint declaration initiative. At Major's insistence, Reynolds had distanced himself from the statements made by Hume and Adams,[58] being told that any association with the latter made the initiative unworkable. Now, much to his surprise, Reynolds discovered that the British government was itself in dialogue with Sinn Féin, and had been for some time. Having been largely forthcoming about their own contacts with the republican movement, Reynolds and his officials felt badly let down by their British counterparts. This sense of indignation naturally bolstered Reynolds's resistance against Major's idea of a joint declaration aimed at restarting inter-party talks. The Taoiseach now insisted that the two governments return to the original proposal of a joint statement directed primarily towards republicans.[59]

The Downing Street Declaration

The DSD was not a direct product of the discussions that took place between Hume and Adams from the mid-1980s to the early 1990s. However, it was heavily influenced by the terms of this dialogue. Also, thanks largely to the Irish government – and in particular the persuasive powers of Reynolds[60] – the DSD was directed towards the same end as the Hume–Adams talks, namely an IRA ceasefire, this as a precursor to fully inclusive negotiations on a new political settlement for Northern Ireland.[61] Of course, though it was based upon an Irish draft, the declaration was significantly altered by British officials, this to produce a document that could win, if not the support, then at least the acquiescence of Ulster unionists. But even in this, Dublin played a crucial role. Reynolds used his own contacts amongst the unionist community, and written inputs from Protestant clergymen, to balance the later texts which his government produced. He also used these contributions to counter British claims that a statement appealing to republicans could not simultaneously carry unionist support.[62]

As a result, green and orange were mixed in way which, somehow, did not produce a lurid mess, but rather an exquisitely ambivalent piece of political craftsmanship.

The DSD, therefore, was the result of many hands' work. However, two key elements in the text can be traced back to the first draft declaration which Hume produced in the autumn of 1991.[63] Firstly, as suggested in Hume's document, the DSD saw the British government repeat the Brooke statement of November 1990, with a formal declaration that it had 'no selfish strategic or economic interests in Northern Ireland'.[64] This served to confirm the argument which Hume had been making to republicans since the AIA of 1985, namely that London was essentially neutral on the future of Northern Ireland, and thus presented no obstacle to a united Ireland achieved by peaceful means. Secondly, again following Hume's first draft, the DSD addressed the issue of Irish self-determination. In doing so, the British government made significant movement towards Hume's idea of 'agreed self-determination'– an exercise involving the whole of Ireland, but achieved through a process of negotiation between the two political traditions on the island, nationalist and unionist. However, in the particular formula used in the DSD, the British government gave much greater weight to the principle of consent than had been the case in Hume's or any Irish version of the proposed declaration.[65] This resulted in a convoluted but crucial statement on Irish self-determination: London acknowledged the nationalist right to pursue a united Ireland, but carefully balanced this with a recognition of the need for majority consent in Northern Ireland as a precondition to this or indeed any other constitutional change:

> The British Government agree that it is for the people of Ireland alone, by agreement between the two parts respectively, to exercise their right of self-determination on the basis of consent, freely and concurrently given, North and South, to bring about a united Ireland, if that is their wish. They reaffirm ... that they will, for their part, introduce the necessary legislation to give effect to this, or equally any measure of agreement on future relationships in Ireland which the people living in Ireland may themselves freely so determine without external impediment.[66]

Also important here was the emphasis that it was 'the people of Ireland alone' who should decide the institutions under which they would live, and that they should do so 'without external impediment'. This dealt with the republican claim that the exercise of Irish self-determination was being prevented by outside interference, namely the British government in its upholding of partition. By recognising that the people of Ireland, by agreement, had the right to undo partition, the DSD supported a revisionist nationalist interpretation. It suggested that the continuation of partition was not a product of British designs, but Irish divisions, the implication being that it could only be ended by first addressing these divisions. Again, this served to underscore the arguments which Hume had been trying to persuade republicans of since the mid-1980s. The British government was declaring that it represented no obstacle to the achievement of a united Ireland, and therefore the way towards this end was to persuade Ulster unionists to embrace it. The DSD thus suggested the viability of a revisionist approach to Irish unity.

However, from a nationalist and, more particularly, a republican perspective, there was a crucial omission from the DSD. In its talks with the SDLP in 1988, Sinn Féin had suggested that the ultimate proof of Hume's assertions of British neutrality would be shown in a commitment by London to join in efforts to convince unionists that their future lay in a united Ireland.[67] Hereafter, republicans had increasingly referred to the potential role of a British government acting as a 'persuaders' for Irish unity.[68] In some respects, this might be seen as movement towards the revisionist nationalist thesis; implicit in republican statements in this period was a recognition that it was unionist attitudes rather than British interests which represented the chief obstacle to Irish reunification. As such, this seeming evolution in republican thinking had been encouraged by both Hume and the Irish government.[69] However, in their eagerness to draw Sinn Féin into the political process, Hume and Dublin might be seen as being either ingenuous or perhaps disingenuous: each overstated the role which the British government might play in advancing a nationalist agenda.

For London to say that it would encourage unionists to join a united Ireland would blur the distinction between consent and compulsion. It would suggest that the British government no longer wished Ulster Protestants to be part of the United Kingdom, and was, ultimately, intent on their removal. As such, to take up the role of persuaders for a united Ireland would not be greatly different to accepting the traditional republican demand for a British declaration of intent to withdraw from Northern Ireland. Moreover, it would likely produce the same destabilising effect on the region. In the DSD, therefore, the British government studiously avoided any commitment to becoming persuaders for Irish unity.[70] Instead, Major said that he wished 'to see peace, stability and reconciliation established by agreement among all the people who inhabit the island', and promised to 'work with the Irish Government to achieve such an agreement'. London thus accepted a part, not promoting Irish unity, but supporting whatever agreement was arrived at through a process of negotiation and consent between the peoples of Ireland: 'The role of the British Government will be to encourage, facilitate, and enable the achievement of such an agreement ... based on full respect for the rights and identities of both traditions in Ireland.'[71]

In this, however, the British government endorsed a model consistent with Hume's notion of an 'agreed Ireland'. Indeed, even Bew and Patterson – formerly scathing critics of this schema[72] – accepted that the idea of an agreed Ireland provided the essential template for solution as adopted by London in the DSD.[73] As such, the declaration saw both governments taking up the positions which Hume and the SDLP had advocated since the late 1970s, acting as joint sponsors of a process of constitutional negotiation, leading to an agreed settlement between the two traditions on the island of Ireland.

Whilst Hume and his party colleagues could, therefore, see much of their own thinking in the text, there remained a concern that the DSD would fail to secure its essential objective: an IRA ceasefire. Without a British commitment to become persuaders for a united Ireland, there was a question as to whether republicans would accept the document. As such, Hume now found himself acting as persuader for the DSD, hoping to convince republicans that it offered the basis for peaceful progress. In a private letter to Adams, he made clear his own position:

> I believe that the Downing Street Declaration contains the substance of the proposed joint declaration that arose from our dialogue ... [It] contains a clear affirmation of what our June document[74] asked the British government to say in relation to its own interests ... [and] accepts the fundamental principles that we proposed to them privately and publicly ... Is whatever difference there is between our June document and the joint Declaration, and I see no difference in substance, worth the cost of a single human life?[75]

In public, too, Hume made his case for the DSD, emphasising those key points which republicans had challenged him to prove, and which he had included in his first draft of a potential joint statement: 'the British government makes clear, not only that it has no longer any selfish, strategic or economic interests in Ireland, but that it is for the people of Ireland alone, North and South, to come to agreement, and that the British government is committed, not only to promoting such agreement, but to legislating for whatever its outcome. Clear self-determination!' Accordingly, Hume called on the IRA to recognise the potential that now existed for a peaceful political strategy, one which would allow republicans to join forces with the other proponents of Irish nationalism, and to push for a just solution to the Northern Ireland conflict:

> They [republicans] cannot be unaware of the mass movement and strength of the Irish at home and abroad that the peace process has created and that strength will achieve more than any guns or bombs ... For the first time in 70 years the energies and talents of all Irish people at home and abroad, including the enormous political clout of our friends in the US and Europe, would be united and at our disposal.[76]

However, in these comments, Hume was belying the efforts which he and other actors had already made to demonstrate to republicans the power of Irish nationalism working in a peaceful consensus.

America's new Irish agenda

As seen in Chapter 6, since the 1970s, Hume had made a conscious effort to engage Irish-America with the Northern Ireland problem. With the help of senior Democratic politicians such as Ted Kennedy and Tip O'Neill, he sought to counter Irish-American support for the IRA, and to articulate the constitutional nationalist case in the US. After the Irish government joined his efforts, Hume found that he was also able to influence the White House, and in turn to pressure the British government into adopting a more progressive policy on Northern Ireland. This strategy had produced great political dividends, adding to the momentum which produced the AIA of 1985.[77]

However, since that time, a new political lobby had emerged in Irish-America. 'This group', John Dumbrell stressed, 'was not merely an out-growth of the Hume-Kennedy network.'[78] Indeed, the 'Americans for a New Irish Agenda' (ANIA) were supportive of Sinn Féin rather than the SDLP. In particular, they wished to aid republicans' burgeoning 'peace strategy'.[79] In this respect, the ANIA did have the same ultimate end as Hume. However, the group provided Sinn Féin with its own credentials in Washington: the ANIA included well-respected Irish-American activists, a number of them leading members of the US business community. Also, the group had links to Bill Clinton, and had been making efforts to engage him on the issue of Northern Ireland from the moment that he won the Democratic nomination for the White House.[80]

The ANIA pushed one idea in particular: that Adams be given a visa allowing him to visit the US. The ANIA felt that giving Adams access to the US would enhance his credibility as a politician. This, it was argued, would bolster the efforts which he appeared to be making to draw the republican movement away from the armed struggle. However, the ANIA's influence over the Clinton administration was shown to have clear limitations. Twice in 1993, Adams applied for an American visa, and twice he was denied.[81] Behind the scenes, both Hume and the Irish government were advising the White House that it was too early to make any significant move on Northern Ireland. In particular, Dublin was concerned not to offend British opinion whilst it was still in the delicate process of negotiating what would become the DSD.[82]

After the DSD, however, the situation changed dramatically. Now Hume and the Irish government felt that an American visa for Adams might help him to convince the republican rank and file that a political approach was a viable option. Indeed, London's opposition to such a concession might even aid the effect, suggesting that American policy on Northern Ireland was no longer determined by British sensibilities, and that Washington would, therefore, support Irish nationalists' efforts to achieve a just political settlement. Accordingly, Hume and Reynolds began to make the case to the Clinton administration that the time was now right to allow Adams a visa. Of course, their task was made much easier by the fact that Clinton had appointed Ted Kennedy's sister, Jean Kennedy-Smith, as American Ambassador to Ireland. Once she was won over, Kennedy-Smith brought the idea to the attention of her brother. Ted Kennedy was interested, but first wanted to discuss the matter directly with Hume. After doing so, he was convinced, and so began to use his considerable influence on the visa issue.[83] Despite this, significant sections of the American government – the State Department, the Justice Department, and the CIA – all remained steadfastly opposed.[84] The State Department in particular was fearful of the damage that might be done to relations with America's closest ally, the UK, which strongly objected to the idea of Adams gaining entry to the US in advance of an IRA ceasefire.

Within the White House itself, however, Hume had the ear of members of Clinton's own staff, and in particular that of Nancy Soderburg, a senior member of the National Security Council. Having previously worked in Ted Kennedy's office, Soderburg had come to know Hume and to trust his instinct. 'John Hume played an extraordinarily important role in sensitising me that things on the ground [in Northern Ireland] were changing', she recalled. 'And I remembered very distinctly that he said, "I really think that the IRA is moving towards a ceasefire."'[85] Though Reynolds's role was also crucial, it is clear that Hume's opinion on the state of play within the republican movement was decisive for figures like Soderburg and the Kennedys,[86] figures who in turn could influence Clinton. Even Niall O'Dowd, one of the leading members of the ANIA, who made enormous efforts to promote the visa issue, recognised the latter point: '[Ted] Kennedy was the king on Irish issues on Capitol Hill and every American president would seek his counsel ... In the case of Clinton it was inconceivable that he would act on an Irish issue without checking with Kennedy first.'[87] However, as noted, Kennedy would not act without checking with Hume first, thus giving the SDLP leader a crucial role in the matter. Ultimately, though, the greatest credit must be given to Clinton. At the end of the day, it was the President alone – against the advice of various sections of his government – who made the extremely bold decision to admit Adams to the US on a temporary visa in February 1994.

This represented a crucial breakthrough for Sinn Féin. It seemed to suggest that, in the post-Cold War world, the US would no longer defer to the British government on Northern Ireland. Hume was aware of the impact this would have on republican thinking. He also knew that it would strengthen Adams's hand in making a case for a change in republican strategy, suggesting that the Sinn Féin leader had explained as much during their confidential talks: 'I knew it was central because Adams told me it was central in our dialogue ... I realised that he needed to persuade people. If he didn't get the visa it would have been a very serious setback.'[88]

By aiding Adams's entry to the US – against fierce opposition from London – Hume was seeking to demonstrate to republicans the power of Irish nationalists working together in a wholly peaceful strategy. Hume had learnt how the US could be brought into play with such an approach, with the Carter statement of 1977, and the trans-Atlantic pressure which had helped to produce the AIA in 1985. Now, he hoped to show the republican movement how a similar coalition might again advance the nationalist position, pressing the British government towards real political change in Northern Ireland. Hume, along with the Dublin government and Irish-America, was demonstrating what could be achieved if republicans committed to constitutional methods.

All of this seemed in vain, however, when Sinn Féin appeared to reject the DSD at a specially convened *ard fheis* held in Letterkenny, Co. Donegal, in July 1994. But in retrospect, this conference can be seen as a piece of republican theatre. For the political leadership of the movement was already determined to change strategy. Indeed, before the Letterkenny meeting, a paper had been circulated amongst the republican rank and file, a paper which proposed, and essentially endorsed, an IRA ceasefire.[89]

The 'TUAS document'[90] provided a critical assessment of the republican position in the early 1990s. Underlying the paper was one key argument: 'republicans at this time and on their own do not have the strength to achieve the end goal [of Irish reunification]. The struggle needs strengthening; most obviously from other nationalist constituencies led by the SDLP, Dublin government and the emerging Irish-American lobby.'[91] Implicit in this reasoning was the idea that republicans should suspend the armed struggle in order to join a political alliance with constitutional nationalists in Ireland and the US.[92] However, TUAS recognised one individual as being vital to this shift: 'Hume is the only SDLP person on the horizon strong enough to face the challenge.'[93] This was considerable praise from a movement which once vilified Hume as a 'collaborator' and a 'West Brit'. However, over the years, republicans had come to accept the integrity of Hume's motives. As Adams later suggested: 'given John's stature ... it was just critical and crucial that he stayed the course [in the early peace process] in terms of republicans who just didn't trust politicians ... or who didn't trust the Irish government, who didn't trust the British government ... the fact that John stayed the course was absolutely crucial to persuading people.'[94] In addition, republicans recognised Hume's vital role in creating a nationalist coalition which was strong enough to move the British government. Moreover, they realised that it was only through Hume that they had any hope of steering this coalition towards their own ends. 'We couldn't get the Dublin Government without Hume', said one senior republican, 'and we recognised we couldn't get the American Government without Dublin'.[95]

The TUAS document clearly signalled a significant change in republican strategy. But this was more than purely pragmatic. The paper also showed signs of deeper ideological shifts, however subtle. This was most notable in the final point in a list of 'principles' which the TUAS document offered to provide the basis for a new nationalist consensus. It suggested that the traditional republican objective of a united Ireland was becoming more nuanced: 'An agreed united and independent Ireland is what republicans desire. However, an agreed Ireland needs the allegiance of varied traditions to be viable.'[96] Like the British government in the DSD, republicans in the TUAS document were edging towards Hume's idea of an agreed Ireland. This, contrary to the interpretation of commentators like Conor Cruise O'Brien, suggested that the Hume–Adams dialogue had affected the latter more that the former. Moreover, the impact of this engagement was not limited to the Sinn Féin leader. For here was an IRA document suggesting that unionist support was necessary for any form of all-Ireland constitution. Republicans were inching their way towards acceptance of the principle of consent, the key tenet of revisionist nationalism.

Ceasefires

For the republican movement, the DSD did not go far enough. However, it was considered as a step forward. Thus, after much deliberation, on 31 August 1994, the IRA declared a ceasefire. Of course, this is not to suggest that the DSD was *the* reason for the change in republican strategy. Various factors were involved in this, many of them internal to the Provisional movement, and most predating the 1990s. Indeed, a number of authors have shown how republicans were, from as far back as the 1970s, moving towards a more political approach.[97] Naturally, events such as the hunger strikes of the early 1980s, and the subsequent emergence of Sinn Féin as a credible electoral force, served to galvanise this process. However, arguably the most important factor in producing the IRA ceasefire was the realisation by republicans that, though they could not be defeated, neither could they force the British state from Northern Ireland.[98] By the late 1980s, leading republicans had accepted this reality, and were thinking of ways to move beyond the stalemate. This provided an opportunity, both for those within the Provisional movement who were looking for a more political strategy, and those without, figures like Hume, who saw the value of engaging such elements. Thus, the arguments that Hume was making in this period – and the fact that republicans were prepared even to consider them – must be seen within the context of a more general rethink within the movement, and particularly a questioning of the efficacy of the armed struggle.[99]

This said, it is also clear that Hume, working in conjunction with others in the wider nationalist family, helped to provide republicans with a credible alternative to the armed struggle. Since the 1970s, he had played a crucial role in building a political consensus between constitutional Irish nationalists, both in Ireland and America. By the early 1990s, republicans were seriously considering the gains that could be made by joining this consensus. Indeed, this was the essential rationale behind the TUAS document. In this paper, the Provisional leadership was able to make the case for republicans entering an alliance with constitutional nationalism, the combined power of which would outweigh the potential for progress achieved through the armed struggle. As such, shifts *within* republicanism came first, but these received vital encouragement from outside actors, initially Hume, then the Dublin government, and finally Irish-America. This created a dynamic which ultimately led to the IRA ceasefire of August 1994.

A reciprocal move by loyalists was not immediately forthcoming. For a period, there was suspicion that the republican cessation was the product of a secret deal between the IRA and the British government. However, once they had received assurances that this was not the case, the main loyalist paramilitaries also declared a ceasefire on 13 October 1994.[100] But the fact that the guns had stopped did not of itself make the path to a peace settlement a smooth or an easy one.

Notes

1 Thatcher, *The Downing Street Years*, p. 415.
2 This is something which Hume expressed great admiration for; see the *Observer*, 27 April 1986.
3 See O'Kane, *Britain, Ireland and Northern Ireland*, ch. 4; and O'Leary and McGarry, *The Politics of Antagonism*, ch. 7.
4 On the gradual shifts within unionism in the aftermath of the AIA, see Cochrane, *Unionist Politics*, chs 6–9; and Farrington, *Ulster Unionism*, pp. 74ff.
5 See Murray, *John Hume and the SDLP*, pp. 15–16.
6 For example, consider the terms in which Hume welcomed the AIA in the House of Commons (see above, p. 129), and his article in the *Irish Times*, 13 September 1986.
7 Bew and Gillespie, *Northern Ireland: A Chronology*, pp. 237, 238, 240; O'Leary and McGarry, *The Politics of Antagonism*, p. 313.
8 *Hansard*, sixth series, vol. 188, col. 765, 26 March 1991.
9 O'Leary and McGarry, *The Politics of Antagonism*, pp. 259, 316; Ruane and Todd, *The Dynamics of Conflict*, p. 136.
10 *Irish Times*, 13 January 1989; LHL, NIPC, SDLP Box 3, J. Hume, 'Shaping the Future', address to SDLP annual conference, November 1990.
11 For further detail on this proposal, see below, p. 195.
12 Bew, Gibbon and Patterson, *Northern Ireland, 1921–2001*, p. 213; Bew and Gillespie, *Northern Ireland: A Chronology*, pp. 260, 265, 267–8.
13 Major, *The Autobiography*, p. 439; Mallie and McKittrick, *The Fight for Peace*, pp. 154–5.
14 Mallie and McKittrick, *The Fight for Peace*, p. 117.
15 Adams, *Hope and History*, p. 98.
16 *Ibid.*, pp. 98, 128; Mallie and McKittrick, *Endgame*, p. 103.

17 Mallie and McKittrick, *The Fight for Peace*, pp. 117–20; Routledge, *John Hume*, pp. 237–8.

18 Various accounts have suggested that the idea of a joint declaration actually came from Fr Alec Reid; Adams, *Hope and History*, pp. 105–6; Coogan, *The Troubles*, p. 394; Mallie McKittrick, *The Fight for Peace*, pp. 72, 117–18; Mansergh 'The background to the Irish peace process', p. 17.

19 Cited in Mallie and McKittrick, *The Fight for Peace*, p. 119.

20 See Sinn Féin, *The Sinn Féin/SDLP Talks: January–September 1988* (Dublin: Sinn Féin Publicity Department, 1989), *passim*.

21 LHL, NIPC, P3395, letter from Hume to Gerry Adams, 17 March 1988, p. 3.

22 LHL, NIPC, P3394, Sinn Féin, 'Sinn Féin statement on the present round of Sinn Féin/SDLP talks', 5 September 1988, p. 5.

23 Cited in Mallie and McKittrick, *The Fight for Peace*, p. 119.

24 See above, pp. 84ff. As noted here, when Hume spoke about an agreed Ireland in the late 1970s, he seemed to envisage a settlement which would involve the effective withdrawal of the British state from Northern Ireland. But this reflected a belief amongst significant sections of the SDLP that disengagement from the region was London's real objective in this period. However, as Hume continued to articulate and to develop the concept of an agreed Ireland in the 1980s, it seemed to be much less influenced by the idea of a British withdrawal from Northern Ireland. Again, this may have reflected the perceived intentions of the British government, which under Thatcher showed no signs that it intended to leave Northern Ireland – notwithstanding unionist misconceptions of the AIA. Indeed, with the Falklands conflict of 1982, Thatcher made clear that she would not relinquish British territory even on the other side of world, thus reinforcing views regarding her commitment to the Union with Northern Ireland. This may have influenced Hume's conception of a likely settlement in the region, allowing him to return to a version of an agreed Ireland which was closer to that which he spoke of in the immediate aftermath of Sunningdale (see above, p. 66) – essentially involving power-sharing and an Irish dimension, and thus leaving the Union intact. Certainly, the way that Hume spoke about 'agreement' in his autumn 1991 draft of a potential inter-governmental statement did not suggest the necessity of a British withdrawal. Instead, it simply emphasised the need for London to support and actively encourage efforts towards a comprehensive political settlement. Moreover, the fact that Hume recognised that this 'cannot be achieved without the agreement of the people of Northern Ireland' – thus giving unionists an effective veto on any proposed settlement – made it fairly clear that he no longer thought in terms of a British departure, even in the medium term; Mallie and McKittrick, *The Fight for Peace*, pp. 118–19.

25 Mallie and McKittrick, *The Fight for Peace*, p. 119.

26 However, one account – to which the present study is much indebted – appears particularly well informed, especially considering the various Irish drafts of the joint declaration included in its appendix. This is the Mallie and McKittrick book, *The Fight for Peace*. However, this text focuses mainly on the Irish side of the initiative, and perhaps understates London's role in the making of the DSD. O'Kane's book, *Britain, Ireland and Northern Ireland*, helps to balance the Mallie and McKittrick narrative by drawing on extensive interviews with British as well as Irish officials involved in the process. Also, for first hand

accounts of the initiative, see Adams, *Hope and History*, pp. 106ff.; Séan Duignan, *One Spin on the Merry-Go-Round* (Dublin: Blackwater Press, 1995), pp. 96ff.; Fergus Finlay, *Snakes and Ladders* (Dublin: New Island Books, 1998), pp. 110–13, 180–204; Major, *The Autobiography*, pp. 447ff.; and Mansergh 'The background to the Irish peace process', pp. 17–19.

27 Mallie and McKittrick, *The Fight for Peace*, pp. 171ff., 190ff.
28 M. Cunningham, 'The political language of John Hume', *Irish Political Studies*, 12 (1997), p. 15; B. Girvin, 'Constitutional nationalism in Northern Ireland', in B. Barton and P. J. Roche (eds), *The Northern Ireland Question: Perspectives and Policies* (Aldershot: Avebury, 1994), p. 43.
29 O'Brien, *Memoir*, pp. 421–4.
30 *Irish Times*, 26 April 1993.
31 O'Brien, *Memoir*, p. 423; emphasis in original.
32 *Irish Times*, 26 April 1993.
33 O'Brien, *Memoir*, pp. 421–2.
34 Mallie and McKittrick, *The Fight for Peace*, pp. 121ff.
35 Finlay, *Snakes and Ladders*, p. 184; Major, *The Autobiography*, pp. 447, 448–9.
36 It is possible that the IRA's attempt to assassinate Major and his cabinet in February 1991 also contributed to his doubts over an emergent republican pacifism.
37 Major, *The Autobiography*, p. 447.
38 O'Kane, *Britain, Ireland and Northern Ireland*, p. 108.
39 Mallie and McKittrick, *The Fight for Peace*, pp. 187–8.
40 Adams, *Hope and History*, p. 133.
41 *Irish Times*, 27 September 1993.
42 Nonetheless, this statement led to wild speculation regarding the contents of the supposed report, or the 'Hume–Adams document' as the media termed it. In truth, there was no such document, at least not in the sense of particular paper handed to Dublin in September 1993. However, Mallie and McKittrick have suggested that, among the numerous draft statements which exchanged hands between republicans, Hume, and the Irish government in this period, one became known as 'Hume–Adams'. This was a version that was completed over a year earlier, but which was considered crucial in that it had gained the approval of the IRA leadership, thus suggesting its ability to deliver a ceasefire; Mallie and McKittrick, *The Fight for Peace*, pp. 150, 375–7.
43 Adams, *Hope and History*, pp. 120, 133.
44 Major, *The Autobiography*, p. 450.
45 O'Kane, *Britain, Ireland and Northern Ireland*, p. 121.
46 *Hansard*, sixth series, vol. 231, col. 35, 1 November 1993.
47 *Irish Times*, 5 November 1993.
48 Finlay, *Snakes and Ladders*, p. 201; Mallie and McKittrick, *The Fight for Peace*, pp. 192–3, 228–30.
49 Mallie and McKittrick, *The Fight for Peace*, pp. 171ff.; 190ff.
50 *Ibid.*, pp. 214–17.
51 Routledge, *John Hume*, pp. 253–5.
52 J. McGarry and B. O'Leary, *Explaining Northern Ireland: Broken Images* (Oxford: Blackwell, 1995), p. 389.

53 Mallie and McKittrick, *Endgame*, pp. 119–21, 136. There may have been a
    further reason that Hume made the September statement with Adams. A
    number of Irish officials involved in the joint declaration process have sug-
    gested that there was some competition between Hume and Albert Reynolds
    over the ownership of the initiative. Both, it seemed, wanted to gain the credit
    if the IRA did end its violent campaign. Following this interpretation,
    Reynolds's efforts to publicly distance himself from the Hume–Adams state-
    ments may not have been simply an act of political diplomacy. Similarly,
    Hume's decision to issue statements with Adams may not have been simply a
    means to put pressure on the two governments, but also a way to show that
    any subsequent declaration was a product of his endeavours. If so, Hume's
    judgement here can be questioned, as his and Adams's public association with
    the initiative made it much harder for the British government to subsequently
    adopt; Duignan, *One Spin on the Merry-Go-Round*, p. 149; O'Kane, *Britain,
    Ireland and Northern Ireland*, p. 107; Mallie and McKittrick, *The Fight for
    Peace*, p. 191.
54 Mallie and McKittrick, *The Fight for Peace*, pp. 233–6.
55 *Observer*, 28 November 1993.
56 *Ibid.*
57 For Major's own account of this dialogue, see his *Autobiography*, pp. 431ff.
58 However, there may also have been other reasons that Reynolds obliged in
    this regard; see above, n. 53.
59 Duignan, *One Spin on the Merry-Go-Round*, pp. 122–5; Finlay, *Snakes and
    Ladders*, pp. 194, 201–3; Major, *The Autobiography*, pp. 450–1; Mallie and
    McKittrick, *Endgame*, pp. 148–50, 152–5; Mallie and McKittrick, *The Fight
    for Peace*, pp. 219–21, 229, 255ff.; Major, *The Autobiography*, p. 452;
    O'Kane, *Britain, Ireland and Northern Ireland*, pp. 106, 113–14, 115, 116.
60 Finlay, *Snakes and Ladders*, p. 203; Mallie and McKittrick, *The Fight for
    Peace*, pp. 256ff.
61 Even in agreeing to make the joint declaration, it seems that the British gov-
    ernment doubted that it would lead to an IRA ceasefire. This would explain
    London's seeming reluctance to commit to the initiative, and the appearance
    that it was Dublin who really drove the early peace process. However, in fair-
    ness to the British government, it had far more to lose if the declaration failed
    to win over republicans, and yet served to provoke the Protestant community.
    By contrast, the Irish government could afford to be optimistic: it did not bear
    ultimate responsibility for the situation in Northern Ireland, but would win
    plaudits if a ceasefire was achieved. As such, it can be said that Major took
    more of a risk than Reynolds, and deserves considerable credit for eventually
    committing to the initiative. For a sympathetic account of Major's handling of
    the early peace process, and one which redresses more nationalist interpreta-
    tions, see O'Kane, *Britain, Ireland and Northern Ireland*, chs 5–6.
62 Mallie and McKittrick, *The Fight for Peace*, pp. 222–4, 228–9, 257–8, 264;
    M. Mansergh, 'The background to the peace process', *Irish Studies in Inter-
    national Affairs*, 6 (1995), pp. 154–5; E. O'Kane, 'Anglo-Irish Relations and
    the Northern Ireland peace process: from exclusion to inclusion', *Contempo-
    rary British History*, 18:1 (2004), p. 90; O'Kane, *Britain, Ireland and North-
    ern Ireland*, p. 109. O'Kane shows that unionists also had some input to the
    DSD through the British government. Specifically, Major showed the UUP

leader, James Molyneaux, draft versions of the document. However, Molyneaux's initial response was far from encouraging, and O'Kane suggests that this was one of the reasons that Major sought to abandon the idea of a joint statement appealing primarily to republicans; O'Kane, 'Anglo-Irish Relations', p. 88.

63 See above, pp. 153–4.
64 HMSO, *Text of the Joint Declaration by the Prime Minister, Rt. Hon. John Major, MP and the Taoiseach, Mr. Albert Reynolds, TD on the 15th December, 1993* [The Downing Street Declaration] (Belfast: HMSO, 1993), para. 4; O'Kane notes that Molyneaux tried to have this line removed from the DSD, but was unsuccessful in his efforts. This suggests how crucial the line was considered to be if the text was to have any effect on republican opinion; O'Kane, 'Anglo-Irish Relations', p. 88.
65 Cf. to the texts reproduced in Mallie and McKittrick, *The Fight for Peace*, appendix 1.
66 HMSO, The Downing Street Declaration, para. 4.
67 LHL, NIPC, P3394, Sinn Féin, 'Persuading the British – a joint call', June 1988, pp. 2–3.
68 Murray and Tonge, *Sinn Féin and the SDLP*, p. 182.
69 For example, see the SDLP's contribution to the 1988 talks with Sinn Féin, LHL (NIPC), P3395, 'Comments on Sinn Féin document, 2 May, pages 8 and 9', June 1988, pp. 1–2. This paper was responding directly to Sinn Féin's earlier suggestion that the British government must become persuaders for Irish unity. However, it should be noted that Hume and the SDLP had previously endorsed the idea that London should actively encourage the goal of a united Ireland, most significantly in the party's first published proposals, the *Towards a New Ireland* document of 1972 (see pp. 2–3). Nonetheless, it is also notable that such arguments did not appear in Hume's first draft of a potential British–Irish declaration in the autumn of 1991. This suggests that it was republicans who had insisted that London act as 'persuaders' in later versions of the text (see Mallie and McKittrick, *The Fight for Peace*, pp. 118–19, and appendix 1). If so, it seems that both Hume and Dublin, ever focused on the possibility of an IRA ceasefire, were not inclined to dissuade republicans from such an ambitious objective.
70 Major was also keen to emphasise this point when discussing the DSD in the House of Commons. However, arguably his comments were aimed at the 'unionists' on his own backbenches as well as those representing Northern Ireland; *Irish Times*, 16 December 1993.
71 HMSO, the Downing Street Declaration, para. 4.
72 See above p. 85.
73 Bew, Gibbon and Patterson, *Northern Ireland, 1921–2001*, p. 221; Bew and Gillespie, *Northern Ireland: A Chronology*, pp. xiii, 285; Bew, Patterson and Teague, *Between War and Peace*, p. 207; Patterson, *Ireland*, p. 322. However, what they gave with one hand, Bew and Patterson took with the other, presenting the DSD in these accounts in a way that sought to diminish Hume's influence to one of mere rhetoric.
74 Here Hume appears to be referring to the paper of June 1992 which Mallie and McKittrick suggest had gained the approval of the IRA leadership (see above, n. 42).

75   Cited in Mallie and McKittrick, *The Fight for Peace*, pp. 274–5.
76   *Irish Times*, 13 April 1994.
77   See above pp. 126–7.
78   J. Dumbrell, '"Hope and history": the US and peace in Northern Ireland', in Cox, Guelke and Stephen (eds), *A Farewell to Arms?*, p. 216.
79   On the crucial role which the ANIA played in this, see O'Cleary, *The Greening of the White House, passim*. For a first-hand account, see N. O'Dowd, 'The awakening: Irish America's key role in the Irish peace process', in M. Elliott (ed.), *The Long Road to Peace in Northern Ireland* (Liverpool: Liverpool University Press, 2002).
80   O'Cleary, *The Greening of the White House*, pp. 18ff.; Dumbrell, '"Hope and history"', p. 216.
81   Dumbrell, '"Hope and history"', p. 216.
82   O'Cleary, *The Greening of the White House*, pp. 34, 39–40, 42.
83   Briand, 'Bush, Clinton, Irish America and the Irish peace process', pp. 173, 180; Coogan, *The Troubles*, pp. 442–3; Dumbrell, '"Hope and history"', p. 219; Mallie and McKittrick, *Endgame*, p. 179; O'Cleary, *The Greening of the White House*, pp. 78–80, 90–1; A. J. Wilson, 'From the Beltway to Belfast: The Clinton Administration, Sinn Féin, and the Northern Ireland Peace Process', *New Hibernia Review*, 1:3 (1997), pp. 29–30.
84   Dumbrell, '"Hope and history"', pp. 218–19.
85   Quoted in O'Cleary, *The Greening of the White House*, pp. 61, 94.
86   O'Cleary, *The Greening of the White House*, pp. 61, 78, 80–1, 94.
87   O'Dowd, 'The Awakening', p. 73.
88   Quoted in O'Cleary, *The Greening of the White House*, p. 81.
89   Mallie and McKittrick, *The Fight for Peace*, pp. 298–9, 311–13.
90   TUAS was initially thought to stand for 'Totally Unarmed Strategy'. However, later commentators suggested a formula more correlative to the acronym, and perhaps more accurate in its suggestion of a continued republican ambivalence: 'Tactical Use of Armed Struggle'.
91   Cited in Mallie and McKittrick, *The Fight for Peace*, pp. 382–3.
92   The sense that this was a tactical and possibly time-limited manoeuvre was arguably necessary to sell the idea of a ceasefire to republican activists. However, this approach added to the uncertainty of unionists and the British government when the ceasefire did arrive, and thus helps to explain the problems in achieving immediate political progress thereafter.
93   Cited in Mallie and McKittrick, *The Fight for Peace*, p. 383.
94   Gerry Adams; interview with author, Belfast, 2 March, 2009.
95   Quoted in B. O'Brien, *The Long War: The IRA and Sinn Féin* (Dublin: O'Brien Press, 2nd edn, 1999), p. 320.
96   Cited in Mallie and McKittrick, *The Fight for Peace*, p. 383.
97   See English, *Armed Struggle*, pp. 187ff.; Moloney, *A Secret History of the IRA*, pp. 149ff.; Murray and Tonge, *Sinn Féin and the SDLP*, pp. 104ff; and H. Patterson, *The Politics of Illusion: A Political History of the IRA* (London: Serif, 1997), pp. 180ff.
98   English, *Armed Struggle*, p. 307.
99   In this interpretation, it should be clear that republicans' adoption of a wholly political strategy was not, as some commentators seem to imply, an inevitability. Indeed, during the 1980s, the IRA had continued to build its military

capacity, aided in particular by a number of large arms shipments from the Libyan government. Had the Libyan arsenal given republicans any advantage in their conflict with the British state, the IRA would have been keen to continue its campaign in the hope of a 'final victory'. Under such circumstances, Hume's arguments would have had little impact.

100 Bew and Gillespie, *Northern Ireland: A Chronology*, p. 297; Mallie and McKittrick, *Endgame*, pp. 203–4.

10

Sunningdale for slow learners

Nearly four years passed between the paramilitary ceasefires of 1994 and
the achievement of an actual peace agreement in April 1998. The road
towards that agreement was understandably arduous:[1] over a quarter century of violence had created severe distrust on both sides of the conflict.
On one, unionists and the British government doubted the republican
movement's conversion to wholly peaceful methods, and so argued that
the IRA should decommission its weapons before Sinn Féin was allowed to
the negotiating table. On the other, republicans saw the decommissioning
issue as a ploy, designed to stall the political process, and in doing so to
divide and demoralise the Provisional movement. Accordingly, it had no
intention of disarming in advance of a political deal. However, more moderate sections of nationalist opinion also saw the weapons debate as something which would only be resolved as part of comprehensive settlement.
In addition, it was felt that Unionist MPs were using the issue to exploit
the situation at Westminster, where John Major held onto power with an
ever-diminishing majority. From a nationalist perspective, it seemed that
the UUP was trading its support for a weakened government in return for
a brake on the peace process. Such suspicion, and the continual delay in
moves towards inclusive political talks, eventually led to a breakdown in
the IRA's ceasefire in February 1996.

For over a year, the peace process was in hiatus. However, changes of
government in both London and Dublin helped to move the situation forward. Firstly, in May 1997, Tony Blair led the Labour Party to a landslide
victory in the British general election. The strength of this administration,
with no need to look for Unionist support at Westminster, led republicans
to believe that real progress was now possible. A month later, Fianna Fáil
returned to power in Dublin, displacing a Fine Gael-led coalition which
Sinn Féin had felt was too focused on unionist concerns. Thus, the election
of a 'greener' Irish government also encouraged republicans to reconsider
their position. But co-operation between the new governments was vital,
too. Within weeks, they agreed on a way around the decommissioning
issue, advocating a process of parallel talks and disarmament, with the
establishment of an independent international commission to oversee the
latter. In addition, Blair made clear that Sinn Féin would be admitted to

inter-party negotiations within weeks of an IRA cessation.[2] This proved
enough to convince the republican leadership, and in July the IRA
announced that it was restoring its ceasefire, thereby finally allowing Sinn
Féin to enter into talks towards a new settlement.

Despite his importance in creating the basis for inclusive negotiations,
Hume had a relatively minor role in these discussions. Instead, party colleagues took the lead.[3] However, it can be argued that, by this stage, the
essential parameters of a settlement had already been established, and that
Hume had played a significant role in this. Indeed, reflecting on the final
outcome of these negotiations, the GFA of April 1998,[4] his ideological
imprint is clearly evident. Of course, the precise contents of the Agreement
were a product of bargain and compromise between the Northern Ireland
parties, and the British and Irish governments.[5] But the basic shape of the
settlement clearly owed much to the thinking of Hume and the SDLP.

The Good Friday Agreement

Séamus Mallon, the SDLP deputy leader, and one of chief negotiators of
the GFA, famously described the settlement as 'Sunningdale for slow learn-
ers'. On one level, his meaning was obvious. The GFA was based on effectively the same formula as the Sunningdale Agreement: power-sharing and
an Irish dimension. But Mallon's comment could also be read as a rebuke
to both republicans and unionists. Each had, after a further two decades
of conflict, finally accepted that which the SDLP had long advocated as the
essential ingredients of any political settlement: power-sharing and an Irish
dimension. However, whilst there were certainly similarities between the
GFA and Sunningdale, there were also crucial differences between the two
accords.

Firstly, the GFA was, in numerous respects, a far more comprehensive
settlement than Sunningdale. Most significantly, it included a much
broader range of political opinion, involving loyalists and republicans as
well as nationalists and unionists. Unlike Sunningdale, which sought to
marginalise the political extremes, the process leading to the GFA had
tried to incorporate these elements. In so doing, the GFA held an obvious
but crucial advantage over its predecessor: it followed a formal cessation
of hostilities, and looked to build political structures that would cement
this peace. By contrast, Sunningdale was constructed amidst a situation of
ongoing violence. Accordingly, it was informed by the optimistic hope that
the successful operation of the new dispensation would gradually erode
support for political extremism and paramilitarism in both communities.

As demonstrated in the previous two chapters, Hume had played a
crucial role in encouraging London and Dublin to move away from the
Sunningdale strategy and its focus on the political centre ground. However, in fairness to the two governments, it should be emphasised that this
was not a viable option until the early 1990s. A fully inclusive approach

only became possible after the political extremes in each community, first republicans and later loyalists, signalled that they might be willing to participate in a democratic settlement in Northern Ireland. But, even then, the British government seemed more likely to maintain its former strategy of negotiating with political moderates and marginalising the extremes. In the end, Hume forced the issue by refusing to acquiesce in the more limited talks process that had begun under Brooke and Mayhew. Indeed, Mayhew and other NIO officials believed that Hume effectively vetoed these talks, instead opting to pursue his dialogue with Adams, and thereby to bring republicans into the settlement process.[6] In doing so, Hume obliged the British government to respond with the DSD, which opened the way towards an agreement that would include all sections of opinion in Northern Ireland.

The GFA was also more comprehensive than Sunningdale in the assurances that it offered to unionists. Most importantly, the Irish government gave unequivocal recognition of Northern Ireland's status as part of the United Kingdom. As a result, the GFA led to changes to Articles 2 and 3 of *Bunreacht na hÉireann*. These saw the removal of Dublin's territorial claim over Northern Ireland, and an acceptance that reunification could only take place with the consent of a majority in the region. In addition, the GFA created new political structures linking Britain and Ireland, these to counterbalance the Irish dimension of the Agreement. Most notable was the British–Irish Council, which would include representatives from the London and Dublin governments, but also from the new devolved institutions in Northern Ireland, Scotland and Wales. This provided a more unionist-friendly, British Isles umbrella to the 1998 settlement.

But with respect to its all-Ireland institutions, the GFA was similar to Sunningdale. Although the powers of these institutions were more clearly defined than had been the case in 1973,[7] again they were intended to facilitate co-operation in areas of mutual interest between the North and South of Ireland. However, as with Sunningdale's Council of Ireland, the GFA's North–South Ministerial Council had a limited remit, which could only be extended with the agreement of both the new Northern Ireland Assembly and the Oireachtas. The GFA and the Sunningdale Agreement both encouraged cross-border co-operation, but neither predetermined the unification of North and South.

Of course, Sinn Féin – in a way not unlike the SDLP in 1973–74 – chose to sell the 1998 Agreement to its supporters as a staging post on the road to a united Ireland. But the GFA was no more this than was Sunningdale. Instead, like Sunningdale, it provided a political framework within which nationalists, North and South, might co-operate with unionists and perhaps, over time, demonstrate the logic of increasing integration between the two parts of Ireland.[8] However, it cannot deliver Irish unity without first creating the consent of a majority in Northern Ireland. In this, the GFA, again like Sunningdale, can be seen as a product of revisionist

nationalist thinking. It accepted the need for unionists' agreement in order
to reunify Ireland, but also allowed nationalists to pursue that end by
democratic means, and reaffirmed the British government's commitment to
accept such an outcome if it becomes the wish of a majority in Northern
Ireland. In this, the GFA confirmed the arguments which Hume had been
making to republicans since the mid-1980s, namely that Britain represented no obstacle to a united Ireland, and that there was, therefore, a
peaceful path towards that goal. Similarly, it endorsed the argument that
Hume had first made in his seminal *Irish Times* article of 1964, namely
that nationalists should be allowed to participate in the state and society
in Northern Ireland without any sacrifice to either their identity or their
aspiration to Irish unity.[9]

Also vitally important for nationalists were the reforms which the GFA
promised in the fields of policing and justice in Northern Ireland. As Hume
had argued at the time of Sunningdale, such changes were crucial if the settlement was to gain full acceptance from the minority. However, unlike
Sunningdale, as the GFA followed an end to mainstream paramilitary violence, the British government was now able to contemplate radical change
to the system of law and order in Northern Ireland. Most important in this
was the replacement of the RUC with a police force capable of representing
both sides of the religious divide.[10] Finally, the GFA provided a commitment
to further reform to achieve full social and economic equality in Northern
Ireland.[11] In this, the Agreement also promised to fulfil the demands which
had first led Hume into political action in the civil rights era.

The Good Friday Agreement and self-determination

Another crucial difference between Sunningdale and the GFA is that the
latter directly addressed the issue of national self-determination. It did so
through the dual-referenda mechanism that was used to endorse the
Agreement in both parts of Ireland, thereby allowing voters across the
island to express their opinion on the new constitutional arrangements.
However, interestingly, it was Hume who first suggested such a scheme at
the time of the Sunningdale Agreement, arguing that its use would remove
the claim to legitimacy which republicans took from the 1918 general election – the last occasion when the whole of Ireland voted as one,[12] and
when the original Sinn Féin party had won a landslide victory. But Brian
Faulkner rejected Hume's proposal, fearing that a majority of unionists
would vote against Sunningdale.[13]

Despite this, in the years that followed, the SDLP continued to push
Hume's proposal. Indeed, in the Constitutional Convention of 1975–76,
the party argued that one of the problems with Sunningdale was that it
lacked a popular mandate. As a result, the SDLP suggested that any new
agreement should be presented to voters in Northern Ireland, but also – to
increase its democratic legitimacy – the electorate in the South of Ireland:

'In this way, the authority of all the people of Ireland could be thrown behind the institutions of government, North and South. For the first time the people of Ireland would be united on how they wished to be governed – North and South.'[14]

After Hume began his dialogue with Adams in the late 1980s, he returned to this idea, seeing it as a way to address the republican argument that partition denied the Irish people their right to self-determination.[15] Accordingly, in discussions with Dublin in the early stages of the joint declaration initiative, Hume continually emphasised the need to hold referenda in both parts of the island, this to bolster the legitimacy of any new settlement, but also to allow for the exercise of self-determination in an all-Ireland context. Again, his intention in this was to override the result of the 1918 election, and thus remove republicans' claim that the armed struggle was directed towards the achievement of the democratically expressed will of the Irish people.[16]

In the DSD itself, there was no explicit reference to the idea of dual-referenda, but the crucial paragraph on Irish self-determination suggested that any new agreement would have to secure popular consent in both parts of Ireland.[17] Thus, in effect, the British government accepted Hume's dual-referenda mechanism as the means by which any new institutions would be endorsed, and so it was in May 1998 that the GFA was put to the electorate in both parts of Ireland. However, for Hume it was also vital that these polls were held on the same day. This meant that he could argue that the people of Ireland had, *together*, exercised their right to self-determination – just as in 1918. But eighty years on, by both supporting the GFA, Irish nationalists and Ulster unionists agreed on how this right would be expressed,[18] thus providing a mandate for new political structures that would allow for peaceful and democratic governance across the island. Thus, in Hume's mind, the people of Ireland had now achieved the state of 'agreed self-determination' which he had proposed in the very first draft of what eventually became the DSD.[19] As a result, immediately after the GFA referenda, Hume returned to the argument which he had first mooted at the time of Sunningdale, suggesting that republicans could no longer claim a mandate for violence in a vote that took place decades earlier:

> The fact that this was the first all-Ireland vote since 1918 sends out a clear message ... to paramilitary groups who claim to be acting in the name of the Irish people. The Irish people have spoken very clearly now and I hope the will of the Irish people will be totally respected by all such groups. Friday's vote was for the implementation of the agreement and that means the creation of democratic institutions which will be shared by all sections of our people.[20]

Hume clearly felt the need to articulate this case, as only a few weeks earlier the IRA had released an official statement on the GFA which rejected the legitimacy of the dual-referenda mechanism as a device for the exercise of Irish self-determination. However, it did so in equivocal terms, and even provided helpful advice to prospective voters: 'In our view, the two imminent referenda do not constitute the exercise of national self-determination and voters' attitudes to the referenda should be guided by their own view and the advice of their political leaders.'[21] Given that the political leaders of the republican community, Sinn Féin, had helped to negotiate the GFA – and thus had implicitly accepted the dual-referenda mechanism that was proposed to endorse the accord – it would be difficult for the IRA to reject the outcome of these polls. Though republicans obviously would have preferred a settlement that involved the whole of Ireland voting as one single constituency, it did not appear that they were about to return to armed struggle as a means to enforce the result of the 1918 election. They would acquiesce in, if not openly accept, the 1998 enactment of Irish self-determination.

However, beyond the republican constituency, others have questioned whether the 1998 referenda can really be viewed as an exercise in Irish self-determination. For example, Jonathan Tonge has suggested that these polls were better seen as providing an act of 'codetermination', as the outcome was also dependent on the choice of the unionist majority in Northern Ireland, and Irish nationalists were being offered only one constitutional option as a means to their self-determination:

> No alternatives to the deal [the GFA] were placed before the electorates of Northern Ireland and the Irish Republic, and whichever way the referendum had gone in the Irish Republic it would not have made any difference to Northern Ireland's constitutional status as part of the United Kingdom. Hence the 1998 referendum was not an exercise in Irish self-determination, but rather a limited device for partial codetermination.[22]

Of course, it could be argued that any population which history deems lucky enough to vote on the constitution under which they live will rarely be offered a range of options from which to choose. More likely, they will be presented with the opportunity to endorse or to reject one particular system of governance. The nature of this system will normally be decided by political elites, but if they hope to gain the assent of their would-be citizenry, they will devise a constitution that is likely to win acceptance among all significant sections of the population. In short, elites will fashion a political compromise which reflects the nature of the society over which they intend to govern. The same can be said of the GFA. It may not have been the first choice of either Irish nationalists or Ulster unionists, but it offered a compromise, negotiated by their political representatives, and then offered for their endorsement or rejection.

Nonetheless, Tonge's idea of 'codetermination' may be an appropriate description of what took place in Ireland in May 1998. Indeed, it is likely that Hume would accept this as an alternative expression of what he called 'agreed self-determination'.[23] For Hume had always argued that nationalist self-determination must be exercised in conjunction with unionist self-determination – that the nationalist right to self-determination would, in effect, be conditioned by the consent of a majority in Northern Ireland. However, Hume's dual-referenda mechanism meant that the same applied in reverse: unionists' right to self-determination was conditioned by the consent of Irish nationalists. As Brendan O'Duffy explains, when London and Dublin first adopted this mechanism in the DSD, 'the citizens of the Irish Republic were being given a veto on unionists' preferences for self-determination (currently, *inter alia* further integration into the United Kingdom; independence; and majoritarian devolution)'.[24] Indeed, unionists could not expect southern Irish voters to endorse these preferences, which offered little to nothing for northern nationalists. Thus, whilst Tonge is right to suggest that the Irish electorate could not, alone, bring any change to Northern Ireland's status as part of UK, neither could unionists, alone, decide the constitutional future of the region.

In this regard, the dual-referenda mechanism provided an effective guarantee to northern nationalists. It meant that unionists would have to offer a constitutional compromise which was acceptable to southern Irish voters. Southern voters, in turn, were only likely to agree to the minimum acceptable to northern nationalists, namely some form of power-sharing and an Irish dimension. However, at the same time, unionist voters – as a majority in Northern Ireland – also maintained veto, and thus a means to ensure a settlement which provided the minimum acceptable to them. Clearly, they would not vote for a set of institutions which were predetermined towards the creation of a united Ireland. Accordingly, nationalists had a veto over the way that unionist self-determination was expressed, and unionists had veto over the way that nationalist self-determination was expressed. As a result, and as Hume had long argued, the two would have to agree on how they should exercise self-determination – neither could ignore or override the rights of the other. In this, it could be said that Hume's dual-referenda formula provided an ingenious way to balance the minority status of nationalists in Northern Ireland, and the minority status of unionists on the island of Ireland. With each retaining a veto over the other's right to self-determination, they had to compromise with one another, and find a settlement that offered the minimum acceptable to each side. It is this which led O'Duffy to argue that the GFA provided what he termed a 'sufficiently consensual' expression of self-determination for both nationalist and unionist.[25]

This interpretation also contradicts those who, at the outset of the peace process, had been critical of Hume's dialogue with Adams, suggesting that this was leading the SDLP towards an essentially republican interpretation of the Northern Ireland problem. In particular, the early Hume–Adams statements were condemned for placing the issue of self-determination in an all-Ireland context, and rejecting any internal settlement of the Northern Ireland problem. In this, it was argued, Hume was supporting an approach that was simply incompatible with unionist rights.[26]

This critique of the Hume–Adams dialogue ignores the fact that that the SDLP had, from the time of its first published proposals in 1972, rejected the possibility of an internal solution in Northern Ireland[27] – a position which it held to hereinafter. As such, it cannot be argued that the Hume's discussions with Adams were 'greening' his or his party's thinking in this regard. However, it was Sinn Féin who introduced the subject of national self-determination into its debate with the SDLP in 1988. But, in responding, Hume and his colleagues held a revisionist line, accepting the principle of self-determination, but arguing the need for people of Ireland to agree on the means towards it exercise.[28]

By considering the concept of self-determination in an all-Ireland context, but stressing the need for agreement between the people of the island on the means towards its exercise, Hume was trying to reconcile nationalist and unionist claims on the same principle. But some commentators did not appreciate the subtlety in his arguments. For example, Michael Cunningham suggested that Hume's emphasis on the people rather than the territory of Ireland was 'insufficient to distinguish his position from that of Sinn Féin since it makes no material difference in that it does not permit self-determination for Northern Ireland (or its unionist constituency)'. Admittedly, there was an ambiguity in Hume's arguments, which even Cunningham accepted 'may in part be influenced by … difficult discussions with Sinn Féin'.[29] Indeed, Hume would have found it impossible to make any progress with Adams if he insisted on explicit recognition of the unionist right to self-determination and the principle of consent in their joint *communiqués*. But these statements do show that Hume was, albeit gradually, steering Sinn Féin towards a conception of Irish self-determination that would require unionist assent.[30]

For pragmatic reasons – that is, to ease republicans into the political process – the Hume–Adams dialogue was unavoidably ambiguous on the relationship between unionist consent and Irish self-determination. However, what was not ambiguous was Hume's continued emphasis – right throughout his talks with Adams – on the idea of using dual-referenda to reconcile the two. Moreover, it is clear that Hume intended this approach to reassure unionists of his party's continued commitment to the principle of consent. Indeed, directly after his first public talks with Sinn Féin, in a newspaper interview with the former chief executive of the UUP, Frank Miller, Hume was eager to make this point: 'I am saying that I accept, before we start [negotiations on a possible replacement for the AIA], that any outcome of that must have the agreement of both [nationalists and unionists] and that in order to assure them of that, before they go to that [talks] table, they should devise a mechanism to ensure that the people on each side have a means of expressing their view on whatever agreement is reached.' Asked directly by Miller whether this meant that any agreement would have to be ratified on both sides of the border, Hume was unequiocal: 'That's precisely what I am proposing.'[31] Thereafter, he continued to argue the case for dual-referenda as a way to ensure unionist consent for any new settlement, but also to allow nationalists to exercise their right to self-determination in an all-Ireland context:

> any agreement reached should be endorsed in a referendum by a majority in each part of the island and if either says no, the agreement fails. To us that reassures the Unionist people that their agreement is necessary, and for the rest of Ireland for the first time the people of Ireland as a whole would have spoken, they would have expressed their right to self-determination, in agreement.[32]

Whatever the opacity of the Hume–Adams statements, this shows that – contrary to Cunningham's interpretation – Hume was committed to a political process that allowed for unionist self-determination. However, his dual-referendum formula also meant that unionists would have to offer a settlement which could win the support of the southern Irish electorate, thus providing an effective guarantee for northern nationalists. As such, unionist Ulster and nationalist Ireland would have to compromise. Both had a right to self-determination, but neither had an absolute right – that is a right to override the wishes of the other. As a result, they had to find a means to achieve Hume's notion of 'agreed self-determination'. With this concept, Hume attempted to square the circle between Irish nationalism and Ulster unionism – to allow both traditions, in both parts of Ireland, to exercise their right to self-determination. In keeping with his idea of an 'agreed Ireland', Hume proposed that unionists and nationalists would have to reach a consensus on how they exercised that right, creating political institutions that could accommodate them both. In the GFA, arguably they did find a form of agreed Ireland, and in the dual-referenda used to endorse the settlement, the people of Ireland did find a means to agreed self-determination.

The Good Friday Agreement and sovereignty

Though the GFA appeared to resolve the dispute over self-determination in Ireland, its implications for political sovereignty on the island were more open to interpretation. Unionist supporters of the Agreement, unsurprisingly, claimed vindication for their position: Northern Ireland remained part of the UK, and British sovereignty over the region was undiminished. In fact, in an article in the *Irish Times* in the approach to the referenda on the Agreement, the UUP leader, David Trimble, argued that the accord actually served to strengthen the Union with Britain. In doing so, he focused particularly on the proposed changes to the Irish constitution. These, he suggested, provided '*de jure* recognition of British territorial sovereignty' over Northern Ireland.[33] Of course, though a barrister by trade, it was clear that Trimble was making a political as well as a legal argument in this piece. Nonetheless, the case which he presented was broadly supported by those with expertise on constitutional law. Indeed, one such commentator went as far as to suggest that the changes to British legislation which accompanied the GFA were, in their implications for Westminster's sovereignty over Northern Ireland, 'legally, of no significance'.[34]

However, political sovereignty is not a subject which is defined solely by constitutional documentation. It also has practical effects, and it was these that nationalist supporters of the GFA focused upon. Firstly, under the terms of the Agreement, whilst Northern Ireland remains part of the United Kingdom, it no longer exists in a purely British political framework. The Union between Britain and Northern Ireland now has a counterbalance in the new all-Ireland institutions. Of course, these do not carry the same political weight as the Union, but British sovereignty is clearly qualified by the Irish dimension of the GFA. In particular, and arguably more important than the new North–South structures which the Agreement created, is the continuing role which it allows for Dublin in the governance of Northern Ireland. For though the 1998 settlement ostensibly 'transcended' the AIA, the essential architecture of the former accord remains in place. Most notably, the 'Intergovernmental Conference' of the AIA was recreated as the 'British–Irish Intergovernmental Conference', this serving much the same purpose as its predecessor. As Ruane and Todd explain: 'Nationalists saw the continuation of some form of intergovernmental conference as essential, both to ensure continued Irish influence [in Northern Ireland] in such areas as policing and justice and as a fall-back mechanism should the Assembly fail to function as envisaged.'[35]

On the latter point, nationalist negotiators of the Agreement showed particular foresight, as the Assembly clearly did fail to function as envisaged during the troubled implementation of the GFA.[36] However, when this occurred, the governance of Northern Ireland simply reverted to 'direct with a green tinge'. In this, it was clear that Dublin had retained the role which it had held since 1985, as mouthpiece of the minority's grievances, and the guardian of its vital interests. This unique political arrangement clearly suggests a diminution, or at least conditioning, of British sovereignty over Northern Ireland.

Since the AIA, Hume and the SDLP had consistently defended Dublin's role in the governance of Northern Ireland, arguing that this protected Catholic interests, but also provided effective recognition of the minority's Irish identity. However, in the GFA, such recognition was enhanced. Indeed, in the Agreement, the London government accepted that people in Northern Ireland had the right to claim Irish rather than British citizenship, or indeed to hold dual citizenship.[37] This was essentially a symbolic gesture, as southern Irish law has always allowed those born in Northern Ireland to claim an Irish passport.[38] However, by affirming this right, the British government formally acknowledged the duality of identity in the region. In this, again, it built on the logic of the AIA, wherein London first accepted the legitimacy of the nationalist identity in Northern Ireland. But the various provisions of the GFA – the North–South institutions, the continued guardian role of the Dublin government, and the recognised right to hold an Irish passport – together create a more explicit 'bi-nationalism' to the Northern Ireland polity. This also changes the nature of British sovereignty in the region.

Most importantly of all, the GFA has made clear that British sovereignty over Northern Ireland is dependent on the will of its people: while they continue to favour the Union with Britain, this wish will be upheld; but if they decide to join the Republic of Ireland, this wish will also be given effect. It is this which allowed nationalists, and particularly the SDLP, to argue that British sovereignty had been replaced by the sovereignty of the Irish people.[39] This interpretation emphasises that the political structures now existing in Ireland were created by the express will of voters in both parts of the island. Moreover, under the terms of the GFA, any change in these arrangements can only be effected by the same means. Accordingly, even academic commentators have found sympathy with the argument that political sovereignty, and thus the political future of Ireland, now rests with the people of the island rather than the British government: 'The institutions of the Agreement are a product of Irish choices, North and South, and not the choices of Great Britain's parliament or people. ... the partition of Ireland now rests on a decision of the people of Ireland, North and South.'[40]

However, despite such assertions, pro-Agreement unionists – and indeed dissident republicans – will argue that the GFA has seen nationalists accept partition. This is true, but they have endorsed a settlement quite different to that which partitioned Ireland. This difference centres on the principle of consent. By endorsing this principle in the GFA, the vast majority of nationalist Ireland has accepted that Irish unity can only be achieved by winning the agreement of a majority in Northern Ireland. This, clearly, can be presented as a victory for Ulster unionism.[41] But this interpretation ignores the issue of *nationalist* consent. The GFA has also won, for the first time, the assent of Irish nationalists for political institutions across the island the Ireland. Until 1998, nationalist Ireland had never accepted the partition of the country. The Irish Free State government may have recognised the border in 1925, but the Irish people, and particularly the Irish people of Northern Ireland, did not. Indeed, even the 1920–21 settlement, though it was accepted by the people of the 26 counties under threat of war from the British government,[42] was certainly not endorsed by the northern minority. But, in the GFA, nationalists in both parts of Ireland have consented to partition. They have accepted the Northern Ireland state – and tacitly British sovereignty over the region – on certain conditions. These include the right to social and economic equality within Northern Ireland; a role for nationalists in the governance of the state; the creation of law and order arrangements which reflect the religious balance in the region, and which ensure impartial treatment of all; recognition of

nationalists' cultural and the political identity; an institutional expression
of this identity through formal linkages with the Republic of Ireland; a
guarantee of nationalists' rights and interests through the role of the
Dublin government; an acceptance of the legitimacy of their aspiration to
a united Ireland; and a political framework in which they might work
towards this end by peaceful means. In summary, through the GFA, northern nationalists can feel that they have attained equality, and have exercised their right to self-determination and sovereignty. However, this has
been achieved without denying any similar rights to Ulster unionists.

After the Good Friday Agreement

Though far more comprehensive than Sunningdale, the GFA did not
resolve all matters relating to the Northern Ireland problem. Most notable
amongst these was the issue of decommissioning, which had already
caused such problems in early stages of the peace process. In order to
ensure that Sinn Féin would accept the deal, the clause in the GFA that
dealt with this subject was left without any binding commitment.[43]
Accordingly, all parties promised to 'use any influence they may have, to
achieve decommissioning of all paramilitary arms within two years following the endorsement in referendums North and South of the agreement
and in the context of the implementation of the overall settlement.'[44]

The ambiguity of this formula caused much dispute in the aftermath of
the Agreement. On the one hand, unionists were understandably unwilling
to sit in government with republicans whilst they retained a huge military
arsenal. On the other, republicans could argue that the GFA made no
explicit link between the issue of decommissioning and Sinn Féin's right to
hold seats in the executive. But decommissioning was not the only problem affecting the implementation of the GFA: there were related disputes
over the UUP's commitment to the new structures of government; the
reform of policing in Northern Ireland; the process of British demilitarisation; and the continued organisational and criminal activities of elements
within the republican movement.[45] Together, these problems served to
undermine the operation of the power-sharing executive and other political institutions, which worked only intermittently in the years immediately
following the GFA. During this time, unionist support for the accord –
only achieving a slim majority in 1998[46] – steadily fell away. This disillusionment was clearly reflected in subsequent elections, which saw the continued decline of the UUP, and the gradual rise of the anti-Agreement DUP.

The difficult implementation of the GFA, and the continued polarisation
of attitudes in the two communities, also saw a decline in the SDLP's electoral fortunes, and a corresponding rise in support for Sinn Féin. In the
Westminster election of 2001 – Hume's last before stepping down as party
leader – the Sinn Féin vote edged ahead of the SDLP's, and continued to
rise thereafter. Of course, there had always been those of his colleagues

who had questioned the wisdom of Hume's engagement with the republicans,[47] and who feared that it would eventually lead to the scenario which now unfolded, with Sinn Féin displacing the SDLP as the leaders of the nationalist community. Hume–Adams, it seemed, had fathered the SDLP's electoral nemesis. But questions were also raised about the organisation of the SDLP, with suggestions that this had been severely neglected during Hume's time as leader.[48] In particular, there was an apparent failure to bring new blood through the ranks of the party. This left the SDLP facing an electoral battle with a younger, more dynamic, extremely well-organised, and increasingly well-funded opponent. Even with a spirited fight-back by the new party leader, Mark Durkan, in the Westminster election of 2005, there remained considerable doubts about the political future of the SDLP. Sinn Féin had now established itself as the dominant party within northern nationalism.

However, whilst the SDLP may have lost the electoral battle, the party certainly won the ideological war. Sinn Féin's recent success is undoubtedly a consequence of extremely effective political leadership, and tremendous organisation and effort amongst the party's rank and file. It is also a result of demographic shifts, and Sinn Féin's ability to attract votes, particularly amongst the young, of an expanding nationalist electorate. But all of this is built upon an acceptance of what is, in essence, the SDLP's political programme.[49] After reaching an electoral ceiling in the mid-1980s, Sinn Féin's growth from the early 1990s clearly coincides with its movement towards a peaceful, reformist strategy. After 1998, its continued success has been based on its commitment to an agreement which was largely negotiated by the SDLP. Thus, as Kevin Bean suggested, 'Sinn Féin has distinguished itself from the SDLP as simply the more effective, the more principled and the better organized wing of the new nationalist consensus.' As such, anticipating Sinn Féin's emergence as the leading nationalist party in Northern Ireland, Bean argued that 'it will only do so within the broad parameters laid down by the politics of the SDLP and the Belfast Agreement.'[50] That said, it should be recognised that, during the implementation of this accord, republicans played an astute game. In one sense, they stood firm, ensuring that there would be no retreat from the Agreement's promise of racial reform.[51] However, at the same time, the republican leadership moved considerably, deftly managing the demilitarisation of the movement required by the spirit if not the letter of the GFA.[52] But this does not disguise the fact that Sinn Féin was working a settlement shaped essentially by the SDLP. Power-sharing and North–South structures were not the aims of Provisional republicanism. Instead, they are the long-standing objectives of the reformist northern nationalism. The irony is that it seems it will be Sinn Féin rather than the SDLP that has the opportunity to show their transformative potential over the long term.

Of course, similar arguments can be made with respect to the changes in unionist politics. Despite its claimed intention, first to dismantle, then to renegotiate the GFA, the DUP has now accepted constitutional arrangements which were brokered by the UUP. The St Andrews Agreement of 2006 made some procedural changes to the GFA,[53] but it did not alter the essential architecture of the 1998 accord. In truth, St Andrews was an agreement on the implementation of GFA, providing a plan to deal with all outstanding issues, and thus allow the restoration of the executive in May 2007. Indeed, the only real difference in the new dispensation is that it is led by Sinn Féin and the DUP rather than the SDLP and UUP. But this is a consequence of electoral shifts rather than any significant change to the GFA. On the face of it, these shifts led to the rise of more 'extreme' parties in each communal bloc. But, in reality, Sinn Féin and the DUP have both moved towards the political centre, and both have adopted the positions of their moderate rivals.[54]

However, to push the argument further, it could be said that the DUP was also accepting an agreement which, although brokered by the UUP, was essentially a creature of the SDLP's creation. Indeed, more than any other party to the conflict – including the two governments – the SDLP provided the thinking behind the 1998 settlement.[55] In this, the party drew on ideas first articulated as early as the 1950s, with the initial stirrings of reformist northern nationalism. These ideas were developed and further refined in the 1960s and 1970s, with the SDLP, and particularly Hume, playing a major part in this.[56] Through the 1980s and early 1990s, under the leadership of Hume, the SDLP began to insert these ideas into the thinking of the other parties to the conflict: influencing the Irish government in the NIF; Dublin and London in the AIA and the DSD; and the republican movement through the dialogue between Hume and Adams from the mid-1980s. Even in the Brooke and Mayhew talks, based on the SDLP's three-strands schema, the party created the basic framework within which unionists were expected to negotiate. In this, Hume and the SDLP defined the ideological parameters of the peace process, and the essential structures of the agreement arising from this. As such, it can be argued that the GFA broadly vindicates the thinking of Hume, the SDLP, and revisionist Irish nationalism.

Notes

1   There is not room here to detail this process, but it has been well documented by other authors. For a range of interpretations, see Arthur, *Special Relationships*, pp. 244ff.; Bew, Gibbon and Patterson, *Northern Ireland, 1921–2001*, ch. 7; Dixon, *Northern Ireland*, chs 9–10; Hennessy, *The Northern Ireland Peace Process*, 88ff.; O'Kane, *Britain, Ireland and Northern Ireland*, chs 6–7; and Tonge, *Northern Ireland*, pp. 158ff.
2   Bew and Gillespie, *Northern Ireland: A Chronology*, p. 343.
3   Hennessy, *The Northern Ireland Peace Process*, p. 120; Murray, *John Hume and the SDLP*, p. 262.

4 For a detailed analysis of the GFA, see B. O'Leary, 'The Nature of the British-Irish Agreement', *New Left Review*, 233 (1999). R. Wilford (ed.), *Aspects of the Belfast Agreement* (Oxford: Oxford University Press, 2001), provides a series of essays which look at specific dimensions of the Agreement, its operation, and early problems in its implementation.

5 For a detailed account of these negotiations, see Hennessy, *The Northern Ireland Peace Process*, parts III–IV.

6 B. O'Duffy, 'British-Irish conflict regulation from Sunningdale to Belfast. Part II: Playing for a draw 1985–1999', *Nations and Nationalism*, 6:3 (2000), p. 410; Mallie and McKittrick, *The Fight for Peace*, pp. 303–4.

7 J. Tonge, *The New Northern Irish Politics?* (Houndmills: Palgrave Macmillan, 2005), p. 164.

8 Of course, it could equally be argued that the GFA allows for a more progressive form of unionism, which seeks to persuade nationalists that the Northern Ireland state can work for them, too, and in this secures the link with Britain.

9 See above, pp. 12–13.

10 On this, see Tonge, *The New Northern Irish Politics?*, ch. 10.

11 On this, see C. McCrudden, 'Equality and the Good Friday Agreement', in J. Ruane and J. Todd (eds), *After the Good Friday Agreement: Analysing Political Change in Northern Ireland* (Dublin: UCD Press, 1999).

12 This excepting the very different elections to the European Parliament.

13 White, *John Hume*, p. 157.

14 SDLP, *Proposals for Government in Northern Ireland: Report to Parliament* (Belfast: SDLP, 1975), XII.

15 This was most evident in Hume's party conference speeches in this period; see LHL, NIPC, SDLP Box 3.

16 Information gained from the author's participation in a 'Witness Seminar' with actors involved in the making of the DSD; hosted by University College Dublin, 2 June 2008.

17 HMSO, the Downing Street Declaration, para 4.

18 It should be noted that that the GFA won support amongst a slim but, in terms of its legitimacy, vital majority of unionists in the referendum in Northern Ireland; Bew and Gillespie, *Northern Ireland: A Chronology*, p. 395.

19 See above, p. 154.

20 *Irish News*, 25 May 1998.

21 *Irish Times*, 1 May 1998.

22 Tonge, *The New Northern Irish Politics?*, p. 47.

23 Interestingly, one of Hume's closest party colleagues, Seán Farren, also described the redefining of self-determination in an Irish context as a movement towards 'co-determination'; see S. Farren and B. Mulvihill, 'Beyond self-determination towards co-determination in Ireland', *Études Irlandaises*, 21:1 (1996).

24 O'Duffy, 'British-Irish conflict regulation from Sunningdale to Belfast. Part II', p. 413.

25 B. O'Duffy, 'British-Irish conflict regulation from Sunningdale to Belfast. Part I: Tracing the status of contesting sovereigns, 1968–1974', *Nations and Nationalism*, 5:4 (2000), p. 524.

26 Cunningham. 'The political language of John Hume', p. 15; Girvin 'Constitutional nationalism in Northern Ireland', p. 43; O'Brien, *Memoir*, p. 423.
27 See above, p. 41.
28 LHL, NIPC, P3395, letter from Hume to Adams, 17 March 1988, p. 3.
29 Cunningham, 'The Political Language of John Hume', p. 15.
30 See above, p. 151.
31 *Irish Times*, 13 January 1989.
32 LHL, NIPC, SDLP Box 3, J. Hume, 'Shaping the future', address to the SDLP annual conference, November 1990, p. 9.
33 D. Trimble, 'At long last Dublin recognises British territorial sovereignty', *Irish Times*, 18 May 1998.
34 B. Hadfield, 'The Belfast Agreement, sovereignty and the state of the Union', *Public Law* (1998), p. 615.
35 J. Ruane and J. Todd, 'The Belfast Agreement: context, content, consequences', in Ruane and Todd (eds), *After the Good Friday Agreement*, p. 11.
36 On this, see the following section.
37 HMSO, *The Belfast Agreement: An Agreement Reached at the Multi-Party Talks on Northern Ireland* [The Good Friday Agreement] (London: HMSO, 1998), Cmnd 3883, Constitutional Issues, Article 1(vi).
38 In 2004, changes in Irish law meant that those born in either part of Ireland were not automatically entitled to Irish citizenship. However, these changes were intended to deal with the issue of migrants from non-EU countries claiming Irish citizenship, and did not adversely affect the right of those living in Northern Ireland to obtain an Irish passport.
39 J. Todd, 'The reorientation of constitutional nationalism', in J. Coakley (ed.), *Changing Shades of Orange and Green: Redefining the Union and the Nation in Contemporary Ireland* (Dublin: UCD Press, 2002), p. 78.
40 J. McGarry and B. O'Leary, *The Northern Ireland Conflict: Consociational Engagements* (Oxford: Oxford University Press, 2004), p. 42.
41 For example, see P. Bew, 'The unionists have won, they just don't know it', *Sunday Times*, 17 May 1998; and D. Trimble, 'At long last Dublin recognises British territorial sovereignty'.
42 J. M. Regan, *The Irish Counter-Revolution, 1921–1936: Treatyite Politics and Settlement in Independent Ireland* (Dublin: Gill and Macmillan, 1999), p. 69.
43 Mallie and McKittrick, *Endgame*, pp. 278–9.
44 The Good Friday Agreement, Decommissioning Section, Article 3.
45 For a more detailed account of the troubled implementation of the GFA, and an explanation of the issues relating to this, see Dixon, *Northern Ireland*, ch. 10.
46 Bew and Gillespie, *Northern Ireland: A Chronology*, p. 395.
47 Mallie and McKittrick, *The Fight for Peace*, pp. 319–22; Mallie and McKittrick, *Endgame*, pp. 194–5; Murray, *John Hume and the SDLP*, pp. 175ff, 195, 204.
48 On this, see Murray, *John Hume and the SDLP*, ch. 11.
49 K. Bean, 'Defining republicanism: shifting discourses of new nationalism and post-republicanism', in M. Elliott (ed.), *The Long Road to Peace in Northern Ireland* (Liverpool: Liverpool University Press, 2002), pp. 133, 140.
50 *Ibid.*, p. 140.
51 Murray and Tonge, *Sinn Féin and the SDLP*, pp. xiv, 209, 211, 212.

52 *Ibid.*, pp. 223ff.
53 Dixon, *Northern Ireland*, pp. 312–13.
54 P. Mitchell, B. O'Leary and G. Evans, 'Flanking extremists bite the moderates and emerge in their clothes', *Parliamentary Affairs*, 54:4 (2001); P. Mitchell, B. O'Leary and G. Evans, 'The 2001 elections in Northern Ireland: moderating "extremists" and the squeezing of the moderates', *Representation*, 39:1 (2002).
55 A. Maginness, 'Redefining northern nationalism', in Coakley (ed.) *Changing Shades of Orange and Green*, p. 35; S. Farren, 'The SDLP and the Roots of the Good Friday Agreement', in Cox, Guelke and Stephen (eds), *A Farewell to Arms?*; Murray, *John Hume and the SDLP*, p. 261; Murray, 'The Good Friday Agreement: an SDLP analysis of the Northern Ireland conflict'; Murray and Tonge, *Sinn Féin and the SDLP*, pp. xiv, xvi, 200–3.
56 Todd, 'The reorientation of constitutional nationalism', pp. 75, 83.

11

A new Ireland in a new Europe

In December 1998, John Hume and David Trimble were joint winners of the Nobel Peace Prize, this recognising their efforts in brokering the GFA. In his acceptance speech in Oslo, Hume stressed one source of inspiration in particular:

> [The] European Union is the best example in the history of the world of conflict resolution. It is the duty of everyone, particularly those who live in areas of conflict, to study how it was done and to apply its principles to their own conflict resolution ... The peoples of Europe ... created institutions which respected their diversity ... but allowed them to work together in their common and substantial economic interest. ... That is precisely what we are now committed to doing in Northern Ireland. Our Agreement ... creates institutions which respect diversity but ensure that we work together in our common interest.[1]

As noted in Chapter 6, Hume had used his role as an MEP to bring a significant European influence to bear on Northern Ireland. Exploiting his contacts and the good favour which he had among the European elite, he was able to secure special financial aid for the region, and to create considerable debate on the conflict in the Strasbourg parliament.[2] In doing so, Hume also shaped European thinking in a way that was favourable to the SDLP. As Brigid Laffan noted: 'Hume played the European card with skill and used his position in the European Parliament's Socialist Group to garner support for his analysis of the conflict and its resolution'.[3] This, in turn, put pressure on the British government, encouraging it to adopt a more progressive policy on Northern Ireland, and in particular to act more closely with its Irish counterpart in a joint effort to resolve the problem.[4]

However, beyond these practical effects, Hume was deeply influenced by the actual ideology of European integration – as the above comments clearly suggest. Of course, his critics would question the integrity of this influence, arguing that Hume merely used integrationist ideas to create a more progressive image for the SDLP.[5] But it is clear that Hume's Europhilia was far from *ad hoc*. Indeed, he found much in the founding philosophy of the European project which coincided with his own belief – emphasised from his earliest writings in the mid-1960s – in practical co-operation as a means to political reconciliation.[6] Nonetheless, Hume's pro-Europeanism, and the questions which his critics have raised about this, both have relevance to nationalism. As such, it is worth exploring this aspect of Hume's thinking in more depth.

A formative influence

As early as February 1971 – when the SDLP was still in its infancy, and British and Irish entry into the EC was still in progress – Hume wrote an article for the *Fortnight* magazine in which he made the case for Europe as a context in which the Northern Ireland problem should be easier to resolve: 'while countries like France and Germany, who only 25 years ago were engaged in mutual carnage are today building bonds of friendship, in Ireland there is little or no sign of the communities coming together. It seems somewhat contradictory that each part of Ireland seems willing to participate separately in the planned integration of Europe, but not in the planned integration of this little island.'[7] However, even these early comments – and in particular the last line of this quotation – suggested that Hume's thinking went beyond the idea of Europe providing a model of political reconciliation. It also appeared that he saw the process of European integration as means towards Irish reunification.[8]

Such thinking was carried through to the SDLP's first published political proposals, the *Towards a New Ireland* document of 1972. As noted in Chapter 3, although this paper drew on contributions from a number of policy-makers in the early SDLP, Hume wrote the final version, and his pro-Europeanism shows though. Most notably, like Hume's *Fortnight* article, *Towards a New Ireland* celebrated the European project as paragon of political reconciliation: 'Old and bitter enemies are settling their differences and are working together in a new and wider context of a United Europe. We in this Island cannot remain in the seventeenth century. We cannot participate in this vision while at the same time continuing our outdated quarrel.' However, *Towards a New Ireland* was more explicit than Hume's *Fortnight* piece in its proposed solution to this quarrel: 'it would be in the best interests of all sections of the Communities ... if Ireland were to become united on terms which would be acceptable to all the people of Ireland.'[9] To this end – and again evoking the European model – *Towards a New Ireland* suggested political institutions which would facilitate co-operation between the North and South of Ireland, harmonising structures and services in the two jurisdictions, and paving the way towards their eventual unification.[10]

Like many of the ideas in *Towards a New Ireland*, this neo-functionalism – common to theories of European integration in this period[11] – would remain central to the thinking of Hume and the SDLP. In articulating a peaceful, gradualist approach to Irish reunification, Hume frequently used the history of post-war Europe as an example of how co-operation in areas of common social and economic interest could, in time, lead to political reconciliation. Similarly, Hume used the model of European integration to support his arguments in favour of a pluralist constitution, capable of accommodating all traditions and identities in Ireland:

> the peoples of Europe have been locked in the savagery of two world wars … that goes far beyond anything that we have experienced on this island. Yet … as a result of an agreed process, they have been able to create one parliament to represent them, one community – and the Germans are still German, the French are still French. They … have a unity in diversity. … Can we too build a unity in diversity?[12]

Of course, this type of discourse served only to heighten unionist distrust of Hume. In Protestant eyes, his pro-Europeanism was merely window-dressing for a traditional nationalist objective: the achievement of a unitary Irish state.[13]

Over time, however, Hume began to use Europe in a more nuanced way. Indeed, by the early 1990s – when the integrationist project itself was moving into a new phase – he was speaking more of how Europe provided an example of ways in which Northern Ireland could move beyond traditional modes of governance and state sovereignty.[14] In doing so, Hume came to be associated with the ideology of 'post-nationalism' – something of an intellectual fashion in the early 1990s.[15] But unionists and other critics remained suspicious, and dismissed any idea that Hume had abandoned the goal of a united Ireland. As Denis Kennedy argued, Hume's ideology was not post-nationalist, but simply 'traditional nationalist thinking dressed up in new European clothes'.[16]

Despite this, Hume and his party did adopt a more radical approach to the Northern Ireland problem in the early 1990s. Most notable in this respect was the *Agreeing New Political Structures* document which the SDLP presented to the Mayhew talks in 1992.[17] As noted in Chapter 9, this suggested an elaborate scheme of joint British–Irish governance over Northern Ireland, but one which also included a political role for the European Union (EU). In addition, the party proposed a 'North–South Council' – clearly modelled on the EU's Council of Ministers – to develop co-operation between the two parts of the island and, as one of its special functions, to deal with European issues which had an all-Ireland dimension.[18]

Unsurprisingly, the unionist representatives at the Mayhew talks immediately rejected the SDLP's proposals. As ever, they opposed any idea that Dublin should play a role in the administration of Northern Ireland, but felt that the involvement of the EU would signal a further dilution of British sovereignty over the region. However, aside from unionist objections, the British government was not hugely impressed by the SDLP's plan for a European role in Northern Ireland. Even more significantly, when he was asked to comment on the party's proposals at a Belfast press conference, the President of the EC, Jacques Delors, explicitly rejected the idea that Brussels could be directly involved in the governance of the region.[19]

It has been suggested that the SDLP were not serious about the proposals which it advanced in the *Agreeing New Political Structures* document. Indeed, when it later became known that Hume was still in dialogue with Gerry Adams, this reinforced the belief that his party had purposely overplayed its hand at the Mayhew talks. In this interpretation, Hume knew that the SDLP's proposals were too ambitious to be accepted by any other party, but was more concerned about bringing republicans into the political process. Accordingly, the *Agreeing New Political Structures* document may actually have been part of a delaying tactic. However, this interpretation does explain the way that Hume resolutely defended the paper. Indeed, after unionists dismissed the idea of Brussels' involvement in Northern Ireland, he even went public with his party proposals, using an interview on local radio to argue his case for a European role in the region:

> we proposed that there be a British Commissioner and an Irish Commissioner and more importantly a European Commissioner. We thought that if we asked the European Commission to nominate a Commissioner, that would ensure that Northern Ireland got major attention in that the European Community would do all in its power to make up for the major economic losses of the last twenty years.[20]

From this it seems that, whatever the practicality of these proposals, and however ambitious they appeared, Hume was serious in putting them forward for discussion at the Mayhew talks. Perhaps influenced by the radical changes taking place in Europe in the early 1990s, he believed that Brussels could make a radical contribution to the resolution of the Northern Ireland problem.[21]

Europe and the Good Friday Agreement

The GFA did not create political institutions as ambitious as those proposed by Hume and his party in either 1972 or 1992. Clearly, unionists were not prepared to allow anything that might equate with joint British–Irish authority over Northern Ireland. Similarly, though they did, eventually, accept an all-Ireland dimension to the settlement, unionist negotiators opposed any structures that might be seen as paving the way towards Irish reunification, with the spectre of Sunningdale's Council of Ireland always looming large in their minds.[22] Thus, the UUP adopted a particularly hard line in the 'Strand Two' talks – those dealing with new North–South structures. Indeed, in the final days of the negotiations, London and Dublin had reached their own agreement on this part of the deal, but found the UUP delegation vehemently opposed to their proposals, and threatening to walk out of the talks. As a result, this aspect of the settlement was renegotiated to produce North–South institutions that were far more modest than the SDLP, or indeed the two governments, had originally envisaged.[23]

Despite this, the all-Ireland structures of the GFA still bear an essential resemblance to the European-style cross-border arrangements long championed by Hume and the SDLP. Most obviously, like the institutions of the EU, they provide formal mechanisms of inter-jurisdictional co-operation. Moreover, though their competencies are circumscribed, the scope and powers of the GFA's North–South structures can be extended by agreement between the Northern Ireland Assembly and Dáil Éireann. Accordingly, the SDLP hoped that these structures would instigate a process similar to that seen in post-war Europe, where increased contact and co-operation between elites from the two parts of Ireland would build both personal trust and political momentum. In this, it was clear that neo-functionalism continued to influence the thinking of Hume and his colleagues.

The main all-Ireland institution to be created by the GFA was the North–South Ministerial Council (NSMC). Though less powerful than the North–South body which the SDLP had suggested at the Mayhew talks, the NSMC clearly drew upon the party's 1992 proposals. In particular, as with the SDLP's version, the NSMC showed a particularly European influence. Indeed, even in its basic mode of operation – meeting in both plenary and in different sectoral formations – this institution closely resembles the practice of the EU's Council of Ministers. Also, again like the SDLP's 1992 model, the NSMC was given specific authority to deal with EU matters which have an all-Ireland dimension.[24]

In addition to the NSMC, the GFA also created a number of cross-border 'implementation bodies'. These were intended to promote co-operation in particular areas of common interest between the two parts of Ireland, for example agriculture or tourism. However, one of the new bodies was given an exclusively European remit. The Special EU Programmes Body (SEUPB) assumed responsibility for the administration of all existing and future cross-border programmes developed by Brussels. In this, by developing an all-Ireland basis to the management of certain EU matters, both the NSMC and the SEUPB are close to the thinking of Hume and the SDLP, and reflect specific proposals which they had submitted to the settlement process.[25]

However, there were European influences beyond Strand Two of the GFA. Indeed, partly because the UUP was allowed to dilute the potential of the North–South institutions, in return, the SDLP had much of its way in the negotiations in Strand One. Most importantly, the Unionists accepted the SDLP's proposals for executive-level and fully inclusive power-sharing arrangements.[26] Again, this created a system with European parallels, consociationalism having a distinctly continental pedigree.[27] Moreover, the idea of an inter-communal coalition can be seen in the SDLP's earliest proposals, with *Towards a New Ireland* suggesting a

Northern Ireland assembly elected by proportional representation and then selecting an executive by the same method.[28] However, the party's thinking on this subject can be traced back even further. Indeed, in an interview with the *Irish Press* more than a year before the publication of *Towards a New Ireland*, Hume had suggested exactly the same executive system that was proposed in the 1972 document. This shows that, even before the fall of Stormont, Hume had been considering the possibility of communal power-sharing. Moreover, his musings made clear that Europe was his source of inspiration, as he cited the Swiss example as one alternative to Westminster-style majoritarianism:

> I'm not suggesting that the Swiss model should be imported into Northern Ireland. All I'm saying is that there are different kinds of constitutions besides the British one and some of these have been specifically geared to cope with minority problems. I'm suggesting that we should examine these and in the light of what we learn from them make radical changes in the constitutional framework of Northern Ireland which would help bridge the sectarian divide.[29]

Over a quarter of a century later, Europe continued to provide ideas for Hume and his colleagues as they sought to negotiate a new system of government for Northern Ireland. In particular, despite resistance from the UUP, the SDLP insisted that the new executive should be elected by the d'Hondt method – the same mechanism that is used to allocate political offices according to the share of seats in the European parliament. As the SDLP argued, this was the surest method towards proportional representation in the executive, thus guaranteeing nationalists that there would be no return to a majoritarian Stormont system.[30]

In summary, the GFA did not provide a set of institutions as radical as those envisaged by the SDLP in its submissions to the talks process, and certainly not as dynamic as those first suggested by the party in its *Towards a New Ireland* proposals. However, the structures which it did create certainly showed a European influence, for which Hume and his party bear some responsibility. In particular, the power-sharing executive and the institutions for North–South co-operation were both ideas that were mooted in *Towards a New Ireland*, and were consistently championed by the SDLP thereafter. However, unlike the party's 1972 proposals, the institutions of the GFA are not predetermined towards the reunification of Ireland. That said, it could be argued that the new structures are actually truer to the revisionist nationalist ideology on which the SDLP was founded. Through power-sharing and the North–South institutions, the GFA provides a political framework within which nationalists in both parts of Ireland can co-operate with unionists and, through this, gradually build more positive relations. Though some may hope that this creates a situation in which attitudes towards Irish unity might evolve, the GFA, like revisionist nationalism, promises that any move towards a unified Ireland will only come about with unionists' consent. In this respect, the GFA is also true to the spirit of the post-war European project. It is based on an acceptance of existing borders, but provides a context in which these do not act as barriers to peaceful co-operation, and political reconciliation.

Hume, 'post-nationalism' and the Good Friday Agreement

Numerous commentators have raised questions over Hume's Europeanism and what Paul Hainsworth described as his 'declared "post-Nationalist" politics'.[31] However, there is a need for caution here. Even in his most pro-European moments in the early 1990s, Hume did not 'declare' himself a post-nationalist. Mark Durkan, Hume's eventual successor as SDLP leader, and his closest aide in this period, is adamant on this point: 'John Hume never called himself a post-nationalist. He ... talked about a post-nationalist *world* and a post-nationalist *Europe*. He never branded himself a post-nationalist or his party.'[32] A close analysis of Hume's writings and speeches in the early 1990s tend to support this claim. They show Hume arguing that Northern Ireland, like the rest of the developed world, was moving into a post-nationalist age. This age, he reasoned, created new problems and challenges, from the economy to environment, which transcended nation-state boundaries. Accordingly, Hume suggested the need for international structures and collaborative approaches which did the same.[33] However, he clearly articulated this case in a way that supported the SDLP's position on the Northern Ireland problem. In particular, Hume used this thinking to strengthen the SDLP's arguments in favour of political institutions which broke with traditional notions of absolute or indivisible sovereignty, and thus could accommodate both political communities in Northern Ireland.

In devising such institutions, Hume continued to point to Europe as the exemplar.[34] With the development of the Single European Market in the late 1980s, and then the birth of the EU in 1992, he assumed that a wholly new political order was in the making. Accordingly, his arguments at this time became ever more optimistic of the part that Europe might play in helping to resolve the Northern Ireland problem.[35] Of course, with the benefit of hindsight, it is clear that Hume was being overly optimistic, and indeed was over-estimating the dynamic of European integration. However, he was not alone in this. In the late 1980s to early 1990s, the period in which the integrationist project achieved perhaps its greatest momentum, many pro-Europeans believed that they were witnessing the emergence of a new and truly supranational polity. In this context, various commentators on Northern Ireland began to speak – in a way not dissimilar to Hume – of how the process of European integration could help to resolve the conflict. Undoubtedly, the optimism of this period was also encouraged by the burgeoning peace process, which began to open up debate on Northern Ireland. However, in time, this debate became coloured by a particularly European discourse, which many referred to as 'post-nationalism'.[36]

Hume also imbibed something of this discourse, as was clearly evident in an article which he wrote in 1993, 'A new Ireland, in a new Europe'. His arguments in this piece were products of their time, influenced by specifically European developments, but also broader, global issues of the day: the growing debate on the environment; the technological and communications revolutions of the early 1990s; and the related advance of transnational economic activity. In different ways, all of these developments appeared to further erode the boundaries and challenge the capacities of the traditional nation-state system. Accordingly, Hume was clearly thinking beyond the Northern Ireland problem when he claimed that

> the democratic nation-state is no longer a sufficient political entity to allow people to have adequate control over the economic and technological forces that affect people's opportunities and circumstances. The task is ... to optimise the real sovereignty of the peoples of Europe rather than ossify our democratic development around limited notions of national sovereignty that only give space to multinational vested interest.[37]

However, in making this case, Hume was not claiming that nationalism was no longer relevant. Rather, he was suggesting that previous conceptions of national independence and sovereignty, ideas rooted in the nineteenth century, were simply not appropriate to the late twentieth-century world:

> the nation-state is not the last word in polity creation. There is an increasing acceptance that policies and agencies operating only on a nation-state basis cannot properly cope with wider economic and technological forces and trends which bear on our social circumstances and impact on our environment. ... Shared sovereignty and interdependence are therefore the issue because they are the method by which we can optimise democratic policy-making in so many matters. The traditional notions of absolute sovereignty and territorial jealousy are now so inadequate that their promotion is destructive.[38]

In this, Hume was moving beyond his previous support of Europe as a model of conflict resolution, or even a means to Irish reunification. He was also suggesting that the new modes of sovereignty and inter-state co-operation in Europe provided the most effective way to deal with the problems of an increasingly globalised world.

Nonetheless, Hume still felt that changes in the European order had particular implications for Northern Ireland, arguing that the conflict there stemmed from a broader failure to resolve issues of sovereignty in Britain and Ireland: 'All this clearly has significance for Ireland given that the historic difficulties in relationships within the island and between Britain and itself have hinged on attitudes and aspirations concerning sovereignty ... The new European scene offers a psychological framework in which such issues can no longer be pushed in absolutist terms.' In addition, he felt that the European experience could have an 'educative effect' on the two communities in Northern Ireland: 'People can see others with deep and marked historical and cultural differences working together, compromising and co-operating without any sacrifice of principle. ... There are lessons in that for our quest for political arrangements that can accommodate different interests and identities, promote co-operation, provide for common needs, and allow for agreed development and adjustment in the future.' As such, Hume hoped that the European example might encourage the two communities in Northern Ireland to move away from a zero-sum conception of their conflict:

> I believe that we are benefiting from exposure to a political ethos and modalities which are not as psychologically constraining as the ethos of 'winner takes all' ... The changes that have taken place in Europe offer, then, the prospect that bitter conflict and tension can be replaced by co-operation and partnership without anyone being cast as the victor or the vanquished and without anyone loosing distinctiveness or identity.[39]

From this it is clear that Hume was not arguing for the abandonment of nationalism or even the transcendence of national identity. Rather, he was suggesting that Europe, by moving away from restrictive forms of national sovereignty, was successfully adapting to the complexities and challenges of an increasingly interdependent world. At the same time, Hume was reinforcing and augmenting arguments in which he had previously linked the situation in Northern Ireland to the process of political reconciliation in Europe. In particular, he was suggesting that the European model provided an example of how conflicting national identities could be accommodated in more plural and flexible forms of governance. Hume hoped that this example might influence attitudes in Northern Ireland, but also more broadly, throughout Britain and Ireland, thus easing the path towards a comprehensive resolution of political relations within and between the two islands. In short, Hume was using the European model to try to move the thinking of all parties to the conflict away from absolutist notions of political sovereignty, to encourage thoughts of constitutional compromise, and thus to aid the infant peace process.

Towards the end of the 1990s, it was clear that European integration was not having the radical impact on the nation-state system which Hume and others had anticipated at the outset of the decade. Similarly, it was evident that Europe had not had the radical impact on Northern Ireland which Hume and others had hoped for. Nonetheless, the European experience did have some influence on the peace process, and the eventual achievement of the GFA. As Ruane and Todd suggested: 'The institutions set up under the ... Good Friday Agreement, were not copies of EU institutions, but they would not have been possible without the loosing of notions of sovereignty exemplified in the EU.'[40]

Other authors have also noted the subtle and indirect influence that European integration has had on Northern Ireland, suggesting that it helped to provide an environment more favourable to political compromise.[41] Even John McGarry, who generally questions the impact which Europe has had on Northern Ireland, accepts this argument: 'European integration has created a context in which the aspirations of nationalists' for meaningful recognition of their national identity through all-island political institutions can be reconciled with unionists' preparedness to accept such institutions providing they are functionally useful'.[42] However, in the same work, McGarry used a wealth of electoral and survey data to refute the suggestions of those who believed that European integration has caused any significant erosion or even softening of political identities in Northern Ireland.[43] In doing so, he dismissed the idea that the GFA represented a move 'beyond' nationalism. Indeed, rather than transcending traditional identities, he argued that the Agreement was designed to accommodate the political differences between the two communities.[44]

Of course, it could be argued that it is this approach, rather than any post-nationalist prescription, which is more commonly associated with Hume and the SDLP. Indeed, the idea of accommodating the two political identities in Northern Ireland goes back to Hume's 'two traditions' thesis of the 1970s[45] and the bi-national arguments contained in the NIF report of 1984. Moreover, Murray and Tonge suggest that it was this strand of Hume's thinking rather any post-nationalist ideology which fed into the GFA.[46] However, other commentators – some intimately associated with the post-nationalist ideas of the early 1990s – have criticised this bi-national approach. By building a settlement based on a recognition of the two main identities in Northern Ireland, they argued that the GFA served to institutionalise and so to 'freeze' those identities. In particular, critics took issue with the communal voting mechanisms of the new Northern Ireland Assembly, the operation of which required members to designate themselves as 'unionist' or 'nationalist'.[47] This system, it was argued, served to maintain and even promote sectarian alignment in Northern Ireland. As such, critics suggest that the GFA will actually frustrate any movement towards the kind of post-nationalist scenario which some had hoped for at the outset of the peace process in the early 1990s.[48]

Responding to this critique, it might be argued that the bi-nationalism of the GFA is a necessary response to the reality of the problem in Northern Ireland, where society is still, essentially, divided along the traditional nationalist–unionist fault-line. Any solution which does not recognise this division – that does not accept that most people in Northern Ireland, at present, want to be represented by unionist or nationalist politicians – would be unlikely to gain widespread acceptance. What the GFA does is to recognise this division, but also attempt to harness it. In doing so, it allows previously conflicting communities not only to co-exist, but also to work together in areas of common social and economic interest. Thus, as

McGarry argues: 'Rather than entrenching divisions as some post-nation-alists suggest, the Agreement's institutions offer the possibility of national-ists and unionists co-operating with each other and building the trust that will allow them to transcend their differences in the longer term.'[49]

It could further be argued that recognition of Northern Ireland as a bi-national society does represent progress. As part of the GFA, London and Dublin accepted the right of Northern Ireland's citizens to be British, Irish, or indeed to claim both identities, and to hold both national pass-ports. This, in itself, allows for a certain 'hybridity' of identity, where Northern Ireland citizens can perceive of themselves as being both British and Irish, and perhaps more one than the other according to circumstance and situation.[50] Moreover, the GFA does not rule out identities beyond the British–Irish or unionist–nationalist binaries. Indeed, though critics focus on the designation rule which underpins the Assembly's communal voting mechanisms, they say less on the fact that members can forgo identifica-tion with either the unionist or nationalist blocs, and instead assign them-selves as a non-aligned 'other'. Thus, Assembly members are not forced to be unionists or nationalists – they can be liberals, socialists, environmen-talists, or any other political category that they choose. Moreover, the elec-torate are free to vote for such representatives. At present, the vast majority does not, instead voting for unionist or nationalist candidates, and critics will cite this as evidence that the GFA is failing to encourage any movement towards a more plural society. However, such change was obviously not going to happen overnight, and certainly not in the years immediately after the Agreement, when its troubled implementation pro-vided grounds for renewed inter-communal contest. But that difficult phase appears to have been successfully negotiated,[51] and the new institu-tions are finally working as intended. Thus, it may only be now, after a period of sustained political stability, that any fair judgement of the GFA might begin to be formed.

However, for critics of the GFA, the fact that it is Sinn Féin and the DUP that are leading the current dispensation still gives reason for concern. Indeed, they argue that the rise to prominence of these parties is evidence of the continued polarisation of society in Northern Ireland, a situation which they feel the Agreement has actually encouraged.[52] But Sinn Féin and the DUP are clearly not the parties that they once were, having both moved onto the political terrain of their more moderate rivals, the SDLP and the UUP respectively.[53] As such, it is questionable whether their elec-toral supremacy should be read in the way that critics of the GFA do, that is as evidence of a more sectarian society. Indeed, the very fact that Sinn Féin and the DUP are now working together in the governance of Northern Ireland is surely evidence of progress rather than polarisation. Moreover, whatever their ideological differences, as these parties are obliged to con-tinue their co-operation in the administration of Northern Ireland, and as they are held accountable for the decisions they make regarding the region's social and economic development, this is surely what they will be judged upon. Bread and butter politics will, gradually, evolve, because the traditional issues of dispute – over Northern Ireland's constitutional status, and then over decommissioning, policing, and so on – have now been addressed.[54] Of course, this is not to say that all will be sweetness and light in Northern Ireland from now on. But, over time, social and economic issues are bound to become increasingly important in terms of political debate in the region. Also, by allowing this development of more normal political competition, in time, Northern Ireland may see the emergence of new alignments which span the religious divide, for example socialist or environmental parties. This, in turn, will allow for further movement away from traditional communal politics, as those of a post-nationalist persuasion hope for. However, arguably, such a scenario is only possible because the GFA has, in the first instance, secured the identities and essential interests of the two main communities in Northern Ireland, and thus ended the conflict which hitherto prevented any normal mode of politics.

But the question remains: is the GFA, or the type of thinking which Hume was promoting in the early 1990s, post-nationalist? Arguably, the answer depends on how the term 'post-nationalism' is defined. If post-nationalism involves a decisive break with or a complete transcendence of traditional forms of national identity, then the answer is clearly no. However, even for some of those who support a post-nationalist agenda, it does not seem that this is the intention. Indeed, Richard Kearney – perhaps the most celebrated commentator on post-nationalism in an Irish context – from the opening page of his *Postnationalist Ireland* (1997) was adamant that his aim was 'not to denounce nationalism – Irish or British – out of hand, but to reinterrogate its critical implications'.[55] As such, Kearney did not dismiss the role of national identity. Rather, he advocated new ways of thinking about, accommodating and expressing such identity, not only in Ireland, but also in Britain, this to end the historic conflict of nationalisms between and within the two islands.[56]

Meanwhile, for those who do see post-nationalism as involving a wholesale movement beyond nationalist forms of identification, they are clearly pursuing a chimera. Indeed, for even Western Europe – where the ideas of post-nationalism appeared to find their greatest hopes – has not witnessed any great erosion of national identity. Instead, it has seen an increasing interaction of different identities and cultures. This is a result, not only of European integration, but also of the wider processes of globalisation, such as increased population movements, a revolution in methods of international communication, and the growth of trans-state networks. Together, these developments are creating more multi-cultural and more complex societies, where people may have nested or hybrid identities, and thus where traditional national loyalties are no longer as singularly dominant as they might have been for much of the nineteenth and twentieth centuries. And it is exactly this that Hume recognised when he talked of post-nationalism. He anticipated the emergence of a socio-political order where traditional identities would not be abandoned, but could co-exist alongside other allegiances:

> Simultaneously or successively, we can be Europeans, British, Irish, Northern Irish, Derrymen or Derrywomen – whatever we choose. In this new world, there are no incompatibilities between identities, there is no superiority of one identity over another, we can be free to invent ourselves. Ultimately identity will simply become a matter of comfort and convenience, not a sign of tribal loyalty. This is the world we must seek and perhaps, invent.[57]

The GFA has certainly not invented a Northern Ireland as plural as Hume suggested here. However, it has provided a basis from which such pluralism can evolve. Of course, it will only be after the region enjoys a sustained period of stable government, and therein the gradual normalisation of relations between the two communities, that such an evolution might take place. But what is crucial is that the GFA does not preclude or prohibit such a development.

The GFA protects and, as some critics suggest, arguably privileges the two currently predominant identities in Northern Ireland.[58] But it does so to remedy the previous situation, wherein the two communities were so distrustful – and felt their identities to be so threatened by the other – that Northern Ireland could not be governed in a peaceful or democratic manner. However, now that these previously conflicting identities have been secured, a more normal society is emerging, one which may, in time, allow other allegiances to develop. For example, in post-Agreement Northern Ireland, there is no reason why someone with a strong British–unionist identity, whilst not abandoning that identity, might now feel that she can afford to concern herself more with social and economic issues at election time, and thus vote for a socialist candidate. Similarly, someone with a strong Irish nationalist identity, feeling that this identity is now respected in Northern Ireland, might be more able to concern himself with environmental issues, and perhaps become involved in cross-community political action on that basis. Also, beyond the nationalist–unionist binary, the extensive equality agenda of the GFA means that the rights and identities of other sections of society – women, people with disabilities, migrant workers, and so on – are all given strong legal protection.[59] In this, whilst the Agreement does, in the first instance, seek to resolve the conflict between the two main identities in Northern Ireland, it can also accommodate other groups, and does allow for the emergence of multiple and cross-cutting identities.

In summary, the GFA is not, in itself, a post-nationalist solution to the Northern Ireland problem. However, it does provide the basis for the development of a society which is more tolerant and plural, and ultimately where national identity – or any other identity – need not be a cause of conflict. With this, Northern Ireland can become as post-national as any other region of the world. Indeed, for it does not seem that any society has experienced a transcendence of national identity, but rather that all developed regions are engaged in an ongoing process of adaptation, as each seeks to deal with the social and political realities of an increasingly globalised world.

Of course, for some, this will not answer the question as to where, exactly, Hume would stand on this debate. As Todd has noted, there are still those who wish to pin down his thinking, and 'to fit it into clear nationalist or post-nationalist categories. ... [Thus] Hume's ideology is either seen as essentially post-nationalist with nationalist residues, or essentially nationalist with a post-nationalist veneer.'[60] Todd's own interpretation is that Hume's thinking is dualist, drawing on both nationalist and more universal non-nationalist principles,[61] and this is an entirely reasonable conclusion. However, the present study takes a different tack, arguing that neither a simple nationalist nor a post-nationalist label is appropriate to describe Hume's ideology. For he was clearly not a post-nationalist – at least not in the sense that he abandoned Irish nationalist aspirations, or sought to transcend Irish nationalist identity. But neither was he, as Kennedy claims, a 'traditional nationalist ... dressed up in new European clothes'.[62] Instead, this study has sought to show that Hume is best considered as a revisionist nationalist – clearly part of the Irish nationalist tradition, but changing key elements in the ideology of that tradition. Thus, he maintained the aspiration to Irish unity, and upheld the right of northern nationalists to express their Irish identity, but developed new ways of realising these goals. Accordingly, for Hume, the aim was not to unite a territory, but rather the people that shared it. To that end, he did not see Irish identity as something which need be oppositional to or exclusive of the Ulster unionist tradition, and did not believe that its political and institutional expression should diminish the same right of expression for unionists. Indeed, Hume's vision was of an Ireland where Irish nationalist and Ulster unionist would find mutually acceptable political arrangements which would allow them not only to co-exist, but also to interact, and through this to reshape their relations with one another. Hume's vision, much inspired by the European ideal, was what he termed a 'unity in diversity'[63] – an Ireland which would accommodate rather than eliminate difference, and thus respect the diversity of its people. In his contribution to the GFA, he has helped to create a situation in which such an Ireland can emerge.

Notes

1   J. Hume, Nobel Peace Prize acceptance speech, 10 December 1998; available at: www.sdlp.ie/news_speeches_07.html (accessed 30 April 2007).
2   Ruane and Todd, *The Dynamics of Conflict*, p. 282.
3   B. Laffan, 'The European context: a new political dimension in Ireland, North and South', in J. Coakley, B. Laffen and J. Todd (eds), *Renovation or*

Revolution? New Territorial Politics in Ireland and the United Kingdom (Dublin: University College Dublin Press, 2005), p. 175.

4 Guelke, *Northern Ireland*, p. 160; Kennedy, 'The European Union and the Northern Ireland question', p. 179.

5 Cunningham, 'The political language of John Hume', pp. 17–18; Kennedy, 'The European Union and the Northern Ireland question'; pp. 167, 185; D. Kennedy, 'Europe and the Northern Ireland problem', in D. Kennedy (ed.) *Living with the European Union: The Northern Ireland Experience* (Basingstoke: Macmillan, 2000), p. 166.

6 See above, p. 12. Hume's strong belief in the power of co-operative action was likely to have been learned though his work with the Credit Union movement. On this, see Hume, *A New Ireland*, pp. 27–8.

7 Hume, 'John Hume's Ireland', *Fortnight*, 5 February 1971, p. 5.

8 Hume was not the first Irish nationalist to use the European project in this way. Indeed, when he submitted Ireland's original application to join the EC in 1961, Seán Lemass maintained that it would advance the cause of Irish reunification. This argument was taken up by many subsequent southern Irish leaders, in particular Garret FitzGerald. As has been noted (see above p. 132, n. 18), FitzGerald and Hume were very similar in their political thinking, particularly on Northern Ireland, and this was also the case in the way that they related Europe to the problem. For example, see FitzGerald's *Towards a New Ireland*, which was written in the same period that Hume was making his first published comments on Europe, and may, therefore, suggest an interchange of ideas between the two men.

9 SDLP, *Towards a New Ireland*, p. 2.

10 *Ibid.* p. 6.

11 See E. B. Haas, *The Uniting of Europe: Political Social and Economic Forces, 1950–1957* (Stanford, CA: Stanford University Press, 1968).

12 Hume, 'The Irish question', p. 310.

13 Kennedy, 'Europe and the Northern Ireland problem', p. 167; C. McCall, 'Postmodern Europe and the resources of communal identities in Northern Ireland', *European Journal of Political Research*, 33 (1998), p. 398; C. McCall, *Identity in Northern Ireland: Communities, Politics and Change* (Basingstoke: Palgrave, 1999), pp. 83, 101, 106, 170; Mitchell and Cavanagh, 'Context and contingency: constitutional nationalists in Europe', p. 259.

14 This was most evident in Hume's conference party speeches in this period; see LHL, NIPC, SDLP Box 3.

15 See below, pp. 199ff., for further discussion of this subject.

16 Kennedy, 'The European Union and the Northern Ireland question', p. 185.

17 Another idea with which the SDLP was associated in this period was that of a 'Europe of Regions'. This concept was also popular with commentators of a 'post-nationalist' persuasion, who argued that the nation-state system would be further eroded, not only by the continued transfer of sovereignty to Brussels, but also by a significant devolution of powers to sub-national regions of Europe. However, some related this thinking to Northern Ireland specifically as a means to transcend the conflict there. The idea in this was that a Northern Ireland polity could exist as part of a larger federation of similar-sized European regions. This, it was argued, would help to delink Northern Ireland from the source of its conflicting nationalisms – the British

and Irish nation-states – create a more common regional identity amongst its citizens, and make its constitutional position less anomalous in relation to other European regions. On this thinking, see G. Delanty, 'Northern Ireland in a Europe of regions', *The Political Quarterly*, 67:2 (1996) and R. Kearney and R. Wilson, 'Northern Ireland's future as a European region' (submission to the Opshal Commission, Belfast, 2 February 1993), in R. Kearney *Post-Nationalist Ireland: Politics, Culture, Philosophy* (London: Routledge, 1997). However, whilst the SDLP also spoke in terms of a Europe of Regions, it seems that what it meant by this was simply that it favoured a significant decentralisation of political power in Europe (see SDLP, *SDLP Manifesto: A New North, A New Ireland, A New Europe* (n.p., Watermark Press: 1992), p. 12). The party did not, at least explicitly, argue that a Europe of Regions would be a panacea for the conflict in Northern Ireland – though it did advocate the devolution of power to the region, and specifically the co-operation of the two communities in its exercise, as a means to aid their reconciliation. Moreover, Hume's most detailed exposition on the idea of a Europe of Regions shows that he was more concerned with the social and economic advantages of regionalisation – and this in the South of Ireland as much as the North – rather than the political effects that it might have on the latter. See J. Hume, 'Europe of the Regions', in R. Kearney (ed.), *Across the Frontiers: Ireland in the 1990s* (Dublin: Wolfhound, 1988).

18 Kennedy, 'Europe and the Northern Ireland problem', pp. 156, 158; McCall, *Identity in Northern Ireland*, p. 47.
19 *Irish Times*, 4 November 1992.
20 Quoted in Murray, *John Hume and the SDLP*, p. 218.
21 Whilst Hume was unable to persuade the EU to assume any political role in the Northern Ireland peace process, he did gain further economic aid. Indeed, in the wake of the 1994 ceasefires, he played a major part in securing a generous financial package from Brussels which was designed to support peace initiatives in the region; Murray, *John Hume and the SDLP*, pp. 213–14.
22 Hennessy, *The Northern Ireland Peace Process*, p. 133.
23 Bew, Gibbon and Patterson, *Northern Ireland, 1921–2001*, p. 236; Mallie and McKittrick, *Endgame*, pp. 260–6; Tonge, *The New Northern Irish Politics?*, pp. 166, 187.
24 Laffan, 'The European context', pp. 173, 181.
25 *Ibid.*, p. 182; Kennedy, 'Europe and the Northern Ireland problem', p. 156, 158; Murray, *John Hume and the SDLP*, pp. 205–6, 217, 218.
26 Bew, Gibbon and Patterson, *Northern Ireland, 1921–2001*, pp. 236–7; Mallie and McKittrick, *Endgame*, pp. 266–70.
27 See A. Liphart, *Democracy in Plural Societies: A Comparative Exploration* (New Haven, CT: Yale University Press, 1977).
28 SDLP, *Towards a New Ireland*, pp. 4–5.
29 *Irish Press*, 18 March 1971.
30 Hennessy, *The Northern Ireland Peace Process*, p. 125.
31 P. Hainsworth, 'European Community Membership', in A. Aughey and D. Morrow (eds), *Northern Ireland Politics* (Harlow: Longman, 1996), p. 130.
32 Mark Durkan; interview with author, Belfast, 6 April 2009 (Durkan's emphasis).
33 Hume, 'A New Ireland in a new Europe', pp. 227, 229. See also his party conference speeches in the early 1990s; LHL, NIPC, SDLP Box 3.

34 Hume, 'A new Ireland, in a new Europe', *passim*.
35 *Ibid.*, *passim*. Also see his party conference speeches in the early 1990s; LHL, NIPC, SDLP Box 3.
36 For examples of literature on Northern Ireland that was influenced by this pro-European and post-nationalist discourse, see K. Boyle, 'Northern Ireland: allegiances and identities', in B. Crick (ed.), *National Identities: The Constitution of the United Kingdom* (Oxford: Blackwell, 1991); G. Delanty, 'Habermas and post-national identity: theoretical perspectives on the conflict in Northern Ireland', *Irish Political Studies*, 11 (1996); V. Geoghegan, 'Socialism, national identities and post-nationalist citizenship', *Irish Political Studies*, 9 (1994); R. Kearney, *Post-Nationalist Ireland: Politics, Culture, Philosophy* (London: Routledge, 1997); E. Meehan, 'Citizens Are Plural', *Fortnight*, 311 (1992).
37 Hume, 'A new Ireland in a new Europe', p. 227.
38 *Ibid.*, pp. 229–30.
39 *Ibid.*, pp. 230–1.
40 J. Ruane and J. Todd, 'A changed Irish nationalism? The significance of the Good Friday Agreement of 1998', in J. Ruane, J. Todd and A. Mandeville (eds), *Europe's Old States in the New World Order: The Politics of Transition in Britain, France and Spain* (Dublin: UCD Press, 2003), p. 129. See also J. Ruane and J. Todd, 'The Northern Ireland conflict and the impact of globalisation', pp. 116, 121–2.
41 Laffan, 'The European context', p. 173; E. Meehan, 'Europe and the Europeanisation of the Irish question', in M. Cox, A. Guelke and F. Stephen (eds), *A Farewell to Arms?: Beyond the Good Friday Agreement* (Manchester: Manchester University Press, 2nd edn, 2006), pp. 338, 352.
42 J. McGarry, 'Globalization, European integration, and the Northern Ireland conflict', in M. Keating and J. McGarry (eds), *Minority Nationalism and the Changing International Order* (Oxford: Oxford University Press, 2001), p. 313.
43 See McCall, *Identity in Northern Ireland*, *passim*, for an alternative reading of how European integration and other processes of 'post-modernity' may have a subtle, long-term effect on identities in Northern Ireland.
44 McGarry, 'Globalization, European integration, and the Northern Ireland conflict', pp. 307, 314. See also, J. McGarry, 'Europe's Limits: European Integration and Conflict Management in Northern Ireland', in J. McGarry and M. Keating (eds), *European Integration and the Nationalities Question* (London: Routledge, 2006).
45 See above, pp. 69ff.
46 Murray and Tonge, *Sinn Féin and the SDLP*, p. 258; J. Tonge, 'Commentary' on M. Cunningham's 'The Political Language of John Hume', in C. McGrath and E. O'Malley (eds), *Irish Political Studies Reader: Key Contributions* (London: Routledge, 2008), p. 145.
47 The essential purpose of this scheme is to provide group vetoes, this to avoid a communal majority overriding the interests of a communal minority on key issues.
48 A. Oberschall and L. K. Palmer, 'The failure of moderate politics: the case of Northern Ireland', in I. O'Flynn and D. Russell (eds), *Power Sharing: New Challenges for Divided Societies* (London: Pluto, 2005), pp. 77, 79, 89;

I. O'Flynn, 'The problem of recognising individual and national identities: a liberal critique of the Belfast Agreement', *Critical Review of International Social and Political Philosophy*, 6:3 (2003), pp. 140, 144, 151; R. Taylor, 'Northern Ireland: consociation or social transformation', in J. McGarry (ed.), *Northern Ireland and the Divided World: Post-Agreement Northern Ireland in Comparative Perspective* (Oxford: Oxford University Press, 2001), pp. 38, 47–8; R. Taylor, 'The Belfast Agreement and the politics of consociationalism: a critique', *The Political Quarterly*, 77:2 (2006), pp. 218–19; R. Wilson, 'Towards a civic culture: implications for power-sharing policy makers', in O'Flynn and Russell (eds), *Power Sharing*, p. 206; R. Wilson and R. Wilford, 'Northern Ireland: a route to stability?' (2003), pp. 2, 5–6, 7–8, available at: www.devolution.ac.uk/pdfdata/Wilson_&_Wilford_Paper.pdf (accessed 31 March 2009).

49 McGarry, 'Globalization, European integration, and the Northern Ireland conflict', p. 308.

50 Survey data suggests that many people in Northern Ireland already do this, and that the GFA is, therefore, simply validating and thus encouraging such hybridity and flexibility of identity. Also, some commentators have noted evidence suggesting a shift towards a unique 'Northern Irish' identity by significant elements in both communities in recent years; Ruane and Todd, 'A changed Irish nationalism?', pp. 135–6; Tonge, *The New Northern Irish Politics?*, p. 176. If such trends continue, they may aid the diminution of communal opposition and identity conflict in Northern Ireland. For a comprehensive discussion of identity and identity change in the region, which draws upon the most up-to-date survey data, see J. Coakley, 'National identity in Northern Ireland: stability or change?', *Nations and Nationalism*, 13:4 (2007).

51 The one major outstanding issue is the devolution of policing and justice powers, which was meant to be dealt with under the terms of the 2006 St Andrews Agreement. At the time of writing, it seems that the Northern Ireland parties are close to finding a way to move forward on this issue whilst retaining the confidence of their respective support bases.

52 Oberschall and Palmer, 'The failure of moderate politics', p. 90; O'Flynn, 'The problem of recognising individual and national identities', pp. 142–3; Taylor, 'The Belfast Agreement, pp. 219–20; R. Wilson, 'Towards a civic culture: implications for power-sharing policy makers', in O'Flynn and Russell (eds), *Power Sharing*, p. 213.

53 Mitchell, O'Leary and Evans, 'Flanking extremists bite the moderates and emerge in their clothes'; Mitchell, O'Leary and Evans, 'The 2001 elections in Northern Ireland'.

54 However, see above, n. 51.

55 Kearney, *Post-Nationalist Ireland*, p. 1.

56 *Ibid., passim.* See also Kearney's 'Introduction: thinking otherwise', in R. Kearney (ed.), *Across the Frontiers: Ireland in the 1990s* (Dublin: Wolfhound, 1988).

57 Hume, *A New Ireland*, p. 155.

58 O'Flynn, 'The problem of recognising individual and national identities', p. 144; Taylor, 'The Belfast Agreement, p. 219.

59 On this, see McCrudden, 'Equality and the Good Friday Agreement'.

60 J. Todd, 'Nationalism, republicanism and the Good Friday Agreement', in Ruane and Todd (eds), *After the Good Friday Agreement*, p. 53.
61 *Ibid.*, pp. 53–6.
62 Kennedy, 'The European Union and the Northern Ireland question', p. 185.
63 Hume, 'The Irish question', p. 310.

Conclusions

> The great historical legacy of the SDLP, and of John Hume in particular, lies in redefining Irish nationalism. I deliberately do not say Northern nationalism, as I believe the SDLP has radically changed the thinking of the mainstream political parties in the South, as well as the broad mass of constitutional nationalist thinking in both North and South. Not only do I make that wider claim, but I also further claim that the SDLP has radically changed the thinking of physical force nationalism or republicanism as well. (Alban Maginness)[1]

Despite the boldness of this assertion – and, indeed, despite the fact that it is made by one of Hume's party colleagues – it has a certain credibility. Of course, as demonstrated in this study, Hume was not the sole originator of the ideas that redefined Irish nationalism. Even before entering into politics, he had started to feed on the thinking abroad in his community. Thereafter, as an elected representative of that community, Hume imbibed ideas from various sources. Accordingly, much of what might be considered his political philosophy may in fact find its genesis in the thoughts of SDLP colleagues, the suggestions of Irish government officials, or the musings of opinion-formers in the media.[2]

Recalling the SDLP's formative years, Austin Currie is keen to emphasise this point:

> Hume initially made a mark at our meetings because of his capacity to write a statement expressing the consensus of our discussions. ... He had to be watched, however, as he had a tendency to introduce certain words, Humespeak, easily identifiable as his and which gave the impression that that he was responsible for the proposal or idea. Sometimes he was, sometimes he was not. ... He had a formidable capacity to analyse a situation and present it as part of a consistent argument. He was an original thinker, but also extremely good at picking up points made by others and presenting them as his own.[3]

But even in this, Currie tacitly admits that Hume, long before he was party leader, became the SDLP's chief spokesperson. In assuming this role, Hume also became the voice of a new form of Irish nationalism. He did so because of his innate ability to pull together the ideas of those around him, assemble them into a coherent discourse, and then express them in a highly persuasive manner.

Hume was, therefore, both a propagator and broker of revisionist nationalism. Also recalling the SDLP's early years, Paddy Devlin asserted that Hume consciously sought to play this role:

> He had a tendency to identify the most powerful and influential people among those we encountered and go off into corner-huddles with these pace-setters and opinion-formers. Editors of important newspapers and TV programmes were the most regularly endowed with these special briefings, which laid the ground-stones for his later reputation as a political visionary and fixer *extraordinaire*.[4]

But Hume was influential amongst the political as well the media establishment. Indeed, as noted in Chapter 3, through his contacts in Iveagh House, Hume was also able to shape the thinking of the Dublin government from the earliest days of the Troubles. However, it was not until the early 1980s, with the NIF, that he had the opportunity to fully impress his ideas upon the Irish state and society. For as well as the huge media coverage which this initiative secured, it also allowed Hume and his colleagues to fully integrate themselves with the political elite in the Republic. Thereafter, successive Irish governments saw the Northern Ireland problem in terms which were greatly influenced by the SDLP.[5] The NIF thus created an essential ideological consensus among constitutional nationalists, a consensus which Hume played a major part in shaping.

In time, the republican movement was also drawn into this consensus. However, on this point, again it should be stressed that, by the late 1980s, the Provisional leadership had already begun to question the efficacy of the armed struggle. Nonetheless, republicans' re-appraisal was clearly encouraged by the prospect of exchanging their military campaign for a place in the powerful nationalist coalition that had been created through the NIF. Thus, it might be argued that, even without Hume's dialogue with Adams, the politicisation of republicanism would eventually have led to Sinn Féin's 'peace strategy'. However, Hume's intervention undoubtedly hastened the process. His engagement with the Provisionals – at a time when they were still considered political pariahs – was extremely risky, but also extremely important in facilitating their entry into the democratic mainstream. Indeed, though the movement's leadership may have realised the redundancy of the armed struggle, Hume's efforts were essential in gaining the commitments and public declarations from London and Dublin which were necessary to steer the republican rank and file behind Sinn Féin's new departure. In the course of this transition, republican leaders also came to adopt a phraseology not unlike that of Hume and the SDLP.[6] Over time, absolutist terms such as 'self-determination' and 'sovereignty' were replaced by more conciliatory notions of 'inclusiveness' and 'agreement', and, as they were, so republicans also joined the ranks of revisionist nationalism.

But Maginness might even have included another party in his list of con-verts to the creed of the SDLP: the international community. Again, Hume was the chief missionary in this. His arduous efforts – stretching as far back as the early 1970s in terms of his courtship of Ted Kennedy – won support for the SDLP's position from Washington to Strasbourg. This also helped to both consolidate and empower the revisionist consensus. Indeed, without American assistance in particular, the NIF report might have been left to gather dust, and the AIA – arguably the first real step in the peace process – might never have been achieved. Of course, during the peace process, a new Irish-American elite came to prominence, one supportive of Sinn Féin rather than the SDLP. However, even then, Hume's old guard still showed its importance. Indeed, though the idea of inviting Adams to the US came from the ANIA, it is unlikely that his 1994 visa would have been attained without pressure from such notables as Ted Kennedy. He, in turn, would not have acted without Hume's assent, and thus again the SDLP leader greatly aided republican efforts to create a peaceful political strategy.

Overview

At the outset of his political career – indeed, before Hume had even thought to enter into formal politics – the focus of his thinking was on change *within* Northern Ireland. His speech to a group of activists in London in August 1965 may have been the one and only time that he spoke explicitly of an 'internal solution' to the Northern Ireland problem, but it was as notable as it was unique. At this point, it seemed that Hume was concerned less with political division in Ireland, and more with communal division in Northern Ireland: 'It is my belief that the problem can only fully be solved by the people there themselves and only then when the mental border that divides the community has been largely eradicated'.[7]

However, Hume never rejected the aspiration to a united Ireland. In his seminal *Irish Times* article of May 1964, he argued the validity of this goal, but suggested that it could only be achieved by first winning Protestant support. In this, it was clear that Irish unity was very much a long-term ambition in Hume's mind. His chief concern was that the two communities in Northern Ireland should work together as a means to overcome their differences. For this reason, he deferred the prospect of constitutional change:

> If one wishes to create a United Ireland by constitutional means, then one must accept the constitutional position. ... a United Ireland, if it is to come, ... must come about by evolution, i.e. by the will of the Northern majority. It is clear that this is the only way in which a truly United Ireland (with the Northern Protestant integrated) can be achieved. ... If the whole Northern community gets seriously to work on its problems; the unionist bogeys about Catholics and a Republic will, through better understanding, disappear. It will of course take a long time.[8]

Hume's arguments here typified the more conciliatory tone of northern nationalism in the mid-1960s. But Stormont's continued failure to respond to this created the frustration that led to the later civil rights movement. Despite the slogan of 'British rights for British citizens', few in this movement had completely abandoned the ideal of a united Ireland. However, this was not the objective of the civil rights campaign, as Hume was at pains to make clear from the outset of his involvement: 'It has been said against this movement that its purpose is to unite Ireland … This movement has no political ends. … Civil rights is not about a political issue but a moral issue. We are seeking fair play for *all within the existing state*.'[9]

It was the unionist community's refusal to accept this claim which led Hume, in November 1969, to put forward his idea of having a periodic plebiscite on the border. His intention in this was 'that the constitutional question should be taken out of politics … so that elections could be real elections based on real political issues'. In effect, Hume was hoping to kick the constitutional question into the long grass, and to focus minds on the reform of Northern Ireland and the development of 'politics based on normal right or left political attitudes'.[10]

In his assessment of this proposal, Eamonn Gallagher, of the Irish Department of External Affairs, provided perhaps one of the most revealing insights into Hume's early political thinking. Clearly having been taken into his confidence, Gallagher suggested that Hume did envisage some form of Irish unity, but only after such reform had taken place in Northern Ireland as to effect a natural evolution in attitudes on both sides of the political divide:

> [The idea of holding periodic referenda on the border is] consistent with Mr. Hume's strategy of working towards a decent society within the present system while it reserves the right to change the constitutional basis of the system through normal democratic processes. He does not himself advocate reunification which he believes to be unattainable … in the current situation. By remaining silent on the issue he hopes to attract support from moderate opinion generally in favour of a new deal in the Northern society and thus bring about an easing of community relations; his private opinion is that a normalised society would eventually reconsider the real place of Northern Ireland in an Irish society.[11]

In this interpretation, Hume's thinking was not predetermined towards Irish reunification. Indeed, at this time, Hume did not even appear to be overly preoccupied with the issue of partition. His main aim, as publicly stated, was to change society in Northern Ireland – from this point on, political developments might take their own course. Though Hume imagined that this course would, ultimately, lead to some form of *rapprochement* between the North and South of Ireland, his approach was not dictated by this goal. Irish unity, if it was to occur, would come of its own accord.

In the months that followed this proposal, the continued resistance to reform in Northern Ireland, the onset of serious political violence, and the repression and radicalisation of the minority community, all brought about significant change in Hume's position. By July 1971, with the SDLP's withdrawal from Stormont, it was clear that he no longer believed that the Northern Ireland state could be reformed; it would have to be completely reconstituted. The introduction of internment the following month served only to confirm this opinion, suggesting that the existing regime had decided to suppress rather than address Catholic grievances. To most nationalists, it now seemed that the Stormont system was simply incapable of accommodating their community on terms of equality.

With the subsequent change to the tone of his writings, Hume clearly reflected the more pessimistic conclusions that his community was now drawing. Indeed, whilst many commentators have noted the late 1970s as a period of shift in Hume's thinking, in fact, it was in the early part of the decade, before the fall of Stormont, that his interpretation of the Northern Ireland problem underwent its most significant change. From this point on, he was convinced that only a radical reworking of the 1920–21 settlement would create the conditions for peace in Ireland. In this, Hume broke decisively with the previous ideas he had entertained of creating a purely internal solution in Northern Ireland. Though he did not, explicitly, call for the dissolution of the border, Hume's arguments now contained an implicit critique of partition. Thus, exactly two years on from his plebiscite proposal – suggested as a means to facilitate Northern Ireland's reform – Hume now asserted that a state 'so drawn as to provide a permanent majority for Protestant ascendancy' made it irremediable. Unionist resistance to reform, he argued, was tied into the fact that any form of change threatened to end this ascendancy. As such, while the British government continued to uphold the existing regime, there could be no political progress in Hume's view: 'It is Unionist power and privilege inextricably bound up with the whole system of government in Northern Ireland that the British Army is defending today.'[12]

By the time London finally did bring an end to Stormont, the nationalist community had become thoroughly radicalised. After Bloody Sunday in particular, equality for Catholics in Northern Ireland was far from the issue. Instead the issue was the presence of an alien and aggressive state, made manifest in the seemingly wilful violence of the British army. And this was the feeling which Hume communicated in his infamous 'united Ireland or nothing' statement. As argued in Chapter 2, this was not his own opinion, but an expression of the sentiment then prevailing in the Catholic community – a sentiment which he and his party colleagues could not afford to ignore. It was also a sentiment which allowed the republican movement to become a genuine force within the nationalist community, and this, too, was something which the SDLP could not ignore. Though the Provisionals did not, at this time, present an *electoral* challenge to the party, they did offer a revolutionary alternative to its reformism, and so always presented a *political* challenge to the SDLP.

However, it was not just the pressures which the party endured, but also the opportunities which it perceived, that led the SDLP to adopt such a stridently 'unificationist' agenda after the fall of Stormont. For example, the relative quiescence of the Protestant community in this period encouraged even moderate sections of nationalist opinion to believe that unionists had resigned themselves to the inevitability of Irish reunification. Similarly, and perhaps more significantly, there were the signals from Westminster – coming from as high up as the leader of the opposition in the form of Harold Wilson's 'Fifteen Point Plan' for Irish unity – suggesting that the British establishment was now determined to rid itself of the Northern Ireland problem. It was, therefore, understandable that Hume and his colleagues began to consider a united Ireland as a medium- rather than a long-term objective. But Provisionals' continued efforts to physically force the British state from Northern Ireland also affected the SDLP's approach. As a means to build confidence in its evolutionary strategy – and so draw off support for the IRA's revolutionary method – the party began to pursue a policy which would – and would be *seen to* – facilitate a process of British disengagement and Irish reunification.

As a result, the SDLP went into the Sunningdale negotiations with a sense of historic opportunity. Hume in particular appeared to believe that an assertive approach, supported by the Dublin government, would create a dynamic towards Irish unification. Indeed, it seemed that such a positive strategy would both exploit the sense of resignation then apparent within the unionist community, and deprive the Provisionals of their claimed rationale. It would also allow the London government to pursue a path which leading figures in the British political elite already seemed set upon. However, in their eagerness to seize this opportunity, Hume and his colleagues lost sight of the SDLP's founding principles: they appeared to assume that Irish unity could be achieved through unionists' acquiescence rather than their active assent.

The manner of Sunningdale's collapse quickly disproved this thesis. The Protestant mobilisation of May 1974 made abundantly clear that unionists would not accept any process which seemed predestined to end in a united Ireland. In this respect, the UWC strike may have acted as a wake-up call to the SDLP, as the party began to pursue a more realistic political strategy in its aftermath. At first, this change in approach was not immediately discernable. Indeed, post-Sunningdale, the SDLP continued to emphasise power-sharing and an Irish dimension as the prerequisites to any new settlement. But behind the rhetorical continuity, a subtle shift did take place. Now the party was at least open to discussion as to how the aims of power-sharing and an Irish dimension might find institutional expression. Thus, gone was the predetermination of its approach from 1972 to 1974. Also absent was the kind of language which, up until Sunningdale, had suggested that the SDLP's strategy was inextricably linked with the construction of a unitary Irish state. Indeed, from 1974 onwards, Hume's discourse in particular suggested that, whatever structures gave the two communities a joint role in the governance of Northern Ireland, and whatever arrangements allowed at least some form of affiliation with the southern state, would in themselves constitute Irish unity: 'If we get an agreed Ireland that is unity. What constitutional or institutional forms such an agreed Ireland takes is irrelevant because it would represent agreement by the people of this country as to how they should be governed.'[13]

Whilst the SDLP refused to abandon the Irish dimension, talks with unionists from the mid-1970s – limited as they were – focused essentially upon the possibility of power-sharing. In public, Hume and his colleagues still spoke of an Irish dimension, but in private negotiations the idea of all-Ireland structures received much less attention. Neither were they articulated as a means towards the ultimate integration of North and South, as had been the case with the abortive Council of Ireland. 'Partnership' became the leitmotif of the SDLP's parlance, and whilst this would involve recognition of both 'traditions' in Ireland, in reality the emphasis was on relationships between the two communities in Northern Ireland, as had been the case at the time of the party's inception.

However, as in the early part of the decade, the political conditions of the late 1970s served to deflect the SDLP from this more conciliatory approach. Most important in this was the attitude of the unionist leadership, which refused to contemplate any real compromise with the SDLP. But the policy of the British government also played a part. Its truce and subsequent talks with the IRA, and then the excuse for an initiative that was the Constitutional Convention, again led to thoughts within the SDLP that London was intent on extricating itself from Northern Ireland, and by whatever means possible. Even when the initial fear of an actual evacuation of British troops receded, the effective withdrawal of the British state – achieved by a combination of military containment and political quarantine – continued to undermine any attempt by the SDLP to pursue a constructive policy.

This appeared to drive the party in a more nationalist direction. But in fact, and in large part due to Hume, the SDLP actually developed quite a considered and far-sighted political approach in the late 1970s. With this, the party asked that the British and Irish governments work together to change the context of the Northern Ireland problem, and through this to create the conditions for a local settlement. Critics interpreted this approach, and the renewed emphasis which it placed on the Irish dimension, as evidence of the 'greening' of the SDLP.[14] But Hume's and his colleagues' thinking in this period was no more nationalist than it had been in the early 1970s. Indeed, in many respects, they were simply returning to the conclusions reached at that time, and particularly the idea that the Northern Ireland problem could not be resolved by a purely internal political settlement. Unionists' continued opposition to power-sharing, even within such an internal arrangement, merely confirmed the SDLP's thinking in this respect.

With the development of the Anglo-Irish process in the early 1980s, it seemed that the two governments also became convinced of the need to broaden their approach the problem. Although the hunger strikes appeared to derail the process, the outcome of this crisis actually forced London and Dublin to proceed with the more radical ideas that they may only have considered up to this point. Indeed, the rise of Sinn Féin acted as a wake-up call in both capitals. It suggested the frustration that had built up even in more moderate sections of the Catholic community – sections which would normally be solidly behind the SDLP, but which the two governments now feared would be swayed by republicanism. It was this concern which produced the essential momentum towards the AIA of 1985.

Although responding to the rise of electoral republicanism, the AIA also showed an acceptance of many of the ideas which Hume and his colleagues had been promoting since the fall of Sunningdale: the institutionalisation of an inter-governmental approach to the Northern Ireland problem; the establishment of an Irish dimension; and the promise of power-sharing in the event of agreement between the two communities. Even the rhetorical commitments of the AIA – recognising the legitimacy of the aspirations and identities of the two traditions in Ireland, and the need to accommodate both on terms of equality – captured the essence of the SDLP's ideology. However, from Hume's perspective, the AIA was most important in terms of its potential to end the unionist veto on political change. Since Sunningdale, he had consistently argued that this would only be achieved if London revised the terms of the guarantee which it gave to the majority in Northern Ireland. In Hume's eyes, the unconditional nature of this commitment – assuring unionists in their basic political objective, namely to remain part of the United Kingdom – gave them no incentive to engage in dialogue with the nationalist community. However, by involving Dublin in the governance of Northern Ireland, Hume felt that the AIA demonstrated London's commitment to change: 'The guarantee is no longer an unconditional guarantee.'[15] As a result, he believed that 'the unionist people … will finally embrace real politics, real dialogue and sit down with the rest of us to begin the long process of breaking down the barriers of prejudice and mistrust which for so long have disfigured this country.'[16] For Hume, therefore, the Agreement had the potential to break the political stalemate in Northern Ireland.

Of course, the AIA did not work quite as Hume had hoped or the two governments had intended. Rather than bringing unionists to the negotiating table, it sent them into the streets, creating the largest Protestant mobilisation since Sunningdale. However, on this occasion, the British government was more steadfast in its response, and unionists were, ultimately, forced to talk their way out of the AIA. But in its principal objective the Agreement was less successful. It may have stemmed but it did not reduce support for radical republicanism. Indeed, ironically, rather than marginalising republicans, the AIA provided the basis for bringing them into the political process. For in his claim that the accord represented a statement of British neutrality on Northern Ireland, Hume provoked a response from Sinn Féin, which was determined to challenge this interpretation. Thus, rather than talks between the SDLP and unionists, the AIA first produced an intra-nationalist dialogue.

In agreeing to talks with Sinn Féin, Hume was clearly building on the efforts of individuals like Fr Alec Reid, who were already encouraging republicans to think beyond the armed struggle. In particular, Reid hoped to demonstrate the viability of an approach which would bring together the various strands of Irish nationalism in a common, peaceful strategy. Hume effectively ran with this idea, aiming to show republicans that they could, on the condition of a ceasefire, join with other nationalists to create a momentum for political progress in Northern Ireland.

Ultimately, the support of the Irish government would prove crucial to this endeavour. However, in the early stages of the peace process, it was Hume who took the risk – both personal and political – to openly engage with Sinn Féin. Mitchel McLaughlin, one of the Sinn Féin members involved in these early discussions, recognised the importance of this. Though he stressed that republicans were reaching out to various groups in this period, he noted that: 'Hume was the first political leader to respond ... the first person that agreed to meet and started the process ... I would give him his due credit and I do generously, because he was the only one who had the backbone ... he was the only one at that time.'[17] Of course, after Hume began more formal talks with Sinn Féin, Fianna Fáil also agreed to hold discussions with republicans. But the latter were both secret and short-lived. At a time when the IRA showed no signs of ending its campaign of violence, a governmental party could not afford to maintain contacts with the republican movement. However, Hume saw the need to remain engaged, and through this to encourage the changes that were slowly taking place within republicanism.

In order to aid this process, Hume also convinced the British government to make helpful statements. Thus, whilst it was unlikely that the Margaret Thatcher ever intended the AIA to represent a declaration of British neutrality on Northern Ireland, Peter Brooke was prepared to effectively endorse this interpretation in his famous 'no selfish strategic or economic interests' speech. Encouraged by Hume, and possibly the information he was receiving from British intelligence, Brooke recognised the impact that these words would have on republican thinking. This they did, and so when Hume came to Dublin with the first draft of what became the DSD, the Irish government could believe that his proposal was something worth pursuing.[18] This was vital: without the political weight of Dublin behind the initiative, it would be impossible to convince republicans that progress could be achieved by purely peaceful means.[19] Accordingly, it could be argued that, at this point, the Irish government took on the baton from Hume. For only Dublin could provide the political influence that was necessary to move the process on from here. When it did so, persuading the British government to commit to the DSD, it also opened the way to American involvement. Most notable in this respect was the granting of Adams's visa in January 1994, which clearly demonstrated to republicans the gains that could be made by adopting a peaceful strategy. However, with both initiatives – the DSD and Adams's visa – Hume had a hand. He was able to open doors in Dublin and Washington, and in this to fulfil the promise of Alec Reid's early efforts, showing republicans that there was a credible alternative to the armed struggle.

But there was an obvious downside to all of this. By dealing with republicans, even after such atrocities as the Shankill bombing, Hume forfeited any little trust which the Protestant community had in him. This exposed the essential paradox in Hume's political strategy. By engaging with Sinn Féin, he hoped to bring an end to violence in Northern Ireland, and thus create the conditions for genuine negotiations between the two communities. However, for most unionists, Hume's initiative with Adams, and the subsequent support which it received from Dublin and Washington, represented a fearful alliance of nationalist forces. As such, rather than creating a basis for inter-communal reconciliation, Hume's efforts actually served to heighten anxieties within unionism.

Of course, Protestant fears were also stirred by the content of the statements emanating from the Hume–Adams talks. In particular, there was concern over the two leaders' agreement that there could be no internal solution to the Northern Ireland problem, and the related emphasis on an all-Ireland exercise of self-determination. From a unionist perspective, it seemed that Hume was surrendering ground to Sinn Féin, and endorsing an approach which could only end in a united Ireland.

However, as noted above, Hume had long since abandoned the position he held in the 1960s, when he had spoken in terms of an internal solution. Indeed, as late as November 1969, in his plebiscite proposal, Hume had accepted that the people of Northern Ireland alone had the right to determine the future of the region, suggesting that this was the only way to still unionist fears of reform, and so maintain the process of change. But the failure of this process – with unionists continuing to resist reform, and republican activity only bolstering their resistance – led Hume to the conclusion that the problem could only be resolved by returning to its origins: the 1920–21 settlement, which gave unionists an unassailable majority, and so an effective veto on political change. It was this thinking which led to the defining statement made on the opening page of the SDLP's first published proposals in 1972: 'Any re-examination [of the 1920–21 settlement] must therefore take place, not in a purely Six County context, but in an Irish context.'[20] This is a position which Hume and his party continued to hold to from hereinafter.

It was also this position which allowed Hume to share some common ground with Adams in their public dialogue two decades later. But this did not mean that he was conceding to a republican reading of the Northern Ireland problem. Hume's opposition to an internal solution was informed by his own experience with the failure of such an approach in the early 1970s. Furthermore, whilst his talks with Adams did lead Hume to consider the issue of self-determination in an all-Ireland context, he reconciled this with his own revisionist interpretation. In this, it was not partition, but rather divisions between the people of Ireland which impeded their exercise of self-determination. Thus, for Hume, the people of Ireland had to address their divisions, and thereby find agreement on how they should express the right to self-determination. But they could only do this, he argued, through a process of peaceful negotiation. And this, in essence, was the approach adopted by London and Dublin in the DSD. Whatever the changes made to the other terms of the Hume–Adams dialogue, both governments accepted Hume's idea of 'agreed self-determination', achieved through inclusive talks, then exercised and endorsed through referenda in both parts of Ireland.

In this, it can be argued that Hume helped to revise another tenet of traditional Irish nationalist thinking: the principle of self-determination. In his dual-referenda formula, he devised a means by which both political traditions in Ireland could exercise their right to self-determination. By doing so, Hume helped to resolve a debate which had long divided both participants to and commentators on the Northern Ireland problem.[21] Of course, some would argue that the peace process and the GFA did not end this dispute: pro-Agreement unionists presented the accord as a means to secure the link with Britain; pro-Agreement republicans, and indeed many nationalists, presented it as a means to advance the goal of a united Ireland.[22] However, it could be said that this is the true beauty of the Agreement: it allows both communities to pursue their constitutional preferences by peaceful, consensual means. By facilitating co-operation between the two parts of Ireland, nationalists and republicans hope that the outworking of GFA will persuade unionists of the benefits of a unified state. Conversely, by reforming Northern Ireland, unionists hope that the outworking of the GFA will demonstrate to nationalists that they can be accommodated within the existing constitution. Achievement of a united Ireland, or maintenance of the Union, are both projects which can legitimately be pursued through the GFA. The success of either will depend on the ability of its proponents to persuade their opponents. In this, whatever the outcome, it will be achieved by peaceful means, and still in keeping with Hume's idea of agreed self-determination.

'Hume-speak'

Reviewing Hume's career, it becomes clear that it was not just his political thinking, but also his manner of political expression, which evoked such distrust among the unionist community. In a short essay examining

Hume's distinctive language, Michael Cunningham considers the reasons for this.

The paper begins with a quotation from a Protestant clergyman, which Cunningham claims 'neatly encapsulates criticisms that have been levelled at John Hume': 'Protestants are really puzzled by what they feel is the ambiguous attitude of Catholics and their failure to define ordinary concepts in a clean, straightforward way. ... Protestants sometimes find it very difficult to understand the sophistry, the playing with words which we (sometimes) get from Catholics.'[23] Cunningham also cites the Protestant literary critic, Edna Longley, who claims that Hume's language 'has much in common with George Orwell's metaphor for Marxist jargon: "prefabricated phrases bolted together like the pieces of a child's Meccano set"'.[24] The invocation of Orwell is quite apposite, for essentially Cunningham's paper posits a critique of 'Hume-speak', with all the undertones of *Nineteen Eighty-Four* which that appellation conveys. Cunningham suggests that, in the Protestant mind, the central motifs of Hume's political discourse – 'agreement' and 'reconciliation', 'aspiration' and 'accommodation' – are all merely verbal camouflage, beneath which hides his true objective: a united Ireland.

However, it should be said that there has always been an element of wilful misinterpretation of Hume's position by many Protestants, the 'it's a united Ireland or nothing' comment providing the classic example. For some unionists, it served their purpose to suggest that the achievement of a unitary Irish state was Hume's sole political motivation, thereby supporting their claim that there could be no compromise with the SDLP. Thus, nearly two decades after Bloody Sunday, Ian Paisley still felt the need to remind an interviewer: 'You can't trust John Hume ... For him, it's a united Ireland or nothing.'[25]

Ivan Cooper, co-founder of the SDLP, and still the most senior Protestant member in the party's history, believes that unionists have seriously misjudged Hume:

> The tragedy for Ulster Protestantism is that they never recognised the moderation and the basic decency of Hume. ... He paid the price in Protestant eyes of being a civil rights leader, and people say: 'He started all this trouble; he is the originator of the IRA.' They couldn't be further from the truth because, if ever there was a fair-minded, non-sectarian man, it's Hume ... Hume has never been committed to a united Ireland; Hume's vision of Ireland is a new Ireland, a totally new Ireland ... Hume has never favoured being subservient, sucked up by, taken over by this united Ireland that Sinn Féin talk about.[26]

Cooper is right to suggest that Hume's conception of Irish unity is fundamentally different from that traditionally supported by republicans. He may also be right in claiming that Hume has never been 'subservient, sucked up by, taken over by' the notion of a united Ireland. Nonetheless, Hume has consistently refused to renounce this aspiration, and for this reason unionists have never been able to trust his intentions.

This aspiration, and indeed Hume's understanding of Irish unity, was best articulated in his idea of an 'agreed Ireland'. Of course, this was also one of the concepts which evoked the most searing criticism from those suspicious of 'Hume-speak'. As noted,[27] Bew and Patterson were amongst such commentators, dismissing Hume's agreed Ireland as '[t]he verbal sleight of hand by which notions of reconciliation and agreement simply serve[ed] to obscure the central and traditional notion – that the British state has the capacity and obligation to create the conditions in which Protestant consent [for constitutional change] would be forthcoming.'[28] Undoubtedly, when he first began to promote the concept of an agreed Ireland in the late 1970s – a time when unionists were refusing to countenance any form of compromise with the SDLP – Hume certainly emphasised that the British government had a vital role to play in changing Protestant attitudes. But his thinking cannot be reduced to this alone.

In the first interview in which he discussed in detail his idea of an agreed Ireland, Hume suggested that it involved an entirely new conception of Irish unity. In articulating this, he made clear that Irish nationalists, as well as the British government, must help to change unionist attitudes:

> We have to be very clear what is meant when we talk about unity. Failure by the Irish political parties in the past to spell out the meaning of this word – or their meaning of it, or their concept or vision of it – has meant that loyalists have easily been able to interpret it as something the Protestant people of the North ought to be afraid of – something which would trample on their rights and coerce them into a hostile State. It is necessary, therefore, to make it very clear that is not what we mean when we say that is our objective. What we want is agreement in an agreed Ireland.[29]

At times, Hume was more explicit in what he was saying: 'Agreement between all sides need not necessarily be the emergence of a unitary state.'[30]

Despite this, as he continued to communicate his concept of an agreed Ireland, Hume recognised that the Protestant community remained deeply suspicious. For this reason, at the SDLP conference of 1981, he spoke directly to unionists, asking them to recognise that an agreed Ireland was something which they would help to make, and which would have to win their assent: 'I know that many of you do not realize that when we say that we are proposing an "Agreed Ireland" we mean those words absolutely literally. We mean an "Agreed Ireland" that you would decisively help to shape.' Accordingly, he called on unionist politicians to sit down with the SDLP and the two governments, and to negotiate structures that would satisfy all parties. By way of assurance, he also put forward his idea of holding dual-referenda on any resulting agreement, this to ensure that the unionist community as a whole accepted the arrangements which their representatives negotiated: 'we would insist that the result of such talks would have to be ratified in two separate referenda, one in the

North, the other in the South. ... The principle of consent will be truly respected.'[31] With this, Hume made clear that unionist assent was integral to his idea of an agreed Ireland. Whatever constitutional form it took, an agreed Ireland would have to be endorsed by polls on either side of the border, thus ensuring that it had the consent of both traditions on the island.

Into the 1990s, when his dialogue with Adams again led unionists to question Hume's intentions, he continually sought to reassure them. This was most notable in an article he wrote in 1994 for the *Belfast Telegraph*, a paper with a large Protestant readership. Here, once more, he insisted that an agreed Ireland required unionist consent, but also nationalist consent, both achieved through dual referenda:

> The SDLP has always espoused and respected the principle of consent and remains committed to the creation of an agreed Ireland. ... Our commitment to real agreement and respect for the legitimacy of both traditions has been reflected in our proposal that any Agreement arising from talks should be subject to dual referenda, i.e. in the north and the south on the same day. This ... means that such an agreement would earn and enjoy the allegiance of Unionists because it would be validated by a majority in the north. Equally, it would earn and enjoy the allegiance of nationalists because it would be validated by a majority of the people of Ireland as a whole.

Of course, this ruled out the first preferences of either tradition – a traditional unitary Irish state for nationalists, or a purely British Northern Ireland for unionists. Instead, Hume proposed that any settlement would represent a compromise between two: 'We are not therefore seeking a solution made solely in the image of the nationalist tradition. Nor can we accept as a solution arrangements made solely in the image of the Unionist tradition.'[32]

Once again, Hume's arguments suggested that, whatever the ambiguity of his agreed Ireland in Protestant minds, it would involve a settlement process that depended on their full participation and – with dual referenda used to endorse its outcome – their full consent to validate it. However, the same approach, by requiring the input of the Irish government and the assent of the southern electorate, would ensure a balanced agreement that was also acceptable to northern nationalists. In this, it could be argued that Hume's idea of agreed Ireland was purposely ambiguous. Its lack of definition was meant to suggest Hume's open-mindedness towards the particular structures which would give it institutional expression. However, the term 'agreed Ireland' did encapsulate what were, for Hume, the two essential requirements of any settlement: that it had an all-Ireland dimension, and won the agreement of both political traditions on the island.

In this respect, Hume's agreed Ireland was also ambiguous because he intended it to appeal in different ways to each tradition. Firstly, to unionists, it was meant to express the idea that 'Irish unity' did not, for the

SDLP, mean a unitary Irish state, but rather consensus on the political structures used to govern the island: 'If we get an agreed Ireland that is unity. What constitutional or institutional forms such an agreed Ireland takes is irrelevant because it would represent agreement by the people of this country as to how they should be governed.'[33] In this respect, the phrase also sought to articulate Hume's conception of Irish unity as something which could not be achieved without unionists' active contribution and consent. Whatever its constitutional complexion, whatever its political architecture, an agreed Ireland would have to be decided through a process of consultation with unionist representatives, and verified by a vote that required the assent of the broader Protestant population. Thus, Hume's agreed Ireland was an attempt to convey his conviction that Irish unity was only feasible, and indeed was only meaningful, if it had the allegiance of both traditions in Ireland.

Meanwhile, to nationalists, Hume's idea of an agreed Ireland was meant to assure them that the SDLP would not accept an internal settlement in Northern Ireland. Any agreement would have an all-Ireland dimension, providing structures which allowed northern Catholics to feel some form of political association with the Irish Republic – the state which they felt best represented their national identity. Without such an approach, it is unlikely that Hume and his party could have delivered nationalist support for a settlement.[34] Indeed, the minority community would no more accept political arrangements which denied their Irish identity and desire for formal linkages with the Republic than the majority community would accept a deal which threatened to diminish their British identity or bring an end to the Union.

At its most basic level, therefore, Hume's agreed Ireland was an attempt to square the circle between Ulster unionism and Irish nationalism – to provide political structures which would satisfy both. Moreover, it can be argued that Hume's idea did provide the conceptual framework within which compromise was eventually achieved. Indeed, as noted,[35] even Bew and Patterson, the foremost critics of Hume's schema, accepted that the notion of an agreed Ireland supplied the essential template for solution after it was adopted by the two governments in the 1993 DSD. However, Bew has also argued that the concept of an agreed Ireland provided the means by which nationalist Ireland was eventually able to accept the Northern Ireland state in the form of the GFA.[36] This is quite true. Hume's idea of agreed Ireland did create the ideological paradigm within which Irish nationalists could consent to partition. But this should not be confused with endorsement of the partitionist settlement of 1920–21, something which most Irish nationalists, and particularly northern nationalists, have never accepted as just. The GFA has fundamentally revised the 1920–21 settlement: the Northern Ireland state no longer exists in a purely British constitutional context. Partition has been accepted, but it has been made permeable; the all-Ireland institutions of the Agreement are such that northern Catholics do not reside in a polity entirely separate from that of their co-nationals in the South. Thus, the structures of the GFA serve to recognise the Irish identity of the minority. By the same token, the Union between Great Britain and Northern Ireland remains intact, and so unionists' British identity has in no way been diminished. The 1998 settlement has, therefore, created a political framework capable of accommodating both political traditions on the island of Ireland. Hume's contribution to the conception of this framework, and in particular his notion of an agreed Ireland, has been highly significant. Whatever the criticisms of his political discourse – of the ambiguity within it, and the intentions behind it – Hume-speak did offer a flexibility of thought, and thereby helped to create an ideological space within which a political compromise over Northern Ireland could be devised.[37]

Despite this, it could be argued that, ultimately, Hume failed in what he intimated was his foremost political objective: the reconciliation of the two traditions in Ireland. The GFA has brought peace, but not – as yet – reconciliation.[38] Of course, the Agreement did not have the best start, its troubled implementation serving to further polarise the two communities in Northern Ireland, and to set back hopes of a new era of co-operation between North and South.[39] However, the fact that the GFA has survived is a testament in itself. Indeed, and it may yet be some time – after its institutions have worked without interruption over a sustained period – before it is fair to judge the Agreement in terms of its impact on both intercommunal and North–South relations. Arguably, Hume was fully aware that this would be the case. He always spoke of a process rather than a definitive act of reconciliation, citing the history of post-war Europe as an example of how practical co-operation would, gradually, lead to changed political relations. The GFA has provided a framework for such a process. Thus, whilst he may not see its full impact in his own lifetime, Hume – in the practical efforts he made to bring an end to violence in Northern Ireland, and the ideological contribution which he made to the resulting political settlement – has helped to create a situation in which the two traditions in Ireland can, in time, reach a deeper understanding, and a more genuine reconciliation.

The limits of Hume's revisionism

The question remains to be answered: how far has Hume moved Irish nationalism on from its traditional assumptions as defined by John Whyte, namely that: (1) the people of Ireland form one nation; and (2) the fault for keeping Ireland divided lies with Britain?

From his earliest commentary on the problem – his *Irish Times* article of May 1964 – Hume had suggested the need to accept the legitimacy of both political aspirations in Northern Ireland. This mode of argument was further developed in the 'two traditions' discourse which Hume began to use from the mid-1970s. In this, he presented the problem as a conflict between two religio-political identities – one Catholic and Irish, the other Protestant and British – which could only be resolved by creating political institutions which accommodated both. Seemingly implicit in this thesis was an acceptance that the people of Ireland were not one nation, but two – one which straddled the border, the other which was part of the larger people of Britain.

This thinking reached its apogee in the NIF of 1983–84. Here, Hume went further than at any previous point in his career in recognising that unionists' political identity was as significant, if not more, than their religious interests: 'The Protestant ethos I am talking about is not merely theological ... It contains also and perhaps more importantly a strong expression of political allegiance to Britain which we cannot ignore and which we cannot wish away.'[40] However, even this statement was qualified. Acknowledging 'a strong expression of political allegiance to Britain' was not the same as accepting that unionists are, in fact, British. To use Hume's own term, unionists were seen as a different 'tradition', but not, necessarily, a different *nation*. Thus, whilst they have a different religious outlook to the rest of Ireland, and indeed a very different relationship with Britain, Ulster unionists were still seen as, essentially, an *Irish* tradition. This explains Hume's emphasis – most evident in the NIF – on political relations on the island of Ireland. Inherent in this was a belief that, if these relations were dealt with in the correct manner, unionists could be accommodated under some form of all-Ireland constitution, howsoever that was shaped. With this, it seems that there remained in Hume's thinking an underlying assumption that unionists were a constituent part of the Irish people, and a desire to persuade them of this.

In spite of the efforts of Hume and his party to accept the authenticity of unionists' British identity, this aspiration always undermined their intentions. Even in the SDLP's first published proposals, *Towards a New Ireland*, this was evident. On the one hand, advocating joint British–Irish sovereignty over Northern Ireland did suggest a genuine recognition of unionists' political identity, and the need to protect this in new structures of government. But, on the other hand, the idea that joint rule would be only an interim arrangement – allowing a gradual transition to a united Ireland, and thus the eventual disengagement of the British state – implied that unionists' political identity was not as rooted as nationalists'. This was confirmed by the paper's intimation that a new and non-confessional Irish constitution would convince unionists that they could be accommodated in a unitary state. It is this nationalist imperative which made Hume's thinking just that – essentially nationalist. He may have come further than any previous nationalist leader in his attempts to address the reasons for unionists' opposition to a united Ireland,[41] but his refusal to surrender this ambition suggests that he was unable to move beyond the basic premise that the people of Ireland are one nation.

With regard to Whyte's second assumption, Hume was more successful in changing nationalist thinking. Overall, he played a major role in encouraging nationalists to accept that division in Ireland was not, in a contemporary context, the result of British intervention. Indeed, the central debate that gave rise to the peace process revolved around Hume's contention that the British government was not opposed to Irish unity, and would in fact endorse this end if only a majority in Northern Ireland so consented. Proceeding from this, Hume was able to argue that it was unionist objections rather than British interests that prevented Irish reunification. His part in persuading the republican movement of this interpretation – and his success in getting the British government to publicly affirm its validity – played a crucial role in paving the way towards the GFA.

Of course, the origins of this interpretation can be traced as far back as the late 1950s, to the thinking of groups such as National Unity and the NDP. Hume followed in their footsteps, his earliest remarks on Northern Ireland describing a problem of internal communal division rather than external political interference.[42] Indeed, in these commentaries, the role of Britain was notable only in its absence. On the basis of this thinking, Hume – like many minority activists in the 1960s – felt that the only way to achieve progress was to accept the existing constitution, and then to work within it for change.

However, the frustration of this approach forced Hume to reconsider his position. By the early 1970s, he had already arrived at the conclusion that the Northern Ireland problem could not be resolved without reference to its historical origins. Indeed, Hume now came to see the conflict as but a legacy of a broader and more long-standing struggle between the nations of Britain and Ireland:

> the real problem wasn't just relations within Northern Ireland, it was a British-Irish problem. It was the failure of Britain and Ireland to resolve their differences in the 1920s and they pushed the failure into a corner called Northern Ireland. ... Northern Ireland today represents unfinished business between our two islands. It represents the residual area of failure of the peoples of the two islands to work out their interlocking relationships in a satisfactory way.[43]

Implicit in this argument was a belief that the 1920–21 settlement had failed. Lloyd George's 'solution' to the Irish Question had only created the Northern Ireland Question; it had quarantined but not resolved the problem.

The failure of successive political initiatives in the 1970s simply made Hume more certain of this reasoning. By the end of the decade, he was convinced that only a complete restructuring of Anglo-Irish relations would create the conditions for a settlement between the two communities in Northern Ireland. However, at this time, London was largely resistant to such ideas. Rather than opening up the Northern Ireland problem, the

British government was looking to contain it. Whilst it continued on this path, Hume saw no prospect of progress in Northern Ireland. Accordingly, from the late 1970s, he turned his attention from the idea of a local settlement, and began to focus almost exclusively on the position of the British government.[44] While he still considered the problem to be essentially aboriginal, Hume, like most nationalists at this time, came to perceive London as the primary obstacle to its resolution.

It was not until 1985 that Hume was able to revise his opinion in this regard. The sole reason for this was the AIA, and the British commitment therein to legislate for Irish reunification in the event of majority support in Northern Ireland. This allowed Hume to return to the logic of his early thinking, arguing that it was internal division rather than any outside interest that was the real cause of conflict in the region. The DSD in 1993, and then the GFA and dual referenda of 1998, can all be seen as proceeding from this premise. All of these developments looked to confirm the view that the continued partition of Ireland was not the will of the British government, but rather the will of the people of the island, whose agreement was the only precondition to its dissolution.

Through the various shifts in British policy on Northern Ireland, so Hume changed his view of London's role in the conflict. Thus, the first Wilson administration was considered an ally for pressing reform on the Unionist government, but the second was scorned for its failure to confront the UWC strike; the Heath government was condemned for allowing Stormont to attempt a security solution in the early years of the conflict, but then feted for achieving the Sunningdale Agreement; Thatcher was criticised for her intransigence over the hunger strikes, but then championed for her steadfastness in upholding the AIA; Major was applauded for delivering the DSD, but was then chided for delaying moves towards inclusive political talks. However, through all of this, Hume rejected the simplicity of the orthodox nationalist interpretation and its assertion that the British government, in upholding partition, was the true cause of division in Ireland:

> Partition is not the Irish problem. It simply institutionalised and exacerbated the differences that had been there for centuries. ... Indeed, is it not a deep misunderstanding of the Ulster Protestant tradition that it is only British influence and not their own deeply-felt reasons that up until now have made them want to live apart from the rest of the people of Ireland, reasons that go back beyond partition.[45]

On this basis, Murray and Tonge concluded that there was definite continuity in Hume's thinking throughout his career:

> The core of SDLP analysis of the Northern Ireland conflict, that the root cause of the problem is attributable to the division of the people in the island of Ireland, was the conviction and constant claim of John Hume. He firmly opposed the traditional Republican viewpoint that the British occupation of

Northern Ireland was the modern cause of the problem, whatever Britain's historical responsibilities.[46]

With regard to Whyte's second assumption of traditional nationalism, it can thus be argued that Hume did not believe – and indeed played a great part in dissuading others – that the fault for keeping Ireland divided lay with Britain.

Whilst Hume's ideology remained nationalist at its core, he encouraged major changes in Irish thinking on partition and the prospect of a united Ireland. For him, partition was a symptom, not a cause, of division in Ireland. Thus, the issue was not the political separation of the island, but rather the psychological barriers between its people. Proceeding from this, Irish unity was not, in Hume's mind, a territorial imperative. Instead, it was seen as the means by which the people of Ireland might resolve their relationships, and accommodate their differences. For Hume, Irish unity did not require the realisation of a unitary Irish state. Rather, it was an open-ended ideal, the ultimate composition of which might only be decided through the co-operation, interaction, and progressive reconciliation of the island's people. Whatever constitutional shape it should assume, Hume's conception of Irish unity was pluralist and consensual. A united Ireland was only possible – and indeed would only be worth achieving – if it secured the agreement of all its citizens. In this, Hume moved Irish nationalism away from a conception of partition as being a British imposition, and away from the idea of Irish unification as an irredentist impulse. Instead the focus has been placed on the people of Ireland, their division being the problem, and their agreement equating with Irish unity.

Leader or follower?

> It is fatuous to assume that followers follow wherever leaders lead. Rather, they follow only if they are being led in a direction they believe is preferable to the available alternatives. (Donald Horowitz)[47]

Shortly after the collapse of the Sunningdale experiment in 1974, a seemingly despondent Hume gave an earnest, even unguarded, interview with the *Belfast Telegraph*. Here, he appeared to give subjective credence to Horowitz's interpretation of elite activity in the context a deeply divided society:[48]

> there are serious limitations to political leadership in Northern Ireland; people can only be led as far as they want to be led. There is ample evidence to demonstrate the truth of that, and therefore a great deal of what happened has been the inevitability of events rather than being particularly shaped by anyone.
>
> It's not the way I wanted it to be, when I set out. I was prepared for a much more gradual development. I believed that the original civil rights campaign, which was in many respects a cautious movement, had the support of quite a number of Protestants at the beginning. And that strict non-violence was the

right way forward and would have brought us much more slowly but more surely to a better future.[49]

Hume's comments here also seem to confirm one of the underlying arguments of this study – the idea that, whatever, exactly, his vision of 'a better future' was, Hume had hoped for a far more incremental, evolutionary and consensual approach towards its achievement, but that circumstances often forced him to act otherwise.

From the outset of his political career, Hume did envisage some form of political unity between the North and South of Ireland. But he thought that this would be achieved by an organic process; it would advance of its own accord rather than having to be engineered. To recall his 'three Rs' approach: reform would presage reconciliation in Northern Ireland, and reconciliation would, in its own time, lead to the reunification of Ireland. For this reason, in his early career, Hume had sought to avoid even mentioning the issue of the border. Indeed, even in his very first election manifesto, in February 1969, there was no specific reference to Irish unity.[50] But in time, a combination of factors – unionist resistance to reform, the repression and radicalisation of the minority, and the revival of the republican movement in that context – brought the constitutional question back to centre stage. This, in turn, obliged Hume to become more open about his objectives. What had hitherto been articulated only in aspirational terms – and for the main was an addendum to his arguments – began to take an ever more prominent role in his reasoning. Having hoped to avoid any reference to Irish unity for fear of alienating unionists,[51] Hume found that he had to become more vocal on the subject if he was to retain the support of nationalists.

Even the SDLP's adoption of a policy of unity by consent was, essentially, an attempt to postpone the constitutional debate and reassure potential Protestant supporters. The objective in this was to win the backing of a broad, cross-community constituency, which would allow the pursuit of a radical reformist programme. The underlying hope was that substantial reform would create a wholly different political environment in which, over time, Protestant attitudes towards reunification might evolve of their own accord.[52] But an aspiration towards Irish unity had to be maintained in order to ensure the support of the Catholic masses. Moreover, as events unfolded in the early 1970s – as the minority community radicalised, as alienation from the Stormont system deepened, and as republicans tried to convert this disaffection into a campaign that would unite Ireland by force – Hume and the SDLP had to move beyond the idea of Irish unity as merely a long-term aspiration. Instead, they were obliged to articulate a concrete and viable strategy towards its achievement, this to provide a non-violent alternative to the Provisionals' approach.

Of course, the SDLP's increasing predetermination towards Irish unity – and the violence and polarisation that came with the outbreak of the Troubles – only made it less likely that the party would win any significant

Protestant support. Thus, the SDLP came to rely almost exclusively on Catholic votes. In turn, this meant that the party became even more subject to the minority's ambition of Irish unity. Any idea of abandoning or even demoting this objective and concentrating on the internal reform of Northern Ireland became politically untenable. Hume's original intention of sidelining the constitutional question – imagining that it would be addressed only after division within Northern Ireland had been overcome – became impossible. He and his party had to be seen to uphold and to pursue the end of Irish reunification if they were to maintain nationalist support.

However, the same approach naturally deepened unionist distrust of the SDLP. In Protestant eyes, the party was determined to bring them into a united Ireland, with or without their consent. This perception played a considerable part in undermining the Sunningdale Agreement. Thereafter, unionists asserted that they could only enter into government with the SDLP if the party gave unqualified acceptance of Northern Ireland's constitutional position. The standard position of UUUC members during the 1975–76 Convention was that they could not be expected to share power with those whose ultimate ambition was to 'overthrow' the state. Thus, in effect, the SDLP was asked to renounce its aspiration to Irish unity as a prerequisite to political compromise.[53] But, in this, unionists were asking the impossible of Hume and his colleagues. As leaders of the nationalist community, they could no more surrender the ambition of Irish unity than a unionist party could forsake the Union. Seán Farren, later Chair of the SDLP, made this clear when discussing the reasons why the party continued to defend the aspiration to a united Ireland: 'The minute you stopped it, was the minute that certainly a party like the SDLP would lose its credentials ... The people who voted for the SDLP would say: "These guys abandoned what I feel I want in my blood." ... the electorate didn't expect us to [constantly talk about Irish unity], but if they perceived you as having abandoned it, then you were in trouble.'[54]

This was the Catch-22 faced by Hume as a political leader operating in a deeply divided society. Unless he upheld the aspiration of Irish unity, he would not have maintained the support of the nationalist community. But by continuing to articulate this aspiration, he could never hope to win unionists' confidence. For this reason, despite his ideas of reaching across to the Protestant community and achieving reconciliation between the two traditions in Ireland, Hume was still an essentially nationalist leader. The question is, though, how far did he lead Irish nationalism?

In answering this question, it may here be useful to make a comparison with Hume's ideological *bête noire*, Conor Cruise O'Brien. O'Brien's approach to Irish nationalism, at least since the onset of the Troubles, was overtly iconoclastic.[55] He asked far more painful, far more searching, and perhaps more important questions of the nationalist tradition than did Hume. But O'Brien's impact on Irish nationalist thinking was, overall, much less significant than was Hume's. O'Brien may have won support from intellectuals on both sides of the political divide in Ireland – something which Hume clearly failed to do – but his broader influence on public opinion, North and South, was more circumscribed. In short, O'Brien did not bring a sizeable constituency along with his political project. Indeed, this is what allowed O'Brien to be so critical of Irish nationalism: for all but a short period of his multi-faceted career, he did not have any political constituency to consider. Put simply, O'Brien was a political thinker before he was a political leader.

For Hume, the opposite was the case. His contribution to changes in Irish nationalist thinking was always conditioned by the realities of being a political leader – a political leader working in a divided society, and a state of ongoing communal conflict. Given this context, as Horowitz suggests, there were bound to be limitations to what he could achieve, and to how far he could lead his followers. That considered, Hume has been a remarkably successful politician. He may not have led his constituency, nor Irish nationalism, as far as critics like O'Brien would have liked, but, reviewing his career, he certainly covered considerable ground. He was one of the first nationalist leaders, not only to advocate, but himself to sit in a power-sharing government at Stormont, and thus to accept and wholeheartedly work the Northern Ireland state; he influenced the policies of successive Irish governments, and maintained Dublin's constructive engagement in the region through a quarter-century of conflict; he altered the attitudes of the Irish-American political elite, and won its support for a patient but far-sighted diplomatic strategy on Northern Ireland; he played a highly significant role in bringing the Provisional movement into the political process, resulting, eventually, with even republicans taking part in a Stormont government; and he eased the path of nationalist Ireland as a whole towards acceptance of a reformulated partition of the island. Though such acts, Hume brought more nationalists further, and changed more minds, than his detractors might ever have dared.

Even those who worked alongside Hume through the most trying times of the Troubles – those who knew him intimately, and so might feel more justified in criticising him – still recognise his stature. Austin Currie is one such person:

> I have never been among those who put forward John's entitlement to sainthood. ... However, and I say this without reservation, from the vantage point of history, John Hume will be recognised as a towering figure, in the same league of Irish history as O'Connell and Parnell. He was courageous, had strategic vision and never for one moment departed from a complete insistence on the non-violent approach, despite all the pressures on him, his family and his electorate. ... Whatever else might be said about John Hume, one thing is incontrovertible: he was the prime mover in bringing about the process that brought peace to Ireland, and in doing so displayed considerable

moral, physical and political courage. There are many people alive today who
would be in their graves save for John Hume.[56]

As Currie suggests, undoubtedly Hume's greatest asset was his political
vision. But, in this respect, perhaps the best epithet of all comes from
Gerry Fitt, albeit also relayed by Currie:

> Gerry's pithy description of John, expressed in terms of praise and begrudgery
> and epitomising their relationship, was, 'He was a far-seeing c***.' Unlikely
> to be on his tombstone, but a considerable tribute indeed given the source
> from whence it came.[57]

Notes

1 Maginness, 'Redefining northern nationalism', p. 33.
2 Currie, *All Hell Will Break Loose*, p. 417; White, *John Hume*, pp. 213–14.
3 Currie, *All Hell Will Break Loose*, p. 206.
4 Devlin, *Straight Left*, pp. 137–8.
5 Murray, *John Hume and the SDLP*, pp. 123, 141.
6 Bean, 'Defining republicanism', pp. 134, 135; Murray, *John Hume and the SDLP*, p. 255.
7 *Derry Journal*, 6 August 1965.
8 *Irish Times*, 18 May 1964.
9 *Derry Journal*, 22 October 1968 (author's emphasis).
10 *Ibid.*, 11 November 1969.
11 NAI, DFA, 2000/5/48, report by E. Gallagher on Hume's proposal for a border poll, 13 November 1969.
12 *Irish Times*, 6 November 1971.
13 *Ibid.*, 17 June 1974.
14 Bew and Gillespie, *Northern Ireland: A Chronology*, pp. 124, 125; Patterson, *Ireland Since 1939*, p. 252.
15 Quoted in Murray, *John Hume and the SDLP*, p. 152.
16 *Guardian*, 21 January 1986.
17 Mitchel McLaughlin; interview with author, Belfast, 28 January, 2009.
18 Martin Mansergh, one of the key Irish officials involved in the negotiation of the DSD, described Brooke's statement as 'a foundation block around which some of the first drafts of the joint declaration were built'; Mansergh, 'The background to the peace process', p. 153.
19 Adams, *Hope and History*, pp. 80, 82.
20 SDLP, *Towards a New Ireland*, p. 1.
21 For an overview of this debate, including a more general discussion of the principle of self-determination and the problems associated with its application, see M. Gallagher, 'Do Ulster unionists have a right to self-determination?', *Irish Political Studies*, 5 (1990).
22 Oberschall and Palmer, 'The failure of moderate politics', p. 81; O'Flynn, 'The problem of recognising individual and national identities', pp. 146–8; Taylor, 'The Belfast Agreement and the politics of consociationalism, pp. 221–2; Wilson and Wilford, 'Northern Ireland: a route to stability?', pp. 2, 6–7. It should be noted that none of these critics provides any persuasive alternative to the GFA in terms of its 'answer' to the constitutional question.

23 Cited in Cunningham, 'The political language of John Hume', p. 13.
24 Cited in *ibid.*, p. 19.
25 Quoted in P. O'Malley, *Northern Ireland: Questions of Nuance* (Belfast: Blackstaff, 1990), p. 33.
26 Ivan Cooper; interview with author, Derry, 30 June, 2004 (Cooper's emphasis).
27 See above, p. 85.
28 Bew and Patterson, *The British State*, p. 99.
29 *Irish Times*, 16 February 1978.
30 Quoted in White, *John Hume*, p. 215.
31 J. Hume, speech to SDLP's annual conference, 1981, cited in R. Aldous, *Great Irish Speeches* (London: Quercus, 2007), p. 152.
32 *Belfast Telegraph*, 23 August 1994.
33 *Irish Times*, 17 June 1974.
34 Ruane and Todd analysed a series of datasets on northern nationalist attitudes towards a political settlement, showing that a significant and, over time, growing majority favoured either a united Ireland or an agreement involving an Irish dimension. By the 1990s, around 80 per cent of nationalists supported one of these two options, but the greater number were prepared to settle for some form of Irish dimension short of a unitary state; J. Ruane and J. Todd, 'A changed Irish nationalism? The significance of the Good Friday Agreement of 1998', in J. Ruane, J. Todd and A. Mandeville (eds), *Europe's Old States in the New World Order: The Politics of Transition in Britain, France and Spain* (Dublin: UCD Press, 2003), pp. 138–9.
35 See above, p. 161.
36 Bew and Gillespie, *Northern Ireland: A Chronology*, p. 404.
37 Todd, 'Nationalism, Republicanism and the Good Friday Agreement', p. 53.
38 On this, see Tonge, *The New Northern Irish Politics?* pp. 208ff.
39 For an overview on North–South co-operation since the GFA, see J. Coakley and L. O'Dowd (eds), *Crossing the Border: New Relationships between Northern Ireland and the Republic of Ireland* (Dublin: Irish Academic Press, 2007).
40 Hume, opening speech to the New Ireland Forum, in Dublin Stationery Office, *New Ireland Forum Public Sessions, 1–13*, p. 23.
41 His friend and often political ally, Garret FitzGerald would be his only challenger in this respect.
42 *Derry Journal*, 6 August 1965; *Irish Times*, 18 and 19 May 1964.
43 Hume, *A New Ireland*, pp. 61, 71.
44 Indeed, this focus was apparent even in the title of his *Foreign Affairs* article of 1979: 'The Irish question: a British problem'.
45 Hume, *A New Ireland*, p. 123.
46 Murray and Tonge, *Sinn Féin and the SDLP*, p. 259.
47 D. Horowitz, *Ethnic Groups in Conflict* (London: University of California Press, 2nd edn, 2000), p. 342.
48 For a more thorough application of Horowitz's model of ethnic party leadership to the development of the SDLP, see P. J. McLoughlin, 'Horowitz's theory of ethnic party competition and the case of the SDLP, 1970–79', *Nationalism and Ethnic Politics*, 14:4 (2008).
49 *Belfast Telegraph*, 27 October 1974.
50 *Irish News*, 7 February 1969.

51 NAI, DFA, 2000/5/48, report by E. Gallagher on Hume's review of Terrence O'Neill's *Ulster at the Crossroads* for the *Irish Times*, 28 October 1969.
52 NAI, DFA, 2000/5/48, report by E. Gallagher on Hume's proposal for a border poll, 13 November 1969.
53 Northern Ireland Constitutional Convention Debates, pp. 285, 286, 287, 19 June 1975.
54 Seán Farren; interview with author, Coleraine, 25 February 2009.
55 See C. C. O'Brien, *States of Ireland* (London: Hutchinson, 1972); and *Ancestral Voices: Religion and Nationalism in Ireland* (Dublin: Poolbeg, 1994).
56 Currie, *All Hell Will Break Loose*, pp. 416, 417.
57 *Ibid.*, p. 417.

Bibliography

Public collections

National Archives of Ireland (NAI)
Department of the Taoiseach (D/T) papers
Department of the Foreign Affairs (DFA) papers

Public Records Office of Northern Ireland (PRONI)
SDLP papers

Interviews

Gerry Adams, Belfast, 2 March 2009
Ben Caraher, Belfast, 25 June 2004
Ivan Cooper, Derry, 30 June 2004
Mark Durkan, Belfast, 6 April 2009
Séan Farren, Coleraine, 25 February 2009
Garrett FitzGerald, Dublin, 22 March 2004
Denis Haughey, Cookstown, 30 July 2004
John Hume, Derry, 12 August 2004
Alban Maginness, Belfast, 3 July 2009
Eddie McGrady, Downpatrick, 25 August 2004
Mitchel McLaughlin, Belfast, 28 January 2009

Parliamentary records

Dáil Éireann Debates
House of Commons Debates
House of Commons (Northern Ireland) Debates
Northern Ireland Assembly Debates
Northern Ireland Constitutional Convention Debates

Newspapers and magazines

Belfast Telegraph   *Derry Journal*
Belfast News Letter   *Fortnight*

Guardian   Observer
Irish Independent   Sunday Independent
Irish News   Sunday Press
Irish Press   Sunday Times
Irish Times   The Times
Magill

Official publications

Dublin Stationery Office, *Agreed Communiqué issued following the Conference between the Irish and British Governments and the parties involved in the Northern Ireland Executive (designate) on 6th, 7th, 8th, and 9th, December, 1973* [The Sunningdale Agreement] (Dublin: Dublin Stationery Office, 1973)

Dublin Stationery Office, *New Ireland Forum Public Sessions, 1–13* (Dublin: Dublin Stationery Office, 1984)

Dublin Stationery Office, *New Ireland Forum Report* (Dublin: Dublin Stationery Office, 1984)

HMSO, *Disturbances in Northern Ireland: Report of the Commission Appointed by the Governor of Northern Ireland* [The Cameron Report] (Belfast: HMSO, 1969), Cmnd 532

HMSO, *The Future of Northern Ireland: A Paper for Discussion* (Belfast: HMSO, 1972)

HMSO, *Northern Ireland: Constitutional Proposals* (London: HMSO, 1973), Cmnd 5259

HMSO, *The Northern Ireland Constitution* (London: HMSO, 1974), Cmnd 5675

HMSO, *Northern Ireland Constitutional Convention Report: Together with the Proceedings of the Convention and other Appendices* (London: HMSO, 1975)

HMSO, *The Government of Northern Ireland: A Working Paper for a Conference* (London: HMSO, 1979), Cmnd 7763

HMSO, *Agreement between the Government of the United Kingdom of Great Britain and Northern Ireland and the Government of the Republic of Ireland* [The Anglo-Irish Agreement] (London: HMSO, 1985), Cmnd 9657

HMSO, *Text of the Joint Declaration by the Prime Minister, Rt. Hon. John Major, MP and the Taoiseach, Mr. Albert Reynolds, TD on the 15th December, 1993* [The Downing Street Declaration] (Belfast: HMSO, 1993)

HMSO, *The Belfast Agreement: An Agreement Reached at the Multi-Party Talks on Northern Ireland* [The Good Friday Agreement] (London: HMSO, 1998), Cmnd 3883

Books, articles and other publications

Adams, G., *The Politics of Irish Freedom* (Dingle: Brandon, 1986)

Adams, G., *Free Ireland: Towards a Lasting Peace* (Dublin: Brandon, 1995)

Adams, G., *Hope and History: Making Peace in Ireland* (Dingle: Brandon, 2003)

Aldous, R., *Great Irish Speeches* (London: Quercus, 2007)

Anderson, B., *Imagined Communities: Reflections on the Origin and Spread of Nationalism* (London: Verso, 1983)

Arthur, P., 'Anglo-Irish relations and constitutional policy', in P. Mitchell and R. Wilford (eds), *Politics in Northern Ireland* (Oxford: Westview, 1999)

Arthur, P., '"Quiet diplomacy and personal conversation": track two diplomacy and the search for a settlement in Northern Ireland', in J. Todd and J. Ruane (eds), *After the Good Friday Agreement: Analysing Political Change in Northern Ireland* (Dublin: UCD Press, 1999)

Arthur, P., *Special Relationships: Britain, Ireland and the Northern Ireland Problem* (Belfast: Blackstaff, 2000)

Aughey, A., *Under Siege: Ulster Unionism and the Anglo-Irish Agreement* (Belfast: Blackstaff, 1989)

Bean, K., 'Defining republicanism: shifting discourses of new nationalism and post-republicanism', in M. Elliott (ed.), *The Long Road to Peace in Northern Ireland* (Liverpool: Liverpool University Press, 2002)

Bew, P., *Ireland: The Politics of Enmity, 1789–2006* (Oxford: Oxford University Press, 2007)

Bew, P. and G. Gillespie, *Northern Ireland: A Chronology of the Troubles, 1968–1999* (Dublin: Gill and Macmillan, 1999)

Bew, P. and H. Patterson, *The British State and the Ulster Crisis: From Wilson to Thatcher* (London: Verso, 1985)

Bew, P. and H. Patterson, 'The new stalemate: unionism and the Anglo-Irish Agreement', in P. Teague (ed.) *Beyond the Rhetoric: Politics, the Economy and Social Policy in Northern Ireland* (London: Lawrence and Wishart, 1987)

Bew, P., H. Patterson and P. Teague, *Northern Ireland: Between War and Peace: The Political Future of Northern Ireland* (London: Lawrence and Wishart, 1997)

Bew, P., P. Gibbon and H. Patterson, *Northern Ireland, 1921–2001: Political Forces and Social Classes* (London: Serif, 2002)

Bloomfield, K., *Stormont in Crisis: A Memoir* (Belfast: Blackstaff Press, 1994)

Boyce, D. G., *Nationalism in Ireland* (London: Routledge, 3rd edn, 1995)

Boyce, D. G., *The Irish Question and British Politics, 1868–1996* (Basingstoke: Macmillan, 2nd edn, 1996)

Boyce, D. G. and A. O'Day (eds), *The Making of Modern Irish History: Revisionism and the Revisionist Controversy* (London: Routledge, 1996)

Boyle, K., 'Northern Ireland: allegiances and identities', in B. Crick (ed.), *National Identities: The Constitution of the United Kingdom* (Oxford: Blackwell, 1991)

Boyle, K. and T. Hadden, *Ireland: a Positive Proposal* (Harmondsworth: Penguin, 1985)

Boyle, K. and T. Hadden, *The Anglo-Irish Agreement: Commentary, Text and Official Review* (London: Sweet and Maxwell, 1989)

Boyle, K., T. Hadden and P. Hillyard, *Ten Years on in Northern Ireland: The Legal Control of Political Violence* (London: Cobden Trust, 1980)

Brady, C., '"Constructive and instrumental": the dilemma of Ireland's first "new historians"', in C. Brady (ed.), *Interpreting Irish History: The Debate on Historical Revisionism, 1938–1994* (Dublin: Irish Academic Press, 1994)

Brady, C. (ed.), *Interpreting Irish History: The Debate on Historical Revisionism, 1938–1994* (Dublin: Irish Academic Press, 1994)

Briand, R. J., 'Bush, Clinton, Irish America and the Irish peace process', *The Political Quarterly*, 73:2 (2002)

Buckland, P., *A History of Northern Ireland* (Dublin: Gill and Macmillan, 1981)

Coakley, J., 'Religion, ethnic identity and the Protestant minority in the Republic', in W. Crotty and D. E. Schmitt (eds), *Ireland and the Politics of Change* (London: Longman, 1998)

Coakley, J., 'National identity in Northern Ireland: stability or change?', *Nations and Nationalism*, 13:4 (2007)

Coakley, J. and L. O'Dowd (eds), *Crossing the Border: New Relationships between Northern Ireland and the Republic of Ireland* (Dublin: Irish Academic Press, 2007)

Cochrane, F., *Unionist Politics and the Politics of Unionism since the Anglo-Irish Agreement* (Cork: Cork University Press, 2nd edn, 2001)

Coogan, T. P., *The Troubles: Ireland's Ordeal 1966–1996 and the Search for Peace* (London: Hutchinson, 1996)

Coulter, C., 'The character of unionism', *Irish Political Studies*, 9 (1994)

Coulter, C., 'Direct rule and the unionist middle classes', in R. English and G. Walker (eds), *Unionism in Modern Ireland* (Dublin: Gill and Macmillan, 1996)

Cronin, S., *Irish Nationalism: A History of its Roots and Ideology* (New York: Continuum, 1981)

Cunningham, M., 'The political language of John Hume', *Irish Political Studies*, 12 (1997)

Cunningham, M., *British Government Policy in Northern Ireland, 1969–2000* (Manchester: Manchester University Press, 2001)

Curran, F., *Derry: Countdown to Disaster* (Dublin: Gill and Macmillan, 1986)

Currie, A., *All Hell Will Break Loose* (Dublin: O'Brien, 2004)

Delanty, G., 'Habermas and post-national identity: theoretical perspectives on the conflict in Northern Ireland', *Irish Political Studies*, 11 (1996)

Delanty, G., 'Northern Ireland in a Europe of regions', *The Political Quarterly*, 67:2 (1996)

Devlin, P., *Straight Left: An Autobiography* (Belfast: Blackstaff, 1993)

Dixon, P., *Northern Ireland: The Politics of Peace and War* (Basingstoke: Palgrave, 2nd edn, 2008)

Doherty, P., *Paddy Bogside* (Cork: Mercier, 2001)

Drower, G., *John Hume: Peacemaker* (London: Victor Gollancz, 1995)

Duignan, S., *One Spin on the Merry-Go-Round* (Dublin: Blackwater Press, 1995)

Dumbrell, J., 'The United States and the Northern Ireland conflict, 1969–94: from indifference to intervention', *Irish Studies in International Affairs*, 6 (1995)

Dumbrell, J., '"Hope and history": the US and peace in Northern Ireland', in M. Cox, A. Guelke and F. Stephen (eds), *A Farewell to Arms?: From 'Long War' to Long Peace in Northern Ireland* (Manchester: Manchester University Press, 2000)

Elliott, S. and W. D. Flackes, *Northern Ireland: A Political Directory, 1968–1999* (Belfast: Blackstaff Press, 1999)

English, R., 'Defining the nation: recent historiography and Irish nationalism', *European Review of History*, 2:2 (1995)

English, R., 'The same people with different relatives? Modern scholarship, unionists and the Irish nation', in R. English and G. Walker (eds), *Unionism in Modern Ireland: New Perspectives on Politics and Culture* (Dublin: Gill and Macmillan, 1996)

English, R., 'The state in Northern Ireland', in R. English and C. Townshend (eds), *The State: Historical and Political Dimensions* (London: Routledge, 1998)

English, R., *Armed Struggle: A History of the IRA* (London: Macmillan, 2003)

Evans, J. A. J., J. Tonge and G. Murray, 'Constitutional nationalism and socialism in Northern Ireland: the greening of the Social Democratic and Labour Party', *British Elections and Parties Review*, 10 (2000)

Fanning, R., 'Playing it cool: the response of the British and Irish governments to the crisis in Northern Ireland, 1968–9', in *Irish Studies in International Affairs*, 12 (2001)

Fanning, R., 'The Anglo-American alliance and the Irish question', in J. Devlin and H. B. Clarke (eds), *European Encounters: Essays in Memory of Albert Lovett* (Dublin: UCD Press, 2003)

Farrell, M., *Northern Ireland: The Orange State* (London: Pluto Press, 2nd edn, 1980)

Farren, S., 'The SDLP and the roots of the Good Friday Agreement', in M. Cox, A. Guelke and F. Stephen (eds), *A Farewell to Arms?: From 'Long War' to Long Peace in Northern Ireland* (Manchester: Manchester University Press, 2000)

Farren S. and B. Mulvihill, 'Beyond self-determination towards co-determination in Ireland', *Études Irlandaises*, 21:1 (1996)

Farren, S. and R. F. Mulvihill, *Paths to a Settlement in Northern Ireland* (Gerrards Cross: Colin Smyth, 2000)

Farrington, C., *Ulster Unionism and the Northern Ireland Peace Process* (Basingstoke: Palgrave, 2006)

Faulkner, B., *Memoirs of a Statesman* (London: Weidenfeld and Nicolson, 1978)

Fennell, D., *The Revision of Irish Nationalism* (Dublin: Open Air, 1989)

Finlay, F., *Snakes and Ladders* (Dublin: New Island Books, 1998)

Finnegan, R. B., 'Irish-American relations', in W. Crotty and D. E. Schmitt (eds), *Ireland on the World Stage* (London: Longman, 2002)

FitzGerald, G., *Towards a New Ireland* (Dublin: Gill and Macmillan, 1972)

FitzGerald, G., *All in a Life: An Autobiography* (London: Gill and Macmillan, 1991)

FitzGerald, G., 'The origins and rationale of the Anglo-Irish Agreement of 1985', in D. Keogh and M. H. Haltzel (eds), *Northern Ireland and the Politics of Reconciliation* (Cambridge: Cambridge University Press, 1993)

Foster, R. F., *Luck and the Irish: A Brief History of Change, 1970–2000* (London: Allen Lane, 2007)

Gallagher, M., 'Do Ulster unionists have a right to self-determination?', *Irish Political Studies*, 5 (1990)

Gallagher, M., 'How many nations are there in Ireland?', *Ethnic and Racial Studies*, 18:4 (1995)

Garvin, T., *The Evolution of Irish Nationalist Politics* (Dublin: Gill and Macmillan, 1981)

Gellner, E., *Nations and Nationalism* (Oxford: Blackwell, 1983)

Geoghegan, V., 'Socialism, national identities and post-nationalist citizenship', *Irish Political Studies*, 9 (1994)

Gillespie, G., 'The Sunningdale Agreement: lost opportunity or an agreement too far?', *Irish Political Studies*, 13 (1998)

Gilligan, C., 'The Irish question and the concept of "identity" in the 1980s', *Nations and Nationalism*, 13:4 (2007)

Girvin, B., 'Constitutional nationalism in Northern Ireland', in B. Barton and P. J. Roche (eds), *The Northern Ireland Question: Perspectives and Policies* (Aldershot: Avebury, 1994)

Girvin, B., 'Northern Ireland and the Republic', in P. Mitchell and R. Wilford (eds), *Politics in Northern Ireland* (Oxford: Westview, 1999)

Goodhall, D., *The Anglo-Irish Agreement of 1985 and its Consequences* (Liverpool: Liverpool University Press, 1995)

Guelke, A., *Northern Ireland: The International Perspective* (Dublin: Gill and Macmillan, 1988)

Guelke, A., 'The United States, Irish Americans and the peace process', *International Affairs*, 72:3 (1996)

Haas, E. B., *The Uniting of Europe: Political Social and Economic Forces, 1950–1957* (Stanford, CA: Stanford University Press, 1968)

Hadfield, B., 'The Belfast Agreement, sovereignty and the state of the Union', *Public Law* (1998)

Hainsworth, P., 'Northern Ireland in the European Community', in M. Keating and B. Jones (eds), *Regions in the European Community* (Oxford: Clarendon, 1985)

Hainsworth, P., 'European Community Membership', in A. Aughey and D. Morrow (eds), *Northern Ireland Politics* (Harlow: Longman, 1996)

Hayward, K., 'The politics of nuance: Irish official discourse on Northern Ireland', *Irish Political Studies*, 19:1 (2004)

Hayward, K., *Irish Nationalism and European Integration: The Official Redefinition of the Island of Ireland* (Manchester: Manchester University Press, 2009)

Heath, E., *The Course of My Life: My Autobiography* (London: Coronet, 1998)

Hennessy, T., *A History of Northern Ireland, 1920–96* (Dublin: Gill and Macmillan, 1997)

Hennessy, T., *The Northern Ireland Peace Process: Ending the Troubles?* (Dublin: Gill and Macmillan, 2000)

Hennessy, T., *Northern Ireland: The Origins of the Troubles* (Dublin: Gill and Macmillan, 2005)

Hewitt, C., 'Catholic grievances, Catholic nationalism and violence in Northern Ireland during the civil rights period: a reconsideration', *The British Journal of Sociology*, 32: 3 (1981)

Hewitt, C., 'Discrimination in Northern Ireland: a rejoinder', *The British Journal of Sociology*, 34:3 (1983)

Hewitt, C., 'Catholic grievances and violence in Northern Ireland', *The British Journal of Sociology*, 36:1 (1985)

Hewitt, C., 'Explaining violence in Northern Ireland', *The British Journal of Sociology*, 38:1 (1987)

Horgan, J., *Seán Lemass: The Enigmatic Patriot* (Dublin: Gill and Macmillan, 1997)

Horowitz, D., *Ethnic Groups in Conflict* (London: University of California Press, 2nd edn, 2000)

Hume, J., 'John Hume's Ireland', *Fortnight*, 5 February 1971

Hume, J., 'The Irish question: a British problem', *Foreign Affairs: An American Quarterly Review*, 58:2 (1979)

Hume, J., 'A new Ireland – the acceptance of diversity', *Studies*, 75:300 (1986)

Hume, J., 'Europe of the regions', in R. Kearney (ed.), *Across the Frontiers: Ireland in the 1990s* (Dublin: Wolfhound, 1988)

Hume, J., 'A new Ireland in a new Europe', in D. Keogh and M. H. Haltzel (eds), *Northern Ireland and the Politics of Reconciliation* (Cambridge: Cambridge University Press, 1993)

Hume, J., *A New Ireland: Peace, Politics and Reconciliation* (Boulder, CO: Roberts Rhinehart, 1996)

Ivory, G., 'Revisions in nationalist discourse among Irish political parties', *Irish Political Studies*, 14 (1999)

Jackson, A., *Ireland: 1978–1998* (Oxford: Blackwell, 1999)

Jackson, A., *Home Rule: An Irish History, 1800–2000* (London: Weidenfeld and Nicolson, 2004)

Kearney, R., 'Introduction: thinking otherwise', in R. Kearney (ed.), *Across the Frontiers: Ireland in the 1990s* (Dublin: Wolfhound, 1988)

Kearney, R., *Post-Nationalist Ireland: Politics, Culture, Philosophy* (London: Routledge, 1997)

Kearney, R. and R. Wilson, 'Northern Ireland's future as a European region' (submission to the Opshal Commmission, Belast, 2 February 1993), in R. Kearney, *Post-Nationalist Ireland: Politics, Culture, Philosophy* (London: Routledge, 1997)

Kennedy, D., 'Whither northern nationalism', *Christus Rex*, 8:4 (1959)

Kennedy, D., 'The European Union and the Northern Ireland question', in B. Barton and P. J. Roche (eds), *The Northern Ireland Question: Perspectives and Policies* (Aldershot: Avebury, 1994)

Kennedy, D., 'Europe and the Northern Ireland Problem', in D. Kennedy (ed.), *Living with the European Union: the Northern Ireland Experience* (Basingstoke: Macmillan, 2000)

Kennedy, M., *Division and Consensus: The Politics of Cross-Border Relations in Ireland, 1925–1969* (Dublin: Institute of Public Administration, 2000)

Kennedy-Pipe, C., *The Origins of the Present Troubles in Northern Ireland* (London: Longman, 1997)

Kennedy-Pipe, C., 'From war to peace in Northern Ireland', in M. Cox, A. Guelke and F. Stephen (eds), *A Farewell to Arms?: From 'Long War' to Long Peace in Northern Ireland* (Manchester: Manchester University Press, 2000)

Kovalcheck, K. A., 'Catholic grievances in Northern Ireland: appraisal and judgment', *The British Journal of Sociology*, 38:1 (1987)

Laffan, B., 'The European context: a new political dimension in Ireland, North and South', in J. Coakley, B. Laffen and J. Todd (eds), *Renovation or Revolution? New Territorial Politics in Ireland and the United Kingdom* (Dublin: University College Dublin Press, 2005)

Lee, J. J., *Ireland, 1912–1985: Politics and Society* (Cambridge: Cambridge University Press, 1989)

Liphart, A., *Democracy in Plural Societies: A Comparative Exploration* (New Haven, CT: Yale University Press, 1977)

Longley, E., *The Living Stream: Literature and Revisionism in Ireland* (Newcastle-upon-Tyne: Bloodaxe Books, 1994)

Lynn, B., *Holding the Ground: The Nationalist Party in Northern Ireland, 1945–72* (Aldershot: Dartmouth, 1997)

MacDonagh, O., 'What was new in the New Ireland Forum?', *The Crane Bag*, 9:2 (1985)

Maginness, A., 'Redefining northern nationalism', in J.Coakley (ed.), *Changing Shades of Orange and Green: Redefining the Union and the Nation in Contemporary Ireland* (Dublin: UCD Press, 2002)

Major, J., *The Autobiography* (London: HarperCollins, 1999)

Mallie, E. and D. McKittrick, *The Fight for Peace: the Secret Story Behind the Irish Peace Process* (London: Heinemann, 1996)

Mallie, E. and D. McKittrick, *Endgame in Ireland* (London: Hodder and Stoughton, 2001)

Mansergh, M., 'The background to the peace process', *Irish Studies in International Affairs*, 6 (1995)

Mansergh, M., 'The background to the Irish peace process', in M. Cox, A. Guelke and F. Stephen (eds), *A Farewell to Arms?: From 'Long War' to Long Peace in Northern Ireland* (Manchester: Manchester University Press, 2000)

Mansergh, M., 'Mountain climbing Irish-style: the hidden challenges of the peace process', in M. Elliott (ed.), *The Long Road to Peace in Northern Ireland* (Liverpool: Liverpool University Press, 2002)

McAllister, I., 'Political opposition in Northern Ireland: the National Democratic Party, 1965–1970', *The Economic and Social Review*, 6:3 (1975)

McAllister, I., 'Political parties and social change in Ulster: the case of the SDLP', *Social Studies*, 5:1 (1976)

McAllister, I., *The Social Democratic and Labour Party: Political Opposition in a Divided Society* (London: Macmillan, 1977)

McAllister, I., 'The legitimacy of opposition: the collapse of the 1974 Northern Ireland executive', *Éire-Ireland: A Journal of Irish Studies*, 12:4 (1977)

McAlpine, A., *Once a Jolly Bagman: Memoirs* (London: Weidenfeld and Nicolson: 1997)

McCall, C., 'Postmodern Europe and the resources of communal identities in Northern Ireland, *European Journal of Political Research*, 33 (1998)

McCall, C., *Identity in Northern Ireland: Communities, Politics and Change* (Basingstoke: Palgrave, 1999)

McCann, E., *War and an Irish Town* (Harmondsworth: Penguin, 1974)

McCrudden, C., 'Equality and the Good Friday Agreement', in J. Ruane and J. Todd (eds), *After the Good Friday Agreement: Analysing Political Change in Northern Ireland* (Dublin: UCD Press, 1999)

McGarry, J., 'Globalization, European integration, and the Northern Ireland conflict', in M. Keating and J. McGarry (eds), *Minority Nationalism and the Changing International Order* (Oxford: Oxford University Press, 2001)

McGarry. J. and B. O'Leary, *Explaining Northern Ireland: Broken Images* (Oxford: Blackwell, 1995)

McGarry, J. and B. O'Leary, *The Northern Ireland Conflict: Consociational Engagements* (Oxford: Oxford University Press, 2004)

McIvor, B., *Hope Deferred: Experiences of an Irish Unionist* (Belfast: Blackstaff, 1998)

McKeown, M., *The Greening of a Nationalist* (Dublin: Murlough, 1986)

McLoughlin, P. J., 'John Hume and the revision of Irish nationalism, 1964–79' (unpublished PhD thesis, Queen's University Belfast, 2005)

McLoughlin, P. J., 'Horowitz's theory of ethnic party competition and the case of the SDLP, 1970–79', *Nationalism and Ethnic Politics*, 14:4 (2008)

McLoughlin, P. J., '"Humespeak": the SDLP, political discourse, and the Northern Ireland peace process', *Peace and Conflict Studies*, 15:1 (2008)

Meehan, E., 'Citizens Are Plural', *Fortnight*, 311 (1992)

Meehan, E., 'Europe and the Europeanisation of the Irish question', in M. Cox, A. Guelke and F.Stephen (eds), *A Farewell to Arms?: Beyond the Good Friday Agreement* (Manchester: Manchester University Press, 2nd edn, 2006)

Mitchell, J. and M. Cavanagh, 'Context and contingency: constitutional nationalists in Europe', in M. Keating and J. McGarry (eds), *Minority Nationalism and the Changing International Order* (Oxford: Oxford University Press, 2001)

Mitchell, P., 'The party system and party competition', in P. Mitchell and R. Wilford (eds), *Politics in Northern Ireland* (Oxford: Westview Press, 1999)

Mitchell, P., B. O'Leary and G. Evans, 'Flanking extremists bite the moderates and emerge in their clothes', *Parliamentary Affairs*, 54:4 (2001)

Mitchell, P., B. O'Leary and G. Evans, 'The 2001 elections in Northern Ireland: moderating "extremists" and the squeezing of the moderates', *Representation*, 39:1 (2002)

Moloney, E., *A Secret History of the IRA* (London: Penguin, 2002)

Moxon-Browne, E., *Nation, Class and Creed in Northern Ireland* (Bodmin: Robert Hartnoll, 1983)

Murphy, M., *Gerry Fitt: A Political Chameleon* (Cork: Mercier, 2007)

Murray, G., *John Hume and the SLDP: Impact and Survival in Northern Ireland* (Dublin: Murray Irish Academic Press, 1998)

Murray, G., 'The Good Friday Agreement: an SDLP analysis of the Northern Ireland conflict', in J. Neuheiser and S. Wolff (eds), *Peace at Last?: The Impact of the Good Friday Agreement on Northern Ireland* (Oxford: Berghahn Books, 2003)

Murray, G. and J. Tonge, *Sinn Féin and the SDLP: From Alienation to Participation* (London: O'Brien, 2005)

Newe, G. B., 'The Catholic in the Northern Ireland community', *Christus Rex*, 18:1 (1964)

Oberschall, A. and L. K. Palmer, 'The failure of moderate politics: the case of Northern Ireland', in I. O'Flynn and D. Russell (eds), *Power Sharing: New Challenges for Divided Societies* (London: Pluto, 2005)

O'Brien, B., *The Long War: The IRA and Sinn Féin* (Dublin: O'Brien, 2nd edn, 1999)

O'Brien, C. C., *States of Ireland* (London: Hutchinson, 1972)

O'Brien, C. C., *Ancestral Voices: Religion and Nationalism in Ireland* (Dublin: Poolbeg, 1994)

O'Brien, C. C., *Memoir: My Life and Themes* (London: Profile, 1999)

O'Brien, J., *The Arms Trial* (Dublin: Gill and Macmillan, 2000)

O'Cleary, C., *The Greening of the White House: The Inside Story of How America Tried to Bring Peace to Ireland* (Dublin: Gill and Macmillan, 1996)

O'Connor, F., *In Search of a State: Catholics in Northern Ireland* (Belfast: Blackstaff, 1993)

Ó Dochartaigh, N., *From Civil Rights to Armalites: Derry and the Birth of the Irish Troubles* (Cork: Cork University Press, 1997)

O'Donnell, C., 'Fianna Fáil and Sinn Féin: the 1988 talks reappraised,' *Irish Political Studies*, 18:2 (2003)

O'Dowd, N., 'The awakening: Irish America's key role in the Irish peace process', in M. Elliott (ed.), *The Long Road to Peace in Northern Ireland* (Liverpool: Liverpool University Press, 2002)

O'Duffy, B., 'British-Irish conflict regulation from Sunningdale to Belfast. Part I: tracing the status of contesting sovereigns, 1968–1974', *Nations and Nationalism*, 5:4 (2000)

O'Duffy, B., 'British-Irish conflict regulation from Sunningdale to Belfast. Part II: playing for a draw 1985–1999', *Nations and Nationalism*, 6:3 (2000)

O'Flynn, I., 'The Problem of recognising individual and national identities: a liberal critique of the Belfast Agreement', *Critical Review of International Social and Political Philosophy*, 6:3 (2003)

O'Halloran, C., *Partition and the Limits of Irish Nationalism* (Dublin: Gill and Macmillan, 1987)

O'Hearn, D., 'Catholic grievances, Catholic nationalism: a comment', *The British Journal of Sociology*, 34:3 (1983)

O'Hearn, D., 'Again on discrimination in the North of Ireland: a reply to the rejoinder', *The British Journal of Sociology*, 36:1 (1985)

O'Hearn, D., 'Catholic grievances: comments', *The British Journal of Sociology*, 38:1 (1987)

O'Kane, E., 'Anglo-Irish relations and the Northern Ireland peace process: from exclusion to inclusion', *Contemporary British History*, 18:1 (2004)

O'Kane, E., *Britain, Ireland and Northern Ireland since 1980* (Routledge: Abingdon, 2007)

O'Leary, B., 'The Anglo-Irish Agreement: statecraft or folly?', *West European Politics*, 10 (1987)

O'Leary, B., 'The limits to coercive consociationalism in Northern Ireland', in *Political Studies*, 37 (1989)

O'Leary, B., 'The nature of the British-Irish Agreement', *New Left Review*, 233 (1999)

O'Leary, B. and J. McGarry, *The Politics of Antagonism* (London: Athlone, 2nd edn, 1996)

O'Malley, P., *The Uncivil Wars: Ireland Today* (Belfast: Blackstaff, 1983)

O'Malley, P., *Northern Ireland: Questions of Nuance* (Belfast: Blackstaff, 1990)

O'Neill, T., *The Autobiography of Terence O'Neill* (London: Hart-Davis, 1972)

Patterson, H., *The Politics of Illusion: A Political History of the IRA* (London: Serif, 1997)

Patterson, H., 'Seán Lemass and the Ulster question, 1959–65', *Journal of Contemporary History*, 34:1 (1999)

Patterson, H., *Ireland Since 1939* (Oxford: Oxford University Press, 2002)

Phoenix, E., *Northern Nationalism: Nationalist Politics, Partition and the Catholic Minority in Northern Ireland, 1890–1940* (Belfast: Ulster Historical Foundation 1994)

Power, P. F., 'The Sunningdale strategy and the northern majority consent doctrine in Anglo-Irish Relations', *Éire-Ireland: A Journal of Irish Studies*, 12:1 (1977)

Power, P. F., 'Revisionist "Consent", Hillsborough and the decline of constitutional republicanism', *Éire-Ireland: A Journal of Irish Studies*, 25:1 (1990)

Purdie, B., *Politics in the Streets: The Origins of the Civil Rights Movement in Northern Ireland* (Belfast: Blackstaff, 1990)

Rees, M., *Northern Ireland: A Personal Perspective* (London: Methuen, 1985)

Regan, J. M., *The Irish Counter-Revolution, 1921–1936: Treatyite Politics and Settlement in Independent Ireland* (Dublin: Gill and Macmillan, 1999)

Regan, J. M., 'Southern Irish nationalism as a historical problem', *The History Journal*, 50:1 (2007)

Routledge, P., *John Hume: A Biography* (London: Harper Collins, 1998)

Ruane, J., 'Ireland, European integration and the dialectic of nationalism and postnationalism', *Études Irlandaises*, 19:1 (1994)

Ruane J. and J. Todd, *The Dynamics of Conflict in Northern Ireland: Power Conflict and Emancipation* (Cambridge: Cambridge University Press, 1996)

Ruane, J. and J. Todd, 'The Belfast Agreement: context, content, consequences', in J. Ruane and J. Todd (eds), *After the Good Friday Agreement, Analysing Political Change in Northern Ireland* (Dublin: UCD Press, 1999)

Ruane, J. and J. Todd, 'The Northern Ireland conflict and the impact of globalisation', in W. Crotty and D. E. Schmitt (eds), *Ireland on the World Stage* (London: Longman, 2002)

Ruane, J. and J. Todd, 'A changed Irish nationalism? The significance of the Good Friday Agreement of 1998', in J. Ruane, J. Todd and A. Mandeville (eds), *Europe's Old States in the New World Order: The Politics of Transition in Britain, France and Spain* (Dublin: UCD Press, 2003)

Ryder, C., *Fighting Fitt: The Gerry Fitt Story* (Belfast: Brehon, 2006)

SDLP, *Towards a New Ireland* (Belfast: SDLP, 1972)

SDLP, *A New North, A New Ireland* (Belfast: SDLP, 1973)

SDLP, *Proposals for Government in Northern Ireland: Report to Parliament* (Belfast: SDLP, 1975)

SDLP, *Speak with Strength* (Belfast: SDLP, 1975)

SDLP, *Facing Reality* (Lurgan: Ronan Press, 1978)

SDLP, *SDLP Eighth Annual Conference Agenda and Other Reports* (Lurgan: SDLP, 1978)

SDLP, *A New Horizon* (n.p.: 1979)

SDLP, *Towards a New Ireland: A Policy Review* (Belfast: SDLP, 1979)

SDLP, *Stand Firm – Vote SDLP* (Belfast: SDLP, 1982)

SDLP, *SDLP Manifesto: A New North, A New Ireland, A New Europe* (n.p.: Watermark Press, 1992)

Shannon, W. V., 'The Anglo-Irish Agreement', *Foreign Affairs: An American Quarterly Review*, 64:4 (1986)

Sinn Féin, *A Scenario for Peace* (Belfast: Sinn Féin, 1987)

Sinn Féin, *The Sinn Féin/SDLP Talks: January–September 1988* (Dublin: Sinn Féin Publicity Department, 1989)

Staunton, E., *The Nationalists of Northern Ireland: 1918–1973* (Dublin: Columba Press, 2001)

Taylor, R., 'Northern Ireland: consociation or social transformation', in J. McGarry (ed.), *Northern Ireland and the Divided World: Post-Agreement Northern Ireland in Comparative Perspective* (Oxford: Oxford University Press, 2001)

Taylor, R., 'The Belfast Agreement and the politics of consociationalism: a critique', *The Political Quarterly*, 77:2 (2006)

Thatcher, M., *The Downing Street Years* (New York: HarperCollins, 1993)

Todd, J., 'Two traditions in unionist political culture', *Irish Political Studies*, 2 (1987)

Todd, J., 'Northern Irish nationalist political culture', *Irish Political Studies*, 5 (1990)

Todd, J., 'Nationalism, Republicanism and the Good Friday Agreement', in J. Ruane and J. Todd (eds), *After the Good Friday Agreement, Analysing Political Change in Northern Ireland* (Dublin: UCD Press, 1999)

Todd, J., 'The reorientation of constitutional nationalism', in J. Coakley (ed.), *Changing Shades of Orange and Green: Redefining the Union and the Nation in Contemporary Ireland* (Dublin: UCD Press, 2002)

Tonge, J., *Northern Ireland: Conflict and Change* (Harlow: Pearson Education Limited, 2nd edn, 2002)

Tonge, J., *The New Northern Irish Politics?* (Houndmills: Palgrave Macmillan, 2005)

Tonge, J., 'Commentary' on M. Cunningham's 'The political language of John Hume', in C. McGrath and E. O'Malley (eds), *Irish Political Studies Reader: Key Contributions* (London: Routledge, 2008)

White, B., *John Hume: Statesman of the Troubles* (Belfast: Blackstaff, 1984)

Whyte, J., 'How much discrimination was there under the unionist regime, 1921–68?', in T. Gallagher and J. O'Connell (eds), *Contemporary Irish Studies* (Manchester: Manchester University Press, 1983)

Whyte, J., *Interpreting Northern Ireland* (Oxford: Clarendon Press, 1990)

Wichert, S., *Northern Ireland since 1945* (London: Longman, 2nd edn, 1999)

Wilford, R. (ed.), *Aspects of the Belfast Agreement* (Oxford: Oxford University Press, 2001)

Wilson, A. J., *Irish-America and the Ulster Conflict, 1968–1995* (Belfast: Blackstaff Press, 1995)

Wilson, A. J., 'From the Beltway to Belfast: the Clinton administration, Sinn Féin, and the Northern Ireland Peace Process', *New Hibernia Review*, 1:3 (1997)

Wilson, R., 'Towards a civic culture: implications for power-sharing policy makers', in I. O'Flynn and D. Russell (eds), *Power Sharing: New Challenges for Divided Societies* (London: Pluto, 2005)

Wilson, R. and R. Wilford, 'Northern Ireland: a route to stability?' (2003), available at: www.devolution.ac.uk/pdfdata/Wilson_&_Wilford_Paper.pdf (accessed 31 March 2009)

Wolff, S., 'Context and content: Sunningdale and Belfast compared', in R.Wilford (ed.), *Aspects of the Belfast Agreement* (Oxford: Oxford University Press, 2001)

Wolff, S., 'Introduction: from Sunningdale to Belfast, 1973–98', in J. Neuheiser and S. Wolff (eds), *Peace at Last?: The Impact of the Good Friday Agreement on Northern Ireland* (Oxford: Oxford University Press, 2003)

Index

Note: 'n' after a page reference indicates the number of a note on that page.

Lightning Source UK Ltd.
Milton Keynes UK
UKOW052202061212

203273UK00002B/5/P